Cultural Tourism

Cultural Tourism

Edited by

Razaq Raj

Leeds Metropolitan University

Kevin Griffin

Dublin Institute of Technology

Nigel Morpeth

Leeds Metropolitan University

www.cabi.org

CABI is a trading name of CAB International

CABI	CABI
Nosworthy Way	38 Chauncey Street
Wallingford	Suite 1002
Oxfordshire OX10 8DE	Boston, MA 02111
UK	USA

Tel: +44 (0)1491 832111	Tel: +1 800 552 3083 (toll free)
Fax: +44 (0)1491 833508	Tel: +1 (0)617 395 4051
E-mail: info@cabi.org	E-mail: cabi-nao@cabi.org
Website: www.cabi.org	

A catalogue record for this book is available from the British Library, London, UK.

Library of Congress Cataloging-in-Publication Data

Cultural tourism / Razaq Raj, Kevin Griffin, Nigel Morpeth, editors.
    p. cm.
  Includes bibliographical references and index.
  ISBN 978-1-84593-923-6 (hardcover)
  1. Heritage tourism--Management. I. Raj, Razaq. II. Griffin, Kevin. III. Morpeth, Nigel D.

  G156.5.H47C854 2013
  910.68--dc23
               2012040698

ISBN-13: 978 1 84593 923 6

Commissioning editor: Sarah Hulbert
Editorial assistant: Emma McCann
Production editor: Lauren Povey

Typeset by SPi, Pondicherry, India.
Printed and bound in the UK by the MPG Books Group.

Contents

Contributors

Lia Bassa, PhD, graduated as an English/French teacher for linguistics and literature in 1978 and received her PhD in English literature 1982. She was an assistant professor at the Technical University of Budapest and established the postgraduate course for technical interpretation. She was a senior consultant of the Hungarian National Committee of UNESCO World Heritage (2000–2004), and was an assistant professor in the Budapest University of Technology and Economics, Department of Information and Knowledge Management from 2004 to 2007. She has been managing director of the Foundation for Information Society, undertaking research for their UNESCO World Heritage Information Management Research Centre, since 2005. She is author of numerous heritage preservation and visitor-related articles and has been a professional interpreter throughout her career. She has been an invited teacher of culture and communication, and since 2010 has been an organiser of and responsible for the World Heritage MA education at the Budapest College for Communication and Business. Mailing address: Foundation for Information Society, Budapest 1507 P.O.B. 213, Hungary. Email address: bassa.lia@infota.org.

Alan Clarke, PhD, is professor of tourism at the University of Pannonia in Veszprém, Hungary. He has undertaken research on cultural and heritage tourism for over 20 years and continues to do so, both as an academic and as a consultant. His areas of interest concern tourism development, strategy and governance, especially stakeholder relations. Recently his work has focused on the possibilities of co-creation for innovation in tourism, exploring the opportunities for cultural interchange and exchanges. The current projects on religious tourism are an extension of this concern. He lives in a small village in Hungary, exploring the joys of Hungarian wines. Mailing address: University of Pannonia, Veszprém, Hungary. Email address: alanhungary@hotmail.com.

Neus Crous-Costa is a junior researcher at the Faculty of Tourism, University of Girona and tourism communication officer at the Museu d'Art de Girona (Girona province art museum). She graduated in tourism studies and holds a Master's degree in tourism planning and management (cultural tourism programme). She is involved in several research projects about religious tourism products and tourism imagery. Mailing address: Tourism Faculty, University of Girona, Plaça Ferrater Mora, 1, 17071 Girona, Spain. Email address: u1055773@correu.udg.edu.

Jon Edwards, PhD, has been involved in the development of research and taught courses in tourism, agri-food and rural development at Bournemouth University from the outset. He always seeks to add a European/international dimension to his research and is particularly interested in the actions and attitudes of societies as they respond to change. He has published extensively in the area of religious tourism.
Mailing address: Sustainable Development Research Group, School of Tourism, Bournemouth University, Poole, Dorset BH12 5BB, UK. Email address: jonedwards@bournemouth.ac.uk.

Carlos Fernandes, PhD, is an associate professor at the Polytechnic Institute of Viana do Castelo, Portugal. He obtained his BA at Syracuse University (USA), MA at Rutgers University (USA) and PhD at Bournemouth University (UK). His interests include tourism as a strategy for rural development, cultural and creative tourism and destination management. In the last few years, he has conducted research and/or consultancy within various special interest areas, including tourism and gastronomy, cultural tourism, and religious tourism and pilgrimage. Carlos also cooperates in World Tourism Organization (UNWTO) activities including 'training the trainer' courses in Africa (Angola and Zimbabwe), training of entrepreneurship for women in Mozambique and capacity-building initiatives in Ukraine and Moldova for the Council of Europe. Carlos has presented papers at national and international conferences and has a substantial number of publications in his area of interest. Mailing address: Escola Superior de Tecnologia e Gestão de Viana do Castelo, Polytechnic Institute of Viana do Castelo, Avenida do Atlântico, 4900-348 Viana do Castelo, Portugal. Email address: cfernandes@estg.ipvc.pt.

Eimear Ging, BA, PGCert (Hum), MA (Hist) (Open), works in administration in a busy Dublin teaching hospital. At the weekends, however, she leads a secret life as a re-enactor and living historian, with a particular interest in the early medieval period. Email address: eimear.ging@gmail.com.

Catherine Gorman, PhD, lectures in tourism marketing, culture and heritage, sustainable tourism and event management at the Dublin Institute of Technology, Ireland. She is originally a science graduate and has a Master's in both environmental science and business/tourism management. Her PhD in geography (TCD) focused on cooperation and networking within the garden tourism sector in Ireland. Catherine has been involved in the development and marketing of tourism at local, regional and national level for the past 20 years. She has contributed papers and chapters on a number of her research interest areas, including tourism marketing, cooperation and networking, cultural and rural tourism. She also led an INTERREG project examining partnerships and networks in the tourism industry and has undertaken work for a variety of stakeholders within the tourism sector. She is member of ICOMOS Ireland, sitting on the Cultural Tourism NSC. Mailing address: College of Arts and Tourism, Dublin Institute of Technology, Dublin 1, Ireland. Email address: catherine.gorman@dit.ie.

Brendan Griffin, BBS, MBS, PMP, is a PMI PMBoK-certified project manager with more than 10 years of experience in managing technology projects in industries including retail and educational software for major international companies. In addition, Brendan has a decade of experience organising and training re-enactment groups as well as events on a regional and national scale. Email address: brendangrif@gmail.com.

Kevin A. Griffin, PhD, is a lecturer and former head of department in tourism at the Dublin Institute of Technology. He is Chair of the ATLAS Religious and Pilgrimage Tourism Special Interest Group (SIG). His academic interests span sustainable tourism, culture/heritage, local history and education. He has written, presented and edited a range of work on various topics in the sphere of tourism and events. Mailing address: College of Arts and Tourism, Dublin Institute of Technology, Cathal Brugha Street, Dublin 1, Ireland. Email address: kevin.griffin@dit.ie.

Claudia Bauer-Krösbacher, PhD, is a full-time lecturer and researcher at the University of Applied Sciences Krems in Austria. She received her PhD from the Dublin Institute of Technology and holds an MA in economics from the University of Innsbruck. Her research interests are cultural tourism, authenticity, tourism consumer behaviour, and multivariate methods as well as qualitative research methods. Her research has been published in the *Journal of Travel Research* and several books. Claudia also has extensive experience as a lecturer at the Vienna University of Economics and Business Administration and the University of Innsbruck. Mailing address: Tourism & Leisure Management, IMC Fachhochschule Krems, University of Applied Sciences Krems, A-3500 Krems, Austria. Email address: claudia. kroesbacher@fh-krems.ac.at.

Wided Majdoub is assistant professor of marketing at the Faculty of Economics and Management of Sousse, Tunisia. She is member of the Tourism and Development Research Unit and of the UNESCO/UNITWIN Culture, Tourism, Development Network, and has carried out research on issues of cultural tourism, cultural itineraries and creative tourism, tourist planning and management of World Heritage Sites. She works in the field of consumer culture theory, new tourists' consumption behaviour and creative tourism. Her recent works concern cultural itineraries, rehabilitation of the medinas, museums and experiential consumption, nature-based tourism and sustainability. She is working in collaboration with foreign universities and research institutes, with international and local boards in the creation of management plans for the protection and promotion of cultural and tourist resources. Mailing address: Faculty of Economics and Management of Sousse, BP 307 – Cité Riadh. 4023, University of Sousse, Sousse, Tunisia. Email address: wided.majdoub@gmail.com.

Frances McGettigan is a lecturer in tourism at Athlone Institute of Technology and has published papers on religious/spiritual/cultural tourism, archaeotourism, and community tourism. She has presented at national and international conferences on these topics. Frances actively works with various stakeholders within the tourism industry. She is a member of Atlas Religious Tourism and Pilgrimage Special Interest Group and Cultural Tourism Special Interest Group. Mailing address: Department of Hospitality, Tourism and Leisure Studies, Athlone Institute of Technology, Athlone, Co. Westmeath, Ireland. Email address: FMcGettigan@AIT.IE.

Nigel D. Morpeth, PhD, is a senior lecturer in tourism management and holds degrees in government and politics, recreation management and sustainability and tourism. He has published work internationally on sustainable tourism policy, communities and cultural events and festivals, tourism development and aspects of special interest tourism. His current research interests are in religious tourism and pilgrimage and in linkages between the creative industries and tourism, specifically in art, artists and tourism. He is co-editor with colleague Dr Razaq Raj of *Religious Tourism and Pilgrimage Management: An International Perspective*. Mailing address: School of Events, Tourism and Hospitality, Leeds Metropolitan University, City Campus, Leeds LS1 3HE, UK. Email address: n.morpeth@leedsmet.ac.uk.

Wil Munsters, PhD, is director of the Centre for Research on Tourism and Culture and professor of Tourism and Culture at Zuyd University, the Netherlands. He has a strong academic background, including a PhD from the University of Nijmegen focusing on French literature and comparative aesthetics. For the last 20 years his major research interest has been in cultural tourism. He is the author of tourism studies on the Netherlands and Belgium. He has also contributed to numerous national and international conferences on tourism. As a member of ATLAS he has been engaged in the international Cultural Tourism Research Project since 1994. Mailing address: Centre for Research on Tourism and Culture, Zuyd University of Applied Sciences, P.B. 550, 6400 AN Heerlen, the Netherlands. Email address: wil.munsters@ zuyd.nl.

Manon Niesten, MSc, is a researcher at the Centre for Research on Tourism and Culture at Zuyd University, the Netherlands. She obtained her Master's degree in marketing at Maastricht University, the Netherlands. She has been involved in research on contemplative tourism and cultural tourism for a number of years. Mailing address: Centre for Research on Tourism and Culture, Zuyd University of Applied Sciences, P.B. 634, 6200 AP Maastricht, the Netherlands. Email address: manon.niesten@zuyd.nl.

Noëlle O'Connor, PhD, is senior lecturer in tourism and hospitality studies and course director for the Bachelor of Arts (Honours) in business studies with event management programme in

Limerick Institute of Technology, Ireland. She is also an MBA online tutor at Glion University, Switzerland. Noëlle is currently an external examiner for the University of the West of Scotland and Bath Spa University, UK. She has a wide range of industrial experience, having worked in the Irish, British, French and Austrian hospitality industries and her research focus is in the area of film-induced tourism, celebrity endorsement of tourism destinations, destination branding and tourism education. Mailing address: Department of Humanities, School of Business and Humanities, Limerick Institute of Technology, Limerick City, Ireland. Email address: noelle. oconnor@lit.ie.

Milena Oliveras-Schwarz graduated in humanities from Barcelona's Pompeu Fabra University, specialising in art. She also holds a Master's degree in Cultural Tourism from the University of Girona, where she is currently taking part in a research project on tourism and imagery. Mailing address: Tourism Faculty, University of Girona, Plaça Ferrater Mora, 1, 17071, Girona, Spain. Email address: milena.oliveras@gmail.com.

Ivana Pavlic, PhD, received her doctorate of social science in economics in 2007 at the Faculty of Economics, University of Josip Juraj Strossmayer, Osijek. Her doctoral dissertation was titled 'Market position of Croatian tourism products on the Mediterranean under globalization conditions'. In July 2010 she became assistant professor in the field of trade and tourism. She is involved in teaching at the Department of Economics and Business Economics and also at the Department for Public Relations, University of Dubrovnik. She teaches undergraduate courses in tourism economics and consumer behaviour and graduate courses in tourism development and tourism policy, integrated marketing communication and marketing communication in tourism. She actively participates in international conferences in Croatia and abroad. She has published papers in national and international journals in the field of tourism and marketing. She is co-author of a university handbook and also published two book chapters. Her areas of interest are related to tourism, consumer behaviour in tourism, marketing communication and researching the tourism market. She cooperates with several Croatian and international companies and non-profit organizations. Through her research she has made contributions to the regional development of Croatia. Mailing address: Department of Economics and Business Economics, University of Dubrovnik, Lapadska obala 7, 20 000, Dubrovnik, Croatia. Email address: ipavlic@unidu.hr.

Razaq Raj, PhD, is senior lecturer at the UK Centre for Events Management, teaching financial and strategic management. His research interests include community events, outdoor events, economic impacts, religious tourism, cultural festivals and sustainable tourism, cultural diversity in events management and financial management for events. He has published work on special events, financial management in events, information technology, cultural festivals and events, sustainable tourism and religious tourism. He is author of the text books *Religious Tourism and Pilgrimage Management: An International Perspective, Advanced Event Management: An Integrated and Practical Approach* and *Event Management and Sustainability*. He also sits on a number of voluntary sector management boards. He is President for the CIRCLE (The Centre for International Research in Consumers Location and their Environments) and Board member for the ATLAS (The Association for Tourism and Leisure Education). Mailing address: Leeds Metropolitan University, City Campus, Leeds LS1 3HE, UK. Email address: r.raj@leedsmet.ac.uk.

Ian D. Rotherham, PhD, is professor of environmental geography and reader in tourism and environmental change at Sheffield Hallam University. He is an environmental geographer, historian and ecologist and has written over 400 articles, papers, books and book chapters. He also writes and broadcasts on history and environmental issues for newspapers, radio and television, including the BBC History Programme. His work in leisure and tourism is focused on human–nature–heritage interactions and issues of cultural severance. This research is together with long-term case studies on the potential of tourism as a tool for regeneration and for economic and social impacts. Mailing address: Sheffield Hallam University, Faculty of

Development and Society, City Campus, Sheffield S1 1WB, UK. Email address: i.d.rotherham@
shu.ac.uk.

Agnieszka Rozenkiewicz is a PhD student in geography at the University of Wrocław in Poland
(Faculty of Earth Science and Environmental Management), involved in the work of the
Department of Regional and Tourism Geography. Her doctoral dissertation explores the question of archaeological tourism complexes in pursuit of the model of adjustment to visitors'
needs. Agnieszka was conferred the title of Bachelor of Business (Honours) in Tourism and
Hospitality Management at Athlone Institute of Technology in Ireland, where she was awarded
the Student of the Year of the School of Humanities (2010–2011). At present she continues
her education in the MA programme of English language studies at the Philological School of
Higher Education in Wrocław. Mailing address: Institute of Geography and Regional
Development, Department of Regional and Tourism Geography, University of Wrocław, Pl.
Uniwersytecki 1, 50–137 Wrocław, Poland. Email address: agnieszkarozenkiewicz@wp.pl.

Karl A. Russell is a senior lecturer in hospitality management at London Metropolitan University.
He is head of the MA Hospitality Management programme and holds a BA (Hons) in hospitality management, MSc in computer science and a Doctorate in the field of strategic management within the hospitality industry and is a professional member of the Institute of Hospitality
Management. Karl has held teaching posts in the UK, Switzerland, UAE and Iran. His research
interests are in strategic management and competitive advantage within the hospitality industry
and Islamic hospitality within emerging markets. He has extensive research and consultancy
experience in the UK, Switzerland and the Middle East. Mailing address: London Metropolitan
Business School, London Metropolitan University, Stapleton House, 277–281 Holloway
Road, London N7 8HN, UK. Email address: K.Russell@londonmet.ac.uk.

Dolors Vidal-Casellas is Dean and senior lecturer at the Tourism Faculty of the University of
Girona, director of the Official Master in Cultural Tourism, member of the Contemporary
Culture and Art Chair and also member of the Contemporary Art Theories and Higher Institute
of Tourism Studies Research Groups. She is director of the Turisme cultural (cultural tourism)
collection by Edicions Vitel·la (http://www.edicionsvitella.com). She is a member of various
cooperation programmes with universities from Algeria, São Paolo, Piracicaba (São Paolo,
Brazil) and San Martín de Porres (Lima, Peru). She is also a member of international cultural
tourism networks: IBERTUR, ATLAS and the UNITWIN 'Culture, tourisme et development'
(UNESCO) group. Mailing address: Tourism Faculty, University of Girona, Plaça Ferrater Mora,
1, 17071 Girona, Spain. Email address: dolors.vidal@udg.edu.

Ivona Vrdoljak Raguž, PhD, received her doctorate of social sciences in economics in 2009 at
the Faculty of Economics, University of Split (doctoral dissertation titled 'The interdependence
of leadership styles and business performance of large Croatian companies'). In July 2010
became assistant professor in the organization and management branch. In the Department of
Economics and Business Economics, University of Dubrovnik, she teaches fundamentals of
management, purchasing management, sales management and human resource management
at undergraduate level and strategic management at graduate level. She actively participates in
international conferences at home and abroad. She publishes papers, national and international in the field of organization, management and leadership and she has published two book
chapters. Her areas of interest are related to the study of general management, strategic management, decision making, business processes and leadership. She cooperates with Croatian
businesses and participates in the development of professional studies. She is a member of the
Croatian Economic Association. She is fluent in English and Italian. From 2011 she has been
Head of the Department of Economy and Business Economy. Mailing address: Department of
Economics and Business Economics, University of Dubrovnik, Lapadska obala 7, 20 000,
Dubrovnik, Croatia. Email address: ivrdolja@unidu.hr.

Vincent Zammit, MA (Baroque Studies), BA (Mediterranean Studies), was born in Valletta and
studied at the University of Malta. Presently he is a lecturer and the head of the Tourism Studies
Department at the Institute of Tourism Studies (Malta) and coordinator of the Centre for

Cultural and Heritage Studies, where he lectures in history, guiding techniques, and cultural and heritage tourism. He has been involved in Maltese culture, heritage and tourism since 1978. Besides guiding special interest groups, he has published a number of studies and books, and has produced and presented a number of radio and television programmes on Maltese history and culture. For the past 16 years he has been responsible for the preparation of tourist guides in Malta. Mailing address: Institute of Tourism Studies, St George's Bay, St Julian's STJ 3300, Malta. Email address: vincent.zammit@gov.mt.

1 Introduction to Cultural Tourism Philosophy and Management

Kevin A. Griffin,[1] Razaq Raj[2] and Nigel D. Morpeth[2]
[1]*Dublin Institute of Technology, Dublin, Ireland;*
[2]*Leeds Metropolitan University, Leeds, UK*

1.1 Introduction

This chapter introduces conceptual, theoretical, policy and management dimensions of culture and presents various themes and critical discourses that underpin the chapters within this book. With an array of cultural tourism books on the market, this volume is distinctive in its philosophy: the authors link the concept of culture to the notion of identity, both individual and collective. In doing so we recognize the importance of individual, community and national identity formation, through community and national celebrations of culture, through inter-cultural dialogue and engagement and all of these within the frame of tourism. In some cases, the individual chapter authors illustrate host communities 'staging' cultural spectacles for tourist consumption through events and festivals; in others, we see local communities living their daily lives with the consumption

of cultural tourism as a by-product; and in others we see the connection with tourism as a tangential and sometimes even accidental occurrence. However, in all instances we see culture and tourism woven together in a cross-pollinating interaction, whereby both the touristic and the cultural experience is a richer one for all those involved.

1.2 The Concept of Culture

As many commentators have acknowledged, culture is one of those slippery concepts with no simple or single definition and a central intention of this book is to add clarity and focus to the notion of both culture and cultural tourism. We argue that a particular strength of this book is the range and coverage of global cultural contexts and tourism, with case study chapters providing timely and pertinent overviews of discourses, contemporary empirical research of culture and inter-culturalism within multiple societies across a range of continents. Storry and Childs suggest that

> Contemporary ... culture is a mixture of all cultures of the past that people are influenced by but certain figures, symbols and narratives exercise particularly strong control over the ways we imagine ourselves to have been.
>
> (1997, p. 4)

This book moves beyond such a singular (Anglo-centric) perspective of culture and tourism and this chapter in particular provides a reassessment of the increasing linkages and interconnections between tourism and culture on a global, national and community scale. This discussion, therefore, illustrates how culture helps to define tourist destinations but in doing so potentially impacts on the coherence of local culture.

In policy terms, the UK's Department of Media Culture and Sport (2007, p. 1) provides an interesting example of how a government can create distinctive and highly aspirational priorities for culture. These ubiquitous policy objectives were intended to create improvements in 'education, social cohesion, regional regeneration, the quality of ... institutions and ... cultural life'. It is suggested therefore that culture contains a matrix of these diverse functional elements, and that economic impacts (outputs) of culture might be measurable in addition to less tangible social and health-related goals that might be more difficult to quantify. Within a review of literature on culture it is clear that there are both common and disparate elements of what constitutes the phenomenon/phenomena of culture.

When exploring the complex nature underlying the concept of culture, consideration must be given to both its material and immaterial elements and there must be acknowledgement that within different ontological, epistemological and ideological perspectives there are competing discourses and narratives that challenge dominant world-views of what constitutes culture. In doing this, the current volume considers cases of cultural tourism, both community-based and on a global and transnational level like the discussion by MacDonald, whereby culture occupies a crucial

role as both an embodiment of the Nationstate and Nationhood and a key element in

> the nationalist quest for order and mapped boundaries ... where groups ... literally employ physical objects in their constitution of culture (and) are unusually capable among institutions of turning culture into an object: of materializing it.
>
> (1996, p. 7)

Citing Graham's approach to developing this concept further, MacDonald (1996) notes that culture can be a localized (but not necessarily place-related) and spatially focused experience that might provide a 'microcosm of regional, national (and international) heritage in a single manageable and visitable site' (2000, p. 198), thereby transforming recreational structures with 'meaning' into cultural locations. Graham *et al.*'s speculation on the recyclable nature of culture as a 'natural' process of preservation and the concept of moving heritage resources to new locations as replication leads to questions of identity and continuity, the mythologizing of nation state 'in which "high culture" and "low culture" battle for legitimacy' (MacDonald, 1996, p. 14).

Conceptually, in citing the work of Nash (1999) and Merriman (1991), Graham *et al.* remind us that culture as a 'recycler' of the past is the 'product of specific historical circumstances' (2000, p. 32) and should not be seen as merely telling a story (linear narrative) about the past but should be recognized as creating meaning through specific social and political circumstances and indeed most likely reflecting dominant narratives of the prevailing political and social system. For MacDonald this leads to colonial interpretations of history and to narratives with excluded 'voices' (1996, p. 7). This concept is particularly apposite in this book, where there is an emphasis on developing themes of multiculturalism and interculturalism as key elements that underpin discourses of cultural tourism. This is explored in a number of chapters, particularly Chapter 8 by Morpeth, Raj and Griffin.

1.3   Culture and Tourism

For Fjagesund and Symes, culture is part of a traditional elitist association with travel, and a throwback to the 'exclusivity of the Grand Tour' (2002, p. 48), which was articulated through travel literature of the 19th century, most notably poets such as William Wordsworth. The subsequent metamorphosis of the elite cultural traveller into a tourist embodies a process of touristification (Picard, 1996) and change in self-identity – i.e. what it means to be a tourist, perhaps by redefining what an individual 'does' as a tourist. In modern discourse, however, tourism is often seen as an industrial activity that exerts a series of impacts similar to other industrial activities. Taking this viewpoint, McKercher (1993) views tourists as consumers, not 'anthropologists', and essentially sees tourism as a form of entertainment. While he raises questions of how agencies and organizations might ameliorate and 'manage' the externalities of tourism, he argues that modifications to tourist activity might be dependent on the emergence of new forms of tourism. In this respect Palmer (1992) argues that we have an obligation to bequeath 'an undiminished bank of natural resources' and indeed cultural resources to future generations, as part of a sustainable society. To do this, tourism must adopt 'softer cultural development paths' (1992, p. 182).

The resultant study of culture encompasses a diverse range of academic disciplines that traditionally have attracted the attention of a broad community of multidisciplinary academics, including historians, orientalists, classicists, archaeologists, sociologists, anthropologists, linguists, art historians and philosophers. Increasingly, in order to explore these 'softer paths', the study of culture within the context of tourism is combined with these other academic disciplines to express new insights into the significance of culture within contemporary society.

With regards to culture and tourism, Richards identifies that 'Cultural attractions have become particularly important in … modern … tourism' (2001, p. 3) and in citing Urry (1992) goes a step further, suggesting that in fact 'tourism is culture' (2001, p. 4). Urry (1992) identifies the search for artificial pleasure environments as part of the postmodernist condition, which is preoccupied with 'dissolving … the boundaries' (1992, p. 82) of cultural forms in society. Engaging in such activity, tourists are focused on 'pseudo-events and disregarding the "real" world outside'

(1992, p. 7). Jafari (1989) and Poon (1993) echo the words of Burns and Holden (1995), who discuss 'post-modern societies [who are] in search of the alternative as a means of giving new meaning and values to social order' (1995, p. 208). Consistent with this statement is Urry's (1992, p. 13) view on the search for the 'alternative' as consistent with changes from 'post-Fordist' to more individual patterns of consumption, prompting more specialized purchasing and segmentation of consumer preferences. Arguably, this social change results in increasingly specialized patterns of purchasing cultural products.

In part, Urry views the search for new tourist products as disillusionment with mass tourism products and 'contemporary consumerism' (1992, p. 13). Sightseeing is therefore a modern ritual where attractions are venerated though what MacCannell (1976) called sight sacralization. Furthermore, the extension of Richard's thesis is that cultural sites and attractions take on 'symbolic value and meaning' (2001, p. 17). Richards highlights the work of Edensor (1998), who differentiates between 'enclavic' spaces such as hotels and attractions, which have dominant discourses controlled by the 'international tourist industry'. This is contrasted with 'heterogeneous' spaces, which are largely unplanned where 'tourists become literally "performers", creating experiences for themselves and their fellow visitors to consume' (2001, p. 18). In Boorstin's related treatise (1987) on the inauthentic experiences of modern tourism, there are parallels between the perceived qualities of the traveller from previous centuries and the search for authentic experience based on culture. This is further mirrored by Eco's (1983) contention that in fact tourists are more comfortable with the inauthentic. These various discussions around concepts of authenticity are recurring themes for a number of authors within this text.

Richards argues that this commodification has arisen because of 'the problems of growing cultural competition between cities [which] has more recently led to a shift from consumption-led to production-led strategies' (2001, p. 12). Central to this model of development is increasing festivalization and commodification of destinations, wherein 'traditional culture is not sufficient – popular culture must be added to the production mix' (2001, p. 13). Richards

(2001) cites the work of Pine and Gilmore (1999) in suggesting that economies have 'gone through a transition from extracting commodities to making goods, delivering services and currently staging experiences as the primary arena of value creation' (2001, p. 55).

The powerful forces and patterns of globalization and related social narratives have stimulated people to travel to cultural centres in many parts of the world. These social narratives might be expressed through diverse typologies of culture that reflect the consumptive trends of globalization and internationalization. This undoubtedly poses complex challenges for 'managers' of cultural destinations to respond to motivations for visitation. Practical issues of site management have to determine how cultural destinations successfully incorporate different forms of tourism that reflect the mainstream but also move 'in and out of time', departing from simply being sites of daily rituals to become 'centres of society' 'transformed' (Richards and Palmer, 2010). Indeed, in this respect sites need to reflect New Age philosophies of travel and indeed pilgrimage to explore the emergence of New Tourists or 'Esoteric Tourists'. Thus sites need to facilitate engagement in processes of spiritualization and enlightenment.

1.4 Engaging with Cultural Heritage

Intertwined with the concept of new tourists is the engagement of individuals with cultural offerings. There is a wide ethical responsibility for commercial operators, planners and policy makers to review the utilization of culture, ensure meaningful strategic policy and adequate management of their sites. This premeditated commodification of culture must take cognisance of the inherent challenges in facilitating access for all – mindful of Bourdieu's notion (1984) that individuals possess unequal levels of 'cultural capital' and thus perhaps possess varying abilities to engage with culture in a meaningful way.

For Urry (1995, p. 45) there is a fundamental question that prefaces how we understand the scope and nature of culture. This is how we remember the past. In addition, Urry

suggests that our understanding of culture is strongly influenced by the contemporary renegotiation between material and immaterial culture. Cultural products such as museums, which are the epitome of institutionalized Western society, provide representations of the past and are engaged in collectively remembering the past through promoting their specific 'theatre of memory' (Samuel, 1994). Samuel argues that the fostering of museums has lessened the importance of immaterial culture in the sense that there has been a shift from an 'auratic history to a commodified heritage' (1994, p. 46). Within this emphasis on the institutional, there is a heavy reliance on conversion of the past into simple narratives (Urry, 1995, p. 52). Pearce argues that material cultural entities include the 'museum (which) is an institution which collects, documents, preserves, exhibits and interprets material evidence and associated information for the public benefit' (1992, citing the Museums Association, 1991, p. 13). However, in mapping out different phases of cultural expression from modern to post-modern, Pearce identifies that

> In essence, modernity was concerned with the development of meta-narratives, overarching discourses through which objective realities and eternal truths could be defined and expressed.
> (1992, p. 2)

Pearce considers that one of the characteristics of the modern (Western capitalist) meta-narrative is the 'complex relationship with objects – as producers, owners and collectors' (1992, p. 3) and our associated endeavours to understand material culture (for Pearce the whole of cultural expression is fashioned by material culture). The act of the material collection of culture is, according to Pearce, guided by 'inherited social ideas' and 'curators make museum meanings from the material and the traditions which they inherit' (1992, p. 118).

Prior suggests museums as important social entities, not only because they appear to fortify a cultural doxa under threat in postmodern social space (permanence, nationhood, art, history) and represent identities, objects and histories, but also because they are indeterminate, contradictory, shifting spaces that are subject to contested meanings and open acts of (mis)interpretation (2002, p. 211).

1.5 How is Culture Formed/Shaped?

Muensterberger (1995) asked the question: Why do we collect? This is as pertinent for immaterial as it is for material culture. In defining collecting as simply 'selecting, gathering and keeping objects of subjective value' (1995, p. 4), he indicated that, in part, choices and tastes of collectable items reflect the social cultural climate of society. Walsh considered the 'expansion of heritage during the 1970s and 1980s' as a response to disconnection from history and an attempt to develop a sense of rootedness (1992, p. 116). This desperate attempt to become 'connected' opened the door for wholesale commodification of both culture and heritage. Looking at later society highlights a continuation of this trend. Jones has examined the increasingly blurred boundaries between the virtual and real/online and offline worlds and the part that technology plays in creating simulacra and hyper-real (tourist and) voyeuristic experiences. Jones (2002) goes on to identify the growing and ubiquitous nature of virtual cultures – the amalgam of cultures hybridized through cyberspace.

In Staging the Real, Kilborn (2003) used the phrases 'faking the real' and 'new modes of reality formatting'. He suggests that

> As far as artefacts and objects are concerned, the practice of faking is connected with attempts to fulfil the desire of those who wish to own or have access to an original item which, in cultural or material terms, is deemed to be of high value – often on account of its unique qualities. Hence passing something off as original, when in fact it has been copied or cloned, attracts a particular kind of cultural opprobrium.
>
> (2003, p. 127)

Walsh (1992) has criticized superficial representations of the past – which are offered through the guise of a heritage industry that is founded in a market ideology. This is part of what he observed as 'the wider assertion of the New Right, that the individual can experience new forms of emancipation through the market' (1992, p. 121).

Going a step beyond individual cultural elements, and reflecting on this 'market' concept, Prior claims that destinations have a 'cultural history' and engage in 'cultural production', which results from 'culture mediated power relations' (2002, p. 212). Prior (2002) then goes on to remind us that a 'traditional' view of culture is as a conduit for a society's 'most cherished values'. At the apex of 'society', the state is viewed as a custodian or mediator of mass culture. Stallabrass questions this custodian role, however, stating that

> the model of culture to which the state subscribes has become corporatised, and that corporations want to reduce aesthetic experiences to fashion.
>
> (2004, p. 100)

Destinations therefore create cultural patterns within the (often European-influenced) world. For MacDonald this has societal implications, shaping spatial and temporal orders and indeed 'creating cultural contexts' and 'embodiments of temporal relations and social rememberings' (1996, p. 9).

Urry (1992) reminds us that there are inherent contradictions in remembering the past, thus influencing the formation of cultural and heritage values. This thread is taken up by Prior who identifies 'history as palimpsest, delivering a cultural legacy of conflict to a new generation of artistic agents' (2002, p. 212). MacDonald, in citing Lumley and the dubbing of societies as 'Time-machines' (1988, p. 9), adds temporal dimensions to the act of both individually and collectively remembering the past. In fact Urry questions the actual act of abstracting 'historical time' (1995, p. 48), highlighting that the past is constructed in the paramount reality of the present. Each moment of the past is constructed anew, so there is no past or back there. There is only the present, in the context of which the past is constructed anew.

1.6 Cultural Tourism

While providing a sound basis for academic reflection, such ponderings as outlined in the chapter above are mainly of little interest to the tourism industry, which focuses more on culture or more specifically on cultural tourism as a marketable and saleable 'product'. This business-focused linkage between culture and tourism has been explored in depth by a 2009

OECD Report entitled The Impact of Culture on Tourism. This suggests that the growing 'articulation' between culture and tourism was stimulated by a number of factors, which it classifies under Demand and Supply (see Fig. 1.1).

According to the OECD, the resultant cultural tourism product is responsible for influencing approximately 40% of global international trips (OECD, 2009, p. 1), is of growing international importance, and results in the regional/ destination benefits outlined in Fig. 1.2.

The aforementioned growth in importance of cultural tourism as expressed by the OECD has been paramount in prompting the production of this text. The authors, in presenting their work (both conceptual and case-based), aspire to blend the theoretical with the practical and thus bridge the divide between the tourism industry and academia. This blending of practitioner and theoretician is to be seen throughout the chapters of the book, with most authors being more

firmly based in one or other paradigm. However, the majority of contributors comfortably blend the two approaches to provide, in its entirety, a readable, pragmatic, yet theoretically sound work, which we hope will be of interest and use to both academic and practice-based readers.

1.7 Structure of the Book

The following sections provide an overview of the book, identifying the key concepts and ideas of each chapter. In Chapter 2, 'Managing Heritage and Cultural Tourism Resources', Jon Edwards highlights how the culturally motivated visitor goes to a diverse range of cultural and heritage venues, which necessitates the effective and efficient management of cultural resources. The multi-sectoral management focus, he argues, should be on providing a quality experience for visitors, which increasingly

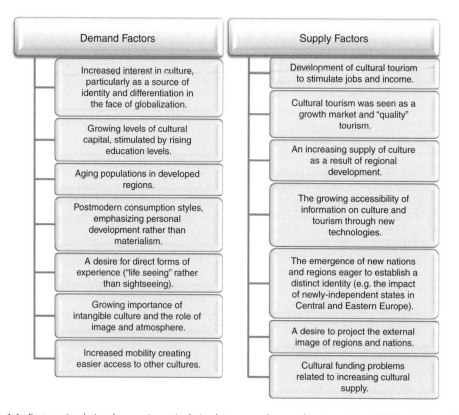

Fig. 1.1. Factors stimulating the growing articulation between culture and tourism. (From OECD, 2009, p. 20.)

Creating jobs and businesses.

Increasing tax revenues.

Diversifying the local economy.

Creating opportunities for partnerships.

Attracting visitors interested in history and preservation.

Increasing historic attraction revenues.

Preserving local traditions and culture.

Generating local investment in historic resources.

Building community pride in heritage.

Increasing awareness of the site or area's significance.

Fig. 1.2. Benefits of cultural tourism. (From National Trust for Historic Preservation in the USA, cited in OECD, 2009, p. 22.)

requires collaborative approaches between managers and visitors to ensure that within the tourist experience they can enjoy a sense of place and an authentic experience or experiences.

In Chapter 3, 'The Impact of Cultural Tourism on Host Communities', Carlos Fernandes, after initially defining the concept of community and its multifaceted elements, considers the problems associated with a range of impacts, including economic, environmental and socio-cultural, and applying the tenets of social exchange theory to the analysis of impacts suggests that community well-being is linked to the perceived benefits that can be accrued from tourism. He argues that capacity building is required for communities to accrue lasting benefits from the development of cultural tourism.

Chapter 4, Cultural Tourism: Issues and Policies', by Razaq Raj, Kevin Griffin and Nigel Morpeth, highlights a range of theoretical models that try to frame cultural tourism, bringing together definitions of culture and tourism and illustrating the constant strain between the terms. In a highly pragmatic approach, while acknowledging various 'higher order' means of exploring culture, the chapter recognizes the almost inevitable commodification of culture that emerges when discussing cultural tourism. The second main theme of the chapter is the

presentation of case studies to illustrate the development of cultural tourism policy in a range of international destinations.

Chapter 5, 'Cultural Sites and their Management: Co-creation of Value or Co-creation of Experience?', by Wided Majdoub, applies different academic discourses to explore how producers and consumers of tourism might collaborate to co-create meanings, values and experiences related to cultural tourism. She argues that while the tourism industry works on a goods-dominant logic, applying both service dominant logic and consumer theory, it is possible to create a theoretical foundation to add to the embryonic field of tourism and leisure research, which is attempting to understand the co-creation of experience. He argues that if customers are to be fully involved in defining experience environments, then cultural tourism managers need to engage customers in communication processes in the planning of those environments.

In Chapter 6, 'Mobile Interpretation at Cultural Attractions: Insights into Users and Non-users of Audio-Guides', Claudia Bauer-Krösbacher posits that quality interpretation can be regarded as a key aspect to the cultural tourism experience, with a key question being how to tell the story around sites and exhibitions. It is suggested that different media applications should underpin strategies that offer the right type of interpretation to different types of visitor. Using insights from research into the museums sector in Vienna, it is argued that ICT increasingly provides opportunities for mobile technologies to create more effective forms of interpretation.

In Chapter 7, 'Emerging Concepts and Case Studies of Eco-cultural Tourism', Ian D. Rotherham emphasizes how expressions of cultural identity in rural destinations become important meeting places for tourists to engage in cultural tourism. He uses case study work in a range of rural locations within Europe, Africa and South-east Asia to further the concept of eco-cultural tourism. He argues that established forms of ecotourism are fast becoming mass forms of tourism, experienced within rural locations, and as such this is a misused and misunderstood concept. The distinctiveness of eco-cultural tourism allows the ecological and cultural dimensions of a landscape to combine in creating a site that forms an attraction for tourists. In exploring the Libyan Green Mountains he demonstrates how Roman settlements along the Mediterranean shore combine to become an effective eco-cultural landscape.

Chapter 8, 'Reinventing British Culture: Multiculturalism, Travel and Cross-cultural Comparisons', by Nigel D. Morpeth, Razaq Raj and Kevin Griffin, provides important multi-cultural perspectives of culture that are intended to present a range of discourses on culture while also seeking to challenge the dominance of Eurocentric and 'white' perspectives of culture, which have become established as the bedrock on which cultural and tourism discourses are recorded in many countries. In using cross-cultural analysis of multiculturalism within the UK and Australia, and examining associated tourism marketing campaigns, conclusions are made about the focus of multiculturalism within the image identity making of tourist destinations.

Chapters 9–19 provide an eclectic group of cultural tourism cases, and combine contemporary empirical insights from a range of international scholars. In Chapter 9, 'Case Study 1: Irish Cultural Tourism – Case Study of Policy Development', Catherine Gorman highlights how over 300 historic houses and gardens in Ireland provide the focus for a cultural tourism

experience, emphasizing the scope for visitors to engage in creative forms of tourism within these locations. In marketing these cultural locations for tourism, it is argued that balance needs to be achieved between access and authenticity. The potential danger of maximizing the economic benefit from these sites may result in losing the cultural significance of the house and garden through over-commodification. Within heritage becoming an important economic driver in Irish society, it is argued that a balance is needed between finding appropriate funding to keep these resources open as cultural attractions and preserving their cultural integrity. This necessitates a strategic approach to policy development for those organizations and agencies managing houses and gardens.

Within Chapter 10, 'Case Study 2: Archaeotourism – The Past is Our Future?', Frances McGettigan and Agnieszka Rozenkie-wicz explore the issue of culture through the concept of archaeotourism as a distinctive form of tourism and more specifically as a distinctive specialized product for Irish tourism, an underresearched area in the view of the authors. The essence of this form of tourism is the conservation of the historical-archaeological sites and how interpretation offers the key for tourists to experience the authenticity of this form of attraction. The authors use the context of Newgrange to determine what motivates the cultural tourist to visit such sites. Their research reveals that the majority of visitors to this World Heritage Site considered that they are archaeological tourists and gained a quality experience through effective management, interpretation and visitor guide services and through impressive marketing.

Chapter 11, 'Case Study 3: Urban Regeneration and Culture: Maltese Example', by Vincent Zammit, uses the cultural context of Malta to demonstrate how in recent decades tourists have developed a greater understanding of the cultural heritage of its islands. This is part due to the role of government-inspired regeneration and tourist board initiatives based on culture, strategically identified through a National Cultural Policy. Festivals and historical re-enactments as the foundation of these community-based regeneration initiatives are highlighted within the chapter, a theme that is picked up later in Chapter 18 where Griffin and Ging present a detailed case study focused entirely on re-enactment. The author concludes that through these initiatives the local population has gained greater cultural awareness, but also that culture is a key aspect of tourist visitation.

In Chapter 12, 'Case Study 4: The Cultural Tourism Sustainability Mix Applied to the Development of Contemplative Tourism in Limburg, the Netherlands', Wil Munsters and Manon Niesten use the context of the Roman Catholic tradition within the province of Limburg to demonstrate how a religious site and its buildings can be utilized as a niche cultural tourist product. The authors highlight the complexity of managing a site that is primarily focused on prayer and worship with the aim of developing so-called contemplative tourism. They apply the conceptual framework of the cultural tourism sustainability mix to demonstrate how, in theory, it is possible to visualize a balance between the preservation of cultural resources with the expectations of contemplative tourists who are seeking an authentic experience in their interaction with the host community. In reality this form of cultural tourism places an obligation on tourists to have sensitivity towards cultural sites that are designed for worship and prayer.

Chapter 13, 'Case Study 5: Network of Hungarian Rural Heritage Farmhouses', presents a good example of built, natural, tangible and intangible cultural preservation using the indispensable contribution of tourism. In doing so, Lia Bassa links with the themes of Chapter 6, highlighting how technologies can be utilized to interpret (and also manage) both individual cultural heritage sites and their overall network; this theme was also touched on by Gorman in Chapter 9, which in addition also focuses on heritage houses and gardens, but constructions of a very different scale. The author in this chapter specifically reports on a rural research project that focuses on a network of over 400 heritage buildings throughout Hungary. In addition the chapter explores the application of ICT technologies at these sites to understand and curate the local histories, which encapsulate a collection of historical cultural memories in a range of different archives. The author reports sadly that not all of these historical archive materials have been preserved.

In Chapter 14, 'Case Study 6: Managing Heritage and Cultural Tourism Resources in Dubrovnik', Ivana Pavlic and Ivona Vrdoljak Raguž focus on the UNESCO World Heritage city of Dubrovnik as an example of an urban cultural tourism development. In promoting the application of a sustainable development model for the better management of cultural sites they advocate incorporating the views of local people. The authors report that the major challenge for city authorities in preserving and managing historical sites within the Old City is a lack of appropriate funding; however, networks of cultural and tourism institutions are emerging to interpret and present the cultural heritage of the Old City. This is somewhat similar to the previous case study of Hungary, which also stresses the need to preserve cultural-historical heritage. It is suggested in this instance that seasonality of tourism demand is a further challenge for the city authorities in creating a sustainable cultural tourism product, as is the over-emphasis on city centre sites to the neglect of more peripheral cultural elements.

Chapter 15, 'Case Study 7: Urban Regeneration and Cultural Development of Girona', by Neus Crous-Costa and Dolors Vidal-Casellas, outlines how Spain has over 900 historical and artistic heritage sites and over 14,000 UNESCO sites. The authors, using the specific context of Girona and its urban recovery plan which stretches over four decades, map out a descriptive overview of the chronology of restoration and preservation. Embedded within this descriptive overview is the theme of emerging/growing tourism and its recognition as an important part of the City Plan, which was implemented in 1994 and had the ambition of making Girona a European city of tourism. At the heart of this plan is the recognition that the cultural heritage of the city, and in particular the Jewish Quarter and Arabian baths, would be promoted for tourism consumption but crucially alongside the regeneration of local-level facilities within the city that conserve the community and cultural dynamic.

In Chapter 16, 'Case Study 8: Reflection on the Constituent Elements of Cultural Tourism: Theatre Festivals. A Case Study of Temporada Alta (Girona, Spain)', Dolors

Vidal-Casellas, Neus Crous-Costa and Milena Oliveras-Schwarz emphasize that the relationship between theatre festivals and tourism is consistent with the way that festivals in general are used as a way of attracting tourists to a destination. In initially reviewing the general qualities of festivals, not least their capacity to enhance a destination's image, they specifically review Girona's 'Temporada Alta' Festival and the focus on theatre, which in their view has revitalized the cultural life of Girona. Nevertheless, they conclude from their analysis that there is scope for a more strategic approach between arts administrators and tourism bodies to have an integrated approach to marketing theatres and festivals within Girona.

In Chapter 17, 'Case Study 9: The London 2012 Olympic Games: The Cultural Tourist as a Pillar of Sustainability', Russell and O'Connor provide a timely reminder written in advance of the 2012 Olympic Games being staged in London of the global scope that the Olympics has, not just in sporting terms but also in its capacity for cultural exchange. The initial part of the chapter provides an overview chronology of the previous modern Olympics. The distinctiveness of this chapter, however, is its treatise on the emergence of possible Olympic hostings in 'the east' and the cultural significance for the event travelling beyond a western cultural focus. However, Russell and O'Connor highlight that with the potential for large numbers of visitors from Islamic countries within the Middle East, there are cultural challenges for both the Olympic organization and indeed the venue hosts and organizers to be able to respond to the cultural needs of these potential visitors and participants. They identify that these cultural tourists will have a need for daily prayer and other cultural sensitivities that organizers have to respect, such as gender segregation, dress code and culturally determined dietary needs.

Grifffin and Ging, in Chapter 18, 'Case Study 10: Re-enactment as an Aspect of Cultural Tourism', set an Irish cultural context as backdrop for the development of cultural tourism, illustrating this by focusing on re-enactment to enliven cultural festivals and sites. They specifically use the example of the twin Midwest towns Ballina and Killaloe on the banks of the Shannon River and their linkage to the historic figure of BrianBorú to demonstrate re-enactment methodologies being used at Féile BrianBorú – a local festival – to raise cultural awareness and thereby promote a particular form of niche tourism. In their case study they raise issues of authenticity and shared experience of events and festivals between communities and visitors (this theme of viewer engagement and co-creation picks up on and illustrates concepts raised by Majdoub in Chapter 5). The authors then discuss how nationally conceived cultural initiatives throughout 2013 will be used to stimulate developing a large Celtic/Gaelic/Viking event in 2014, marking the highly significant Millennium anniversary of the Battle of Clontarf, which resonates throughout the Irish diaspora and neighbouring European countries – particularly those with Viking connections.

Chapter 19, 'Case Study 11: Music, Money and Movement', focuses on the global role of performed music as a cultural resource that has historically adapted to new geographical locations, assimilating the cultural and musical nuances of that location. In this chapter Clarke explores the community dynamic and relationships within performed music and its patterns and traditions, but also the impact of commercialization on music and music as a resource for tourism. In tracking musical change within an historical context, he highlights the role of globalization in cultural change within the context of music. In providing a series of observations about the capacity of musical festivals to attract cultural tourists, Clarke combines an invaluable series of personal insights into the cultural role of music. In his various travels and the resultant musical travelogue, the author has developed cultural insights into a global range of cultural music locations. The chapter is underpinned by theoretical insights on the culture cycle and the role of authenticity in music, performance and cultural contexts.

1.8 Summary

This chapter sets the scene for a re-examination within the second decade of the 21st century of the complex concept that is culture, of its relationship with our understanding of tourism and the phenomena of cultural tourism within different global contexts. This book brings together a range of established and emerging academics, and provides an invaluable insight into contemporary research and case studies that in their cross-cutting themes consider different approaches to the management of cultural tourism within diverse cultural contexts. In providing cultural insights from various perspectives, the volume incorporates a range of multicultural perspectives and examples of both material and immaterial culture.

1.9   Discussion Questions

- What is culture? Consider different definitions of culture.
- What are the distinctions between material and immaterial culture?
- Consider how cultural tourism is expressed within different cultural locations.
- What impact has the so-called 'on-line' world had on our understanding of culture?

References

Boorstin, D. (1987) *The Image: A Guide to Pseudo-events in America*. Harper & Row, New York.

Bourdieu, P. (1984) *Distinction: A Social Critique of the Judgment of Taste*. Routledge & Kegan Paul, London.

Burns, P. and Holden, A. (1995) *Tourism: A New Perspective*. Prentice-Hall, London.

Department for Culture, Media and Sport (2007) *Annual Report*. DCMS, London.

Eco, U. (1983) *Travels in Hyperreality*. Harcourt Brace Jovanovich, San Diego, California.

Edensor, T. (1998) *Tourists at the Taj: Performance and Meaning at a Symbolic Site*. Routledge, London.

Fjagesund, P. and Symes, J. (2002) *The Northern Utopia*. Rodopi, Amsterdam.

Graham, B., Ashworth, G. and Tunbridge, J.E. (2000) *A Geography of Heritage: Power, Culture and Economy*. Oxford University Press, Oxford.

Jafari, J. (1989) Tourism models: the sociocultural aspects. *Tourism Management* 8, 151–159.

Jones, S. (1997) *Virtual Culture: Identity and Communication in Cybersociety*. Sage, London.

Kilborn, R. (2003) *Staging the Real: Factual TV Programming in the Age of 'Big Brother'*. Manchester University Press, Manchester, UK.

Lumley, R. (ed.) (1988) *The Museums Time-Machine: Putting Cultures on Display*. Routledge, London.

MacCannell, D. (1976) *The Tourist: A New Theory of the Leisure Class*. Macmillan, London.

MacDonald, S. (1996) Theorising museums: an introduction. In: MacDonald, S. and Fyfe, G. (eds) *Theorising Museums*. Blackwell, Oxford, pp. 1–18.

McKercher, B. (1993) Some fundamental truths of tourism. *The Journal of Sustainable Tourism* 1, 6–16.

Merriman, N. (1991) *Beyond the Glass Case: the Past, the Heritage, the Public in Britain*. Leicester University Press, Leicester, UK.

Muensterberger, W. (1995) *Collecting: An Unruly Passion*. Routledge, London.

Museums Association (1991) *A National Strategy for Museums*. Museums Association, London.

Nash, C. (1999) Historical geographies of modernity. In: Graham, B. and Nash, C. (eds) *Modern Historical Geographies*. Pearson, London, pp. 13–40.

OECD (2009) *The Impact of Culture on Tourism*. OECD, Paris.

Palmer, J. (1992) Towards a sustainable future. In: Cooper, D. and Palmer, J. (eds) *The Environment in Question: Ethics and Global Issues*. Routledge, London, pp. 181–186.

Pearce, S.M. (1992) *Museums, Objects and Collections: A Cultural Study*. Leicester University Press, Leicester, UK.

Picard, M. (1996) *Bali: Cultural Tourism and Tourism and Culture*. Archipelago, Singapore.

Pine, B.J. and Gilmore, J.H. (1999) *The Experience Economy*. Harvard University Press, Cambridge, Massachusetts.

Poon, A. (1993) *Tourism, Technology and Competitive Strategies*. CAB International, Wallingford, UK.

Prior, N. (2002) *Museums and Modernity: Art Galleries and the Making of Modern Culture*. Berg, Oxford.

Richards, G. (ed.) (2001) *Cultural Attractions and European Tourism*. CAB International, Wallingford, UK.

Richards, G. and Palmer, R. (2010) *Eventful Cities: Cultural Management and Urban Revitalization*. Butterworth Heinemann, Oxford.

Samuel, R. (1994) *Theatres of Memory*. Verso, London.

Stallabrass, J. (2004) *Contemporary Art: A Very Short Introduction*. Oxford University Press, Oxford.

Storry, M. and Childs, P. (1997) *British Cultural Identities*. Routledge, London.

Urry, J. (1992) *The Tourist Gaze: Leisure and Travel in Contemporary Societies*. Sage, London.

Urry, J. (1995) *Consuming Places*. Routledge, London.

Walsh, K. (1992) *The Representation of the Past: Museums and Heritage in the Post-modern World*. Routledge, London.

2 Managing Heritage and Cultural Tourism Resources

Jon Edwards

Bournemouth University, Bournemouth, UK

This chapter explores a range of challenges and issues regarding the management of cultural and heritage tourism. These themes range from how the ownership of a site can influence its philosophy and mission, to a practical discussion of income streams. It then explores the challenges of communicating with visitors, both potential and actual, before, during and after their experience with a site. The chapter highlights the benefits of collaboration and illustrates how a collaborative approach strengthens both the offering and professional management of a site. The final section provides a reflection on some of the key challenges for cultural heritage sites, namely ensuring a successful visitor experience, and consideration of both interpretation and authenticity.

2.1 Introduction

A review of definitions of cultural and heritage tourism demonstrates that it encompasses people who, in their leisure time, are to varying degrees seeking enjoyment, culturally motivated, wishing to gather new information and experiences, wanting to satisfy their human need for diversity, seeking to raise their cultural level and satisfy their cultural needs. For some agencies attendance at a cultural venue or participation in a cultural event is another defining characteristic. The range of cultural and heritage venues, events or products that are frequently included is extensive and may variously include: aboriginal peoples, archaeological sites, breweries and distilleries, castles and forts, created cultural experiences, designated landscapes, gastronomy, gardens, historic houses and palaces, industrial workplaces, museums and art galleries, places of worship, rural areas, steam and heritage railways, wildlife reserves – a list that is by no means exhaustive.

The importance of the effective and efficient management of these resources is clearly apparent in the statistical analyses that are widely published, for example the $17 billion spent by international heritage and cultural tourists visiting Australia in 2008 (Tourism Australia, 2009) who, while typically spending less per day, stay longer than do other international visitors. This level of spend compares with the $9.6 billion spent by domestic visitors. Of equal relevance is the analyses of visits to tourist (visitor) attractions in Scotland in 2009, which indicate that in excess of 60% of the 44.7 million visits were to cultural and heritage attractions (Visit Scotland, 2010). Regardless of the nature of the heritage and cultural resources that are being managed in whole, or more commonly in part, for tourists and visitors, there are a number of factors that impinge on the management of the resource. Given that visitors are welcomed, there will be a constant tension in deciding what resources of management are devoted to preservation, conservation or renovation as opposed to those given over to visitors. In this chapter the focus will primarily be on management that focuses on providing a quality experience for visitors, although inevitably there are a number of management responsibilities that are equally important to both the curatorial staff and those engaged with visitors. The range of topics that may influence management strategies and actions include: ownership, location, access to and within the attraction, finance, provision of facilities, staffing, health and safety provision, and communication with the visitor before, during and after their visit.

2.2 Ownership and Location

Ownership of any tourist attraction will determine in large measure the objectives and priorities of management. Public-sector ownership may well lead to management objectives that include economic development or regeneration, improving residents' quality of life, together with providing leisure and education opportunities while at the same time achieving conservation objectives. It is generally perceived that while private owners may share some of these objectives, profitability will feature. Voluntary-sector owners, while often apparently prioritizing conservation and education, will also be very conscious of managing income generation. A further consideration is the eligibility of the owners of the resource to register as a charity because this may well determine not only their eligibility to seek funding from the voluntary sector, but may also have implications for tax exemption for certain of their activities.

While ownership may determine management priorities, location will determine the catchment area and, in all but the relatively few genuinely global attractions, these areas are finite and generally reflect travel times, whether by car, train or plane. The setting of heritage and cultural resources may determine the overall experience and in many cases strategies that slow the visitor's final approach are actively pursued, not only to assist in creating a sense of place but because the setting is integral to the heritage resource. For example, preserving as pedestrianized the open area or 'close' that surrounds cathedrals, which are typically located in busy urban areas, or reinstating the traditional landscapes that surround many historical cultural resources. The reality is that in many situations the majority of visitors arrive by road, requiring cooperation with the highways authorities in regard to signage and with local authorities in regard to car parking and coach drop-off points. It may be inappropriate or physically impossible to provide car parking adjacent to the site, and in these cases transfer arrangements by some form of people mover is necessary. This again gives time for the visitor to adjust and begin to engage with the heritage or cultural experience. Given that the car parks are under the jurisdiction of the manager, one of the more contentious issues that has to be resolved is whether or not to charge separately for car parking as opposed to either integrating this into the admission charge, if indeed there is one, or providing free parking. Parking problems may be exaggerated if special events are hosted, and inadequate parking will quickly lead to visitors becoming irritated, making the provision of a rewarding visit unnecessarily difficult. Location not only defines the numbers of domestic and international tourists who are likely to visit, it will also affect the numbers of educational and special interest groups to be expected. The importance of educational groups, which may have relatively low levels of visitor spend, should nevertheless not be underestimated.

The location of many cultural and heritage resource-based attractions such as the pyramids of Egypt or Colonial Williamsburg are of course predetermined because they were not originally sited with a view to acting as major tourist attractions and attention focuses on their sympathetic development and management. However, it is increasingly the case that cultural and heritage resources are introduced or relocated, most frequently to stimulate economic development and to enrich the socio-cultural environment. Some developments, such as the Guggenheim in Bilbao, which opened in 1997 partly as a response to the decline in the maritime economy of this northern Spanish town, have assumed almost iconic status, primarily due to architectural qualities. Others, which in terms of the richness of their cultural resources deserve equal recognition such as the Gulbenkian Museum in Lisbon, which opened in 1969, are less well known.

However, investing in the development of heritage and cultural resources is not always successful, as national and regional authorities in the UK have discovered. The Leeds Armoury Museum, which opened in 1996 at a cost of £42.5 million, forecast 1 million visitors annually but in practice received far fewer than this and by 1999 was facing a bleak financial outlook. It is thought that one reason for the disappointing visitor numbers was the £6.95 admission charge, which was dropped in 2001. The museum has in recent years attracted around 280,000 visitors a year. While the Leeds Armoury survived an unpromising start, the same did not apply to the National Centre for Popular Music, which opened in Sheffield in 1999, largely funded by the National Lottery. Like many similar projects, the National Centre was housed in architecturally award-winning purpose-built structures; however, it closed

15 months later, having attracted only 20% of the forecast visitors. Over-optimistic visitor projections are often the cause of failure or disappointment for many visitor attractions. This may relate to the chosen location, but a range of other factors are also relevant, such as the underlying concept, poor marketing and/or the control of costs. A particular danger for small- or medium-sized operations reliant upon tourists and other visitor groups is that the manager or the management team may be inexperienced in managing both the resource and the visitor. In these situations it is more common to find managers who have considerable expertise in managing the cultural or heritage resource, but having far less knowledge and understanding of satisfying visitor expectations. This is particularly critical where income from the visitor is vital for financial viability. Nevertheless, other recent developments of cultural resources have been far more successful. The Lowry Centre on Salford Quays in Manchester, developed at a cost of £120 million, originally forecast 770,000 annual visitors, but has consistently outperformed this since its opening in 2004. Unsurprisingly, authors such as Swarbrooke (2001), when suggesting those factors that are critical to success, refer to sound finances, location and organizational experience. Swarbrooke also suggests that innovation, variety and sound strategic management are vital and for many seeking to build on cultural and heritage resources the main strategic focus should be the delivery of a unique experience. However, as the examples referred to above demonstrate, innovative concepts and the promise of memorable experiences require dependable and continuing financial underpinning, hence Wanhill's (2008) observation that the development of attractions is inherently risky is as applicable to cultural and heritage-based attractions as it is to any other visitor attraction.

2.3 Socio-economic Profile of Visitors

Location will determine in part the socio-economic profile of the visitors, particularly the domestic tourist and day visitor. This is clearly important, both in terms of the cultural appeal and also of setting admission charges and determining potential secondary spend. Not all heritage and culture-based attractions charge for admission, but many do and this variable is frequently used as a basis for classification and in the collection of statistical data. A recent survey for the Association of Leading Visitor Attractions (ALVA) (Morisetti, 2011) of those UK attractions that charge admission indicates that in 2011 the average admission charge for heritage attractions, other than museums, was £7.22. Museums charged somewhat less (an average of £5.07), while admission to leisure attractions was on average considerably higher at £12.92. This survey also revealed that admission prices for heritage and leisure attractions had risen over the previous 3 years, while the mean admission charge for museums had fallen slightly. In addition to income derived from admission charges, levies could be put in place, because income can be derived from other sources once the visitors are on site. Experience demonstrates that when visitors arrive at a venue they most often want toilets and possibly some refreshment. However, while toilets are usually provided, catering facilities are not always in place. While this may be due to physical constraints, the economic arguments for providing catering facilities are significant. While precise data are difficult to identify, available evidence suggests that catering income, at £39 million, accounts for a little under 10% of the UK National Trust's annual income (National Trust, 2011) and for other organizations it may be double this. The ALVA benchmarking study of paying visits referred to above indicates that 60% of the income derived from visitors to heritage attractions comes from admission charges, approximately 20% from catering (mean £1.93) and a further 20% from retailing (£2.17). The analysis of visitors to fee-charging museums indicates that 40% of visitor revenue is derived from admission, a little less than 30% from catering (£1.18) and a little over 30% from retailing spend (£2.23). The importance of quality catering was highlighted a little over 20 years ago, when in 1988 the Victoria and Albert Museum (V&A) in London ran a campaign 'An ace caff with quite a nice museum attached'. This campaign is indicative of a time when the

owners of many cultural and heritage-based attractions realized the need to adopt a more professional approach in understanding and responding to the demands of their existing and potential visitor market. In practical management terms the V&A campaign also highlighted whether or not the public can access the cafeteria before handing over an admission fee.

2.4   Income Streams

The opportunity to draw in customers other than those visiting the attraction is a powerful argument that persuades many managers to encourage this additional income stream. For some cultural sites attracting many tens or hundreds of thousands of visitors, catering provision is contracted out. Such contracts are fiercely contested, as has been recently evidenced in the 2011 award by the Science Museum in London of a contract worth £25 million in sales to the café deli operator Benugo, who will initially invest in excess of £1 million refurbishing four dining areas within the museum (Stamford, 2011), and more recently in the award to the same operator in 2012 of a £40 million 5-year contract by the British Museum (Stamford, 2012). It is relevant to reaffirm that currently neither of these museums charge for admission and between them they receive in excess of 9 million visitors annually. For smaller operations the economics of scale coupled with their location may make the appointment of a specialist caterer less viable, resulting in the operation being brought in-house. This will usually require employment of suitably qualified staff and the challenge of responding to seasonal variations in visitor numbers and the vagaries of the weather, which will significantly influence the demand for different menu items. If the cafe/restaurant is to be available to non-visitors this will clearly determine its size and location, and the more recent trend of hosting events, not least weddings and other celebrations, will have a significant impact on the management of the resource. Some of the same considerations regarding the location of the catering facilities also apply to retail outlets, not least whether they are to be accessible to non-visitors: almost without exception the visitors will be directed to exit the attraction through a retail outlet, although there may also be a range of such outlets throughout the site. For many organizations, their retail outlet presents a real opportunity for reinforcing the theme of the attraction. The increasing professionalism evident in the provision of catering is no less relevant in developing retailing and investing in individuals/consultants with key display skills and others with expertise in public relations who have the potential to inform product development, procurement and retail sales strategies. While not many museums can hope to aspire to the £27 million (*FX Magazine*, 2010) retailing turnover enjoyed by the V&A, it is very evident that many cultural and heritage-based organizations are recognizing not only the commercial opportunities of on-site retailing, but also the relevance of items purchased during a visit in embedding a memory of the visit and thereby encouraging repeat visits and person-to-person recommendations.

While visitors are for some cultural or heritage-based attractions the major source of income and are likely to become increasingly significant in the future, there are other sources that are important, both in terms of revenue and for funding capital investment. These funds may either be direct, in the form of equity or loan capital, or indirect. Obtaining commercially determined funding from the private sector for cultural and heritage-based tourism investments is challenging since such investments are seen as inherently high risk. For commercially focused organizations whose portfolio may include cultural heritage resources, indirect funding may be achieved by franchising, leasing or sale and leaseback arrangements, while for some organizations sponsorship or endowments may represent a very significant income. The Calouste Gulbenkian and Guggenheim Foundations referred to above, and the Courtauld Gallery at Somerset House in London, clearly illustrate the significance of sponsorship in ensuring that a truly international audience has access to global heritage. There are also many examples of national sponsorship. In the UK, the Department for Culture, Media and Sport (DCMS) sponsors 20 museums and galleries, eight of which are in the top ten UK visitor attractions,

attracting between them 43.8 million visitors in 2010/11 (DCMS, 2012). Among those it sponsors are the Royal Armouries with museums in London, Portsmouth, Leeds and Louisville, Kentucky. The Royal Armoury museum in Kentucky, which opened in 2004, resulted from collaboration between the Royal Armouries and the Frazier History Museum who are dedicated to telling the complete cultural story of America including its British and French roots (Royal Armouries, 2012). In addition to national sponsorship, local sponsorship supporting local cultural resources is rarely fully appreciated; for example, the Russell-Cotes Museum in Bournemouth benefits from an undertaking by the local authority to annually donate sufficient funds to make up the shortfall on its operating costs, which until the museum recently introduced an admission charge equated to around £700,000 per annum (Charity Commission, 2010). Sponsorship also originates in the private sector from individuals, corporate organizations and financial institutions. Another important source of funding is legacies, which are very significant for large charitable heritage organizations such as the National Trust, which received £46.3 million in 2010/11 (National Trust, 2011). This represented 11% of the Trust's income compared with the 9.5% derived from their catering operations. While legacies running into millions are few, smaller legacies and gifts are significant for many organizations and are often used entirely or in part to fund capital projects and may indeed be earmarked for such by the benefactor.

In addition to its role as sponsor, the public sector may also be a source of grants, loans and in-kind contributions. It is often portrayed as the source of last resort because not only is matched funding often necessary, there may also be a requirement for the beneficiary organization to address the economic, social and environmental priorities of the public sector. Nevertheless, for the last 20 years culture and heritage organizations, based in long-standing and more recent member states of the European Union, have, in addition to regional and national funds, had access to a wide range of funding opportunities within the EU Culture programme. This scheme will, in the current programming period (2007–2013), disperse a budget of some

€400 million across approximately 300 projects (European Commission – Culture, 2007–2013). There are, in addition, opportunities for seeking finance in other sectors of EU competence, including regional development, media, employment and citizenship.

The third source of funding available to develop heritage and cultural resources, particularly those recognized as being of charitable status, is the voluntary sector, which in the UK is estimated to be the source of about £2 billion annually for charitable organizations. However, it is not uncommon for the beneficiary group to be restricted, i.e. to a particular sub-group of the population or to a geographic area. While being a recognized charity will give access to voluntary-sector funding, it may also have benefits in terms of the payment of tax, particularly of value added tax (VAT); although such benefits appear to be relatively minor and diminishing as evidenced recently in the UK with the government's proposal to remove the zero rating on alterations to buildings listed as being of architectural merit, many of which are owned or are sought by organizations seeking to own or manage such heritage resources.

Outgoings will clearly be influenced by the nature of the resource and the relative prioritization of conservation or preservation, and what are probably best termed visitor services. Overall, staff costs are likely to be never less than one third of expenditures and will often be considerably more – for example, at the Russell-Cotes Museum in 2009 they were two thirds of total expenditure (Charity Commission, 2010) – and will be added to either through the delivery of in-house training or through buying in. In many, probably the majority of organizations, until the last decade of the last century, those occupying senior management positions were almost invariably qualified in conservation and management of cultural heritage. However, an increasing recognition of how dependent such resources are on visitor revenue has led a range of owners, not least those in the private sector who not only own considerable amounts of the United Kingdom's heritage but are amongst its greatest advocates, to look to appoint general managers who, while culturally sympathetic, have considerable experience in managing contemporary commercial attractions. The impacts of these appointments are seen not only in far

more rigorous financial management and improved, frequently aggressive, marketing, but in significant improvements in all aspects of the delivery of a quality experience. The delivery of a quality experience depends not only on the manager but on the performance of all staff. The role and importance of the management of these human resources has been critically examined by Watson and McCracken (2008), based on an analysis of Storey's model of human resource management (Storey, 1991). Storey's model is based on four key tenets, which include the beliefs and assumptions that people are critical to the success of the attraction, that people are a concern at the highest level of management, that line managers are the key players in managing people, and that the culture of the organization and the integration of people management procedures enhances effective people management. While organizations may employ their own human resource manager, many smaller organizations rely on buying-in training for customer services. In the UK a suite of training programmes under the umbrella of 'Welcome to Excellence' have been developed over the last 30 years, originally based on the SuperHost training methodology pioneered in British Columbia (British Columbia Ministry of Tourism, 1991).

Introducing professional approaches to the management of human resources applies not only to the management of paid staff, but also of volunteers, who can be vital to the successful operation of many UK and North American heritage-based attractions and who may outnumber the paid employees by a factor approaching 100 to 1. A statement by the coordinator of volunteers at the Field Museum in Chicago that 'our volunteers are so important to our museum because they deliver such engaging tours' (Levin, 2011) captures the value many culturally based attractions attach to their volunteer programmes. Volunteers are nearly always highly committed and knowledgeable, with considerable experience of implementing responsible management practices. Such management requires a defined skill set if volunteers are to be managed effectively, not least in ensuring they share the organizations' vision regarding delivery of the visitor experience. In considering the management of volunteers, Stamer et al. (2008), focusing principally on the management of volunteers in international art museums, identified three practices: building a community of volunteers, enhancing volunteer learning experiences and fostering the self-management of volunteers, all of which appear to increase the performance of volunteer programmes. Managing paid staff is guided by national legislation, which may not always apply to volunteers, although clearly there are responsibilities for health and safety. Health and safety responsibilities relate to both staff and visitors and may constrain access and activities, requiring management to undertake regular risk assessments of the opportunities of access to different areas and of activities that may be undertaken. Another dimension of health and safety relates to the wellbeing of the resource itself in terms of minimizing wear and tear, accidental damage and occasionally deliberate vandalism. Managing and minimizing deleterious impacts is best addressed both by controlling access and through effective communication as discussed later: for example, the need to conserve furniture and fabrics is one reason why historic properties and their furnishings are often accessible to visitors for only part of the year in order to manage light, temperature and humidity regimes.

2.5   Communication with Potential Visitors

Communicating with invited visitors is an activity central to the management of cultural and heritage resources. While communication is essentially a two-way exchange process, from the perspective of management, the prime purpose is to convey information and messages that may be marketing, advertising or promotional. Some messages, particularly those delivered on site, often seek to be interpretational. The messages may be designed to simply convey information, for example opening times and only demand a cognitive response, or they may attempt to develop an affective response, to arouse feelings and these responses may, it is hoped, lead to a change in behaviour. The recently published *Communicating Heritage – Handbook for the Tourism Sector* (UNWTO, 2011) clearly indicates a desire to encourage sustainable approaches and behaviour when it states that the four guiding objectives of communication of heritage should: facilitate market access, promote particular types of tourism, provide an incentive for more sustainable products and influence visitor behaviour (see Fig. 2.1).

In addition to these four guiding principles, the World Tourism Organization (UNWTO)

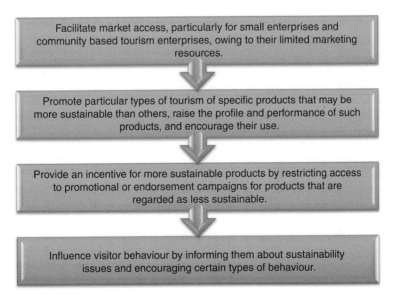

Fig. 2.1. Guiding objectives of communication for heritage. (From UNWTO, 2011.)

suggests a further ten communication objectives, which include: enabling tourists to gain a richer and more satisfying experience from their visit; creating opportunities for new or enhanced tourism products in lesser known and smaller attractions; encouraging visitors to interact more deeply with the place and the local society; encouraging visitors to behave responsibly; and increasing cooperation and coordination between the tourism sector, destination management organizations and heritage site managers in order to provide expanded and improved integration between their various products and services.

Communicating with actual and potential visitors takes place off-site before they arrive, on-site during their visit and after they leave. Off-site communication should ideally begin as an awareness-raising activity in the hope of influencing travel plans and if possible should be maintained on the visitors' journey to the site, within the destination and subsequent to their visit. On-site communication should comprise both practical information and, by means of affective interpretational messages, support the delivery of a memorable experience. In terms of preparing communication materials for a given site or resource, the UNWTO recommend that management should strive to develop the five strategies highlighted in Fig. 2.2.

2.6 Collaboration and Marketing

While the majority of owners and managers invest time and money in addressing these demands, increasing numbers of organizations have given attention to developing collaborative relationships, as we have seen in the case of the Royal Armouries, an approach that Crotts *et al.* (2000) describe as an essential ingredient of organizational longevity in the tourism industry. Fyall and Garrod, both in their contribution to Theobald's *Global Tourism* (2004) and in their subsequent 2005 publication, successfully defend their argument that collaboration is not only integral to the management of tourism, but that it is arguably the single most important aspect of management in determining the success, or indeed failure, of tourism marketing strategies and programmes.

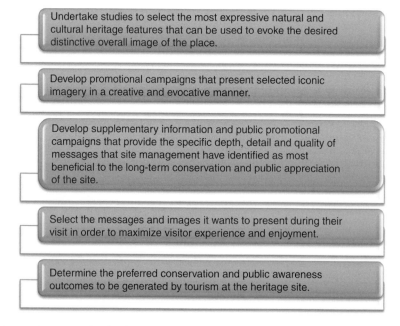

Undertake studies to select the most expressive natural and cultural heritage features that can be used to evoke the desired distinctive overall image of the place.

Develop promotional campaigns that present selected iconic imagery in a creative and evocative manner.

Develop supplementary information and public promotional campaigns that provide the specific depth, detail and quality of messages that site management have identified as most beneficial to the long-term conservation and public appreciation of the site.

Select the messages and images it wants to present during their visit in order to maximize visitor experience and enjoyment.

Determine the preferred conservation and public awareness outcomes to be generated by tourism at the heritage site.

Fig. 2.2. UNWTO strategies for development. (From UNWTO, 2011.)

Funding issues are but one of the drivers of collaboration; others include on-going integration and the development of networks, changing and growing demand, technological advances and the demands of achieving sustainability. In any collaborative process it is important that stakeholders retain their independence, that joint ownership of decisions is accepted and that the stakeholders assume collective responsibility. It should be recognized that collaboration is an emergent process, where collaborative initiatives can be understood as emergent arrangements through which organizations collectively cope with the growing complexity of their environments. Huxham captured the strengths of collaborative actions when he recorded that

> when something unusually creative is produced – perhaps an objective is met – which neither organisation could have produced on its own and when each organisation, through the collaboration, is able to achieve its own objectives better than it could alone.
>
> (1993, p. 609)

One of the main outcomes of effective marketing activities that is sought will either be the maintenance of previously recorded visitor numbers or an overall increase. Therefore ensuring a positive experience for visitors is a strategic imperative for management, given that they wish to remain financially viable, increase the awareness for their visitors of the value of the resource they experience, and

contribute to the preservation and conservation of the resource they are responsible for.

2.7   The Key Visitor Experience Challenges: Experience, Interpretation and Authenticity

Pine and Gilmore succinctly summarized the importance of the experience provided for customers and visitors in their seminal 1999 publication *The Experience Economy*. They argued that today's businesses should offer five basic elements as outlined in Fig. 2.3.

These ideas can also be seen in Weaver's (2007) proposed eight-stage crafted visitor experience model, which suggests that visitors, pass through a series of stages when they visit, from Invitation to Finale (Invitation, Welcome, Orientation, Comfort, Communication, Sensation, Common, Sense, Finale). It is proposed that experiences can be enhanced through five main types of what are essentially communication activities. These include communicating three sets of information relating to the recreational activities available, visitor safety and comfort, and providing information that supports the on-site managing authority and its objectives. The two other communication activities advocated should, it is suggested, create a 'sensation' by bringing a destination 'to life' as well as capitalizing on visitor curiosity and thereby creating an 'actual' experience.

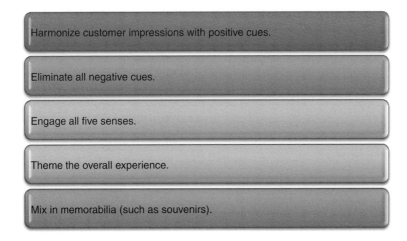

Fig. 2.3. The importance of experience. (From Pine and Gilmore, 1999.)

These last two activities are in essence examples where the communication goes beyond requiring a cognitive response to information, such as the First Aid Cabin is adjacent to the restaurant, to communication that seeks an affective emotional response. On-site communication of this nature is widely referred to as interpretation.

It is no coincidence that the individual accredited with establishing the value and benefit of the interpretation of the resource in order to enhance the visitor experience had a background in the performing arts. Freeman Tilden, more than 50 years ago, argued that communicating with the visitor should be much more than conveying information, rather a process that he termed interpretation being the 'revelation of a larger truth that lies behind any statement of fact', and 'should capitalise on mere curiosity for the enrichment of the human mind and spirit' (Tilden, 1977, pp. 8–9). Tilden proposed six basic principles and although more recent authors have added to these, his six principles (see Fig. 2.4) have stood the test of time and numerous varied applications.

Early definitions and approaches to interpretation communication generally emphasized an educational motive, whereas more recent definitions tend to focus on ethical and personal experiential dimensions. This change of emphasis is evident in those responsible for managing Colonial Williamsburg, who regard interpretation as

> the communication process which aims at helping people to discover the significance of things, places, people and events ... helping people change the way they perceive themselves and their world through a greater understanding of the world and themselves.
> (Colonial Williamsburg, 2012)

At historic sites, heritage interpretation is often experienced as a form of creative art that explains the past in relation to social conditions and activities, typically by bringing it to life in a strongly thematic way (see Chapter 18, this volume). Such an approach requires interpreters to act as more than costumed guides, rather they need to combine acting skills with a detailed knowledge of both the particular resource and the wider historical or cultural context. While definitions may vary, the central principle remains provocation and the revealing of meanings and emotions that are relevant to the experience of the visitor. Given that many visitors will have limited knowledge and awareness of the resource, it is advisable to focus on a clear central theme with its associated messages in order to encourage visitors' first-hand active involvement and use of their senses in order to foster self-discovered insights. These contribute

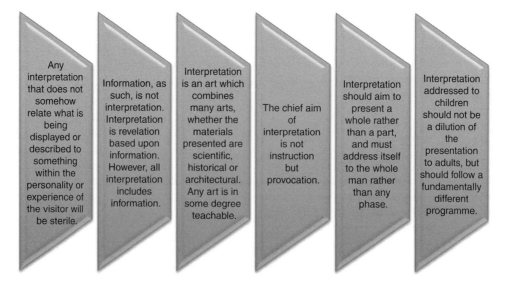

Fig. 2.4. Tilden's six principles of communication (From Tilden, 1977.)

significantly to their experience and to their appreciation of the attributes of the resource. Many first-hand interpreters have identified the importance of the 'discovery' aspect of interpretation and have suggested that the feelings generated within the visitor by such an encounter can be truly profound (Ham, 1992).

Not only can interpretation that is done well and regularly refreshed contribute significantly to what some refer to as the recreational visitor experience, it can also assist management in a number of other ways. These include contributing to the protection of the resource 'through interpretation, understanding; through understanding, appreciation; through appreciation, protection' (Keirle, 2002, p. 173). Interpretation has the potential to contribute to the economic sustainability of the resource by enhancing the quality of the visitor experience and therefore potentially encouraging an increased visitor spend on-site as well as increasing the chance of repeat visitation. The 2011 ALVA Financial Benchmarking Study clearly demonstrated that the more there is for visitors to engage in, the longer they stay and their frequency of using catering, and to a lesser extent retail facilities, increases. Such economic benefits contribute to the financial stability of the managing organization through helping to provide facilities, materials and services. In addition, it can create local employment for people as interpreters and guides. Effective interpretive services can also be useful in promoting the 'image', or indeed the 'visual identity', of the site and its managing authority, as well as promoting its values, objectives and practices. As with many management activities there needs to be an overall interpretive strategy expressed through an interpretative plan that is regularly reviewed. Brochu (2003) argues cogently throughout her discussion of interpretive planning that any interpretive plan should address the audience or markets it proposes to serve, in order that, as Hammitt (1984) argued, the resulting interpretation kindles the visitor's imagination and encourages them to develop a 'sense of place' that stimulates an emotional connection with the site as well as an enjoyable on-site experience.

Sense of place and authenticity are two characteristics of heritage and cultural resources that, while being highly prized by many, have been much debated over the last 50 years. Sense of place is the focus of Schofield and Szymanski's recently published (2011) volume *Local Heritage Global Context: Cultural Perspectives on Sense of Place*. A number of locations, for example the Edinburgh World Heritage Site (UNESCO, 1995), seek to offer a 'sense of place product' to their visitors. In this instance Edinburgh directs visitors to particular locations such as Parliament Square and the Grassmarket (Edinburgh World Heritage, 2012). The equally challenging authenticity debate has been thoroughly reviewed recently by Timothy (2011). The innate intangibility of authenticity and the varying degrees of importance that owners and managers accord to it is reflected in the range of resulting management actions. The management of authenticity is in part culturally determined, as the controversy over the renovation of the Sultan Sanjar Mausoleum, one of the centrepieces of the Merv Archaeological Park World Heritage Site in Turkmenistan, demonstrates (ArchNet 2012).

2.8 Summary

It is appropriate when reflecting on the different challenges faced by those seeking to manage cultural and heritage resources for tourism that while some challenges, most notably those relating to facility provision, appear to lend themselves to solutions drawing on experience in related service sectors such as catering and retailing, other demands such as creating a sense of place and ensuring authenticity are far more difficult to address. Achieving these and other management goals requires either a manager or management team equally competent in developing the tangible dimensions of the visitors' experience and at the same time providing an emotionally satisfying and memorable visit. To achieve success in this regard requires a move away from the traditional curatorial approach to a visitor management paradigm, and one of the most successful methods of ensuring this is to engage in collaboration with other sites and visitor experiences. A further finding of this chapter is the importance of considering the entire cultural tourism experience from pre-visit, through the actual visit onto the post-visit memories and emotional engagement that the visitor takes home with them. The success of a site, therefore, must balance a professional management approach with an organizational philosophy in tune with the unique and special qualities of the particular cultural heritage site, and all of this focused on the creation of a meaningful visitor experience.

2.9 Discussion Questions

- What are the three key sources of funding available to cultural institutions?
- How does ownership of a site influence its management?
- How does collaboration assist in the marketing and management of a cultural tourism site?
- Mindful of issues such as authenticity, what are the main principles to note when interpreting cultural heritage?

References

ArchNet (2012) Sultan Sanjar Mausoleum. http://archnet.org/library/sites/one-site.jsp?site_id=9067 (accessed 14 May 2012).

British Columbia Ministry of Tourism (1991) *SuperHost Japan Seminar Leader's Manual*. British Columbia Ministry of Tourism, Educational Services Department.

Brochu, L. (2003) *Interpretive Planning: The 5-M Model for Successful Planning Projects*. Interpress, Fort Collins, Colorado.

Charity Commission (2010) Summary information return Russell-Cotes Museum and Art Gallery. http://www.charitycommission.gov.uk/SIR/ENDS88%5C0000306288_SIR_09_E.PDF (accessed 10 May 2012).

Colonial Williamsburg (2012) History in motion. http://www.history.org/foundation (accessed 10 May 2012).

Crotts, J., Buhalis, D. and March, R. (2000) *Global Alliances in Tourism and Hospitality Management*. Haworth Hospitality Press, New York.

DCMS (Department for Culture, Media and Sport) (2012) Museums and galleries. http://www.culture.gov.uk/what_we_do/museums_and_galleries/default.aspx (accessed 15 May 2012).

Edinburgh World Heritage (2012) Sense of place. http://www.ewht.org.uk/sense-of-place (accessed 15 May 2012).

European Commission Culture (2007–2013) Culture Programme: a serious cultural investment. http://ec.europa.eu/culture/our-programmes-and-actions/doc411_en.htm (accessed 10 May 2012).

FX Magazine (2010) Retail focus: The fine art of retailing. *FX Magazine* http://www.fxmagazine.co.uk/story.asp?storyCode=3637 (accessed 14 May 2012).

Fyall, A. and Garrod, B. (2004) From competition to collaboration in the tourism industry. In: Theobald, W. (ed.) *Global Tourism*, 3rd edn. Butterworth-Heinemann, Oxford, pp. 52–73.

Fyall, A. and Garrod, B. (2005) *Tourism Marketing: A Collaborative Approach*. Channel View Publications, Clevedon, UK.

Ham, S.H. (1992) *Environmental Interpretation: A Practical Guide for People with Big Ideas and Small Budgets*. Fulcrum/North American Press, Golden, Colorado.

Hammitt, W.E. (1984) A theoretical foundation for Tilden's interpretive principles. *Journal of Environmental Interpretation* 12, 13–16.

Huxham, C. (1993) Pursuing collaborative advantage. *Journal of the Operational Research Society* 44, 599–611.

Keirle, I. (2002) *Countryside Recreation Site Management: A Marketing Approach*. Routledge, Oxford.

Levin, A. (2011) Valued and valuable: the museum volunteer workforce. *Tourist Attractions & Parks* 41, 90–92.

Morisetti, L. (2011) *Attractions Performance 2011: A Financial Benchmarking Survey for the Association of Leading Visitor Attractions*. ALVA, London.

National Trust (2011) *Going Local: Annual Report 2010/11*. The National Trust, Swindon, UK.

Pine, B.J. and Gilmore, J.H. (1999) *The Experience Economy*. Harvard Business Press, Boston, Massachusetts.

Royal Armouries (2012) http://www.royalarmouries.org.uk/visit-us/louisville-kentucky (accessed 14 May 2012).

Schofield, J. and Szymanski, R. (2010) *Local Heritage, Global Context: Cultural Perspectives on Sense of Place*. Ashgate, Farnham, UK.

Stamer, D., Lerdall, K. and Guo, C. (2008) Managing heritage volunteers: an exploratory study of volunteer programmes in art museums worldwide. *Journal of Heritage Tourism* 3, 203–214.

Stamford, J. (2011) Benugo takes Science Museum deal worth £25m from Elior. *Caterer and Hotelkeeper* 8 April 2011. http://www.caterersearch.com/Articles/08/04/2011/337824/Benugo-takes-Science-Museum-deal-worth-16325m-from.htm (accessed 8 May 2011).

Stamford, J. (2012) Benugo wins £40m deal at the British Museum. *Caterer and Hotelkeeper* 28 February 2012. http://www.caterersearch.com/Articles/28/02/2012/342589/benugo-wins-40m-deal-at-the-british-museum.htm (accessed 8 May 2012).

Storey, J. (1991) *New Perspectives on Human Resource Management*. Routledge, London.

Swarbrooke, J. (2001) *The Development and Management of Visitor Attractions*. Butterworth-Heinemann, Oxford.

Tilden, F. (1977) *Interpreting Our Heritage*, 3rd edn. University of North Carolina Press, Chapel Hill, North Carolina.

Timothy, D.J. (2011) *Cultural and Heritage Tourism: An Introduction*. Channel View Publications, Bristol, UK.

Tourism Australia (2009) Cultural and Heritage Tourism in Australia 2008. http://www.ret.gov.au/tourism/Documents/tra/Snapshots%20and%20Factsheets/Cultural_08_v2%20%282%29.pdf (accessed 8 May 2012).

UNESCO (1995) *World Heritage Convention – Old and New Towns of Edinburgh*. UNESCO, Paris.

UNWTO (2011) *Communicating Heritage – Handbook for the Tourism Sector*. UNWTO, Madrid.

Visit Scotland (2010) *The 2009 Visitor Attraction Monitor*. Moffat Centre for Travel and Tourism Business Development, Glasgow Caledonian University, Scotland.

Wanhill, S. (2008) Interpreting the development of the visitor attraction product. In: Fyall, A. Garrod, B. and Leask, A. (eds) *Managing Visitor Attractions – New Directions*, 2nd edn. Butterworth-Heinemann, Oxford, pp. 16–35.

Watson, S. and McCracken, M. (2008) Visitor attractions and human resource management. In: Fyall, A., Garrod, B. and Leask, A. (eds) *Managing Visitor Attractions – New Directions*, 2nd edn. Butterworth-Heinemann, Oxford, pp. 171–184.

Weaver, S. (2007) *Creating Great Visitor Experiences: A Guide for Museums, Parks, Zoos, Gardens, and Libraries*. Left Coast Press, Walnut Creek, California.

3 The Impact of Cultural Tourism on Host Communities

Carlos Fernandes

Polytechnic Institute of Viana do Castelo, Viana do Castelo, Portugal

3.1 Introduction

This chapter explores the various ways in which cultural tourism impacts on host communities. It explores how the pursuit of attracting culture-motivated tourists will require that communities improve their capacity to establish social relationships and encourage a more active role by community stakeholders. Once the participation of the local people is obtained, it is they who often are the most committed and capable guardians of local resources. The new local development approaches are an innovative alternative to conventional needs-based approaches. In this participatory approach, communities are the key participants in local development that should aim for the type of change desired by the local community.

The next four sections aim to understand the impact of cultural tourism development on host communities. Section 3.2 explores the changing meaning of the concept of community. Because pursuit of the development process depends on the involvement of community residents, this section analyses the existing theories and discusses the definitions used in literature on the changing meaning of the concept of community. Section 3.3 describes why tourism is a common strategy of community development and identifies inherent impacts – economic, environmental and socio-cultural – based on studies and specific literature. The subsequent section demonstrates the importance of social exchange theory when developing and attracting tourism to a community, and how the goal is to achieve outcomes that obtain the best balance of benefits and costs for both residents and tourism actors (Ap, 1992).

But communities often start tourism development focusing solely on economic factors, paying little attention to other essential factors, such as cultural, social and environmental costs. Communities seldom realize that impacts of tourism may represent negative consequences for the host community. The social and environmental costs are items that are hardly considered. Communities may not be particularly attentive to the possible negative impacts. It is suggested that such impacts must be avoided so that the natural and cultural heritage in which tourism development is based may be preserved and protected for future generations. This approach to development incorporates the concept of sustainability.

As such, Section 3.4 examines how communitarianism can support the sustainability of cultural tourism, from community organizing as a form of empowering that promotes trust and feelings of involvement (networking), to the nature of participation and the importance of capacity building for acquiring the skills required to obtain benefits from tourism. Entrepreneurship is one example of those skills.

3.2 The Changing Meaning of Cultural Tourism

To set the scene for this chapter, we reflect on the words of Wallerstein, in Sklair's book *Capitalism and Development*:

> There is perhaps no social objective that can find as nearly unanimous acceptance today as that of economic development. I doubt that there has been a single government anywhere in the last 30 years that has not asserted it was pursuing this objective, at least for its own country. Everywhere in the world today, what divides left and right, however defined, is not whether or not to develop, but which policies are presumed to offer most hope that this objective will be achieved. We are told that socialism is the road to development. We are

told that laissez-faire is the road to development. We are told that a break with tradition is the road to development. We are told that a revitalized tradition is the road to development. We are told that industrialization is the road to development. We are told that increased agricultural productivity is the road to development. We are told that delinking is the road to development. We are told that an increased opening to the world market (export-oriented growth) is the road to development. Above all, we are told that development is possible, if only we do the right thing. But what is this right thing?
> (Wallerstein, 1994, p. 3)

However, this reflection does little to suggest what might be the right thing. Much past thinking about development involved pragmatic solutions (conventional) that started with a traditional low-income economy losing its workforce to higher-paying jobs in the new, modern industrial sector. This conventional approach to development is centrally planned and imposed on communities. The communities themselves are viewed as objects of development and are reduced to empirical indicators rather than subjective participants in their own development process. From the conventional arose alternative development paradigms, also known as new local development approaches based on endogenous factors (Casanova, 2004), that allow the community to engage in development in ways that conform to local traditions.

Cultural tourism, it is argued, is considered one such endogenous approach to development, as tourists are keen to visit areas of unspoilt natural beauty and authentic cultural heritage. Many communities are interested in developing tourism, because when it is successfully developed tourism yields many coveted socio-economic benefits (Brown, 2004). However, developing cultural tourism can have negative consequences for the local natural and cultural environment of the community when not developed sympathetically (Dewar, 2004). This implies that the development of cultural tourism will be small scale and will take a long-term perspective and seek not to damage or deplete the natural, built and cultural resources. The unique sense of place and the natural, social and cultural authenticity of the communities have to be respected (Bestard and

Nadal, 2007). It is proposed that once this is done, local people will benefit directly from the increase in number of visitors by owning and managing the facilities and developing attractions and activities (Sharpley and Vass, 2006). While in the short term such compromises at the expense of local interests may seem appropriate courses of action, there may be negative repercussions at a later date (Gill and Williams, 1994). To lower the risk of negative impacts, the development of tourism should be driven by the needs, wishes and aspirations of the community. Involving local people in the development process, and ensuring that residents have a personal stake in the development of cultural tourism, builds the capacity of the community to improve the skills needed to pursue such development and to benefit from it.

3.3 Why Cultural Tourism?

Culture has always been a major object of travel. Actually, nowadays, tourism is culture. Because of the increasing pace of life people have turned to the preservation of the past. It seems that the combination of nostalgia for the past, the need to reassert national and local identities and the perceived economic benefits of cultural development have had a dramatic effect on the supply of cultural attractions.
(Smith, 1999, p. 32)

Culture, traditions, heritage and nature are the reasons for tourists to visit an area. Therefore, cultural tourism depends on these natural and cultural resources. A region's culture can and often does form the basis of tourism development.

Visiting historic sites or participating in historic activities lets visitors to an area learn about the past, experience a variety of recreational opportunities, and enjoy the natural and cultural environment of an area (Swarbrooke, 1996; Sharpley, 2000; Williams, 2001). Cultural heritage describes both material and immaterial forms, e.g. artefacts, monuments, historical remains, buildings, architecture, philosophy, traditions, celebrations, historic events, distinctive ways of life, literature, folklore or education (Nuryanti, 1996).

Tourism is increasingly offering a range of cultural products, from visiting monuments and traditional arts and crafts centres, to participating in historical events and discovering unique lifestyles. It creates an interest in these particular forms of culture, often encouraging the preservation of cultural and historical traditions, contributing to the protection of cultural heritage and to a renaissance of local cultures, cultural arts and crafts. Potentially the relationship between tourism and the cultural sector is highly complementary. The cultural sector creates attractions for the tourist, while tourism supplies extra audiences for cultural events and activities (Tighe, 1991).

It is argued, therefore, that tourism has many potential benefits for communities because it provides them with an opportunity to exploit idyllic landscapes, agricultural products, local customs and traditions, and cultural heritage to cater to the needs of the visitors, outsiders and tourists for economic benefits (Xiao and Li, 2004). Thus, a rich natural and cultural heritage can be a contributory factor in the development of communities, for the benefit of residents and visitors alike.

3.4 Defining the Concept of Community

For almost everyone, the word community has a very positive connotation indeed. It evokes images of personal relationships characterized by warmth, care and understanding; of shared values and more commitments; of social cohesion and solidarity; of continuity in time and place. In many spheres of thought, the ties of community – real or imagined, traditional or contrived – come to form the image of the good society (Nisbet, 1971). Humans need communities – and a sense of community. There is a sense of belonging and identity, a spirit of mutual responsibility (Gardner, 1995).

But what is a community and who forms it? A survey of the literature indicates that beyond the common basis that community deals with people, there is little agreement on a definition. It may be geographical in nature or a community of interest, built on heritage and cultural values shared among community members. In some cases, communities may cluster together beyond their administrative

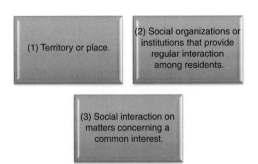

Fig. 3.1. The three elements of community. (From Author.)

boundaries, based on their assessment of the values in working together (Joppe, 1996). For Smit (1990), a community implies a coherent entity with a clear identity and a commonality of purpose. Green and Haines (2007) defined community as including three elements, as outlined in Fig. 3.1.

Communities of place are becoming problematic because people are becoming less attached to their place and more linked to communities of interest. Many issues that concern residents, however, are place based. So, although there are social and economic forces changing the nature of community, place-based issues continue to influence the quality of life of most people (Gunn and Gunn, 1991).

A community thus is a group of people who are socially interdependent (Etzioni, 1995). This implies that in their involvement with one another, people have some of their important needs and interests met by other group members, and that their actions have direct consequences for those with whom they regularly interact (MacIntyre, 1981; Bellah et al., 1985). Community involves people sharing certain practices. These practices are defined as shared activities that are not undertaken as a means to an end, but that are ethically good in themselves (Bender, 1982).

3.5 The Inherent Impacts of Cultural Tourism

Tourists do not visit an area and then leave it unchanged; they need accommodation, restaurants, recreational facilities; they make demands on local shops and firms; they make contact with local people (White, 1974). According to Doxey (1976) and Butler (1980), irritations may develop as a result of the threats posed by tourists to the way of life of permanent residents. Both Doxey's index of tourist irritation and Butler's concept of a tourist area cycle of evolution suggest that as the number of visitors to a region increases, residents who at first were overwhelmingly positive in their attitudes to their guests develop increasing reservations concerning the long-term benefits of the visitors. This may be because the original expectations of benefits were unrealistic (and so are incapable of being fulfilled) or because the benefits are perceived to accrue only to a small number of people. The growing emphasis on tourism development has led to a renewed interest in the impacts of tourism on the environment, society and culture, and the term 'tourism impact' has been gaining increasing attention in the tourism literature.

3.6 Economic Impacts

The degree of support for tourism development has been associated with the perceived economic benefits that residents will derive from it. Due to the increased demand for goods and services, stimulated by the pressure of tourists, tourism is seen to generate economic impacts, such as employment, income, improved living standards, economic diversification, widening economic opportunities and stimulating investment (see Fig. 3.2). But jobs are not only created in facilities directly servicing tourists (Davidson, 1992), tourism also generates local employment in various support and resource-managed sectors.

Cavaco (1995) noted that a revitalization and restoration of local trade businesses might occur; tourism may help to retain local businesses and provide new markets for local products. Tourism helps to diversify the economy and may improve the communities' economic situation and the quality of life of residents.

One of the greatest advantages tourism can bring to communities is increased income and employment (FNNPE, 1993). As such, economic benefits are often the primary

Fig. 3.2. Examples of tourism related businesses. (From Author.)

reasons to develop tourism. Tourism development will lead to more investment and spending, creating new jobs and businesses. Consequently, an increase in income will lead to an increased standard of living. With most residents seeing tourism as an economic development tool (Keogh, 1990), it is not surprising that the findings of most of the studies suggest that, overall, locals have positive attitudes toward tourism (Andereck *et al.*, 2005).

3.7 Environmental Impacts

Negative impacts on the natural environment include erosion resulting from overuse of hiking and riding trails, clashing and unfitting architectural styles, disturbance of animal behavioural patterns, disruption of breeding animals and birds, loss of natural plant cover, loss of soil and rocks, trampling and damage of vegetation, picking of flowers, disturbance to wildlife, loss of quietness, disruption of natural processes, overcrowding, interference with natural sounds, loss of wilderness, pressures and visual impacts of visitor numbers, litter, as well as water, air and noise pollution and traffic congestion (Hardy *et al.*, 2002; Liu, 2003; Andereck *et al.*, 2005).

Although impacts are at times negative, they may bring environmental advantages as well – tourism can be a significant factor in conserving or preserving the natural and cultural patrimony, which might fall into decline otherwise. As a result of tourism there may be an incentive to conserve important natural areas, which might improve the environmental quality of an area. An environment of scenic beauty and interesting features – vegetation, wildlife and clean air and water – offers many of the resources that attract tourists. The more the community residents benefit from tourism, the more, it is argued, they will be motivated to protect the area's natural environment and support tourism activities (McIntyre, 1993).

Also, the presence of supplementary sources of income from tourism will encourage residents to become stewards of their environment (Ross and Wall, 1999). Thus, it is suggested that as a consequence of tourism development the environmental awareness of the local people may increase. They become aware of tourists' interests and the role that they must play in the conservation of landscapes and the quality of the environment. Their involvement in tourism makes local people agents in the conservation of traditional, agricultural and scenic landscapes (Garcia-Ramon *et al.*, 1995). The increased concern with public image stemming from involvement with tourists may encourage enterprises and organizations to undertake landscaping and litter removal, thereby rendering sites more attractive to both locals and visitors (Kelly and Dixon, 1991).

3.8 Socio-cultural Impacts

Socio-cultural disadvantages may result from the development of tourism; not only is local culture open to be exploited as it becomes divorced from the community residents' everyday lifestyle, but it can also be degraded and devalued in the process. Tourists can behave in irresponsible or thoughtless ways that can irrevocably damage local culture (FNNPE, 1993):

> There is a tendency of tourists to become concentrated in relatively small geographical areas, leading to a situation where the indigenous culture can become swamped and overwhelmed by outside influences.
> (Swarbrooke, 1996, p. 455)

These influences include issues such as crowding, disturbance and alienation (Butler, 1992), as community residents try to get on with their everyday lives (FNNPE, 1993; Gilbert and Clarke, 1997; Lindberg and Johnson, 1997; Brunt and Courtney, 1999). Consequently, changes in local attitudes and behaviour may result. The constant pressure of demanding tourists can create an unhealthy mixture of resentment, envy and dissatisfaction, particularly among the young members of the host population, causing further imbalance to the already precarious feeling, common among the local youth in particular, that 'real-life' lies elsewhere (Davidson, 1992; Smith, 1999).

Tourism can also dramatically change the socio-economic balance of communities, when more money can be made from tourists compared with lesser financial rewards from traditional occupations. Healy states that 'social tensions might be brought on when some members of the community benefit more than others from tourism' (1994, pp. 148–149).

> Other socio-economic impacts may include the over-commercialisation, alteration or even loss of authenticity of traditional arts, crafts and ceremonies and increased standardisation of culture (to suit tourist demands), overcrowding and loss of amenities for residents, reinforcement to social inequalities as those with capital and education benefit most from tourism, and local social problems of drugs, prostitution, alcoholism and crime may be exacerbated by tourism.
> (Whelan, 1991, p. 106)

However, there are various socio-cultural advantages to the development of tourism. A first advantage might be a heightened local awareness, a better understanding and appreciation of community culture and lifestyle. The interest of tourists in local culture can result in the conservation and sometimes revitalization of traditional arts, traditional festivals (see Fig. 3.3), handicrafts, folklore, customs, ceremonies and certain aspects of traditional lifestyles (Grahn, 1991; Kelly and Dixon, 1991; FNNPE, 1993; Unwin, 1996; Cohen, 2001; Lindberg et al., 2001; Besculides et al., 2002; Richards, 2005).

'The fact that outsiders come and appreciate the local customs and environment and share the life of the community can re-value in local people's eyes their own traditions' (Davidson, 1992, p. 126). Both Inskeep (1987) and Jurowski (2007), 20 years apart, assert that the development of tourism might lead to renewal of a sense of cultural pride by residents and this renewal can be strengthened when local people observe tourists appreciating their culture.

Tourism is one of many forms of development that encourages social contact between

Fig. 3.3. Visitors taking part in the traditional carnival in a mountain village in Portugal. (From Author.)

people of different backgrounds (Cavaco, 1995; Yueh-Huang and Stewart, 1996; Ross and Wall, 1999; Jurowski, 2007). One benefit of such encounters is how receiving visitors, for some older people, fulfils a social need and it may provide valuable assistance in their struggle against solitude and an unchanging future (Ostrowski, 1987).

Finally, local people may benefit from better community infrastructure facilities and services and from using recreational facilities built for tourists (Perdue *et al.*, 1990). Tourism can support the development and maintenance of public transportation, roads, health care, goods and services, telephones, mail delivery, electricity supply and other services in rural areas where the standards of such facilities may otherwise decline (Pizam, 1978; Inskeep, 1987; FNNPE, 1993; Brunt and Courtney, 1999; Ross and Wall, 1999; Marsden *et al.*, 2002; Liu, 2003).

3.9   Social Exchange Theory

In developing and attracting tourism to a community, the goal is to achieve outcomes that obtain the best balance of benefits and costs for both residents and tourism actors (Ap, 1992; Moore and Cunningham, 1999). But, while many studies have addressed the social interface between residents and tourists, there appears to be little research that specifically addresses the needs of residents in tourist areas. It is suggested that residents evaluate

tourism in terms of social exchange: that is, they evaluate it in terms of expected benefits or costs obtained in return for the service they supply. Figure 3.4 outlines the reasons, according to the principles of social exchange theory, why individuals will engage in exchange.

There is a relatively universal assumption that host resident actors seek tourism development for their community in order to satisfy their economic, social and psychological needs, and to improve the community's well-being.

However, evidence suggests that in economically depressed regions, locals underestimate the cost of tourism development and overestimate the economic gains (Liu and Var, 1986; Sharpley, 2000; Hardy *et al.*, 2002). They are willing to 'put up with some inconvenience in exchange for tourist money' (Var *et al.*, 1985, p. 654).

3.10   Communitarianism to Support Sustainability of Cultural Tourism

The protection of cultural heritage and economic development needs to be promoted as a complementary rather than antagonistic process (see for example Fig. 3.5). As such, the sustainability of attracting culturally motivated tourists to a community entails looking to achieve a situation that provides a high-quality experience for the visitor, maintains the quality of the cultural attractions and benefits the host community (Wahab and Pigram, 1997; Wight, 1998; Paskaleva-Shapira, 2001; Font and

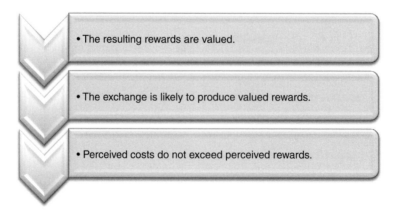

- The resulting rewards are valued.

- The exchange is likely to produce valued rewards.

- Perceived costs do not exceed perceived rewards.

Fig. 3.4. Reasons why individuals will engage in exchange. (Derived from Skidmore, 1975.)

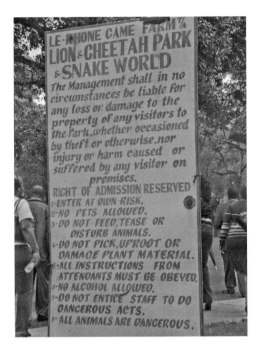

Fig. 3.5. Community initiatives in Zimbabwe. (From Author.)

institution building and local control of programmes. Both of these translate to strong stakeholder involvement. Following this argument, cultural tourism cannot be successfully implemented without the direct support and involvement of those who are affected by it – the different stakeholders. Inskeep (1994) reiterated Murphy's (1985) assertion that sustainable tourism development can be achieved through a community approach in which there is maximum involvement of the community in the planning and decision-making process of tourism and in the actual development and management of tourism and its socio-economic benefits. It is suggested that once community members are informed of the development intent and agree to participate, they sense a stake in the outcome (Guyette, 1996). To achieve this objective, all stakeholders need to be consulted and empowered in tourism decision making (Bramwell *et al.*, 1986; Halme, 2001; Vernon *et al.*, 2005) and particularly the host community must be fully involved in all stages of tourism's development (Ioannides, 1995; Hassan, 2000).

3.11 The Nature of Participation

Paul (1987) argued that the single most important determinant of sustainable development was participation. Given the scale of resource management decisions involved in cultural tourism development, where the physical and social environment can experience substantial change (impacts), it would seem to make good sense to work with the communities likely to be affected by such decisions. To achieve success, development strategies must be consistent with local goals and be sensitive to sustaining a community character and traditions (Brown, 2004), which will require direct participation and involvement of residents.

An active community thrives on the ideas of its residents. It sets clear visions of its priorities and needs as well as agreeing on things that need to be done. Local residents have to act as concerned people interested in working together to improve their communities. Ideas and plans need to be developed by local people, possibly with technical assistance from

Harris, 2004). More recent literature on community development through tourism (e.g. Dredge, 2007; Prentice, 2007; Sirakaya, 2007; Jurowski, 2008) does not differ in its approach to ameliorating the quality of life of the host community, particularly in areas with more extreme needs, assuring a better quality of tourist services and guaranteeing a higher level of tourism development that is compatible with the environment and culture and fulfils the aspirations of the citizens economically, culturally, socially, psychologically and politically.

Thus, sustainability signifies that the demands placed upon the natural and cultural heritage need to be met without reducing the capacity of the environment to provide for future generations. In this sense, economic growth must be based on policies that sustain and expand the environmental and cultural resource base. Meeting the needs of all today without compromising the ability of future generations involves the equitable sharing of resources within and between generations (Ko, 2005) and may lead to sustainable development.

Uphoff (1986) argues that there are two determinants of sustainable development: local outside the community. A wealth of literature (e.g. Long and Nuckolls, 1994) suggests that forging local ties could lead to improved living standards, which, in turn, could determine the success of community development. Creating a mentality of partnership in the local residents and organizations, public agencies and planning officials becomes necessary in order to generate sufficient social capital so that efforts made will be sustainable (Knack and Keefer, 1997; Jones, 2005).

Residents are the ones who suffer most from tourism's effects because the impacts of policy are felt at the local level, by local people and their cultural and physical environments. Tourism will have a big impact on their life, which is why they should have input in the decision-making process. A second reason is safeguarding the sustainability of the development. Community participation in the decision-making process of tourism development is a key issue in ensuring acceptability of tourism, thus contributing to its sustainability (Bramwell and Sharman, 1999; Sharpley, 2000; Hardy et al., 2002; Liu, 2003, 2006; Tosun, 2006). Participation significantly raises the level of commitment by the beneficiaries, thus encouraging them to seek ways and means to sustain the project (Gonzalez, 1998).

But community participation in cultural tourism development can be rather difficult to obtain. First of all, 'some communities may be relatively unconcerned about the long-term ecological and social sustainability of their decisions' (Bramwell and Sharman, 1999, p. 26). Secondly, local experience with tourism is wholly lacking, and people are largely at the mercy of the opinions of those who are presented to them, or who present themselves as 'experts' (de Kadt, 1979). Ordinary people are often found to be sceptical of the participative processes in planning (Jackson and Morpeth, 1999). Furthermore, some studies have demonstrated that those who are locally influential and wealthy will become the spokespersons for communities unless specific measures are taken to counter this pattern (de Kadt, 1979). Power often sits with an established local elite and/or those most 'vocal'; the silent majority and any local minorities may often be superseded (Tosun, 2006). Encouragement of community members to participate in tourism development

requires the opening of power distribution channels and legitimizing issues so local people will have an equal opportunity to participate (Wahab and Pigram, 1997). Without empowerment, tourism development by communities is difficult to attain (Sofield, 2003). Empowerment, it is argued, increases the community's performance and effectiveness in local development initiatives, thus facilitating sustainable development. But empowerment ultimately depends on residents' attitudes toward their surrounding environment and the impacts of tourism development on community quality of life (i.e. the acceptable level of social exchange), and further tourism development.

3.12   Capacity Building

An organized community could motivate and encourage the private sector, foster entrepreneurship by improving institutional facilities for enterprise creation, address the lack of public and private investment, and simplify local formalities that sometimes make local investment more complicated, costly and time consuming. Income generation, increased local control of resources, local institution-strengthening, capacity building, and greater involvement of local organizations and local levels of government, as development mechanisms, are crucial for overcoming the many obstacles to attaining community development objectives.

Developing a community's capacity means building skill and knowledge bases, local institutions, local resources and programmes that empower a community to deal effectively with its own circumstances (Oakley, 1991). Capacity building of community residents through the acquisition of skills, such as technical, leadership or interpersonal values, would contribute to them performing the necessary tasks in the cultural tourism development process. These new skills and abilities enable communities to manage better and have a say in, or negotiate with, existing development delivery systems. Others see it as more fundamental and essentially concerned with enabling communities to decide on and to take actions that they believe are essential to their development.

3.13   Summary

This chapter has described the inherent impacts of cultural tourism on the host community. The concept of community was explored and it was argued that locality is not sufficient to turn a population into a community. Community goes far beyond mere settlement and encompasses all forms of relationship that are characterized by a high degree of personal engagement, emotional depth, moral commitment, social cohesion and continuity in time. In this context, the strength of the community lies in its ability to provide both for its current residents and for their children.

Communities often start tourism development focusing only on economic factors, paying little attention to other essential factors, such as cultural, social and environmental costs. Tourism is seen as an option to provide an improved lifestyle, through the provision of increased income and employment. Tourism helps to stimulate the local economy and, in particular, plays an important role in creating a value-added commercial channel for local products. Residents are more open to support tourism development when it is perceived that personal benefits outweigh the losses.

However, communities seldom realize that impacts of tourism may represent negative consequences for them. Communities may not be particularly attentive to the possible negative impacts. It is suggested that such impacts must be avoided so that the natural and cultural heritage in which cultural tourism is based may be preserved and protected for future generations. This approach to development incorporates the concept of sustainability.

It was also explained how the pursuit of cultural tourism will require that communities improve their capacity to establish social relationships and a more active role by community stakeholders. Once the participation of the permanent residents is obtained, it is they who often are the most committed and capable guardians of local resources. But other capacity-building measures are also required, particularly for developing local services and encouraging business to take advantage of opportunities emerging from the cultural tourism product development.

3.14   Discussion Questions

* Provide a short discussion on the role of cultural tourism in local development.
* What are the main impacts of cultural tourism in a local area?
* According to social exchange theory, why would a local person become involved with cultural tourism development?
* Why is it important to engage the local community in cultural tourism development?
* How could cultural tourism be made more sustainable?

References

Andereck, K., Valentine, K., Knopf, R. and Vogt, C. (2005) Residents' perceptions of community tourism impacts. *Annals of Tourism Research* 32, 1056–1076.

Ap, J. (1992) Residents' perceptions research on the social impacts of tourism. *Annals of Tourism Research* 17, 610–616.

Bellah, R., Madsen, R., Sullivan, W., Swidler, A. and Tipton, S. (1985) *Habits of the Heart. Individualism and Commitment in American Life*. University of California Press, Berkeley, California.

Bender, T. (1982) *Community and Social Change in America*. Johns Hopkins University Press, Baltimore, Maryland.

Besculides, A., Lee, M. and McCormick, P. (2002) Residents' perceptions of the cultural benefits of tourism. *Annals of Tourism Research* 29, 303–319.

Bestard, A. and Nadal, R. (2007) Modelling environmental attitudes toward tourism. *Tourism Management* 28, 688–695.

Bramwell, B. and Sharman, A. (2000) Approaches to sustainable tourism planning and community participation. The case of the Hope Valley. In: Hall, D. and Richards, G. (eds) *Tourism and Sustainable Community Development*. Routledge, London, pp. 17–35.

Bramwell, B., Henry, I., Jackson, G., Prat, A., Richards, G. and van der Straaten, J. (1986) *Sustainable Tourism Management: Principles and Practice*. Tilburg University Press, Tilburg, the Netherlands.

Brown, D. (2004) *Rural Tourism: An Annotated Bibliography*. US Department of Agriculture. http://www.nal.usda.gov/ric/ricpubs/rural_tourism.html (accessed 4 November 2004).

Brunt, P. and Courtney, P. (1999) Host perceptions of sociocultural impacts. *Annals of Tourism Research* 26, 493–515.

Butler, R. (1980) The concept of a tourism area cycle of evolution: implications for management of resources. *Canadian Geographer* 24, 5–12.

Butler, R. (1992) Alternative tourism: the thin edge of the wedge. In: Smith, V. and Eadington, W. (eds) *Tourism Alternatives. Potentials and Problems in the Development of Tourism*. University of Pennsylvania Press, Philadelphia, Pennsylvania, pp. 31–46.

Casanova, F. (2004) *Local Development, Productive Networks and Training: Alternative Approaches to Training and Work for Young People*. Cinterfor, Montevideo, Uruguay.

Cavaco, C. (1995) Tourism in Portugal: diversity, diffusion, and regional and local development. *Tijdschrift voor Economische en Sociale Geografie* 86, 64–71.

Cohen, J. (2001) Textile, tourism and community development. *Annals of Tourism Research* 28, 378–398.

Davidson, R. (1992) *Tourism in Europe*. Pitman, London.

De Kadt, E. (1979) *Tourism – Passport to Development?* Oxford University Press, Oxford.

Dewar, K. (2004) Tourism in national parks and protected areas: planning and management. *Tourism Management* 25, 288–289.

Doxey, G. (1976) When enough's enough: the natives are restless in Old Niagara. *Heritage Canada* 2, 26–27.

Dredge, D. (2007) Community development through tourism. *Annals of Tourism Research* 34, 1097–1099.

Etzioni, A. (1995) *The Spirit of Community*. Fontana Press, London.

FNNPE (Federation of Nature and National Parks of Europe) (1993) *Loving Them to Death? Sustainable Tourism in Europe's Nature and National Parks*. FNNPE, Grafenau, Germany.

Font, X. and Harris, C. (2004) Rethinking standards from green to sustainable. *Annals of Tourism Research* 31, 986–1007.

Garcia-Ramon, D., Canoves, G. and Valdovinos, N. (1995) Farm tourism, gender and the environment in Spain. *Annals of Tourism Research* 22, 267–282.

Gardner, W. (1995) *Tourism Development: Principles, Processes and Policies*. Van Nostrand Reinhold, New York.

Gilbert, D. and Clarke, M. (1997) An exploratory examination of urban tourism impact, with reference to residents' attitudes, in the cities of Canterbury and Guildford. *Cities* 14, 343–352.

Gill, A. and Williams, P. (1994) Managing growth in mountain tourism communities. *Tourism Management* 15, 212–220.

Gonzales, J. (1998) *Development Sustainability Through Community Participation*. Ashgate, Singapore.

Grahn, P. (1991) Using tourism to protect existing culture: a project in Swedish Lapland. *Leisure Studies* 10, 33–47.

Green, G. and Haines, A. (2007) *Asset Building and Community Development*, 2nd edn. Sage, London.

Gunn, C. and Gunn, H. (1991) *Reclaiming Capital: Democratic Initiatives and Community Development*. Cornell University Press, Ithaca, New York.

Guyette, S. (1996) *Planning for Balanced Development*. Clear Light Publishers, Santa Fe, New Mexico.

Halme, M. (2001) Learning for sustainable development in tourism networks. *Business Strategy and the Environment* 10, 100–114.

Hardy, A., Beeton, R. and Pearson, L. (2002) Sustainable tourism: an overview of the concept and its position in relation to conceptualisations of tourism. *Journal of Sustainable Tourism* 10, 475–496.

Hassan, S. (2000) Determinants of market competitiveness in an environmentally sustainable tourism industry. *Journal of Travel Research* 38, 239–245.

Healy, G. (1994) Tourist merchandise as a means of generating local benefits from ecotourism. *Journal of Sustainable Tourism* 2, 137–151.

Inskeep, E. (1987) Environmental planning for tourism. *Annals of Tourism Research* 14, 118–135.

Inskeep, E. (1994) *National and Regional Tourism Planning*. World Tourism Organisation (WTO) Publication. Routledge, London.

Ioannides, D. (1995) A flawed implementation of sustainable tourism: the experience of Akamas, Cyprus. *Tourism Management* 16, 583–592.

Jackson, G. and Morpeth, N. (1999) Local agenda 21 and community participation in tourism policy and planning: future or fallacy. *Current Issues in Tourism* 2(1), 1–38.

Jones, S. (2005) Community-based tourism: the significance of social capital. *Annals of Tourism Research* 32, 303–324.

Joppe, M. (1996) Sustainable community tourism development revisited. *Tourism Management* 17, 475–479.

Jurowski, C. (2007) Tourism and intercultural exchange. *Annals of Tourism Research* 34, 551–552.

Jurowski, C. (2008) Community development through tourism. *Tourism Management* 29, 394–396.

Kelly, I. and Dixon, W. (1991) Sideline tourism. *The Journal of Tourism Studies* 2, 21–28.

Keogh, B. (1990) Public participation in tourism planning. *Annals of Tourism Research* 17, 449–465.

Knack, S. and Keefer, P. (1997) Does social capital have an economic pay-off? A cross country investigation. *Quarterly Journal of Economics* 112, 1251–1288.

Ko, T. (2005) Development of a tourism sustainability assessment procedure: a conceptual approach. *Tourism Management* 26, 431–445.

Lindberg, K. and Johnson, R. (1997) Modeling resident attitudes toward tourism. *Annals of Tourism Research* 24, 402–424.

Lindberg, K., Anderson, T. and Dellaert, B. (2001) Tourism development: assessing social gains and losses. *Annals of Tourism Research* 28, 1010–1030.

Liu, A. (2006) Tourism in rural areas: Kedah, Malaysia. *Tourism Management* 27, 878–889.

Liu, J. and Var, T. (1986) Resident attitudes to tourism impacts in Hawaii. *Annals of Tourism Research* 13, 193–214.

Liu, Z. (2003) Sustainable tourism development: a critique. *Journal of Sustainable Tourism* 11, 459–475.

Long, P. and Nuckolls, J. (1994) Organising resources for rural tourism development: the importance of leadership, planning and technical assistance. *Tourism Recreation Research* 19, 19–34.

MacIntyre, A. (1981) *After Virtue: A Study in Moral Theory.* Duckworth, London.

Marsden, T., Banks, J. and Bristow, G. (2002) The social management of rural nature: understanding agrarian-based rural development. *Environment and Planning* 34, 809–825.

McIntyre, G. (1993) *Sustainable Tourism Development: Guide for Local Planners,* 2nd edn. World Tourism Organization, Madrid.

Moore, K. and Cunningham, W. (1999) Social exchange behaviour in logistics relationships: a skipper perspective. *International Journal of Physical Distribution and Logistics Management* 29, 103–121.

Murphy, P. (1985) *Tourism: A Community Approach.* Methuen, New York.

Nisbet, R. (1971) *The Sociological Tradition.* Heinemann Educational Books, London.

Nuryanti, W. (1996) Heritage and postmodern tourism. *Annals of Tourism Research* 23, 249–260.

Oakley, P. *et al.* (1991) *Projects with People: The Practice of Participation in Rural Development.* International Labour Office, Geneva, Switzerland.

Ostrowski, S. (1987) Polish holiday villages. Secular tradition and modern practice. *Tourism Management* 8, 41–48.

Paskaleva-Shapira, K. (2001) Innovative partnerships for sustainable urban tourism. Paper presented at the TTRA European Conference 'Creating and Managing Growth in Travel and Tourism', Stockholm, Sweden.

Paul, S. (1987) *Community Participation in Development Projects: The World Bank Experience.* World Bank, Washington, DC.

Perdue, R., Long, P. and Allen, L. (1990) Resident support for tourism development. *Annals of Tourism Research* 17, 586–599.

Pizam, A. (1978) Tourism's impact: the social cost of the destination community as perceived by its residents. *Journal of Travel Research* 16, 8–12.

Prentice, R. (2007) Book Review of Murphy, P. and Murphy, A., Strategic management for tourism communities: Bridging the gaps. *Tourism Management* 28, 940–946.

Richards, G. (2005) Textile tourists in the European periphery: new markets for disadvantaged areas? *Tourism Review International* 8, 323–338.

Ross, S. and Wall, G. (1999) Ecotourism: towards congruence between theory and practice. *Tourism Management* 20, 123–132.

Sharpley, R. (2000) Tourism and sustainable development: exploring the theoretical divide. *Journal of Sustainable Tourism* 8, 1–19.

Sharpley, R. and Vass, A. (2006) Tourism, farming and diversification: an attitudinal study. *Tourism Management* 27, 1040–1052.

Sirakaya, E. (2007) Concurrent validity of the sustainable tourism attitude scale. *Annals of Tourism Research* 34, 1081–1084.

Sklair, L. (ed.) (1994) *Capitalism and Development*. Routledge, London.

Smit, D. (1990) Community participation: some realities. In: Seminar on Community Participation in Service Provision for Township Development, Univ. of Witwatersrand, Johannesburg, cited in Abbot, J. Community participation and its relationship to community development. *Community Development Journal* 30, 164.

Smith, E. (1999) The effects of investments in the social capital of youth on political and social behaviour in young adulthood. *Political Psychology* 20, 553–580.

Sofield, T. (2003) *Empowerment for Sustainable Tourism Development*. Pergamon, Amsterdam.

Swarbrooke, J. (1996) Towards the development of sustainable rural tourism in Eastern Europe. *Journal of Sustainable Tourism* 4, 58–65.

Tighe, A. (1991) Research on cultural tourism in the United States. *Travel and Tourism Research Association Proceedings* 387–391.

Tosun, C. (2006) Expected nature of community participation in tourism development. *Tourism Management* 27, 493–504.

Unwin, T. (1996) Tourist development in Estonia. Images, sustainability and integrated rural development. *Tourism Management* 17, 265–276.

Uphoff, N. (1986) *Local Institutional Development: An Analytical Sourcebook with Cases*. Kumarian Press, Hartford, Connecticut.

Var, T., Kendall, K. and Tarakcioglu, E. (1985) Resident attitudes towards tourists in a Turkish resort town. *Annals of Tourism Research* 12, 652–657.

Vernon, J., Essex, S., Pinder, D. and Curry, K. (2005) Collaborative policymaking: local sustainable projects. *Annals of Tourism Research* 32, 325–345.

Wahab, S. and Pilgram, J. (eds) (1997) *Tourism, Development and Growth: The Challenge of Sustainability*. Routledge, London.

Wallerstein, I. (1994) Lodestar or illusion. In: Sklair, L. (ed.) *Capitalism and Development*. Routledge, London, pp. 3–20.

Whelan, T. (1991) *Nature and Tourism: Managing the Environment*. Island Press, Washington, DC.

White, P. (1974) *The Social Impact of Tourism on Host Communities: A Study of the Language Change in Switzerland*. School of Geography, Oxford.

Wight, P. (1998) Tools for sustainability analysis in planning and managing tourism and recreation in the destination. In: Hall, M. and Lew, A. (eds) *Sustainable Tourism. A Geographical Perspective*. Addison-Wesley Longman, Harlow, UK, pp. 75–91.

Williams, D. (2001) Sustainability and public access to nature: contesting the right to roam. *Journal of Sustainable Tourism* 9, 361–371.

Xiao, H. and Li, L. (2004) Villagers' perceptions of traditions: some observations on the development of rural cultural tourism in China. *Tourism Recreation Research* 29, 69–80.

Yueh-Huang, H. and Stewart, W. (1996) Rural tourism development: shifting basis of community solidarity. *Journal of Travel Research* 34, 26–31.

4 Cultural Tourism: Issues and Policies

Razaq Raj,[1] Kevin A. Griffin[2] and Nigel D. Morpeth[1]
[1]*Leeds Metropolitan University, Leeds, UK;*
[2]*Dublin Institute of Technology, Dublin, Ireland*

4.1 Introduction

This chapter explores cultural tourism and its related policies, considering the distinctiveness and pervasiveness of the concept within contemporary society, and how different societies value, plan for and develop policies of this nature. From the application of post-modern discourses, culture, and more particularly cultural tourism, is explored within both developing and developed societies.

The concepts of culture, tourism and cultural tourism relate to a unique part of the tourism industry addressing issues related to a country or local community/region. It is important to understand a country or local community/region/area, because people from these geo-social entities express themselves differently in the form of their art, music, religion, local customs, values, architectural design and so on. Thus, it is evident that culture can form a key ingredient of local distinctiveness from a tourism perspective.

4.2 Cultural Tourism as a Commodity

The linkage of culture and tourism is becoming more and more commonplace. According to the OECD, this is because

> Cultural tourism is one of the largest and fastest growing global tourism markets and the cultural and creative industries are increasingly being used to promote destinations and to increase their competitiveness and attractiveness. The increasing use of culture and creativity to market destinations is also adding to the pressure of differentiating

regional identities and images. A growing range of cultural elements are being employed to brand and market regions. Culture and tourism are therefore essential tools to support the comparative and competitive advantage of regions in global markets.

(OECD, 2009, p. 65)

Many dimensions of contemporary tourism offering are culturally determined elements of everyday society. Figure 4.1 visually illustrates Richards' useful representation of a cultural tourism milieu. In his typology, two scales – past/present form and education/entertainment function – form the axes of the matrix, which contains a broad range of cultural products ranging from those that are often 'performed' primarily for tourism, such as staged pageants or festivals, to forms that can be almost liminal entities for the tourism industry, such as art exhibitions and language courses.

While this is very much a 'product-based' view (OECD, 2009), it is difficult to escape this commodification of culture because there is no denying its importance as a tool for the development of any region seeking to benefit from tourism. Cultural experiences can both enhance the extant offering or attract new tourists to an area, with visitors attracted for many culture-related motivational factors. The 2009 OECD report *The Impact of Culture on Tourism* states that cultural tourism can play a major role in the development of different regions, bringing people with different traditions together by sharing their customs and values.

One of the difficulties with this, according to Raj, is that

The term 'culture' has been debated intensely over the last two decades and no clear definition of the concept has yet been accepted by the community as a whole … [it] … is closely linked to our national identity and the importance that individual people place on local and national social organisations, such as local governments, education institutions, religious communities, work and leisure.

(2012, p. 213)

How therefore can such a personal, amorphous, abstract concept be managed, manipulated and massaged into a tool for the leverage of tourism. The most common approach taken in dealing with cultural tourism is to reduce the intangible to a market product, differentiating it into sub-themes and interrelated concepts of heritage tourism, cultural tourism and creative tourism (see Fig. 4.2).

To simplify the matter, it can be useful to change the lens of investigation from being product-focused to examining the tourist as illustrated in Fig. 4.3. In this model, the indices used are depth of experience sought and the importance of cultural tourism in the decision to visit a destination. Both of these scales are used in later chapters of this book.

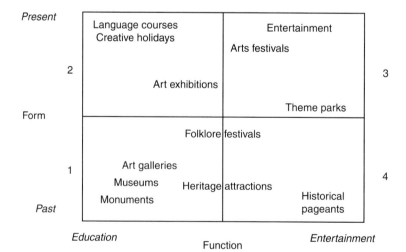

Fig. 4.1. Typology of cultural tourism attractions. (From Richards, 2001.)

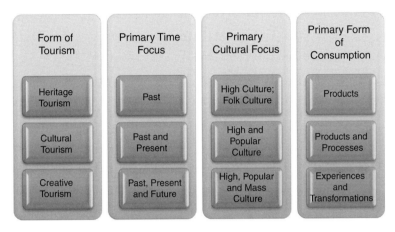

Fig. 4.2. The characteristics of cultural tourism juxtaposed with heritage and creative tourism. (From Richards, 2001.)

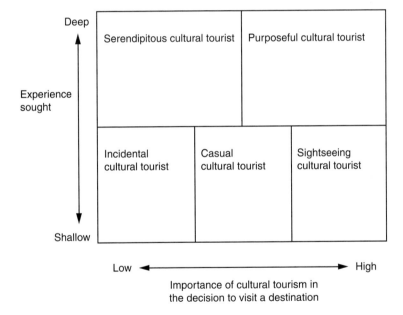

Fig. 4.3. The cultural tourist. (From McKercher and Du Cros, 2002.)

4.3 Cultural Strategies

A review of OECD case studies indicates that for many regions the emphasis on cultural tourism is indeed as a commodified product. The main drivers identified for developing policies that bring together both culture and tourism are outlined in Fig. 4.4 (OECD, 2009, p. 43).

The future of cultural tourism in developing cities or countries relies significantly on event tourism strategies. Therefore it is important for governments to develop clear and effective integrated strategies encompassing culture, event and tourism elements. It is also important for destinations and countries to understand the potential customers'/tourists' needs and expectations and to introduce the

Fig. 4.4. Main drivers for cultural tourism policy. (From Raj, 2012.)

consumer decision-making process for these various product components. In addition, the aim of many policies is to encourage tourism by ensuring that complex and extensive planning strategies are in place for the future. Relying on these elements to generate tourism in the future is difficult to predict, therefore it is essential that governments and other related authorities do not rely on certain singular dimensions to attract tourists, but have a variety of future strategies in place to increase cultural tourism in the 21st century.

Strategic decisions made by a variety of governments in the past have resulted in poor support from the local community. Therefore, it is important for governments to work with local communities to attract visitors to cultural and heritage sites. Also they need to improve transport, accommodation and food facilities in the tourism areas. Governments should also provide tax breaks for those companies that are catering for the local and international tourist at the destination.

Having established the importance of effective planning in preparing for and executing cultural tourism, the remainder of this chapter will discuss the principles behind cultural tourism policy and will then present a range of international case studies that illustrate the diverse approaches and methodologies employed to ensure its successful and sustainable management. Despite the various frames of reference utilized in this chapter for the exploration of cultural tourism, as will be seen, the manifestation of cultural tourism is not static, such that complex sites like Uluru in Australia's outback range across the various dimensions represented, being simultaneously

seen as a high or folk culture entity, and a desirable 'product' for mass cultural consumption (see Fig. 4.2).

4.4 The Importance of Cultural Policy

The importance of planning for culture has motivated the formation of the Cultural Policy Education Group (CPEG), which is an initiative of the European Cultural Foundation to address universities, lecturers, students, scholars and cultural operators dealing with cultural policy issues and professional education. This has evolved from the recognition of growing demand for the provision for students and professionals of a theoretical and practical knowledge on contemporary issues of cultural policy and to thereby develop educational structures to tackle this need. CPEG tackles all aspects of culture, particularly in Eastern Europe and its neighbouring regions, stimulating discussion of cultural policy education and enhancing its academic training opportunities.

According to its website,

> CPEG is closely affiliated with the South East European expert network of the Policies for Culture Programme of the European Cultural Foundation (Amsterdam) and ECUMEST Association (Bucharest). Current CPEG activities target the entire area of Central and Eastern Europe and especially address qualified universities in the countries of Albania, Belarus, Bosnia & Herzegovina, Bulgaria, Croatia, Czech Republic, Estonia, Hungary, Latvia, Lithuania, Macedonia, Moldova, Poland, Romania, Russia, Serbia & Montenegro, Slovakia, Slovenia, Ukraine,

improving research and International cooperation in cultural policies.

(http://www.policiesforculture.org)

However, despite this example of universities (in Europe) becoming increasingly involved in transversal and transnational activities, Bennett and Mercer remind us that

> Cultural policy does not yet exist as a clearly defined area of study with agreed research paradigms and methodologies. It rather comprises a loose articulation of work emerging from different disciplinary origins – from arts management, communication studies, urban studies, cultural studies, cultural economics – and is not yet able to readily identify how its different parts add up to a cohesive whole.
>
> (1998, p. 4)

This general lack of integrated thinking in cultural policy is even more evident when one focuses particularly on policy in relation to cultural tourism. As indicated in Fig. 4.4, there are a multitude of reasons for engaging in cultural tourism, but the economic ones seem to prevail:

> In all regions, however, it is increasingly the case that culture and tourism policy are related to generating externalities which will benefit the local economy.
>
> (OECD, 2009)

To achieve the benefits that they allude to in their statements regarding the importance of cultural tourism, the OECD suggest that a number of central policy areas are commonly identifiable, across a range of case studies that they have evaluated (see Fig. 4.5).

Later in the same report, the OECD point out that reflections on policy seem to focus on either tourism, or culture, but rarely on cultural tourism itself. Therefore,

> [the most] challenging aspect of policy developments linking tourism and culture is to successfully integrate the requirements of stakeholders from the two sectors, which is exacerbated by their different philosophies and approaches: the profit motive vs. non-profit, markets vs. public, etc.
>
> (OECD, 2009, p. 67)

The following sections set out to explore an international sample of cultural tourism policies, ranging from very local to national and even transnational. To provide a focus, this discussion will set out to answer some of the questions posed in this chapter, but will also try to explore how policy makers are tackling and trying to address the main challenges for cultural tourism policy outlined in Fig. 4.6.

4.5 Guidelines for Developing a Cultural Tourism Policy in the Irpinia Region

In 2010 at the First International Conference on Sustainable Tourism in Rural Areas: Issues and Policies from the Irpinia Region, Italy, Razaq Raj presented a discussion on how the region should approach the development of its cultural policy. One of his main strategies was to suggest that the region should allow and facilitate locals to become independent and

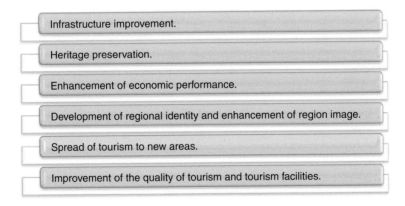

Fig. 4.5. Main cultural tourism policy areas. (From OECD, 2009.)

get engaged with cultural tourism development. Government laws, for example, allow locals to make and sell handicrafts, rent rooms from their own housing as well as cook for tourists. These activities could provide advantages for both the local community as well as the region's economy. Other government strategies, with support from locals, could involve regular improvements on heritage buildings, such as museums, churches and large sport facilities, resulting in the provision of facilities for visitors, which can ensure that locals are not negatively disturbed during their time in the area. Cultural activities, he suggested, can be used to develop community pride, self-sufficiency as well as intercultural communication (Raj, 2012). In his paper, Raj proposes a range of cultural strategies that the region should adopt (Fig. 4.7). It will be interesting to visit the region in the future to ascertain if any or all of these strategies have been adopted.

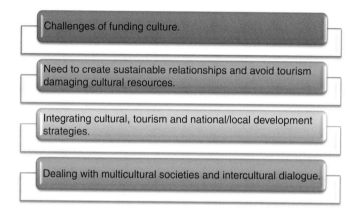

Fig. 4.6. Challenges for cultural tourism policy. (From Authors.)

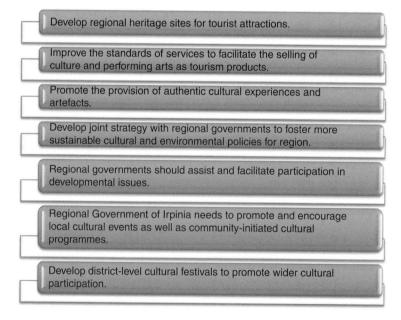

Fig. 4.7. Cultural strategies for the Irpinia region. (From Raj, 2012.)

4.6   Why is Ayers Rock called Uluru?

Globally, one of the best-known contestations of cultural tourism spaces is Uluru or Ayers Rock, located in Uluru–Kata Tjuta National Park, which covers an area of 1326 square kilometres in the very centre of Australia. In the late 19th century two white explorers, Giles and Gosse, were the first 'visitors' to investigate this region. On reaching Kata Tjuta, a group of almost 40 red sandstone domes (located about 30 kilometres west of Uluru), Giles named them 'The Olgas', after the then Queen of Wurttemberg. Gosse, being the first to reach Uluru, an impressive 348-metre high monolith, named it Ayers Rock after Sir Henry Ayers, then Chief Secretary of South Australia.

The nature of how this feature has been named and renamed provides an interesting insight into the changing cultural emphases that have governed its management and recognition as an Aboriginal site:

> In 1873, Ayers Rock and Mount Olga were named by the SA Government (recorded in South Australian Parliamentary Paper 48 of 1873). Since 1894, both Uluru and Kata Tjuta in varying forms have been recorded, though not as widely as their English equivalents, named by the SA Government. On 15 December 1993 this feature was the first officially dual named feature in the Northern Territory – Ayers Rock/Uluru. Following a request from the Regional Tourism Association in Alice Springs, on 6 November 2002 the order of the dual names was officially changed to Uluru/Ayers Rock.
> (Northern Territory Government, 2011)

These subtle alterations in nomenclature are evidence of a long and sometimes contentious debate concerning the cultural significance and even ownership of Uluru. The changes in ownership and control of the site have been documented elsewhere and will not be revisited here, but symbolic of its 'return' to the Aboriginal peoples is the fact that nowadays only 10% of visitors climb what they see as the 'rock', with the remaining 90% respecting the cultural significance of this spiritual site. Extracts from the detailed and extensive *Visitor Guide to Uluru-Kata Tjuta National Park* (Department of Sustainability, Environment, Water, Population and Communities, 2011) illustrate the areas that are particularly sensitive (Fig. 4.8)

from a cultural perspective. The document also presents a cogent and compelling request for visitors to value the site, based on respecting native laws and traditions (Fig. 4.9). In fact, the guide goes beyond asking people to not climb Uluru and suggests that in certain sacred areas visitors should not use film or photography.

From a policy perspective, management of Uluru is governed with reference to the 2009–2019 Uluru-Kata Tjuta National Park Management Plan, which is currently in draft form (Director of National Parks, 2009). Produced by a Board of Management comprising traditional Aboriginal owners and representatives of Parks Australia in a cooperative partnership, the plan is both culturally sensitive and based on sound scientific knowledge. The following lengthy but worthy extract from the plan presents an admirable and perhaps enviable example of multicultural thinking and mutual respect behind a cultural tourism policy, and goes towards justifying why an image of Uluru has been chosen for the cover of this book:

> Board of Management Vision (for The Uluru–Kata Tjuta National Park):
>
> The Uluru–Kata Tjuta landscape is and will always be a significant place of knowledge and learning. All the plants, animals, rocks, and waterholes contain important information about life and living here now and for all time.
>
> Anangu grandparents and grandchildren will always gain their knowledge from this landscape. They will live in it in the proper way. This is *Tjukurpa*.
>
> The special natural and cultural features of this area, which have placed it on the World Heritage List, will be protected. Its importance as a sacred place and a national symbol will be reflected in a high standard of management.
>
> This will be achieved through joint management of Uluru–Kata Tjuta National Park where Anangu and Piranpa will work together as equals, exchanging knowledge about our different cultural values and processes and their application. Together we will apply Anangu *Tjukurpa* and practice and relevant Piranpa knowledge to:
>
> - keep *Tjukurpa* strong
> - look after the health of country and community
> - help Uluru–Kata Tjuta National Park to become known as a place of learning,

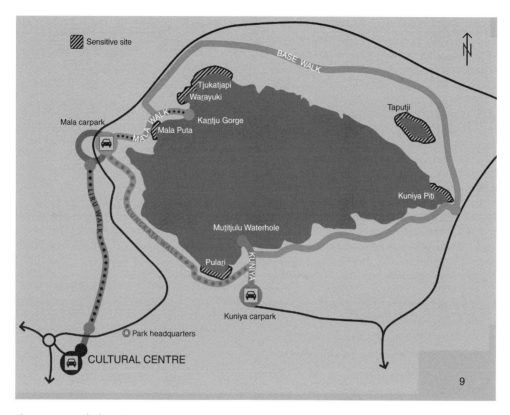

Fig. 4.8. Map of Uluru highlighting the most sensitive areas. (From Director of National Parks, 2009.)

knowledge, and understanding about culture, country and custom

- ensure a strong future for Anangu in the management of the Park and ensure Anangu benefit from the existence of the Park
- protect World Heritage natural and cultural environments of the Park in harmony with Australian social and economic aspirations.

We would like all visitors and people with an interest in this place to learn about this land from those who have its knowledge. We would like you to respect this knowledge, behave in a proper way, enjoy your visit, and return safely to your homes and families to share the knowledge you have gained.

(Director of National Parks, 2009, p. ii)

4.7   Cultural Counter-colonization – the Forts and Castles of Ghana

In a paper published by Addo in the *Journal of Tourism Consumption and Practice*, the author examines how Ghana in West Africa is trying to diversify its tourist landscape, and in particular how it is improving the product offering along its coastal region, where a number of beach and resort hotels are being developed. One of the most interesting cultural features in this zone is a series of European-built coastal fortifications dating back to the late 15th century:

Three castles and about 80 forts were built by Europeans along the entire Atlantic coast of Ghana to serve as trading posts, residences, and strategic defence. Some of the forts are in ruins. The Netherlands built 37%; England, 20%; Denmark, 14%; Portugal, 9%; Sweden, 7%; France, 7%; and Brandenburg (Prussian portion of Germany), 6% of the forts and castles … The three castles … are St. George in Elmina (often called the Elmina Castle) built by the Portuguese in 1482, Carolusburg in Cape Coast (often called the Cape Coast Castle) built by the Swedes in 1653, and Christianborg in Accra (often called the Osu Castle) built by the Danes in 1659.

(Addo, 2011, p. 10)

Wanyu Ulurunya tatintja wiyangku wantima

Please don't climb Uluru

That's a really important sacred thing you are climbing... You shouldn't climb. It's not the real thing about this place. The real thing is listening to everything.

And maybe that makes you a bit sad. But anyway that's what we have to say. We are obliged by *Tjukurpa* to teach people what behaviour is appropriate. It has been the same for us since the beginning.

And all the tourists will brighten up and say, 'Oh I see. This is the right way. This is the proper way: no climbing.'

© Traditional owner

Cultural reasons

What visitors call 'the climb' is of great spiritual significance to us. As a guest on *Anangu* land, we hope that you will choose to respect our law and culture by not climbing. When you visit the Cultural Centre you will learn more about the significance of Uluru to us.

Safety reasons

Traditionally we have a responsibility to teach and safeguard visitors to our land. The climb can be dangerous and over 35 people have died while attempting to climb Uluru - many others have been injured. We feel great sadness when a person dies or is hurt on our land. Please read the safety information on the back of this guide before you decide whether or not to climb.

Fig. 4.9. Extract from National Park guide requesting visitors not to climb. (From Department of Sustainability, Environment, Water, Population and Communities, 2011.)

In his paper, Addo lists 16 other extant forts, which further supplement the supply of tourism product. In 1979 some of the forts and castles were placed on the list of UNESCO World Heritage Sites; however, the author points out that these were sites of slavery, where people were interned, then traded like commodities, and subsequently sent to Europe and 'the New World' where they were enslaved into horrendous work conditions on plantations and other industries:

> Some of the slaves died in chains and dungeons whilst awaiting ships for the forced emigration. The colonial edifices, therefore, undeniably qualify as European 'blackspots' in cultural heritage tourism.
>
> (Addo, 2011, p. 11)

In February 2007 during a meeting of African tourism ministers in Accra, the Ghanian Minister of Tourism and Diasporan Relations (MOTDR) launched an elaborate plan to establish Ghana as the homeland for the African Diaspora via an innovation entitled the *Joseph Project*. Based on the fact that many millions of Africans who were taken into slavery in the Americas passed through these slave castles, which are dotted along the Ghanaian coast, the invitation being sent from Ghana to their descendants is to return to the land of their ancestors:

> Once upon a time, the gangways of the castles and forts leading to the slave ships appeared to be 'the doors of no return', but thanks to the new spirit of reconciliation, the gates have now become 'a new Akwaaba' (welcome) for the African Diaspora, the 'Gates of Return' into their second home, their real home, in Africa.
>
> (Tourism Ghana, 2007, p. 6)

This interesting policy of utilizing the imagery of these forts, which are symbols of darkness (what Addo labels 'blackspots' or elements of dark tourism) in Ghana's past, as a positive for tourism changes the lens of investigation from viewing them as symbols of colonial domination to regarding them as centres from which African culture was spread throughout the Americas and Europe. Tourism Ghana claim that 'However negative the slave trade may have been, through its instrumentality the native African cultural traditions were transplanted to the New World' (2007, p. 9). Having listed a broad range of religious, musical and linguistic developments in African-American culture and their origins in Africa, they finish their overview of this initiative by claiming: 'Such is the legacy of the African-European relationships established on the Gold Coast as these two peoples met at the castles, forts and lodges between 1482–1880'. Thus, through a creative policy initiative, Ghana is embracing its violent colonial past, the ghastly human practice of slavery and generations of forced human displacement and translating this dark period of its history into a cultural positive. Thus, this culturally motivated tourism initiative is linking castles that are symbols of cultural dominance, pain and death, and turning them into symbols of cultural awakening and open-armed welcome.

4.8   Developing a Creative Economy in the USA

In 1982 the President of the United States of America (Ronald Reagan) established the President's Committee on the Arts and the Humanities (PCAH), which advises the White House on cultural issues. Since its foundation, the Committee has undertaken an impressive range of work including major research and policy analysis, and the encouragement of numerous federal cultural programmes. This committee works directly with

> the three primary cultural agencies – National Endowment for the Arts, the National Endowment for the Humanities and the Institute of Museum and Library Services – as well as other federal partners and the private sector, to address policy questions in the arts and humanities, to initiate and support key programs in those disciplines and to recognize excellence in the field. Its core areas of focus are arts and humanities education, cultural exchange, and creative economy.
>
> (PCAH, 2012)

This third area, 'creative economy', recognizes that the arts and humanities are a powerful and positive force in the life of the American economy. More specifically relevant to this chapter is an appreciation that the creative economy 'drives tourism and commerce', and thereby supports jobs. Thus, one of the two component elements of this creative economy strand for the PCAH is 'cultural tourism'. Explaining the importance of this element, the PCAH states:

> Travel industry research confirms that cultural and heritage tourism is one of the fastest growing segments of the tourism industry. The growth and investment in cultural heritage tourism has expanded markets, audiences and consumers, as well as provided a means for sustaining cultural and heritage resources with vital revenue and awareness.
>
> (PCAH, 2012)

Under this theme of cultural tourism, a range of current projects are progressing, with an overall goal to raise awareness regarding the importance of cultural heritage tourism across the United States. The most influential report produced by this group, *A Position Paper on Cultural and Heritage Tourism in The United States*, dates to 2005, but the twelve pages of background and directions it gives still influence the workings of the PCAH, and through that organization, the individual states of America, driving their awareness of policy and planning for this particular tourism sector. In positioning cultural and heritage tourism, the following extract from the paper provides advice that is a relevant and central motivator in much of the cultural and heritage tourism policy in the USA:

> [C]ultural and heritage tourism is different from other 'mass market' travel industry segments in several ways:
>
> – First, many cultural and heritage institutions are nonprofit organizations where tourism is only one strategy that meets their mission. In many cases, funds are dedicated to an artistic or educational mission or the preservation, interpretation and management of a resource rather than to marketing.
> – Second, limited capacity or the fragility of cultural, natural and heritage resources and sites sometimes constrains the number of visitors that can be hosted annually or seasonally ... Overuse or excess capacity can result in negative impact on resources and can diminish the quality of the visitor and resident experience...

– Finally, cultural and heritage assets are traditionally 'one of a kind' and seek to provide unique experiences not replicated in any other community. Additionally, the artistic or educational missions of these institutions, as well as the interests and work of the artists, performers and artisans, all contribute to a place's authenticity ... The travel and tourism industry must work closely with cultural and heritage organizations and the community to provide quality visitor experiences without compromising the integrity of message or negatively affecting these authentic resources and living traditions. Each constituent group should be proactive in helping its partners in learning more about how their respective industries work.

(PCAH, 2005, pp. 3–4)

Examination of the PCAH website and its various outputs in the form of reports and press releases, for example, illustrates many policy successes in the area of cultural heritage tourism. Perhaps these successes are somewhat related to PCAH's political position, which is envied by many such organizations. Firstly, it was set up by the American Presidency, and secondly, since its foundation the Honorary Chairperson has been the First Lady. Perhaps this explains the level of credibility, recognition and influence it enjoys, not to mention its level of administrative integration, which is not repeated in very many jurisdictions.

4.9 The Cold Reality of Cultural Tourism in the Antarctic

While Antarctica may not be seen by many as a destination for cultural tourism, Spennemann (2007) classifies it as a remote heritage area (the main topic of his article includes examining the Moon under this categorization). Documenting the evolution of 'tourism' in the Antarctic, he points out that initial visitations were largely scientific until

commercial tourism commenced in December 1956 with a LAN Chile DC-6 conducting an overflight tour. In 1958 the first ship-based tours, out of Chile and Argentina, began. By 1969, purpose-built cruiseships visited the waters. Between 1977 and 1980, commercial airlines out of New Zealand and Australia

conducted low-level 'flight-seeing' tours, taking some 11,000 tourists over the area in 44 flights. By the late 80s, ship-based tours were mounted to the edge of the pack-ice and landing tourists.

(Spennemann, 2007, p. 899)

According to the International Association of Antarctica Tour Operators, in the 2010–11 season, the combined number of seaborne, airborne landed and cruise-only tourists numbered 33,824, the 2011–12 figure was 26,519 and 2012–13 is estimated to reach 34,950 (IAATO, 2012). While these are relatively small numbers, there is a deep concern that the regulations governing the management of this precious and fragile landscape are constantly being stretched and casually overlooked.

In a paper entitled 'Towards an Antarctic tourism policy: a framework for policy analysts', Greg O'Brien (then based at the Centre for Antarctic Studies and Research at the University of Canterbury) presented an interesting discussion on the importance of regulating Antarctic tourism. He situated his discussion around a basic but useful model of policy development (borrowed from Pollitt and Bouckhaert, 2004), which consists of three conceptual components.

The first, termed *alpha*, is the situation as it is prior to the policy process, the empirical circumstances that the policy will seek to alter. The second, termed *beta*, is the desired situation, the state of affairs that the policy will attempt to bring about. The final category, termed *omega*, is the trajectory connecting the two states, the existing state and the desired state. The trajectory will be one or a group of policies designed to achieve the stated aim.

(O'Brien, 2009, p. 1)

Thus, the concern being expressed about Antarctica is that the universally agreed pristine (*beta*) state of the continent is currently at risk, and thus the *omega* trajectory needs to be strengthened and formalized.

Policy development for Antarctica is developed through the Antarctic Treaty System (ATS) or via methods of self-regulation, such as through the International Association of Antarctic Tour Operators (IAATO), and to date all tourism activities have been assessed as having a minor and transitory impact or lower. However, there are two problems in this assessment: the investigations (Environmental Impact

Assessments) are being undertaken by the tourist operators themselves; and no tourist activity has yet to complete a Comprehensive Environmental Evaluation (CEE), the highest level of EIA under the treaty system.

The extant evaluation criteria for activity in Antarctica are vague and, in addition, based on one-off events rather than considering the cumulative impact of activity. Thus, regular visits to a single site are only evaluated as individual occurrences. This is because the current structure is developed around managing the activities of state science programmes and is ill-equipped to deal with the impacts of tourism. The implication is that a single tourist cruise can fall well below the environmental capacity of the environment (in terms of pollutants and stress on wildlife) and thus be legitimately allowed under the system. However, because there is a series of these cruises, each below the crucial limits individually, the cumulative impacts may be greater.

France and the UK have put forward a number of working papers to develop a vision and structure for managing tourism, however many of the proposals are not designed as policy instruments but non-mandatory and aspirational tools towards the management of Antarctic tourism. There are some suggestions (see O'Brien, 2009) that tourism in Antarctica could/should be regulated according to a 'precautionary approach', similar to that of mining (i.e. limited or banned). However, the precautionary position has not advanced far beyond discussion because of the difficulty in linking specific impacts to tourism, even conceptually:

> While there is broad agreement that there is the potential for cumulative impacts and adverse damage to the environment, there seems to be little in the way of theoretical models of damage that could be used to justify the implementation of the precautionary principle.
> (O'Brien, 2009, p. 25)

In a destination where international diplomacy is at its most sensitive, policies and agreements by governments about the management of tourism will be slow to develop. In the meantime, the IAATO state that 'In more than 40 years of organized tourism to the continent...no discernible impact has been observed' (2012, p. 3). Furthermore, they position managed visitations to the continent as a positive tool both for conservation and as a cultural tool for international peace and harmony:

> Tourism is and should continue to be a driving force in Antarctic conservation. Firsthand travel experiences foster education and understanding, with visitors from all over the world – representing more than 100 different nationalities during the 2011–12 season alone – returning home from Antarctica as ambassadors of goodwill, guardianship and peace for the destination they have visited.
> (IAATO, 2012, p. 4)

4.10 Summary

Examining culture, tourism and cultural tourism reveals a complex and convoluted set of philosophies from a policy perspective. Both culture and tourism are often misunderstood, under-valued and neglected, and this can be magnified even more when the two spheres combine under cultural tourism. However, the new global reality of recessionary times, and the need to think outside the 'industrial box', has led various territories and regions to realize the true worth of exploring their culture and heritage, and often this is operationalized via tourism. Many regions (as illustrated throughout this book), are exploring tools such as urban (re)generation, tourism development and community enhancement, with culture as a main focal point.

This chapter began by recognizing that the most pragmatic way for cultural tourism to be taken seriously as an area for policy development is to acknowledge it in a commodified frame of reference. Thus, the chapter identified a number of approaches to classifying both cultural tourism and the cultural tourist. This theoretical portion of the chapter continued by linking cultural tourism policy to the idea of generating externalities, and commented on the need to engage the multitude of stakeholders who are involved.

The remaining sections of the chapter provided a smorgasbord of case studies, to illustrate various approaches and models of cultural tourism policy. Italy's Irpinia Region is seeking to exploit its cultural heritage, and the chapter gave a brief overview of some of the various measures that are being considered for doing this in a sustainable manner. Uluru in Australia is the quintessential example of conflict between touristic desire to consume a product and local desire to preserve and protect culture. The policies that have evolved in this instance are a wonderful example for any destination facing the challenges of integrating ethnic requirements into the development of tourism. The forts and castles of the Ghanaian coastline are less well known but present a curious example of utilizing a cultural element that represents such a negative experience for a territory. In Ghana these symbols of cultural oppression are being turned into a vibrant and exciting tourism product. The President's Committee on the Arts and the Humanities in the United States of America evidences high level recognition

for cultural tourism, in the context of developing the creative economy of the country. The chapter ended with a discussion on the challenges being faced in the Antarctic, where there is much difficulty navigating the political maze caused by multiple stakeholders sharing jurisdiction over such a fragile yet attractive landscape.

4.11 Discussion Questions

- Who is responsible for developing cultural tourism policy?
- Why do we need to consider developing policies in the area of cultural tourism?
- Identify the policies that impact on culture and tourism in your country, and check if there are any specific to cultural tourism.

References

Addo, E. (2011) Diversification of the tourist landscape on Ghana's Atlantic coast: forts, castles and beach hotel/resort operations in the tourism industry. *Journal of Tourism Consumption and Practice* 3, 26–50.

Bennett, T. and Mercer, C. (1998) Improving research and international cooperation for cultural policy. Paper presented at UNESCO Intergovernmental Conference on Cultural Policies for Development, UNESCO, Stockholm, pp. 1–32.

Department of Sustainability, Environment, Water, Population and Communities (2011) Palya! Welcome to Anangu land: visitor guide to Uluru–Kata Tjuta National Park, Australia. Australian Government Director of National Parks. http://www.environment.gov.au/parks/publications/uluru/pubs/visitor-guide.pdf (accessed 22 March 2012).

Director of National Parks (2009) *Uluru-Kata Tjuta National Park Management Plan 2009–2019*. http://www.environment.gov.au/parks/publications/uluru/draft-plan.html (accessed 29 March 2012).

IAATO (International Association of Antarctica Tour Operators) (2012) *Antarctica Tourism Fact Sheet 2012–2013*. IAATO, Providence, Rhode Island.

Northern Territory Government (2011) *Dual Naming: Policy of the Place Names Committee for Australia's Northern Territory*. http://www.placenames.nt.gov.au/policies/dualnaming (accessed 20 March 2012).

O'Brien, G. (2009) *Towards an Antarctic Tourism Policy: A Framework for Policy Analysts*. Graduate Certificate in Antarctic Studies Project Reports (2008–2009). http://www.anta.canterbury.ac.nz/courses/gcas/reports/Projects%20GCAS%2011.shtml (accessed 22 March 2012).

OECD (2009) *The Impact of Culture on Tourism*. OECD, Paris.

PCAH (President's Committee on Arts and Humanities) (2005) *A Position Paper on Cultural and Heritage Tourism in the United States*. PCAH, Washington, DC.

PCAH (President's Committee on Arts and Humanities) (2012) President's Committee on Arts and Humanities website. http://www.pcah.gov (accessed 28 March 2012).

Pollitt, C. and Bouckaert, G. (2004) *Public Management Reform: A Comparative Analysis*, 2nd edn. Oxford University Press, Melbourne, Australia.

Raj, R. (2012) Contemporary cultural issues and policies for the region. *Palermo Business Review* 6 Special Issue. Facultad de Ciencias Económicas, Universidad de Palermo, Buenos Aires, Argentina. http:// www.palermo.edu/economicas/cbrs/business_review_ed6.html (accessed 20 March 2012).

Spennemann, D.H.R. (2007) Extreme cultural tourism from Antarctica to the Moon. *Annals of Tourism Research* 34, 898–918.

Tourism Ghana (2007) Ghana: Tourism, the World's New Destination. africasia.com, London. http://www. africasia.com/uploads/ghana_march_07_new_african_tourism_special.pdf (accessed 29 March 2012).

5 Cultural Sites and their Management: Co-creation of Value or Co-creation of Experience?

Wided Majdoub
University of Sousse, Sousse, Tunisia

There is growing discussion among researchers relating to how consumers engage with producers to co-create meanings, values and experiences through consumption. The Service-Dominant Logic (S-D Logic) is particularly relevant to tourism management. The tourism sector is based around the customer experience, and as such tourism's suppliers and consumers interact more closely together at all stages of their relationship (Shaw *et al.*, 2011). The changes in the actual competitive environment have caused the latest reformist marketing agenda, the S-D Logic (Vargo and Lusch, 2004). The S-D Logic highlights the value-creation process that occurs when an individual consumes (or uses) a product (or service), as opposed to when the output is manufactured. The customer is the final arbiter of value-in-use through the sharing and integrating of resources with suppliers, especially their skills and knowledge. This recognizes the active involvement of tourists in the development of their own experiences, where the value is created through the interaction process with the

resources in tourism destination. In this context, S-D Logic provides a conceptual framework so that tourism providers can create competitive advantage, understand how the consumer is becoming central to the development of tourism offers and improve co-creation value process management.

We are in this research at the confluence of two major paradigms: Service Dominant Logic and Consumer Culture Theory (Arnould, 2007). Our goal is to examine and understand the concept of co-creation in the field of cultural tourism. How can we define value? And how does value emerge in the co-creation process? Finally, is it about co-creation of value or rather co-creation of experience?

5.1 Introduction

Shaw *et al.* (2011) and Li and Petrick (2008) note the relative failure of tourism research to incorporate research paradigms like the service-dominant logic. This debate is particularly relevant in the field of cultural sites and their management. The aim of this chapter is to link cultural sites studies with two of the latest reformist marketing agenda (service-dominant logic and consumer culture theory) in order to integrate these new frames in further research.

The cultural tourism sector is increasingly based around the customer experience and as such tourism's suppliers and consumers interact more closely at all stages of their relationship (Shaw et al., 2011). This recognizes the active involvement of tourists in the development of their own experiences, where the value is created through the interaction process with the resources in cultural sites. The tourism industry works on a goods-dominant logic (Li and Petrick, 2008, p. 240). At the same time, marketing has moved from a goods-dominant logic to a service-dominant logic (Vargo and Lusch, 2004, p. 2). For Prahalad and Ramaswamy, 'the consumer is networked, active, informed and involved in consumer communities, and co-creation is the result of the changing role of consumers' (2004c, p. 5). The ability of consumers to actively participate in product design and to reinterpret the meaning of products as trademarks redraws the rules of encounter between actors of 'supply and demand'. This principle of co-creation has contributed to the emergence of several theoretical trends in marketing.

Vargo and Lusch have discussed service-dominant logic as a challenging approach to the traditional goods-dominant logic of marketing (2004, 2008a, 2008b, 2008c). One of the central aspects of service-dominant logic is the proposition that customers become *co-creators of value* (Vargo et al., 2008; Vargo and Akaka, 2009). Hence, the service-dominant logic emphasizes the customer perspective, and the customer interacts with suppliers during product design, production and consumption (Payne et al., 2008). Numerous theories are dealing with the new role of the consumer in the market process (consumer empowerment, agency, tribes, resistance, presumption; Cova and Dalli 2007, 2009).

This chapter explores academic discourses on value, co-creation and experience in order to provide a more complete understanding of these concepts, within the cultural sites. From Holbrook's (1996) definition to the Nordic interpretation of experience and co-creation of experience (Grönroos, 2008), we will try to understand the role of value and experience in the co-creation process. More generally value is not in the object of consumption but in the consumption experience itself. For Chen (2009), the experience is the object of value. In a cultural tourism context, Bourgeon-Renault et al. (2006) and more recently Chan (2009) adopt a relational approach to the value, and that value is inherent in the consumption experience itself.

5.2 The Logic of Service-Dominant Logic

Service-dominant logic can be viewed as one such 'emerging thought' in the marketing discipline. We will first try to summarize service-dominant logic by defining the paradigm as service dominant:

> Briefly, marketing has moved from a goods-dominant view, in which tangible output and discrete transactions were central, to a service-dominant view, in which intangibility, exchange processes, and relationships are central.
>
> (Vargo and Lusch, 2004, p. 2)

To clarify their position, Vargo and Lusch (2004) first presented service-dominant logic through eight fundamental premises, and later added a ninth fundamental premise:

> Organizations exist to integrate and transform micro specialized competences into complex services that are demanded in the marketplace.
>
> (Vargo and Lusch, 2006, p. 53)

At that time they also modified their sixth fundamental premise:

> The customer is always a co-creator of value: There is no value until an offering is used – experience and perception is essential to value determination.

The tenth fundamental premise: 'Value is always uniquely and phenomenologically determined by the beneficiary' was added in their 2008 paper and most of the other premises were also modified (Vargo and Lusch, 2008a). In this chapter we will focus specifically on the premise 'The customer is always a co-creator of value' and explore the implications of such a proposal.

In the 2004 version of their model, the sixth fundamental premise is based on the fact that

> The customer becomes primarily an operant resource (co-producer) rather than an operand resource ('target') and can be involved in the entire value and service chain in acting on operand resources.
>
> (Vargo and Lusch, 2004, p. 11)

This distinction between operant and operand resources is underlined: the consumer is viewed as a set of operant resources: a set of knowledge, expertise and skills (Arnould *et al.*, 2006; Baron and Harris, 2008).

> Value, then, becomes a joint function of the actions of the provider(s) and the consumer(s) but is always determined by the consumer.
>
> (Vargo and Lusch, 2006, p. 44)

In a traditional goods-centred view, companies focus on operand resources in order to produce goods and services. By contrast, service-dominant logic shifts the focus to operant resources. Companies have to focus on understanding how consumers engage in the value creation process by viewing consumers as one of their resources. In this paradigm, companies have to employ their core competencies to co-create value with consumers by interacting with them through the 'value proposition'. Peñaloza and Venkatesh (2006, p. 300) believe that the Vargo and Lusch framework does not go far enough, and the first re-conceptualization they propose concerns 'the necessity of re-visioning the creation of value in markets to include meanings' and the nature of value creation.

We are here in the heart of our central question: what is value, value creation and the value-generating process? For Grönroos (2008, 2009) we are talking about offering value proposition and not value-added. The value-in-use can only emerge when goods and services are consumed:

> When customers are using resources they have purchased value is created as value-in-use.

Value-in-exchange is a function of value-in-use. Theoretically, the former only exists if value-in-use can be created. In practice, goods and services may have exchange value in the short term, but in the long run no or low value-in-use means no or low value-in-exchange. Hence, value-in-use is the value concept to build upon, both theoretically and managerially.

(Grönroos, 2009, p. 304)

For Ballantyne and Varey (2008, p. 5), co-production and co-creation are different concepts:

> One subtle but important point of difference is that they use the term 'co-creation' as a rubric, with co-production as one sub-category of co-creation ... that co creation is a distinct form of collaboration. It results in unique value, perhaps starting with a spontaneous idea achieved through dialogical interaction.

5.3 The 'New Customer Perspective' in the Market Process

Hence, service-dominant logic emphasizes the customer perspective, and the customer interacts with suppliers during product design, production and consumption (Payne *et al.*, 2008). For Prahalad and Ramaswamy (2004a, 2004b), the market is viewed as a forum, a space of potential co-creation, through Dialog, Access, Risk-benefit and Transparency, named the DART system (Prahalad and Ramaswamy, 2004b, p. 8). Co-creation of value is then the result of the changing role of consumers. As Prahalad and Ramaswamy underline,

> The consumer is networked, active, informed and involved in consumer communities, and co-creation is the result of the changing role of consumers.
>
> (2004c, p. 5)

The ability of consumers to actively participate in product design and to reinterpret the meaning of products as trademarks redraws the rules of encounter between actors of 'supply and demand'. This principle of co-creation has contributed to the emergence of several theoretical trends in marketing: co-creation of value, co-creation of experience, consumer empowerment, consumer agency, consumer tribes, consumer resistance and presumption. Customer participation itself is not new, but as Bendapudi and Leone (2003, p. 14) clarify, what is new is the recognition that encouraging customers to be co-producers is the next frontier in competitive effectiveness. Bendapudi and Leone (2003, pp. 16–17) present a chronological review of the literature on customer participation in production, asserting that

> Consumers are not just passive receptacles of brand identities projected by marketers; they are active co-producers of brand meanings.
>
> (Bendapudi and Leone, 2003, p. 26)

For Cova and Dalli (2007, 2009), various theoretical trends (lead users, service encounter, consumer resistance, consumer communities, consumer empowerment, consumer agency and working consumers) have shaped the consumer figure as collaborator. The stream of lead users (Von Hippel, 2005) considers the relationship as a cooperation manifested by co-development, co-design and co-production, and highlights consumers mobilizing their creative abilities. The service encounter is the moment of truth that requires consumer participation (Bitner et al., 2000, p. 139).

Concerning consumer resistance, Cova and Dalli suggest that

> Today consumers are more apt to resist corporate marketing actions and possess greater expertise in terms of their consumption and in regards to the products and brands they consume.
>
> (2008, p. 5)

When this movement is a collective one we then talk about 'brand hijack' (Wipperfürth, 2005). In their study, Schau et al. emphasized the fact that consumers can co-create value within brand communities and thereby neutralize the risk of a product being hijacked:

> Value is manifest in the collective enactment of practices, which favor investments in networks rather than firm–consumer dyads; ceding control to customers enhances consumer engagement and builds brand equity; and firms derive added brand value by creatively using willing customer (operant) resources.
>
> (2009, p. 41)

Focusing on managerial implications, Schau et al. (2009, p. 41) advise companies that want to encourage co-creation to foster a broad array of practices and not merely customization. These brand communities are somewhat like spokespersons, prescribers and mark opinion leaders. Because of the strong personal and emotional involvement of consumers in the product life, the balance of relations in business-related individuals is changed. Furthermore, for consumers, this role typically involves producing goods and services for own consumption, i.e. what Toffler (1980) referred to as 'prosumption', which is an acronym for the combined activities of PROduction and conSUMPTION. Xie et al. define prosumption as

> Value creation activities undertaken by the consumer that result in the production of products they eventually consume and that become their consumption experiences.
>
> (2008, p. 110)

It is also a creation process of sociopsychological experiences that allows us to construct and maintain our self-identity and social image (Xie et al., 2008, p. 111), which is consistent with the notion of value co-creation as espoused by Vargo and Lusch.

The theoretical stream of consumer empowerment (Denegri-Knott et al., 2006) argues for a rebalancing of power in the relationship and encourages consumers to control their choices and to control the relationship by taking part in defining its terms. For Holt (2002), in consumer culture theory (Arnould and Thomson, 2005), the co-creation value is viewed in terms of a cultural framework that focuses on how consumers perceive, interpret, understand and interact with the market offering. This is called consumer agency (Arnould et al., 2006), whereby consumers in the communities do not only add holistic value to the process, they co-create value for each other. Eckhardt and Mahi define consumer agency as the ability to transform meanings, arguing that

> Consumers act in an agentic way to shape market preferences while being influenced by the market themselves.
>
> (2004, pp. 137–138)

By sharing experiences with other consumers of the brand the consumer becomes directly involved in the life of the product. This gives meaning to the brand in co-creating identity and symbolic value.

The concept of working consumers depicts consumers who, through their immaterial labour, add cultural and affective value to market offerings. For Cova and Dalli (2009), this way, consumers increase the value of market offerings.

A number of research streams point toward an increasing involvement of consumers in value creation through marketing processes. In addition, these proponents of the collaboration/co-production/co-creation model suggest that integrating customers in the production of market value is not only economically necessary and strategically effective but, most of all, essential for maintaining competitive advantage through innovation (Prahalad and Ramaswamy, 2004a).

While previous marketing research and practices have focused on value-in-transaction (economic value) through the exchange process, service-dominant logic proposes value-in-use or service (Vargo and Lusch, 2004) as a focus of the value co-creation process, but they neither define this term nor develop an

argument as to how it can be assessed. This raises questions regarding the nature of customer value and how it can be assessed.

5.4   Co-creation of Value or Co-creation of Experience

Definition of value is one of the most controversial issues in marketing literature. Through a review of literature, Day and Crask (2000, pp. 53–55) present seven tenets, as outlined in Fig. 5.1.

Extending the work of Woodruff (1997), Sánchez-Fernández and Iniesta-Bonillo define consumer value as

> A cognitive-affective evaluation of an exchange relationship carried out by a person at any stage of the process of purchase decision, characterized by a string of tangible and/or intangible elements which determine, and are also capable of, a comparative, personal, and preferential judgment conditioned by the time, place, and circumstances of the evaluation.
>
> (2006, p. 55)

According to Grönroos, the concept of value is difficult to define, which he indicates by

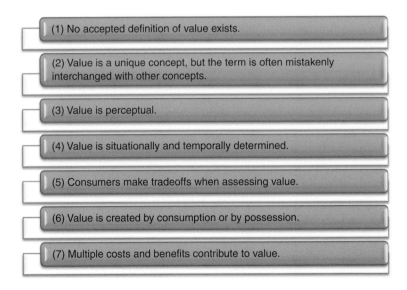

(1) No accepted definition of value exists.

(2) Value is a unique concept, but the term is often mistakenly interchanged with other concepts.

(3) Value is perceptual.

(4) Value is situationally and temporally determined.

(5) Consumers make tradeoffs when assessing value.

(6) Value is created by consumption or by possession.

(7) Multiple costs and benefits contribute to value.

Fig. 5.1. The seven tenets of value. (From Author.)

a very simple definition where a process of value creation is directed:

> Value for customers means that after they have been assisted by a self-service process or a full-service process they are or feel better off than before.
>
> (2008, p. 303)

Value is a complex and multi-dimensional concept (Sánchez-Fernández and Iniesta-Bonillo, 2007; Sánchez-Fernández *et al.*, 2009). A multitude of definitions and categories of value have been proposed, but three perspectives emerge while synthesizing academic literature in marketing. These are value-in-exchange, value-in-possession and value-in-use, as illustrated in Fig. 5.2.

Therefore, it is important to underline that the notion of value in service-dominant logic corresponds to what Vargo (2008, p. 213) and Vargo and Akaka (2009, p. 39) call 'value-in-context' as the situational context of the service encounter:

> Value-in-context highlights the importance of time and place dimensions and network relationships as key variables in the creation and determination of value. Thus, value-in-context is uniquely derived at a given place and time and is phenomenologically determined based on existing resources, accessibility to other integratable resources, and circumstances.

Concerning value typologies, there are a wide range of examples in the literature. However, two classical approaches appear (Gallarza and Gil, 2006): the acquisition versus transaction value difference and the hedonic versus utilitarist value dichotomy. Berthon and John (2006, p. 204) present a typology based on seven dimensions; value is then an interaction from the consumer perspective of these dimensions: content, control, continuation, customization, currency, configuration and contact. Holbrook has developed a typology of value, which includes two or three dimensions, this is one of the more in-depth proposals regarding the concept of value and identifies eight key sources of value: efficiency, excellence, status, esteem, play, aesthetics, ethics and spirituality (1999, p. 12). Holbrook further

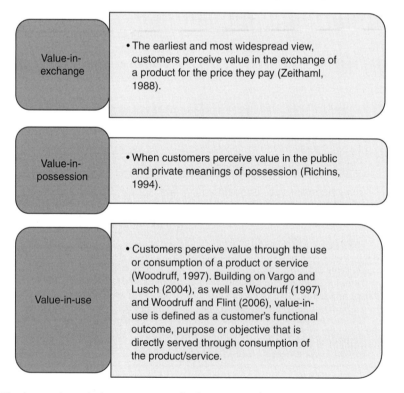

Fig. 5.2. The three main marketing perspectives of value. (From Author.)

deepens the link between value (more precisely value-in-use) and experience:

> Value resides not in an object, a product or a possession but rather in and only in a consumption experience.
>
> (2006a, p. 213)

More generally, in experiential consumption research and consumer culture theory, value is not in the object of consumption but in the consumption experience itself. Customer value is defined as 'an interactive relativistic preference experience' (Holbrook, 2006a, p. 212). Interactive means that no value exists without an interaction between a subject and an object. Relativistic means that customer value is comparative, situational and personal. Value resides in and only in a consumption experience, which Holbrook calls ROSEPEKICECIVECI: Resource-Operant, Skills-Exchanging, Performance-Experiencing, Knowledge-Informed, Competence-Enacting, Co-producer-Involved, Value-Emerging, Customer-Interactive.

Chen (2009, p. 927), while investigating the perceived values of contemporary art collectors and exhibit visitors, defines their experience in the object of value and presents six dimensions: (1) imaginary value, sentiments and pleasure; (2) stimulation and hedonist value; (3) self-orientation and interpersonal orientation; (4) social practice; (5) entertaining and aesthetic value, status, ethic, esteem and spirituality; and (6) distraction, exhibitionism and evangelism.

Vargo and Lusch (2008a, 2008b) have discussed the value of the co-creation process, taking into account the dynamic and multiple dimensions of value, and conclude that it depends on how consumers interpret the consumption of objects through their experience. They underline that

> This partial shift to a value-in-use orientation can be seen creeping into marketing in general in the form of terms like 'coproduction' and 'value co-creation' and 'experience economy'.
>
> (Vargo and Lusch, 2008b, pp. 30–31)

5.5 Applied to Culture

In a cultural tourism context, Prentice emphasizes that

Museums, like many other heritage attractions, are essentially experiential products, quite literally constructions to facilitate experience. In this sense, museums are about facilitating feelings and knowledge based upon personal observation or contact by their visitors.

(1996, p. 169)

We must admit that the dominant cognitivist perspective fails to understand the experience of the public, or tourist, in consuming cultural objects, such as museums, monuments or any artefacts (Holbrook and Hirschman, 1982). For Doering (1999), visitors may be viewed as strangers (who are privileged to be admitted), guests (who gratefully receive what the museum has to offer) or clients (whom the museum is obliged to serve). One of the consequences of viewing visitors as clients, according to Doering, is that we need to understand the meaning and value of a museum visit from the visitor's perspective. In that context, Doering (1999, p. 75) defines four types of experience in a museum, which are illustrated in Fig. 5.3.

Value must be examined from a relational approach, that is to say, in an experiential perspective. The notion of experience entered the field of consumption with Holbrook and Hirschman's pioneering article of 1982 regarding the experiential aspects of consumption; since then, the conceptualization of consumption

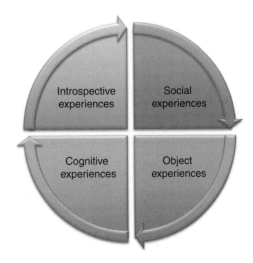

Fig. 5.3. Visitor's experience in a museum. (From Author.)

experience has gained more attention (Carù and Cova, 2007).

Bourgeon-Renault *et al.* (2006) and more recently Chan (2009) adopt this relational approach to value and underline that value is inherent in the consumption experience itself. As we have seen earlier, co-creation of products and services has been seen as a new way to create value, both for customers and for businesses, because co-creation enables customers to co-construct the service or tourist experience to suit their purposes and needs. Value is seen to come increasingly from the relationship and co-creation process between a supplier and a customer (Prahalad and Ramaswamy, 2004c, p. 4). Customers can be involved in product and service development processes in many different ways. In this context must we talk about co-creation of value or co-creation of experience?

A number of authors (Vargo and Lusch, 2004; Holbrook, 2006a, 2006b; Woodruff and Flint, 2006; Payne *et al.*, 2008) argue that value emerges at the point of consumption and that consumers perceive value through the consumption experience. Holt (1995) shows that value emerges when consumers assign meanings or symbolic value to objects; we consume in four ways: as an experience, a classification, integration and to play.

This view of consumption is derived from consumer culture theory and explains how consumers allocate meaning to material resources by negotiating between their cultural lives and social relationships (Arnould and Thompson, 2005). Involvement then emerges as a core concept (Carù and Cova, 2007; Ramaswamy, 2008). But as mentioned by Vargo *et al.*,

> This exploration of value co-creation raises as many questions as it answers. For example: What exactly are the processes involved in value co-creation? How can we measure co-created value and value-in-use?
>
> (2008, p. 151)

To conclude, in tourism literature, despite the potential benefits of its application (Li and Petrick, 2008), these new frames (service-dominant logic and consumer culture theory) have received reduced attention. Shaw *et al.* have stated that

> The engagement of tourism management with research in what can be called 'mainstream management literature' remains highly uneven.
>
> (2011, p. 207)

In tourism and leisure, we are only at the beginning of exploring co-creation experience. We obviously need a more holistic view of customer value, encompassing the full spectrum of the customer experience and all types of value. Particularly, this paradigm change would be of significant worth in the management of cultural sites.

5.6 Summary

This chapter presents a theoretical foundation and a holistic view of customer value, encompassing the large spectrum of consumer experience. We agree with Day (2006) and think that organizations in the cultural and heritage sector that develop a better understanding of value, co-creation of value and experience may develop a significant advantage.

The chapter explores academic discourses on value, co-creation and experience in order to provide a more complete understanding of these concepts within the cultural tourism field. From Holbrook's (1996) definition to the Nordic interpretation of experience and co-creation of experience (Grönroos, 2008), we try to understand the role of value and experience in the co-creation process. According to Grönroos (2008, p. 303), the concept of value is quite difficult to define, and he suggests that value occurs when a customer feels better off after the encounter than they did beforehand. Holbrook (2006, p. 213) further deepens this notion that value is not product- or possession-based but in the actual act of consumption.

More generally, in experiential consumption research and consumer culture theory, value is not in the object of consumption but in the consumption experience itself. For Chen (2009), the experience is the object of value. In a cultural tourism context, Bourgeon-Renault *et al.* (2006) and more recently Chan (2009) adopt a relational approach to value, and that value is inherent in the consumption experience itself. For a number of authors (Day and Crask, 2000; Day, 2002; Sánchez-Fernández *et al.*, 2009), value is an elusive concept, and further research is necessary in order to understand experience and categories of value.

Co-creation of services has been seen as a new way to create value, both for customers and for businesses, because the co-creation enables customers to co-construct the service or tourist experience to suit their purposes and needs (Prahalad and Ramaswamy, 2004c). Value is seen to come more and more from the relationship and co-creation process between a supplier and a customer (Prahalad and Ramaswamy, 2004c, p. 4). Customers can be involved in product and service development processes in different ways. But as mentioned by Vargo *et al.* (2008, p. 151), the investigation of co-creation raises more questions than answers. Questions remain regarding the

processes involved in value co-creation and value-in-use and their measurement.

5.7   Discussion Questions

- What is service-dominant logic, and how can it be used to improve cultural tourism products?
- How does viewing a tourist/visitor as an empty receptacle weaken the opportunity for engagement and positive experience?
- What is co-creation, and what are its implications for the cultural tourism sector?
- Identify a number of ways of demonstrating value in a tourism experience, and discuss the merits of each approach.

References

Arnould, E.J. (2007) Service-dominant logic and consumer culture theory: natural allies in an emerging paradigm. In: Belk, R.W. and Sherry, J.F. (eds) *Consumer Culture Theory: Research in Consumer Behavior*. Elsevier, Oxford, pp. 57–76.

Arnould, E.J. and Thomson, C.J. (2005) Consumer Culture Theory (CCT): twenty years of research. *Journal of Consumer Research* 31, 868–882.

Arnould, E.J., Price, L.L. and Malshe, A. (2006) Toward a cultural resource-based theory of the customer. In: Lusch, R.F. and Vargo, S.L. (eds) *The Service-Dominant Logic of Marketing: Dialog, Debate and Directions*. ME Sharpe, Armonk, New York, pp. 91–104.

Ballantyne, D. and Varey, R.J. (2008) The service-dominant logic and the future of marketing. *Journal of the Academy of Marketing Science* 36, 11–14.

Baron, S. and Harris, K. (2008) Consumers as resource integrators. *Journal of Marketing Management* 24, 113–130.

Bendapudi, N. and Leone, R.P. (2003) Psychological implications of customer participation in co-production. *Journal of Marketing* 67, 14–28.

Berthon, P. and John, J. (2006) From entities to interfaces: delineating value in customer–firm interactions. In: Lusch, R.F. and Vargo, S.L. (eds) *The Service-Dominant Logic of Marketing: Dialog, Debate, and Directions*. M.E. Sharpe, Armonk, New York, pp. 196–207.

Bitner, M.J, Brown, S. and Meuter, M.L. (2000) Technology infusion in service encounters. *Journal of the Academy of Marketing Science* 28, 138–149.

Bourgeon-Renault, D., Urbain, C., Petr, C., Le Gall-Elly, M. and Gombault, A. (2006) An experiential approach to the consumption of value of arts and culture: the case of museums and monuments. *International Journal of Arts Management* 9, 35–47.

Carù, A. and Cova, B. (eds) (2007) *Consuming Experience*. Routledge, London.

Chan, J.K.L. (2009) The consumption of museum service experiences: benefits and value of museum experiences. *Journal of Hospitality Marketing and Management* 18, 173–196.

Chen, Y. (2009) Possession and access: consumer desires and value perceptions regarding contemporary art collection and exhibition visits. *Journal of Consumer Research* 35, 925–940.

Cova, B. and Dalli, D. (2007) Community made: from consumer resistance to tribal entrepreneurship. In: Borghini, S., McGrath, M.A. and Otnes, C. (eds) *Proceedings of the 2007 European Conference*. European Advances in Consumer Research 8.

Cova, B. and Dalli, D. (2008) From communal resistance to tribal value creation. In: proceedings *Colloque International Consommation et Résistance(s) des consommateurs*. Université Paris Est, Créteil, pp. 1–22, http://s2.e-monsite.com/2010/01/11/11/3-Cova-Dalli.pdf (accessed 1 January 2010).

Cova, B. and Dalli, D. (2009) Working consumers: the next step in marketing theory? *Marketing Theory* 9, 315–339.

Day, E. (2002) The role of value in consumer satisfaction. *Journal of Consumer Satisfaction, Dissatisfaction and Complaining Behavior* 15, 22–32.

Day, E. and Crask, M.R. (2000) Value assessment: the antecedent of customer satisfaction. *Journal of Consumer Satisfaction, Dissatisfaction and Complaining Behavior* 13, 52–60.

Day, G. (2006) Achieving advantage with service dominant logic. In: Lusch, R.F. and Vargo, S.L. (eds) *The Service-Dominant Logic of Marketing: Dialog, Debate, and Directions*. M.E. Sharpe, Armonk, New York, pp. 85–90.

Denegri-Knott, J., Zwick, D. and Schroeder, J.E. (2006) Mapping consumer power: an integrative framework for marketing and consumer research. *European Journal of Marketing* 40, 950–971.

Doering, Z.D. (1999) Strangers, guests, or clients? Visitor experiences in museums. *Curator: The Museum Journal* 42, 74–87.

Eckhardt, G.M. and Mahi, H. (2004) The role of consumer agency in the globalization process in emerging markets. *Journal of Macromarketing* 24, 136–146.

Gallarza, M.G. and Gil, I. (2006) Value dimensions, perceived value, satisfaction and loyalty: an investigation of university students' travel behavior. *Tourism Management* 27, 437–452.

Grönroos, C. (2008) Service logic revisited: who creates value? And who co-creates? *European Business Review* 20, 298–314.

Grönroos, C. (2009) Towards service logic: the unique contribution of value co-creation. Working Paper, Hanken School of Economics, 1–28.

Holbrook, M.B. (1996) Special Session Summary Customer Value C: a framework for analysis and research. In: Corfman, K.P. and Lynch, J.G. Jr (eds) *Advances in Consumer Research*, vol. 23. Association for Consumer Research, Provo, Utah, pp. 138–142.

Holbrook, M.B. (1999) Introduction to consumer value. In: Holbrook, M.B. (ed.) *Consumer Value: A Framework for Analysis and Research*. Routledge, London, pp. 1–28.

Holbrook, M.B. (2006a) ROSEPEKICECIVECI vs CCV: the resource-operant, skills-exchanging, performance-experiencing, knowledge-informed, competence-enacting, co-producer involved, value-emerging, customer-interactive view of marketing versus the concept of customer value: 'I can get it for you wholesale'. In: Lusch, R.F. and Vargo, S.L. (eds) *The Service-Dominant Logic of Marketing: Dialog, Debate, and Directions*. M.E. Sharpe, Armonk, New York, pp. 208–213.

Holbrook, M.B. (2006b) Consumption experience, customer value, and subjective personal introspection: an illustrative photographic essay. *Journal of Business Research* 59, 714–725.

Holbrook, M.B. and Hirschman, E.C. (1982) The experiential aspects of consumption consumer fantasies, feelings and fun. *Journal of Consumer Research* 9, 132–140.

Holt, D.B. (1995) How consumers consume: a typology of consumption practices. *Journal of Consumer Research* 22, 1–16.

Holt, D.B. (2002) Why do brands cause trouble? A dialectical theory of consumer culture and branding. *Journal of Consumer Research* 29, 70–90.

Li, X. and Petrick, J.F. (2008) Tourism marketing in an era of paradigm shift. *Journal of Travel Research* 46, 235–244.

Payne, A.F., Storbacka, K. and Frow, P. (2008) Managing the co-creation of value. *Journal of the Academy of Marketing Science* 36, 83–96.

Peñaloza, L. and Venkatesh, A. (2006) Further evolving the new dominant logic of marketing: from services to the social construction of markets. *Marketing Theory* 6, 299–316.

Prahalad, C.K. and Ramaswamy, V. (eds) (2004a) *The Future of Competition: Co-creating Unique Value with Customers*. Harvard Business School Press, Boston, Massachusetts.

Prahalad, C.K. and Ramaswamy, V. (2004b) Co-creation-experiences: the next practise in value creation. *Journal of Interactive Marketing* 18, 5–14.

Prahalad, C.K. and Ramaswamy, V (2004c) Co-creating unique value with customer. *Strategy and Leadership* 32, 4–9.

Prentice, R. (1996) Managing implosion: the facilitation of insight through the provision of context. *Museum Management and Curatorship* 25, 169–185.

Ramaswamy, V. (2008) Co-creating value through customers' experiences: the Nike case. *Strategy and Leadership* 36, 9–14.

Richins, M.L. (1994) Valuing things: the public and private meanings of possessions. *Journal of Consumer Research* 21, 504–521.

Sánchez-Fernández, R. and Iniesta-Bonillo, M.Á. (2006) Consumer perception of value: literature review and a new conceptual framework. *Journal of Consumer Satisfaction, Dissatisfaction and Complaining Behavior* 19, 40–58.

Sánchez-Fernández, R. and Iniesta-Bonillo, M.Á. (2007) The concept of perceived value: a systematic review of the research. *Marketing Theory* 7, 427–451.

Sánchez-Fernández, R., Iniesta-Bonillo, M.Á. and Holbrook, M.B. (2009) The conceptualization and measurement of consumer value in services. *International Journal of Market Research* 51, 93–113.

Schau, H.J., Muniz, A.M. Jr and Arnould, E.J. (2009) How brand community practices create value. *Journal of Marketing* 73, 30–51.

Shaw, G., Bailey, A. and Williams, A. (2011) Aspects of service-dominant logic and its implications for tourism management: examples from the hotel industry. *Tourism Management* 32, 207–214.

Toffler, A. (1980) *The Third Wave*. William Collins Sons, New York.

Vargo, S.L. (2008) Customer integration and value creation: paradigmatic traps and perspectives. *Journal of Service Research* 11, 211–215.

Vargo, S.L. and Akaka, M.A. (2009) Service-dominant logic as a foundation for service science: clarifications. *Service Science* 1, 32–41.

Vargo, S.L. and Lusch, R.F. (2004) Evolving to a new dominant logic for marketing. *Journal of Marketing* 68, 1–17.

Vargo, S.L. and Lusch, R.F. (2006) Service-dominant logic. What it is, what it is not, what it might be. In: Vargo, S.L. and Lusch, R.F. (eds) *The service-dominant logic of marketing: dialog, debate, and directions* M.E. Sharpe, Armonk, New York, pp. 43–56.

Vargo, S.L. and Lusch, R.F. (2008a) Service-dominant logic: continuing the evolution. *Journal of the Academy of Marketing Science* 36, 1–10.

Vargo, S.L. and Lusch, R.F. (2008b) Why service? *Journal of the Academy of Marketing Science* 36, 25–38.

Vargo, S.L. and Lusch, R.F. (2008c) From goods to service(s): divergences and convergences of logics. *Industrial Marketing Management* 37, 254–259.

Vargo, S.L., Maglio, P.P. and Akaka, M.A. (2008) On value and value co-creation: a service systems and service logic perspective. *European Management Journal* 26, 145–152.

Von Hippel, E. (2005) *Democratizing Innovation*. MIT Press, Cambridge, Massachusetts.

Wipperfürth, A. (2005) *Brand Hijack: Marketing Without Marketing*. Portfolio, New York.

Woodruff, R.B. (1997) Customer value: the next source of competitive advantage. *Journal of the Academy of Marketing Science* 25, 139–153.

Woodruff, R.B. and Flint, D.J. (2006) Marketing's service-dominant logic and customer value. In: Lusch, R.F. and Vargo, S.L. (eds) *The Service-dominant Logic of Marketing: Dialog, Debate, and Directions*. M.E. Sharpe, New York, pp. 183–195.

Xie, C., Bagozzi, R.P. and Troye, S.V. (2008) Trying to prosume: toward a theory of consumers as co-creators of value. *Journal of the Academy of Marketing Science* 36, 109–122.

Zeithaml, V. (1988) Consumer perceptions of price, quality and value: a means–end model and synthesis of evidence. *Journal of Marketing* 52, 2–22.

6 Mobile Interpretation at Cultural Attractions: Insights into Users and Non-users of Audio-guides

Claudia Bauer-Krösbacher

University of Applied Sciences Krems, Krems, Austria

The chapter deals with an important issue within cultural tourism, namely the interpretation of heritage attractions. More specifically, this chapter looks at mobile interpretation techniques, discusses their pros and cons, and presents findings from a study on the use of audio-guides conducted at a major museum in Vienna. The findings show that the majority of people used an audio-guide; however, there are also visitors who prefer conventional types of interpretation. The study also revealed that the use of an audio-guide does not lead to a greater depth of experience, but there is evidence that it led to a greater enjoyment of the site.

6.1 Introduction

Interpretation has become an essential part of cultural attractions and designing experiences for the visitor. Culture and heritage, when viewed by people who are not experts, have to be interpreted for them (Dewhurst and Dewhurst, 2006). Moreover, people who come from a different cultural context need detailed on-site information to derive meaning of the culture and heritage presented to them and also to develop a sense of place. Many exhibits and sites cannot be fully understood simply by looking at them. At its basic level, minimalist interpretation requires the visitor to recognize significance and derive meaning from the experience (Hughes and Morrison-Saunders, 2005). Low fulfilment may occur if the visitor is not able to achieve this. For example, in a museum some paintings need interpretation to facilitate understanding that goes beyond enjoying their aesthetic beauty. Interpretation enables tourists to obtain an understanding of the culture and heritage alien to them (Goodall and Beech, 2006). It creates an enhanced appreciation of the site and increases visitors' respect for it. Quality interpretation can therefore be regarded as key to the cultural experience. It has the ability to raise the added value of a site in the eyes of the tourist (Timothy and Boyd, 2003).

When it comes to interpreting sites and their exhibits the question is: which media should be applied to help tell the story? There is general agreement among experts that interpretation needs to be attuned to the type and specific characteristics of the cultural attraction. Goodall and Beech (2006) emphasize that there is no single model of interpretation that can be used in all situations. Similarly, Uzzell (1989, p. 6) argues that there are no stock solutions of interpretation because it is always a function of the uniqueness of place and the individual response that is required to interpret effectively, meaningfully and enjoyably, and that planning and design solutions should reflect local environmental, organizational and cultural circumstances.

However, interpretation can only be effective if the different needs of visitors are recognized. Different groups are looking for different experiences, such as children as opposed to adults, experts as opposed to the lay person, locals as opposed to foreign visitors, and people who have a specific disability and those without. Hence, the challenge is to offer the right interpretation to different types of visitors (Falk and Dierking, 1994).

Interpretation exists in verbal, written or other visual forms (Timothy and Boyd, 2003). Media used to support interpretation include displays, printed brochures and maps, signs, labels, audio presentations, guided tours and live interpreters. It is not just the notion as to how a site should be interpreted that has changed – the tools available for interpretation have also been changing rapidly in recent years. Many institutions within the cultural attraction sector have come to embrace the possibilities of Information and Communication Technologies (ICT) to reach new audiences. Visitors' first contact with the site is often a click on the attraction's website. ICT has opened up an exciting new world of information, education, entertainment and advertising in the attractions sector. Through multimedia technology there are totally new possibilities in the presentation and interpretation of culture and heritage, which have implications on how visitors can experience a cultural attraction. Some tools, such as audio-guides and computer

terminals, have already become commonplace. In the beginning, the use of multimedia technology at museums was pioneered in the US for educative purposes of interpretation (Light, 1995). However, since then multimedia has been developing, acquiring additional roles. In stimulating and arousing visitors' imagination and entertainment, multimedia applications can make a cultural site more exciting, easier to absorb and more meaningful. There are several reasons why ICT nowadays play a crucial role in the provision of cultural products. Moscardo (2000) points out that visitors may arrive with increasing experience of interaction with information through diverse media such as the World Wide Web, and therefore expect greater sophistication and flexibility in their experiences of the site. The new generation of visitors, especially children and young adults, favour an 'up-to-date' presentation and interpretation and are enthusiastic about interactive exhibits (Dierking and Falk, 1998). Nowadays, the attractiveness of a cultural site lies to a great extent in the style of presentation (Boniface, 1995). It is important to communicate through media that a present-day audience not only finds approachable but also appealing. Therefore, new product developments are considered important to create more active visitor participation.

Modern technologies are increasingly used for cultural attractions. However, relatively little knowledge exists with respect to their users and, moreover, to non-users. In the following, different mobile interpretation techniques are discussed, with an emphasis on audio-guides. Results from a visitor survey of users and non-users of audio-guides conducted in November 2008 at a major museum in Vienna are presented. Finally, conclusions on mobile interpretation at cultural attractions are drawn.

6.2 Mobile Interpretation Techniques

When it comes to modern media, audio-guides, also referred to as acoustic guides, are among the most frequently applied forms of interpretation at cultural attractions, and a whole business has developed around this technology. Audio-guides are electronic tools that provide visitors to cultural attractions with spoken information about exhibits. Visitors usually receive the mobile device at the beginning of an exhibition, which they then carry with them (usually with a lanyard around their neck or wrist) through the exhibition. Upon typing in the number of the respective exhibit, they receive the relevant information in the form of audio output. While at the beginning this technology was mainly applied indoors, now an increasing number of open-air attractions offer audio-guides to convey their messages to visitors. The most common form are handheld devices similar to a mobile phone, however, sets with separate headphones are also available (see Fig. 6.1). Cultural attractions offer these mobile devices as an additional service, but this is not always included in the ticket price. In many cases, the service and maintenance of audio-guides is sourced out to an external specialized provider.

Audio-guides are usually designed so that they are easy to use. A key benefit over other interpretation tools is that they allow adaptation for different target groups. For example, they can provide information in different languages, usually contain different layers of information to satisfy lay persons as well as experts in the area, and they can be created in a more entertaining form for children as opposed to adults. Often first-person narration is used to tell the story of an attraction in a more authentic way. Well-known voices of actors or specific dialects can add an extra element of uniqueness to the experience. Also background music to dramatize parts of the story or sound

samples, when appropriate, can be incorporated. Many visitors find listening more convenient than reading information on text panels. Audio-guides can be supportive for people with various disabilities, such as visually impaired or blind people, whereby specific audio-descriptions can be provided to help orientation through the site and give detailed descriptions of, for example, the texture, size and colours of exhibits. For this group it is particularly important how the audio-descriptions and interpretations are activated. If it is necessary to type in a specific number, this should be indicated in Braille script. For people with hearing disabilities wearing a hearing aid, headphones are not usable. For these people it is also important that they are still able to hear background noise in the form of, for example, other visitors.

Audio-guides provide many benefits for the visitor, but they do not come without limitations. All too often they do not work properly, meaning not only maintenance costs but also annoyed visitors. The main disadvantage of audio-guides, however, is the resultant limited or no social interaction with companions. Using an audio-guide may result in quite an isolated experience. Falk and Dierking (1994) claim that people usually have a desire to talk about things they have discovered, what they find interesting, what they like or dislike about an exhibition or site, or what sense they make of certain exhibits and stories. They often relate and compare objects to their own concrete experiences and want to share their ideas with their companions. For heavily

Fig. 6.1. Example of audio-guide. (This model of audio device is currently in use in the Guinness Storehouse, Dublin, and provided by Antenna International. See: http://www.antennainternational.com/content/category/113/622/lang,en_GB/976)

frequented attractions a sufficient quantity of devices needs to be available to give every customer the possibility of using an audio-guide if they wish to do so. Last but not least, hygiene factors need to be mentioned in relation to audio-guides. It is essential that the devices are kept clean.

Different generations of audio-guides exist. The first generation devices emerged in the 1980s and have been replaced by more advanced ones. Audio devices have been improved with respect to both technology and content, such that today's technology, for example, allows tracking the position of visitors. Furthermore, today's devices feature not only audio but also image and video capabilities. The question arises whether audio-guides will become entirely outdated: already the next generation of mobile interpretation in the form of diverse applications continues to gain momentum at an increasing number of attractions.

These applications combine all forms of interpretation and are compatible for iPhones, iPads, Android phones and even ordinary phones. One such application for mobile phones is quick response codes (QR codes). A QR code is a tag in the form of a two-dimensional code, which can be read by scanners or cameras combined with specific software programs that mobile phones or PDAs (Personal Digital Assistant) provide. Originally developed in logistics, QR codes are nowadays used in diverse areas such as the interpretation of sites and their exhibits.

According to Winter (2010), historic sites are now using mobile tagging to provide audio, video and text information. QR codes allow the connection of physical objects and virtual information (Hegen, 2010), such that data can be retrieved directly or users are connected to online data (Canadi et al., 2010). In museums, for example, visitors can scan the code of an exhibit with their smartphone and get redirected to a website with more information, or they are taken to an online version of the audio tour. Mobile tagging is also used in souvenir shops to give consumers access to background information and related products. QR systems also offer options in the field of event information for the combination of printed and online content supporting the actuality of data. In the attractions area they have also gained popularity

regarding ticketing. Online ticket reservation, online payment as well as ticket distribution make the ticketing process more autonomous (Canadi et al., 2010).

QR codes are not limited to indoor use but are used extensively in outdoor environments such as in parks or gardens (see Fig. 6.2). From a consumer perspective, the high flexibility of the QR code system represents a key benefit. At any time and almost everywhere, people have access to information that they can select according to personal criteria. They can support the interpretation of cultural attractions because their handling is easy and people can decide individually if they want more detailed information. A major advantage is that QR codes automatically rule out input errors from the users and also they have a high resistance to dirt and damage, which means that even if a part of the code is missing or damaged it can be read successfully. While many of the abovementioned advantages and disadvantages of audio-guides also apply to mobile applications such as QR codes, there are specific issues to be mentioned.

Although becoming more widespread, these applications show some limitations, which are mainly related to mobile applications in general. Downloading information can incur additional costs and requires an available Internet connection, which is not always the case. Furthermore, users need the software for decoding the QR code. When used outdoors, weather conditions can influence the experience. Dazzling sun might compromise the readability of text or rain can hinder the usage of the mobile device. Account should also be taken of the fact that not everyone is familiar with smartphone applications, which might be the case with older generations. Mobile applications are great tools to support the visitor experience of an attraction. Nevertheless, careful implementation is required, taking interpretation guidelines into consideration.

Managers of sites or exhibitions who are planning a QR code project should be aware of some critical factors for the application of QR codes. It must be ensured that all codes are useable and that all links and URLs to websites are functioning. Furthermore, it is important that websites are optimized for mobile viewing. Also, specific decisions with regard to the size of the codes must be taken. Codes need to be

Fig. 6.2. Example of QR codes in use (advertising Dublin Wax Museum). (From Kevin Griffin.)

larger if the distance to the scanner is bigger, for example if an exhibit is placed in a fenced-off area. When a code is too small it can become unusable because scanners might not register the right definitions in the pattern. Overall, it should be borne in mind that content is more important than features. The question about the best way for mobile technology to support the interpretation of culture and heritage can only be answered in the context of the individual site. The decision process depends not only on the specific characteristics of a cultural attraction but also on the target groups. Canadi *et al.* (2010) argue that the success of QR codes in the context of mobile tagging depends on the diffusion of mobile services. Developments in this sector show that a growing market can be anticipated for the near future.

6.3   Profile of Users and Non-users of Audio-guides

In the following, findings of a study conducted at a historical museum in Vienna are presented. The study aimed to investigate not only users but also non-users of audio-guides in terms of their characteristics, depth of experience and satisfaction with the site. Furthermore, reasons for not using an audio-guide were explored. At the museum 781 of the respondents used an audio-guide, whereas 405 of those surveyed decided to do without this interpretation tool. Hence, users of audio-guides clearly constituted the majority of visitors. Table 6.1 reveals the main demographic and socio-demographic differences between these two groups.

Performing a Pearson chi-square test revealed no significant differences between

Table 6.1. Characteristics of users and non-users of audio-guides.

	Users	Non-users
Gender: (p = 0.150)		
Male	39.6%	44.0%
Female	60.4%	56.0%
Age: (p = 0.038[a])		
18–24	18.9%	14.0%
25–34	35.2%	30.3%
35–44	20.2%	22.3%
45–54	11.3%	15.5%
55–65	10.0%	12.8%
>65	4.5%	5.0%
Companionship: (p > 0.05)[b]		
Alone	9.5%	9.2%
Spouse/partner	53.5%	49.0%
Kid/s	2.3%	4.2%
Other family members	11.6%	11.7%
Friends	22.3%	25.4%
Group	2.7%	3.2%
Business partner(s)	0.8%	1.2%
Other	0.1%	0.2%
Interest in culture: (p = 0.448)		
Highly interested	45.7%	46.0%
Interested	53.0%	51.7%
Generally not interested	1.3%	2.2%

	Users	Non-users
Occupation: (p = 0.317)		
Self-employed	12.9%	15.0%
Executive/managerial employee	21.1%	23.1%
White collar	36.2%	32.0%
Blue collar	3.9%	2.5%
Homemaker	3.0%	2.5%
Student/in training	16.2%	14.7%
Retired	5.8%	8.6%
Other	1.0%	1.5%
Education: (p = 0.224)		
Grade school/primary school	1.3%	3.0%
Apprenticeship/vocational training	8.5%	7.9%
Secondary/high school without A-level/leaving certificate	11.7%	13.5%
Secondary/high school with A-level/leaving certificate	16.3%	14.5%
University	62.2%	61.2%
Length of stay: (p = 0.000*)		
Less than 60 min	1.3%	5.2%
60 min – 90 min	20.6%	39.5%
91 min – 120 min	35.0%	30.5%
121 min – 150 min	30.5%	18.9%
151 min – 180 min	9.3%	5.0%
More than 180 min	3.3%	1.0%
Visitation of the site before: (p = 0.370)		
No	89.6%	87.9%
Yes	10.4%	12.1%

[a]Significant at the 0.05 level.
[b]Percentages total more than 100 as some respondents selected more than one category.

users and non-users of audio-guides with respect to visitors' gender, occupation, level of education, companionship, interest in culture and visitation of the attraction before. The corresponding p-values are all indicated in Table 6.1. However, in terms of their length of stay and age, significant differences occur as p-values remain below the 0.05 level. With respect to length of stay, there is evidence that the use of an audio-guide results in a longer dwell time. This is not surprising because listening to the explanations on the audio-guide is time consuming. When it comes to age, users of audio-guides show a higher percentage in the age categories below 34 years. Among visitors aged above 34 years, non-users outnumbered users of audio-guides. This supports the general notion that the younger generation is more susceptible to the use of modern technologies. However, it should be noted that older people do not completely refrain from using an audio-guide. For the near future it can safely be assumed that they will gradually become acquainted with the use of modern technologies in general and this will also have a positive effect on the use of technologies at cultural attractions.

6.4   Reasons for Not Using an Audio-guide

In order to find out why visitors decided not to use an audio-guide, a question was included in the survey asking individuals to state their reasons for not using an audio-guide, using a predefined list of items (see Table 6.2).

The main reasons why visitors decided not to use an audio-guide were because they did not know that audio-guides were included in the ticket price (39%) and because they did not know that they were available (17%). Of the respondents who did not use an audio-guide 16% stated that they already had a profound knowledge and therefore decided to experience the museum without an audio-guide. However, 8% were forced to do without an audio-guide because there were none available for them. For 10% of the non-users it was too busy at the audio-guide counter and they did not want to make the effort to queue up.

Table 6.2. Reasons for not using an audio-guide.

	%
I did not know they were included in the ticket price	39
I did not know they were available	17
I have already a profound knowledge	16
It was too busy at the audio-guide counter	10
I have reservations about technology	10
No audio-guide was available	8

Therefore, it can be assumed that with better visitor information and communication, the number of audio-guide users would have been significantly higher. All visitors should be given an equal possibility to use an audio-guide. The non-availability of audio-guides and requirement to queue up could result in unhappy and unsatisfied customers. However, besides these organizational problems there are also visitors who have reservations about technology (10%) and prefer to rely on more traditional ways of interpretation. This implies that technology is a great tool to impart knowledge, but conventional forms of interpretation are still important.

Other important reasons why visitors decided not to use an audio-guide were identified through an open-ended question, revealing 181 statements. The statements were categorized as outlined in Table 6.3.

As can be learned from the comments, visitors had not used an audio-guide mainly because of 'time restriction' (20%). They argued that it takes too long to listen to an audio-guide and their time to visit the museum was limited. They wanted to have 'freedom of time' and stated that the audio-guide would 'slow them down'. One respondent explained in this respect that 'I wanted to look around faster than the voice could talk' and another one argued 'no patience, rather want speed'. For some visitors audio-guides provide too detailed information (4%) and are considered 'lengthy'. Such visitors are 'not interested in detailed information' and find that audio-guides provide too much information, arguing that 'there is already enough to see'.

Some visitors prefer to explore the museum by themselves (11%). They claimed, for example, that 'without [the] audio-guide I can see things better and explore by myself' or 'I like to

Table 6.3. Other reasons for not using an audio-guide

		%
1	Time restrictions	20
2	Preference of own exploration of the museum	11
3	Non-availability of audio-guides in specific languages	10
4	Distracting	9
5	Preference to read	9
6	Preference of other guides (human guide, guide book)	9
7	No need/interest	8
8	Social reasons	6
9	Too detailed information	4
10	Dislike of audio-guides	4
11	Uncomfortable	3
12	Other reasons:	6
	I want the exhibits to speak for themselves	
	I like to feel the thing that the museum gives	
	I only wanted to view the museum	
	I thought they are only for non-German speakers	
	It's annoying	
	Already have some knowledge about the matter	
	I did use one on my last visit	
	Took one but did not use	
	Not profound, sometimes I argue with audio-guides	

have my own opinion without the influence of an audio-guide'. In the region of 9% of the non-users found that an audio-guide is distracting. They prefer to walk around the museum and to look at the artefacts without getting the in-depth information from the audio-guide. These visitors see audio-guides as a hindrance rather than support in their experience of the site. They do not want to be tied to the audio-guide. The same is true for visitors who indicated that audio-guides are uncomfortable (3%). This group do not want to carry one around and feel more independent without this interpretation tool. Further comments provided in the open-ended question about non-use of an audio-guide referred to the non-availability of audio-guides in their native languages, such as Chinese, Russian or Dutch (10%), the preference of other guides such as human guides or guide books (9%), or preference of reading texts over listening to an audio-guide (9%).

Social reasons were stated by 6% of the non-users of audio-guides. As explained earlier, when listening to an audio-guide, visitors are quite isolated in their experience because immediate communication and discussion with companions is not really possible. In the remaining statements a dislike of audio-guides (4%) was articulated; some respondents (8%) stated that they just did not want to use one or felt no need of using one. Other comments that were not categorized included, for example, 'took one but did not use it', 'I want the exhibits to speak for themselves' or 'I like to feel the thing that the museum gives'. There are also visitors who already have a profound knowledge of the site; one respondent stated, for example, 'I already had enough knowledge about the matter' or 'sometimes I argue with audio-guides', as expressed by a respondent who seemed to be an expert in the area. Much can be learned from these statements, most notably, that there are justifiable reasons why the use of an audio-guide is not equally conducive to all visitors.

6.5 Depth of Experience and Satisfaction

A further aim of this study was to find out if the use of an audio-guide makes a difference with respect to the depth of the experience and satisfaction with the site. A t-test was performed to evaluate whether there are significant differences in the means of the two groups, i.e. users of audio-guides and non-users of audio-guides. In the questionnaire a 5-point Likert scale was used, ranging from 1 'strongly agree' to 5 'strongly disagree'. The items for each construct and the according mean- and p-values are displayed in Tables 6.4 and 6.5.

With respect to the depth of experience, the results provide little evidence that the use of an audio-guide makes a difference because only the item 'lost the sense of time' is significant at the 0.05 level. Regarding satisfaction, two out of four items proved to be significant. Items 'best museum I have ever visited' and 'museum provides good value for money' are not significant, implying that a positive influence of audio-guides on price–performance

Table 6.4. Depth of experience items with mean- and p-values.

	Items	Mean 'non-users'	Mean 'users'	p-value
1	I felt to be transferred into the world of XY	2.34	2.31	0.671
2	I forgot about the outside world	2.81	2.74	0.364
3	I was deeply immersed in the experience	2.74	2.71	0.642
4	I lost the sense of time	2.72	2.51	0.005*

*Significant at the 0.05 level.

Table 6.5. Satisfaction items with mean- and p-values.

	Items	Mean 'non-users'	Mean 'users'	p-value
1	This is one of the best museums I have ever visited	2.69	2.58	0.063
2	I am pleased to have visited this museum	1.81	1.68	0.015*
3	I have really enjoyed myself at this museum	2.01	1.85	0.005*
4	This museum provides good value for money	2.33	2.24	0.127

*Significant at the 0.05 level.

ratio and excellence compared with other sites cannot be supported. However, the indicated mean values show that users of audio-guides show higher satisfaction when it comes to enjoyment of the museum. Also, users of audio-guides seem to be more pleased to have visited this museum than non-users of audio-guides.

6.6   Summary

Interpretation of sites and their exhibits has become an essential part of the visitor experience at cultural attractions. Developments in the area of ICT have generated a wide array of devices that can help attractions to tell the stories of their exhibits in new ways and to engage visitors. Mobile interpretation techniques have come to be among the most prevalent ones. Results of this study underline the common notion that there is a general openness towards the use of modern technologies at cultural attractions and more specifically towards the use of audio-guides. For many visitors these tools for interpretation have already become an essential part of their experience of a site. However, there are also visitors who prefer to use conventional types of interpretation for various reasons.

This non-engagement with technology is an important message for cultural attraction managers and implies that the site should be made equally 'consumable' with or without a mobile guide. In a positive sense, different tools for interpretation can support each other. However, limitations were also identified in relation to mobile technology. Therefore, further product development is needed in this area. After all, audio-guides and other mobile technologies should not be regarded as an end in themselves but only as a means of improving services and interpretation at cultural attractions. The ultimate aim is to enhance the quality of the visitor experience and there is no doubt that mobile technology can play a significant part in achieving this. Decision makers of cultural tourism institutions should therefore monitor developments regarding innovative technologies that could be applied at the sites.

6.7   Discussion Questions

- What is the role of interpretation in experiencing a heritage site?
- What are the pros and cons of using mobile interpretation at heritage sites from a visitor's point of view?
- What are the pros and cons of providing mobile interpretation at heritage sites from the provider's point of view?
- How can mobile interpretation be adapted to different target groups?

References

Boniface, P. (1995) *Managing Quality Cultural Tourism*. Routledge, London.

Canadi, M., Höpken, W. and Fuchs, M. (2010) Application of QR codes in online travel distribution. In: Gretzel, U., Law, R. and Fuchs, M. (eds) *Information and Communication Technologies in Tourism 2010*. Springer, New York, pp. 137–148.

Dewhurst, P.D. and Dewhurst, H. (2006) Visitor attraction management. In: Beech, J. and Chadwick, S. (eds) *The Business of Tourism Management*. Prentice-Hall, Harlow, UK, pp. 287–303.

Dierking, L.D. and Falk, J.H. (1998) Audience and accessibility. In: Thomas, S. and Mintz, A. (eds) *The Virtual and the Real. Media in the Museum*. American Association of Museums, Washington, DC, pp. 57–70.

Falk, J.H. and Dierking, L.D. (1994) *The Museum Experience*. Whalesback Books, Washington, DC.

Goodall, G. and Beech, J. (2006) The management of heritage and cultural tourism. In: Beech, J. and Chadwick, S. (eds) *The Business of Tourism Management*. Prentice-Hall, Harlow, UK, pp. 486–506.

Hegen, M. (2010) *Mobile Tagging: Potenziale von QR-Codes im Mobile Business*. Diplomica, Hamburg, Germany.

Hughes, M. and Morrison-Saunders, A. (2005) Influence of on-site interpretation intensity on visitors to natural areas. *Journal of Ecotourism* 4, 161–177.

Light, D. (1995) Visitors' use of interpretive media at heritage sites. *Leisure Studies* 14, 132–149.

Moscardo, G. (2000) Cultural and heritage tourism: The great debates. In: Faulkner, B., Moscardo, G. and Laws, E. (eds) *Tourism in the 21st Century. Lessons from Experience*. Continuum, London, pp. 19–27.

Timothy, D.J. and Boyd, St. W. (2003) *Heritage Tourism*. Prentice-Hall, Harlow, UK.

Uzzell, D. (1989) *Heritage Interpretation. The Natural and Built Environment*, vol. I. Belhaven, London.

Winter, M. (2010) *Scan Me – Everybody's Guide to the Magical World of QR Codes*. Westsong Publishing, Napa, California.

7 Emerging Concepts and Case Studies of Eco-cultural Tourism

Ian D. Rotherham
Sheffield Hallam University, Sheffield, UK

This chapter is based on case study work from the UK and elsewhere around the world. The core study regions include areas in the Scottish Highlands, in Cornwall, Yorkshire, the Peak District and Norfolk in England, in the Libyan Green Mountain, in Hungarian Transylvania, in Poland and Ukraine, and in Taiwan. The detailed individual case studies are reported elsewhere (see, for example, Doncaster *et al.*, 2005).

The chapter summarizes the background to the emergence of new concepts in the understanding of landscapes and environmental change. Through extensive stakeholder observation and in-depth case studies, the argument is presented for a new research paradigm and consequent revisions of thinking for tourism practitioners. The chapter introduces ideas and issues surrounding tourism development and the separation into niches such as ecotourism, sustainable tourism, wildlife tourism, nature-based tourism, heritage tourism and cultural tourism.

7.1 Introduction

With emerging concepts of cultural landscapes and cultural ecology (see Rotherham, 2008a), it seems there are opportunities to apply the same conceptual approach to tourism and to its impacts on regional and local economies.

While cultural tourism can seem a very closely-focused field, and indeed one directed very much towards urban cultural capital (for example, Richards, 1996), given a wider remit, it offers the basis for a more inclusive and useful framework. Stebbins (quoting Reisinger, 1994), defined cultural tourism as

> a genre of special interest tourism based on the search for and participation in new and deep cultural experiences, whether aesthetic, intellectual, emotional or psychological.
> (Stebbins, 1996, p. 948)

This goes further than referring to museums, galleries, festivals, architecture, historic ruins, artistic performances and heritage sites, all of which regularly draw tourists and other recreational visitors (Rotherham, 2007). Bachleitner (1999) suggests that cultural tourism is applicable not only to cities but to rural areas too and that it can be important in fostering rural tourism. In this same paper the author highlights the impacts of rural cultural tourism through economics, image improvement and better development prospects. At the same time, Trauer (2006) considers the complexities of special interest tourism and proposes models or frameworks to help structure and direct future research and to guide conceptual development. MacDonald and Jolliffe (2003) also take cultural tourism out of the town and into peripheral rural areas. They note that cultural tourism can help rural areas counter the economic declines of primary traditional industries like fishing and farming. Alongside the emerging concept of cultural tourism has been the development of ecotourism ideas, which are academically interesting but of questionable merit when applied. The challenges of tourism diversification and definition in rural areas have been considered by, for example, Sharpley (2002).

7.2 Setting the Context for Nature-based and Cultural Tourism

Wildlife-based tourism is often assumed to be inherently sustainable (Roe et al., 1997), even though observation confirms that this is not so. However, managing and developing appropriate resources for tourism and leisure can be problematic. Indeed, the relationships between tourism growth, local economic development, indigenous cultures, nature and heritage remain complex and frequently disjointed. Concepts such as 'ecotourism', while accessible and popular, are often misunderstood, misused and in their purest sense refer to something almost unattainable and with limited economic impact. Defined by the Ecotourism Society, ecotourism is nature-based speciality travel centred on 'responsible travel to natural areas which conserves the environment and sustains the well-being of local people' (http://www.ecotourism.org/what-is-ecotourism). This definition is widely-accepted in principle but is not a functional definition for gathering statistics, and there is no globally accepted mechanism for gathering ecotourism data. Also, many researchers consider ecotourism to be a specialty segment of the larger nature-tourism market. However, and here confusion arises, many researchers and practitioners use the terms interchangeably. There is a considerable practitioner and researcher information base with, for example, The Ecotourism Society's bibliography showing hundreds of papers, book chapters and technical reports on the subject. But there remains a question as to how much of this is 'ecotourism' at all and how much is pure 'ecotourism'.

Roe et al. (1997) addressed issues of wildlife tourism and ecotourism aspirations and definitions in some detail. Ecotourism is a fast-growing component of tourism (Higgins, 1996; Herath, 2002), one of the fastest growing sectors of the tourism industry worldwide, according to the World Tourism Organization (1995). Furthermore, it has been described as a niche market (Bell and Lyall, 2002) and Preece et al. (1995) questioned the time and resources dedicated to ecotourism as a small component of tourism. In 1996 Brandon claimed that ecotourism and nature-based tourism had not lived up to expectations, though others suggest that ecotourism and nature-based tourism may 'green' mainstream tourism (Preece et al., 1995). Additionally, Stucker Rennicks (1997) suggested nature-based tourism had come of age for 'green', cultural and nature tourists, and for mainstream tourists enjoying nature-based experiences on holiday. This nature-based tourism, wildlife tourism and adventure tourism is increasingly significant but often this is not ecotourism. Even the degree to which such tourism can be sustained or considered sustainable is open to debate. The need to address more thoroughly the issues and nature of ecotourism has been noted:

> The recent wave of support for ecotourism has been based largely on anecdotal reports of impacts combined with unverified 'common-sense' propositions such as the idea that ecotourism is ecologically benign because ecotourists are environmentally sensitive.
> (Lindberg, 1992, p. 2–3)

Taking the impacts of wildlife- and nature-based tourism further, Roe *et al.* (1997) discuss the potential problems and suggest ways to resolve them. However, these analyses tend to focus specifically on travel to protected sites, areas and reserves, rather than the wider 'ordinary' countryside or rural landscape.

Furthermore, in terms of assessing impacts, the idea of 'sustainable tourism' (Bramwell and Lane, 1993) begs the question of what exactly is being 'sustained' and how this might be evidenced. Reviewing tourism literature, including that on both ecotourism and sustainable tourism, it is clear that the 'eco-' component of the studies is often weak or even non-existent. In that case, how has the delivery of either nature conservation or environmental sustainability been assessed and verified. In part this is a consequence of the separation, certainly in British universities and government agencies, between the disciplines that focus on tourism, leisure, economics, ecology and environmental sciences. Cross-disciplinary dialogues are relatively rare and often only short term; a problem driven home by the brutal purism of government research assessment exercises and the need for mainstream academic discipline-based impacts. The consequence is that much of the 'eco-' in ecotourism is very weak and the history in heritage tourism similarly so. There are attempts (e.g. du Cros, 2001) to help make tourism, and in particular cultural tourism, more sustainable. The latter paper attempts to link tourism and cultural heritage management and to address issues regarding the sustainability of heritage tourism.

7.3   Problems with Definitions and Niches

Observations and action research with stakeholders in the UK and around the world suggest that there are problems with the artificial separation of tourism resource components or what we might term as the 'capital' on which the industry is based. Touristic niches seem to be defined according to the activity of the tourist rather than the nature of the resource, but in attempting to manage the latter sustainably this is not necessarily helpful. These issues were highlighted for the UK in recent papers (Rotherham, 2008a, 2008b). Moreover, the result of the academic and researcher problems noted above is that the separation of different segments or components of tourism and leisure are often unsatisfactory. A consequence is also the separation of financial flows in terms of the costs of resource provision (capital and revenue) and of income from touristic and leisure activities. Essentially, with a few notable exceptions, the costs of resource and access provision are borne by the public purse, but the financial benefits flow to the private sector. The income and outlay are only balanced indirectly by tax revenues from business expenditures, from individual expenditures and from associated employment to treasury coffers.

However, in the current scenarios of the economic downturn, the tax revenue does not flow back to local authority countryside services, National Park authorities and others who provide access and other essential infrastructural support. Very often farmers and others who provide and manage the landscape backdrop to rural tourism are similarly omitted from the economic flow. Unless farmers are able to develop their business through entrepreneurship into activity or accommodation provision, or by diversification into a farm shop, then they are disadvantaged by the emerging tourism-based rural economy. As local and national government support through advisory bodies, agencies and grants is slashed farmers find it even harder to move into new fields of provision. In England the recent demise (2011) of the Farming and Wildlife Advisory Groups, or FWAGs, illustrates the loss of such an advisory service. A consequence of the opaqueness of benefit and cost in tourism development is a lack of conservation of, or investment in, critical eco-cultural capital and infrastructure. The need to foster cross-disciplinary approaches to these problems and to provide the necessary inclusive frameworks for research is ever-more urgent.

It is suggested therefore that an approach that considers leisure and tourism from the perspective of the resource and its management can be helpful. Furthermore, it is argued that this focus for interrogation must recognize that landscape is both ecological and cultural.

7.4 Traditionally Managed Landscapes as a Backdrop to Rural Tourism

Nature and traditionally managed landscapes provide an arena within which much tourism is played out (Doncaster *et al.*, 2005; Rotherham, 2008b). Even leisure and tourism in urban settings often take place against a backdrop of scenery and rural culture. In Britain a significant majority of the visitors to Cornwall, a major tourism destination, were drawn by the 'natural' scenery and the cultural and literary association and mythology of the region. However, the landscape that provides this important setting is the result of long-term and intimate interactions between nature and culture that reflect traditions, heritage and ecology.

7.5 Cultural Severance and its Implications

As discussed in recent papers (e.g. Rotherham, 2008a), the breakdown of traditional management in landscapes across Europe is leading directly to massive declines in ecological quality and associated biodiversity. Furthermore, until very recently, much of this loss and the changes responsible for it have been generally overlooked. However, the implications for leisure, tourism and regional economics are very serious. Declining ecology, derelict landscapes and de-populated rural areas leave little that is positive for the tourist (Rotherham, 2008a, 2008b). Yet often the ecologists see these changes as positive steps and frequently describe them as

re-wilding (Rotherham, 2008b). Furthermore, the suggestion is made that such rural areas as the Pennines can be economically powered by ecotourism, which will replace traditional farming (see Anderson, 2004). Critical questions of who the tourism actors might be in such de-populated landscapes without local communities or 'opportunities to spend' to draw down tourist income were overlooked (Rotherham, 2008b). Fundamental to these misunderstandings and misplaced aspirations is the basic omission of the eco-cultural nature of landscape. This fundamental difficulty carries forward into debates on tourism (for examples of cultural severance, see Figs 7.1 and 7.2).

7.6 The Ecotourism Myth

The term ecotourism has been adopted widely as a generic description of tourism with a primary aim to interact with nature and at the same time to involve minimal negative impacts. There is an assumption that local communities will benefit from such tourism and that in the process of these interactions and activities nature will be conserved (Roe *et al.*, 1997). The phrase that is widely adopted to summarize this is to 'take only photographs, steal only time, leave only footprints', but in most cases this is aspirational rather than practical. Indeed, in order to have the positive economic impacts and benefits that key stakeholders advocate will flow from such tourism development, there must be change in both communities and in the environmental resource. These are not necessarily negative or damaging but they are impacts.

As noted earlier, ecotourism is an interesting concept and an academically fascinating paradigm. However, much so-called ecotourism is in fact mass tourism to watch wildlife or experience nature. According to Xiang Huang (personal communication), ecotourism in the rapidly expanding market-place of mainland China is clearly mass tourism to view wildlife experiences. As such it is not ecotourism and it is not benign but often damaging to the resource. However, much wildlife tourism, while not fulfilling the requirements of ecotourism, is economically and, if managed carefully,

Fig. 7.1. Overgrown heath in the Peak District suffering from cultural severance and abandonment. (From Author.)

Fig. 7.2. Sheringham Common Site of Special Scientific Interest in Norfolk, England, suffering from cultural severance. (From Author.)

environmentally beneficial. Indeed, where strict ecotourism is by definition something that has minimal impact and therefore can only ever yield limited benefits, wildlife tourism, managed effectively, can reap substantial rewards. In this context, Roe *et al.* (1997) consider and assess the various definitions of ecotourism and their relationships with other forms of niche tourism.

I suggest that 'ecotourism' as such, misused and misunderstood as it frequently is, can be a problematic concept. Furthermore, since ecotourism in its correct and purest sense can have little impact on people or environment, in terms of regional economic or community development, it is generally irrelevant. As a largely niche end of tourism it is overlooked in terms of emerging planning issues, but damagingly, it clouds relationships with potentially important growth sectors of wildlife-, nature-based, heritage and cultural tourism. These significant drivers in often-struggling rural economies are already overlooked by planners and regional economics analysts; the ecotourism label and its profoundly limited real-life impacts simply confirm their worst fears. In order to change the limited perceptions of nature-based and wildlife tourism as potential drivers in regional economies and, for example, in rural renaissance, it is necessary to revisit the resource and its assets, and the compartmentalism that hinders effective investigation.

7.7 Nature-based, Wildlife and Cultural Tourism

The potential of nature-based and wildlife tourism has been argued and discussed (Roe *et al.*, 1997; Doncaster *et al.*, 2005, 2006) and development of such provision can help trigger economic renewal through both day-visiting and the growth of tourism. The rapid emergence of a tourism visitor economy in South Yorkshire's Dearne Valley, for example, with 100,000 visitors per year, is just one such case. However, this is clearly a wildlife tourism development and not ecotourism. Furthermore, to continue to grow the tourism economy at this location will require diversification of the experience and the attractions to

encompass a wider market. Already, there is an emerging water-sports synergy and a growth of other recreation and sporting activities on offer, such as golf, cycling, horse-riding, garden visiting and countryside walking. A similar pattern can be seen in the nearby Humberhead Levels, where an asset-rich natural environment is providing a context for wildlife leisure, angling, equestrian activities, garden centre visiting, church and heritage visiting, and canal holidays (Doncaster *et al.*, 2005). However, despite the obvious potential, there is little sign of any significant joined-up thinking on site management and regional branding or marketing to consider the regional tourism capital as a holistic whole. It seems that the separation of the various strands and niches is preventing or impairing the marketing of the overall resource. The experiences, destinations and activities on offer mix nature-based and cultural resources.

Furthermore, if we consider the tourism landscape further east, across to the coastline of the East Riding of Yorkshire and the region known as Holderness, this absence of integrated approaches becomes even starker. A recent study (Anon., 2010) considered aspects of wildlife tourism and nature-based tourism in this dramatically under-performing region. In comparison with the hugely successful tourism economy of the north Norfolk coast, the Holderness coastline attracts mostly bottom-end, highly seasonal, low-spending visitors. The higher-spending visitors are almost exclusively day-visitors to the high-profile RSPB (Royal Society for the Protection of Birds) and YWT (Yorkshire Wildlife Trust) sites at Bempton Cliffs Nature Reserve and Flamborough Head. Observation suggests that these visitors go directly to the sites, which themselves have minimal 'opportunity to spend', bring their own food and drink, and depart immediately and go directly home at the end of a single-day visit. Their economic benefits to the region and to the local people are therefore minimal. A limited number of bed-and-breakfast providers and a few cottage accommodation owners gain some benefit, but this is minimal by comparison with the potential.

The interaction between local visitors, leisure day-visitors and tourists is also unsatisfactory.

From the viewpoint of economic impacts, and especially of local business entrepreneurs, the separation makes little sense. Different categories of visitor will have varying needs or desires to spend money, and a business profile needs to anticipate the likely implications of this. However, from a commercial viability perspective, the bottom-line is that you receive visitors and they spend money. Your services and goods, the 'opportunities to spend', need to be planned to meet the market, but essentially all income will be welcomed. In Yorkshire, for example, the official tourism market-place assessment for the East Coast resorts omitted visitors from within Yorkshire and Humberside since they were not 'importing' economic activity from outside the region. From a business viability perspective, and in terms of planning the visitor economy and the associated services and infrastructure, this is nonsense.

A review of the strengths and weaknesses of the experience on offer here and on the infrastructural base suggests that there is a major problem with the quality of service and provision on offer. This is compounded by an absence of joined-up, integrated marketing and investment in the capital base of the tourism industry here. There seems to be little awareness of what the higher-end tourist might require in this landscape in order to visit more frequently, to come in greater numbers, to stay longer and to spend more money. This situation is surprising given the diverse and rich natural and cultural assets of the region, and the fact that this is a long-established tourist destination area. Somehow, the region is failing to capitalize on its capital. I return to this failure later, but in part, I suggest that a fundamental problem is the absence of a coherent and cohesive conceptual framework through which to consider the rural and coastal tourism resource. For this landscape to deliver more fully its tourism economic potential, it is necessary to bring presently disparate leisure and tourism assets and activities together into a single conceptual framework. In particular, there are few efforts for this region to join the different tourism segments to form a coherent whole. The capital resource of the region supports wildlife leisure and tourism, heritage and church tourism, visiting historic houses and gardens, and outdoor activities such as horse-riding or sea-fishing. Yet these and related elements of the region's mass tourism are fragmented and uncoordinated (see, for example, Anon., 2010).

7.8   The Emerging Need for a Broad Concept of Eco-cultural Tourism

The idea of 'eco-cultural tourism' is not new. There are already papers (e.g. Wallace and Russell, 2004) that use the term 'eco-cultural tourism'. In this case, the concept is presented as one where ecological and cultural aspects of a landscape combine to create a site and attraction for tourists. However, while this is a major contribution to the present concept, there is still benefit in the idea being more over-arching and inclusive. Wallace and Russell focus quite reasonably on the now standard view of ecotourism as a specialist micro-niche. They also consider the merits of various approaches to cultural tourism, from visiting a great cathedral in an urban setting to viewing archaeological ruins in a rural location. In this context, Hobsbawn and Ranger's 1983 contribution on the invention of tradition and the increasing demand for nostalgia is particularly relevant. Issues of balance between high-brow culture and low-brow entertainment are also discussed. Russell and Wallace (2004) also note that ecotourism is not always or necessarily sustainable. These discussions provide a useful platform to develop the idea of eco-cultural tourism for a broadly inclusive sweep of leisure and tourism activities that may be experienced in isolation, in sequence or in combination, as appropriate. However, these definitions of tourism segments are based largely on the behaviour of the tourist and the other tourism stakeholders, rather than on the resource capital – the landscape in which tourism is played out.

Observation confirms that much mass tourism takes place in a context and against a backdrop of natural beauty and cultural richness that provides depth and distinctiveness to a particular locale. In landscape definition terms we would describe this as 'local character', and even if this is not the primary target of the tourism visit, it may be the reason for the indefinable attractiveness of a destination. As noted, Cornwall is a major and important tourism region and one where the post-industrial economy is otherwise limited and weak. Yet despite much of the Cornish tourism industry being firmly 'mass tourism', the over-riding reason for visiting is the natural landscape of moor and tor, and of wild seas and windswept cliff-tops, within which arena the touristic experience is played out. Yet the Cornish visitor is also drawn by the beautifully exotic gardens of this most mild climate of the British mainland, and the historic and cultural heritage and myths of Cornish mines and miners, of seafarers and traders, and a rich literature and art relating to both. The visitor might one day be walking on a cliff-top to see rare flowers, sea birds and basking sharks, and the next day visiting an historic house and a created exotic garden. Evenings may be spent dining on local seafood and drinking distinctive ale from a local brewery, and with a name evocative of regional landscapes and heritage. 'The Beast', for example, is a beer that draws its inspiration from the supposed wild cats of the remote Bodmin Moor; a marketing tool mixing a sense of place, a feel for wild nature and a modern myth.

Cultural tourism frequently takes place in a beautiful landscape where nature is a vital component and contact with local wildlife is an important part of the visit. Gardens and grand houses in dramatic landscape settings offer touristic experiences that combine architecture, culture, heritage, history, food and drink, and nature, both wild and domestic. Many countryside activities involve outdoor sports, which take place in and around places of natural beauty and of heritage value, and bring high-spending visitors to a destination. Additionally, many visitor destinations provide a range of services and opportunities for local visitors, leisure day-visitors and tourists, and yet these stakeholder groups are often considered and treated as separate entities. These individuals and organizations do not fit simply and comfortably into current tourism classifications. As noted for the Yorkshire coast example, for a small business providing services to visitors at a destination, the place of origin and the time of stay are

not relevant except in their influence on the willingness to spend money.

7.9   Stakeholder Synergies and Competition

Planning for and managing a diversity of visitors also demands holistic appraisals and models. With diverse communities of users, there arise conflicts and competition for access to resources such as space and sites. This might, for example, be between anglers and watersports at a lake, or between horse-riders, walkers and off-road vehicles on a bridleway. Recent events in the Peak District National Park (see Fig. 7.3), for example, have demonstrated intense competition for space and resources between recreational walkers, off-road four-by-four vehicles and horse-riders. The bitter rivalries lead to major problems in managing the resources sustainably and also become long-running and expensive disputes for local authorities with reduced budgets. Competition runs deep and may extend off the physical site and into the politics of resource allocation, such as through essential grant aid to support or develop provisions. Outdoor sports groups and nature conservation bodies vie with each other for financial support from bodies such as the Heritage Lottery Fund (HLF). This is an unspoken but acute rivalry. During action research with stakeholders from this sector under the auspices of the Central Council for Physical Recreation (CCPR) (Rotherham et al., 2006) the depth of the rivalries became sharply apparent. In particular, this was manifest in the rivalries between active sports groups and conservation organizations such as the RSPB (external to the CCPR federation), and also within the umbrella of the CCPR itself. The latter showed a reluctance to use the Ramblers' Association (a CCPR member) as an example of good practice in sustainable countryside recreation, preferring instead to promote the case study of off-road motorcycling. So in terms of users and the representational organizations there is a wide variety of stakeholders with varying affinities to concepts of sustainable tourism and recreation but all competing for space and resources.

Fig. 7.3. Monsal Dale in the Peak District National Park: a major eco-cultural tourism destination. (From Author.)

These issues affect vital aspects of tourism management such as destination development and marketing, and a failure to collaborate presents major disadvantages in terms of potential destination development. Case studies and action research with key stakeholders indicate a lack of collaboration (Doncaster *et al.*, 2005; Capriello and Rotherham, 2008). Within sectors such as wildlife visiting, and between different sectoral actors, there is often little collaboration in promotion and profile development since the other stakeholders are competitors and not collaborators. Individual organizations with similar positions and interests, such as the Wildlife Trusts, the Royal Society for the Protection of Birds, and the Wildfowl and Wetlands Trust in say the English Fenlands region, generally behave as competitors rather than collaborators (Doncaster *et al.*, 2005). A further problem is that these organizations frequently fail to engage with mainstream tourism agencies and organizations, and the latter don't see the potential and importance of the major conservation bodies. The situation becomes even more problematic if we extend the review to historic and heritage buildings and sites, and to historic gardens and

garden retail (such as garden centres). The tourism agencies and practitioners overlook major components of this broad church of nature-based and heritage tourism, and a review of garden-based attractions suggested that their stakeholders felt ignored and overlooked. It terms of collaboration between these stakeholders, and those with conservation and wildlife interests, the reviews showed almost no collaboration at all (Rotherham *et al.*, 2002; Doncaster *et al.*, 2005; Rotherham, 2006).

This lack of joined-up thinking or integrated approaches leads to additional problems when destination development requires infrastructural investment, grant-aid draw-down, and effective badging and marketing. All these issues become fragmented and ineffective. There is a further complication in the way that cost and benefit of countryside or rural visitor infrastructure and support are funded and in the way that they may generate revenue. The necessary investment in infrastructure and conservation or management, for cultural and nature-based destinations and resources, is paid by stakeholders who gain little from the visitor economy. Cost and benefit are often not co-located, and tourism can be seen as parasitic and economically fickle, and can be highly seasonal too (Rotherham, 2008b). Displacement of established economic sectors can occur and, unless managed carefully, this may be to the long-term detriment of regional development. Infrastructural improvements are often funded from the public purse but the benefits flow to the private sector. In the current climate of economic austerity, these issues are becoming more deeply ingrained and potentially very damaging.

7.10   The Silos and Consequences of Compartmentalism

In this chapter, I argue that addressing the problems of compartmentalization is fundamental to a better understanding of the separate tourism niches. It is also essential to achieving more effective social, economic and ecological impacts of tourism, or at least avoiding unnecessary damage to ecological and cultural resources. The work was undertaken in an attempt to understand both the resource and the emerging tourism industries. In many cases, observation suggests that tourists and other visitors seek mixed portfolios of visitor experiences, which combine nature, heritage, culture, outdoor activities and cuisine. Furthermore, tourism is often actively encouraged and fostered as a driver of economic development in a region. However, in order to justify such tourism development in a region there must be economic impact, which, like it or not, will bring about a degree of local cultural transformation. Without this there is no visitor economy and tourism will not be sustained. To facilitate the change, local people and communities will adapt and some may be displaced, in contrast, for example, to the purist ethics espoused by 'real' ecotourism.

Indeed, with the development of leisure retail outlets, the 'opportunity to spend' becomes an essential part of the destination development. Shops supplying local needs and resources such as groceries and household goods cannot compete in the inflated marketplace and are soon displaced by sports goods and outdoor clothing shops. Ultimately, in situations such as Bowness or Ambleside in the English Lake District, the local culture of the destination itself metamorphoses to become a haven for the recreational shopper, set in a majestic natural landscape, but completely alien to the indigenous community now displaced. Just as at Castleton in the English Peak District, the visitors now come to a cultural landscape of gift shops, knick-knacks, and outdoor clothing and equipment. Many experience local nature first hand, as they trudge up a mountain path, but many more bond with the new cultural landscape and wild nature from the comfort of a coffee shop or restaurant. In remote locations, low-key tourism may help maintain and sustain vital services such as local shops, but in destinations that are more popular the result is usually cultural displacement. The situation is exacerbated by the knock-on impact of leisure and tourism demand on local house prices for primary residence, second homes or holiday lets. In popular destination regions, such as National Parks and some coastal areas, local communities are squeezed out of their towns and villages by inflated prices. With reduced local services, high prices in shops and for homes, residence becomes increasingly expensive and exclusive. However, in losing the indigenous community there is a further danger that local heritage and the distinctiveness of local 'cultural capital' will decline.

It is clear from case studies across Europe and the UK, in North Africa, and in Asia, that in managing leisure and tourism it is essential to recognize the core components of the underpinning resources. This needs to be within a conceptual framework that allows us to better understand relationships, interactions and potential play-offs between resources and actors within this dynamic landscape. The emerging vision encapsulates both natural and cultural capital and players. Only then will it be possible to manage the tourism resource capital in a way that will allow it to be both sustained and developed. If cultural tourism is to be developed to enhance local economies then it is necessary to identify the critical facets of the resource base that may facilitate growth. Furthermore, it becomes vital to understand what assets can be compromised or traded and those that are irreplaceable. In developing approaches to these issues for tourism it is useful to borrow models and ideas from other disciplines such as the environmental sciences or economics.

7.11   Critical Resource Capital

In recent decades there have been increasing attempts to find synergies between impact assessment techniques for economics and for the natural environment. These provide useful conceptual ideas that apply to tourism development. Approaches from the natural environmental sciences, nature conservation and countryside recreation management can be informative and adaptable to this broader use. For example, ideas of 'limits of acceptable change' (Sidaway and Thompson, 1991; McCool, 1994) and resource 'carrying capacity' (Hardin, 1991; Sayre, 2008) are useful and can aid assessment of development and resource-use impacts. In particular, however, the concept of 'natural capital' (Ekins *et al.*, 2003) is potentially very useful. The term 'capital' is used to describe a stock or resource from which revenue or yield can be extracted. Human well-being arises from the combined use of various types of capital – social capital, human capital and built capital – but these are all based on natural capital. Four basic categories of natural capital are generally recognized: air, water (fresh, groundwater and marine), land (including soil, space and landscape) and habitats (including the ecosystems, flora and fauna, which they both comprise and support) (see Fig. 7.4. for a composite example of multiple natural assets, utilized as a successful eco-cultural tourism destination). This idea emerged in the 1990s, in order to try to resolve apparent conflicts between economic resource evaluations and natural resource conservation. The concept can perhaps form a cornerstone for a broader understanding of tourism uses of, and impacts on, natural or heritage resources.

Natural capital is taken as a way to identify and define the assets of the natural world that perform or provide various useable services. The idea that elements of the resource base are irreplaceable (i.e. critical) and interchangeable or rechargeable (i.e. tradable) provides a basis for assessing the likely impacts of exploitation

Fig. 7.4. Carsington Water in North Derbyshire: an eco-cultural tourism destination with a million plus visitors per year. (From Author.)

or displacement of natural, heritage or cultural assets. 'Critical natural capital' (CNC) is defined as the natural environment that performs important and irreplaceable functions (Gillespie and Shepherd, 1995; Chiesura and De Groot, 2003). In the early days, most of the work in this regard addressed natural sciences issues, mostly relating to life-support systems and ecological services. Little attention was given to socio-cultural functions, human health benefits or well-being. However, current thinking attempts to provide more rounded consideration of critical functions and associated values in relation to health, recreation, amenity, education, heritage and local economies (e.g. Defra, 2007; TEEB, 2010). These functions provide many socioeconomic benefits that can be assessed through both qualitative and quantitative valuation methodologies, and are relevant to tourism destination development. Integration of ecology, sociology and economics provides more balanced environmental planning and decision making. Natural capital is a hybrid concept, on the one hand borrowed from economics, and on the other relating to environmental quality, resilience and integrity. It lies at the core of human well-being and long-term sustainable economic activity. However, natural capital differs from human-made or manufactured capital in several ways, as Fig. 7.5 highlights.

The hybridization of these concepts can be continued to include culture and heritage, alongside nature itself. As noted, ideas have been developed to consider the balance between critical natural capital, which cannot be replaced or repaired if lost or damaged, and that which might be 'tradable' and replaceable. For an emerging tourism destination, the assessment and evaluation of 'natural capital', 'heritage capital' and 'cultural capital' provides an overarching vision to better inform any models of potential development and possible conflicts. These approaches may be applied in the emerging context of 'eco-cultural tourism', which recognizes that the actors and stakeholders cross boundaries, share resources and compound any influences on the hosts. In particular, this idea reflects recent developments in environmental history that assert the cultural nature of many landscapes and environmental systems around the world. These concepts are being developed with exemplar case studies. Far from being 'natural', most landscapes and their associated ecologies are semi-natural or eco-cultural, and their richness or distinctiveness reflects an often intimate lineage of human exploitation and usage (Berkes and Folke, 1992).

The logic of natural capital outlined above is mirrored in the assessment of tourism assets and actors in the tourism landscape. This leads

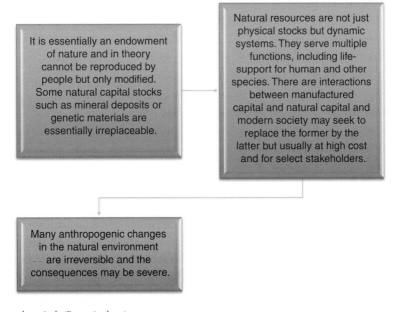

Fig. 7.5. Natural capital. (From Author.)

us to consider an integrated or hybrid concept of 'eco-cultural tourism' based on stakeholders with broadly based interests and resources that combine ecological, heritage and cultural assets. If these are to be managed to best effect, and adverse consequences of use and exploitation are to be avoided, then regional tourism development must be considered in terms of this more holistic conceptual framework. Furthermore, in assessing investment and development needs, infrastructural requirements and potential impacts, ideas of carrying capacity and limits of acceptable change can be applied. Taking this further still, we can begin to apply the tests of sustainable development to this wider tourism concept, by means of the triple bottom line (Ma et al., 2011). Within the conceptual framework for analysis, it is desirable to consider the three pillars of sustainable development: society or community, economy and environment. Because we are considering here the concept of an emerging eco-cultural tourism, then the need to establish genuinely robust assessments of impacts on people (community) and on the environment (ecology, wildlife, vegetation, landscape, etc.) is paramount. Without a joined-up vision of the emerging and developing tourism sector and the assets on which it is based, assessments are generally undertaken that omit key players and essential assets. This suggests that the long-term sustainability of the tourism assets, and therefore of the industry itself, may be jeopardized or compromised through the shortcomings of the conceptual models that are applied. A key thrust of this argument is that the separation of the various tourism segments or niches can be helpful in understanding tourist behaviour, but must also recognize the intimate intertwined relationships between nature and culture. Without effective recognition of the cultural and natural components of landscape, for example, the leisure and tourism that depend on the capital resources may fail and/or be damaging.

7.12   Natural Areas as Eco-cultural Landscapes

The idea and concept of 'natural area tourism' presupposes that landscapes are indeed 'natural', which they are not (O'Connor, 2000;

Newsome et al., 2002). If we apply this concept to the Green Mountain region of eastern Libya, the country's major National Park, for example, then there is a real danger of misunderstanding the resource capital and the tourism or recreation potential. While Green Mountain has spectacular natural features with deep canyons and rolling hills, its major touristic attractions are heritage features, historical associations and archaeology. Furthermore, for the visitors, the obvious links of the region are to the coastal ruins of the great Roman settlements along the Mediterranean shore. This is an eco-cultural landscape with eco-cultural features and capital.

So-called 'natural areas' such as National Parks, wetlands, mountains and forests, for example, have strong natural elements, but they are essentially cultural or eco-cultural landscapes formed by long-term human/nature interactions (see Fig. 7.6). A Mediterranean scrub and grassland landscape, or the ancient lanes, hedgerows and field patterns of England's Somerset Levels, may provide a backdrop to thriving tourism industries. Furthermore, many of the critical interactions that deliver these attractive and biodiverse landscapes have evolved over centuries to become traditions or customs. Many of the cultural manifestations, which are now tourism attractants, have themselves emerged from these complex and intimate relationships. It is these features, through buildings and archaeology, landscape patterns such as field systems, ancient hedgerows and trees, and through festivals and ceremonies, that give distinctive character to places and communities. This distinction and character is often what the tourist, knowingly or unknowingly, seeks.

7.13   Summary

To understand the complexities of the various inter-relationships outlined in this chapter, it is important to improve knowledge of tourism resources and their functioning. However, it is also necessary to recognize that the tourism and leisure visitors often take part in mixed portfolios of experiential activities that mix nature and culture, and these are not easily or exclusively classified. While separation into

Fig. 7.6. The Lizard in Cornwall: a classic eco-cultural tourism destination. (From Author.)

niches may aid some forms of assessment and evaluation, the effective management and support, especially for emerging tourism destinations, may benefit from more inclusive and over-arching approaches.

Applying such broad approaches may be challenging and, as I have indicated in this chapter, it requires genuine multidisciplinary collaborations. In current climates of academic and agency austerity, it is likely that the problems and misunderstandings will worsen rather than ease. Given the importance now being attached to emerging concepts of the cultural nature of landscapes, it is vital that leisure and tourism researchers and practitioners recognize the issues. Secondly, with the imperative of cultural severance and the need to support rural economies, it is necessary to address subjects with more genuinely multidisciplinary

approaches than has previously been the case. It is time to put the 'eco-' into ecotourism and to recognize the roles of culture in nature.

7.14 Discussion Questions

• Discuss the concept of ecotourism and comment on how and why it is often misrepresented in literature.
• When considering local small-scale tourism products, why might it be important to consider a more holistic definition of tourist?
• Why is a failure to collaborate so damaging for a tourism destination?
• What is 'natural capital' and how does a consideration of this assist in the management of landscape resources?

References

Anderson, P. (ed.) (2004) Upland ecology, tourism and access. *Proceedings of the 18th Conference of the Institute of Ecology and Environmental Management*, Buxton, 25–27 November 2003. IEEM, Winchester, UK.

Anon. (2010) *The Economic Potential of Nature Tourism in Eastern Yorkshire. Final report to the Yorkshire Wildlife Trust*. ICRT, Leeds Metropolitan University, Leeds, UK.

Bachleitner, R. (1999) Cultural tourism in rural communities: the residents' perspective. *Journal of Business Research* 44, 199–209.

Bell, C. and Lyall, J. (2002) *The Accelerated Sublime. Landscape, Tourism and Identity*. Praeger, Westport, Connecticut.

Berkes, F. and Folke, C. (1992) A systems perspective on the interrelations between natural, humanmade and cultural capital. *Ecological Economics* 5, 1–8.

Bramwell, B. and Lane, B. (1993) Sustainable tourism: an evolving global approach. *Journal of Sustainable Tourism* 1, 6–16.

Brandon, K. (1996) Ecotourism and conservation: a review of key issues. Environmentally and socially sustainable development. *Environment Department Papers: Biodiversity Series Paper 033*. Global Environment Division, The World Bank, Washington, DC.

Capriello, A. and Rotherham, I.D. (2008) Farm attractions, networks, and destination development: a case study of Sussex, England. *Tourism Review* 63, 59–71.

Chiesura, A. and De Groot, R. (2003) Critical natural capital: a socio-cultural perspective. *Ecological Economics* 44, 219–231.

Defra (2007) *An Introductory Guide to Valuing Ecosystem Services*. Defra, London.

Doncaster, S., Rotherham, I.D. and Egan, D. (2005) Nature-based leisure and tourism in England's Humberhead Levels. *Current Issues in Tourism* 8, 214–230.

Doncaster, S., Egan, D., Rotherham, I.D. and Harrison, K. (2006) The tourism economic argument for wetlands: a case study approach. *Proceedings of the IALE Conference, Water and the Landscape: The Landscape Ecology of Freshwater Ecosystems*, 296–300.

du Cros, H. (2001) A new model to assist in planning for sustainable cultural heritage tourism. *International Journal of Tourism Research* 3, 165–170.

Ekins, P., Simon, S., Deutsch, L., Folke, C. and De Groote, R. (2003) A framework for the practical application of the concepts of critical natural capital and strong sustainability. *Ecological Economics* 44, 165–185.

Gillespie, J. and Shepherd, P. (1995) Establishing criteria for identifying critical natural capital in the terrestrial environment: a discussion paper. *English Nature Research Report No. 141*. English Nature, Peterborough, UK.

Hardin, G. (1991) Paramount positions in ecological economics. In: Costanza, R. (ed.) *Ecological Economics: The Science and Management of Sustainability*. Columbia University Press, New York, pp. 47–57.

Herath, G. (2002) Research methodologies for planning ecotourism and nature conservation. *Tourism Economics* 8, 77–101.

Higgins, B.R. (1996) The global structure of the nature tourism industry: ecotourists, tour operators, and local businesses. *Journal of Travel Research* XXXV, 11–18.

Hobsbawn, E. and Ranger, T. (eds) (1983) *The Invention of Tradition*. Cambridge University Press, Cambridge, UK.

Lindberg, K. (1992) International issues in ecotourism management with applications to Kenya. In: Gakahu, C.G. and Goode, B.E. (eds) *Ecotourism and Sustainable Development in Kenya*. Wildlife Conservation International, Nairobi, pp. 1–13.

Ma, S.C., Rotherham, I.D. and Egan, D. (2011) A conceptual TBL framework for managing sports mega-events to ensure sustainability for host destinations. *Journal of Sustainable Tourism* 19, 79–96.

MacDonald, R. and Jolliffe, L. (2003) Cultural rural tourism: evidence from Canada. *Annals of Tourism Research* 30, 307–322.

McCool, S.F. (1994) Planning for sustainable nature dependent tourism development: the limits of acceptable change system. *Tourism Recreation Research* 19, 51–55.

Newsome, D., Moore, S.A. and Dowling, R.K. (2002) *Natural Area Tourism: Ecology, Impacts, and Management*. Channel View Publications, Clevedon, UK.

O'Connor, M. (2000) Natural capital, environmental valuation in Europe. *Policy Research Brief No. 3*. Cambridge Research for the Environment, Cambridge, UK.

Preece, N., van Oosterzee, P. and James, D. (1995) Two way track. Biodiversity conservation and ecotourism: an investigation of linkages, mutual benefits and future opportunities. *Biodiversity Series Paper No. 5*. Environment Australia: Department of Environment and Heritage, Canberra, Australia.

Reisinger, Y. (1994) Tourist–host contact as a part of cultural tourism. *World Leisure & Recreation* 36(2), 24–28.

Richards, G. (1996) Production and consumption of European cultural tourism. *Annals of Tourism Research* 23, 261–283.

Roe, D., Leader-Williams, N. and Dalal-Clayton, B. (1997) Take only photographs, leave only footprints: the environmental impacts of wildlife tourism. *Wildlife and Development Series No. 10*. International Institute for Environment and Development, London.

Rotherham, I.D. (2006) Opportunities and pitfalls in ecotourism development. In: Dixit, S. (ed.) *Promises and Perils in Hospitality and Tourism Management*. Aman Publications, New Delhi, pp. 148–167.

Rotherham, I.D. (2007) *Sacred Sites and the Tourist: Sustaining Tourism Infrastructures for Religious Tourists and Pilgrims*. CAB International, Wallingford, UK, pp. 64–77.

Rotherham, I.D. (2008a) The importance of cultural severance in landscape ecology research. In: Dupont, A. and Jacobs, H. (eds) *Landscape Ecology Research Trends*. Nova Science, Hauppauge, New York, pp. 71–87.

Rotherham, I.D. (2008b) Tourism and recreation as economic drivers in future uplands. Shaping a vision for the uplands. *Aspects of Applied Biology* 85, 93–98.

Rotherham, I.D., Egan, D. and Doncaster, S. (2002) *The Humberhead Levels Sustainable and Nature-based Tourism and Leisure Project. Stakeholder Interviews and Feedback*. Sheffield Hallam University and Countryside Agency, Sheffield, UK.

Rotherham, I.D., Egan, D. and Egan, H. (2006) *A Review of the Economic Value of Countryside Recreation and Sports*. TECRU (SHU), Sheffield, UK/Sport England, Manchester, UK/CCPR, London.

Russell, A. and Wallace, G. (2004) Irresponsible ecotourism. *Anthropology Today* 20, 1–2.

Sayre, N.F. (2008) The genesis, history, and limits of carrying capacity. *Annals of the Association of American Geographers* 98, 120–134.

Sharpley, R. (2002) Rural tourism and the challenge of tourism diversification: the case of Cyprus. *Tourism Management* 23, 233–244.

Sidaway, R. and Thompson, D. (1991) Upland recreation: the limits of acceptable change. *ECOS* 12, 31–39.

Stebbins, R.A. (1996) Cultural tourism as serious leisure. *Annals of Tourism Research* 23, 948–950.

Stucker Rennicks, J. (1997) Nature-based tourism. *Business & Economic Review* 43(2) http://www.theziels.org/BandE/bande43/43n2/nature.htm (accessed September 2012).

TEEB (2010) The economics of ecosystems and biodiversity for local and regional policy makers. http://www.TEEBweb.org.

Trauer, B. (2006) Conceptualizing special interest tourism – frameworks for analysis. *Tourism Management* 27, 183–200.

Wallace, G. and Russell, A. (2005) Eco-cultural tourism as a means for the sustainable development of culturally marginal and environmentally sensitive regions. *Tourism Studies* 4, 235–254.

World Tourism Organization (1995) *Tourism Market Trends (1985–1995)*. World Tourism Organization, Madrid.

8 Reinventing British Culture: Multiculturalism, Travel and Cross-cultural Comparisons

Nigel D. Morpeth,[1] Razaq Raj[1] and Kevin A. Griffin[2]

[1]Leeds Metropolitan University, Leeds, UK;
[2]Dublin Institute of Technology, Dublin, Ireland

This chapter compares and contrasts discourses of multiculturalism in both British and Australian society, to consider how these societies, with an inescapably linked history, have expressed their human and physical geography as multicultural resources for tourism consumption. After initially considering redefinitions of cultural tourism, and then different perspectives on the concept of multiculturalism, the first part of the chapter has a particular focus on the cultural context of Australia, highlighting the question of multiculturalism as a contested concept within contemporary society, and compares this with Britain. It demonstrates the challenge for contemporary societies to understand the origins of their (multi-)cultural identities and in turn the capacity to attract multicultural tourists to engage with multicultural hosts and audiences.

The chapter then reviews tourism marketing promotions to draw out different observations about the nature of multiculturalism within these two societies and the tensions that occur when cultural diversity is replaced by monocultural stereotypes as a cultural reference point for visiting tourists. Particular scrutiny is made of Australian filmmaker Baz Luhrmann's 2009 'Walkabout' video with an Aboriginal Australian boy as the central character, replacing the controversial Tourism Australia's, 'So Where the Bloody Hell Are You?' campaign, which resonated with a populist Australian nostalgia, represented in part by the Crocodile Dundee film character. Focusing then on the British Tourist Authority's (BTA) Great British marketing campaign, there are uneasy parallels between the cultural contexts of Britain and Australia, with a chauvinistic and colonial past seeming to resonate with the representation of Britain during the year of London 2012 and cultural identity focusing on a homogenized British society.

8.1 Introduction

Nuryanti reminds us of the linkages between culture, heritage and tourism, stating that

> studies of cultural heritage and tourism (Hewison 1987; Heeley 1989; Hall and McArthur 1993) have tended to concentrate on the power of tradition, which implies stability or continuity, whereas tourism involves change.
>
> (1996, p. 395)

It is not surprising, therefore, that dialogue concerning the two is sometimes characterized by a series of contradictions. While different theoretical approaches have been used to analyse relationships between cultural heritage and tourism, a number of authors have chosen to address the linkages between the two by examining the structural ties between the production of culture and tourism consumption (MacCannell, 1976; Cohen, 1988; Urry, 1990; Watson and Kopachevsky, 1996).

Within the context of this chapter there are contradictions in the national narratives that are constructed around the notion of culture and national identity in the UK and Australia, narratives that have promoted and marketed distinctive images of Englishness and Australianness that thereby reveal the unresolved tensions that have festered over decades on what it means to be English/British and Australian. Arguably, there are multiple unspoken narratives of cultural difference and dissonance, which over a series of decades have resulted in the emergence of privileged cultural stereotypes, such as in the case of England the quintessential cultural and physical landscapes of 'England's Green and Pleasant Land'. In the case of Australia, over successive generations, this finds a parallel in a whites-only society, in which indigenous Australians exist as a ghostly presence on the margins of society. Further complexity is added by the inescapable and intertwined history of post-colonized Australia and its linkages to England, which has seen Australia use Britain as the cultural template to perpetuate the myth of an Anglo-Saxon Australia, rather than an Australia that is geographically and culturally part of the south-east Asia region.

8.2 Culture and Image

Morgan and Pritchard note how

> Tourism identities are packaged according to certain value systems and meanings. Just as tourism sites are associated with 'particular values, historical events and feelings', so values, feelings and events are used to promote such sites, reinforcing the dominant ideologies ... Tourism marketers through their marketing images create identities which represent certain ways of seeing reality, images which both reflect and reinforce particular relationships in societies. These are relationships which are grounded in relations of power, dominance and subordination which characterise the global system.
>
> (1999, p. 3)

They argue then (and this would seem to remain the status quo) that the relationship between power and tourism is an under-researched area of tourism investigation. This in part, they argue, is due to duality in the study of tourism, with a lack of synergy between those academics concentrated on a business approach to the study of tourism and those academics who advocate a sociological paradigm to make sense of it.

For Morgan and Pritchard the basis of their paradigm for the study of tourism and in particular 'theoretical ways of seeing tourism' is

> that tourism processes manifest power as they mirror and reinforce the distribution of power in society, operating as mechanisms whereby inequalities are articulated and validated.
>
> (1999, p. 7)

They argue that, historically, in selling the 'dream' of the tourist experience, that image promotion has been dominated by images of the 'whiteness' of the stereotypical tourist. This is consistent with Hylton's (2009) discourses of whiteness and the creation of racialized ideologies, in which racial stereotypes are propagated in different spheres of society:

> power minorities, that is, individuals or groups in society, reinforcing or challenging their own subordination in a system that can alienate and disenfranchise them.
>
> (2009, p. 4)

It is important to realize that the symbolism of branding-images for destinations reflects the wider world of social values and as such are important cultural symbols 'charged with social significance' (Morgan and Pritchard, 1999, p. 27). In essence, it is not possible to separate the actions and processes of tourism, from the so-called real world. Thus, by necessity, all tourism has ideological considerations. What we need to be able to do is to read the semiotics of these images/constructs and interrogate their underlying relationships. Furthermore, Morgan and Pritchard argue that

> Tourism is grounded in real world relationships – historical, economic, political, social and cultural. Culture is about meanings which are communicated via representational systems within these systems. We make use of signs or symbols to interpret these meanings. Language is 'one of the media' through which thoughts and ideas and feelings are represented in a culture, language which is not merely verbal but also visual.
>
> (1999, p. 31)

They argue that the construction of ethnicity is a disputed concept and that 'tourism defines tourists as 'us' who interact with 'others', the non-whites, the visited or 'them'. These terms entail the 'notion of power over ways of talking about and representing subjects and peoples' (1999, p. 211). In their discussion of the exotic they use the phrase the 'white-tourist gaze', in which the generalized power relationship is that tourists 'look down' on local indigenous people, with locals 'looking up to tourists'. They argue that this is reflected in the way that tourist marketers create narratives and images of the tourist–host relationship. They further suggest that

> in the marketing of destinations, we can particularly observe how the language of tourism mediates the exotic with the familiar. This is a familiarity which often juxtaposes exoticism with well known European geography.
>
> (1999, p. 211)

In the late 1990s, on a Thomas Cook holiday, British tourists could enjoy 'an Oriental Journey beyond the wildest dreams of Marco Polo', where they could visit the likes of Bangkok ('the Venice of the East') and Hong Kong ('where Britain meets China') (Morgan and Pritchard, 1999, p. 216). Juxtaposed with the exotic of these trips is the notion of 'home away from home', which is equally important. Colonial

relationships inform interactions between the old and the new world, and in the constructing of destination identities, places such as Jamaica in the Caribbean are viewed as 'playgrounds of the rich and famous'. The sanitization of these destinations for the developed world market and the representations of ethnic people who appear in the tourist literature severely limit local identities and acceptable spheres of action. In the case of the Caribbean, for example, these touristic constructs combine to rewrite a history that is built on plantations, slavery and brutality, and develop an image that facilitates western consumption (1999, p. 216).

Later in this chapter, it is argued that the London Olympic Boroughs, with some of the highest concentration of multicultural communities in the UK, have received similar marketing and branding treatments as discussed above, in the sense that contested racialized landscapes, which received negative media coverage during the 2011 'summer of riots', are now marketed as 'safe' tourist territories, to be visited by international tourists during the London 2012 Olympics.

8.3   Defining Multiculturalism

That a lexicon definition of multiculturalism should suggest a nation is made up of several cultural or ethnic groups tells an incomplete story. Vertovec states that there are multi-multiculturalisms, suggesting that

> it is apparent that multiculturalism currently means no single thing – that is, it represents no single view of, or strategy for contemporary complex societies.
>
> (1999, p. 25)

This raises further questions of the meaning of culture and the issues of cultural assimilation and dissonance (Berger *et al.*, 1984). Cooper states that

> Multiculturalism is sometimes taken to mean that different cultural communities should live their own ways of life in a self-contained manner. This is not its only meaning and in fact it has long been obsolete. Multiculturalism basically means that no culture is perfect or represents the best life and that it can therefore benefit from a critical dialogue with other cultures. In this sense multiculturalism requires

that all cultures should be open, self critical, and interactive in their relations with each other.
(2009, p. 159, citing Parekh from the BBC News, 2004, p. 2)

A full interrogation of the concept of multiculturalism, and indeed the parallels and distinctions with interculturalism, are beyond the scope of this chapter; however, reflecting on the work of Vertovec (2007) and that of Meer and Modood (2012) helps to identify how interculturalism can include

the diversity of the locations from where migrants and ethnic minorities herald, give rise not to a creation of communities or groups but a churning mass of languages, ethnicities and religions all cutting across each other and creating a superdiversity.
(Meer and Modood, 2012, p. 186)

For Meer and Modood, interculturalism is akin to multicultural dialogue and the opportunity for people to engage and learn from different cultural traditions. They argue that multiculturalism as a term can 'encapsulate a variety of sometimes contested meanings' (2012, p. 179).

In applying considerations of multiculturalism to cultural contexts, Storry and Childs talk about the concept of 'Little England' as being a

version of the nation based around cultural or ethnic purity as well as a version of the past as essentially rural and aristocratic. This version is based on the idea of 'Great' Britain, a country with a glorious imperialist past that was in fact built on slave-trading and colonising the 'dark' continents. This nostalgic appeal to history is premised on narrow ethnic stereotypes, a Britain that is WASP (white, Anglo-Saxon and Protestant).
(1997, p. 321)

The reality of this colonial past was emphasized by Hill in his treatise on the origins of the slave trade in the 16th century, which fuelled the development of this 'white' Britain. Negroes were taken from West Africa to be sold in the Spanish colonies of the West Indies:

The basis of the whole business, the actual trade in slaves itself, was as simple as it was diabolical. Every year at a number of settlements on the West African coast like Cormantine and Cape Coast Castle, there assembled crowds of wretched negroes, men and women alike. They had been captured in the ceaseless tribal wars, and this was the

penalty of defeat. The victorious chiefs sold them like so many cattle to the slave-traders, who packed them on board their ships.
(Hill, 1975, p. 57)

The comments made by Storry and Childs (1997), whilst made prior to the new millennium, observed a Britain that thought of itself as essentially white, exemplified by the concept of 'Englishness' that was resistant to emerging multicultural identities, which moved beyond a collective white identity.

There are parallels between this myopic British viewpoint and the conceptualization of Australian culture and society, which until the 1970s was the embodiment of reinforcing 'white identity' through its 'whites only' immigration policy. This policy was one element of the attempt to promote an external image that denied both Australia's south-east Asian geography and the indigenous Australian population. Subsequent multicultural policies were developed and it is argued (by Meer and Modood, 2012, p. 180, for example) that these operated more as a means to better integrate new immigrants, by easing expectations of rapid assimilation, than it was truly a tool for multiculturalism. Levey (2008) notes that this policy did not include Indigenous Australians until the end of the 1970s with the Galbally Report (1978), which spoke of multiculturalism being a policy for 'all Australians, including Indigenous Australians'. However, despite this government pronouncement, there appears to be an ingrained racism within Australia (which it is argued also exists in the UK), and arguably this is an impediment to developing a culturally diverse civil society.

8.4 Searching for a National Identity?

Arguably, the UK and Australia share a similar heritage in terms of their tolerance of racism, leading to what Walker (1977) describes as the 'respectability of racism'. Within the context of the UK, Walker noted how the emergence of the so-called Monday Club was a faction of the Conservative Party that espoused anti-immigration sentiments and noted 'links and flirtations of Club members with the NF (National Front)' (1977, p. 126). This was at a time when NF members were engaged in anti-immigration marches and were keen to see compulsory repatriation of (black) immigrants. Arguably these perceptions of immigration and immigrants still remain part of the psyche of the Conservative Party. Indeed these views are consistent with the observations of Storry and Childs, who argued that

> The identity of Indian and other people in Britain is complicated by a history of colonial relations … Since the nineteenth century, certain theories regarding the relations between race, nation and culture have led to the development of ideas which cast immigration and ethnicity in a very negative light.
>
> (1997, p. 260)

They concur with the views of Walker in recognizing racist and xenophobic violence that emerged in the UK in the 1960s and 1970s. They view this type of racism to be what they categorize as an 'older-biological' form, in contrast to the 'newer, cultural form of racism (which) is more subtle'. For example, one former UK politician caused controversy in the 1990s with his 'cricket test'; Lord Norman Tebbit argued that if people living permanently in Britain support other nations in sporting or other cultural events then they have not sufficiently adapted themselves to British life and cannot therefore legitimately be called British. Tebbit used the example of the way in which many black Britons support the West Indies cricket team, but the point was intended to apply to any instance of cultural 'treason'. Storry and Childs noted that

> Indeed, the issue of sporting affiliation has become even more heated since the publication of an article in a prestigious cricketing journal in 1995 which suggested that it would be a mistake to expect any 'ethnic' sportsperson selected to represent Britain, even if born here, to be as committed as a 'real' (that is, white) Briton.
>
> (1997, p. 261)

At the time of writing this chapter it is both puzzling and perplexing to see that this debate about the notion of identity and national identity, and indeed 'Britishness', continues to be fuelled by politicians. Fuelled without a sense of resolution and, as Storry and Childs have alluded above, there are both stereotypes

and expectations of what it means to be British. In a recent editorial in the *Guardian* newspaper, entitled 'Identity parade', the challenge of defining 'Britishness' stated that it is politically problematic because

> Under the combined late 20th century pressures of the collapse of industrial Britain, the weakening of post-war national institutions, the growing importance of the European Union, the rise of immigration and the Conservative party's increasing militant English-based British nationalism, Labour has struggled with the changing politics of Britishness.
>
> (*Guardian*, 2012, p. 36)

Hylton (2009) uses the notion of critical race theory to consider how racism is embedded within institutions in society, arguing that racism is endemic in all areas of society not least within the sphere of sport and sports policy. In observing the 'salience of race in society', this theory notes that

> In the public sector, underlying the development of equal opportunities policies and the 'race relations industry' since the 1950s has been a worldview that draws its reasoning from racialised, race-based discourse.
>
> (Nanton, 1989, p. 549)

Focusing on Australia, Jupp (1994, p. 74) acknowledges this constant search for the meaning of identity, emphasizing the notion of a lack of national identity. Particularly within the context of Australia's colonial past, initially dominated by the cultural and economic influence of Britain, emphasizing that it was the Aborigines not the colonists who were oppressed.

> Australian self-definition was racist towards immigrants and Aborigines. Racism was quite explicit in ostensibly radical publications such as the Bulletin, with its masthead 'Australia for the White Man' only removed in 1961.
>
> (Jupp, 1994, p. 74)

Jupp noted that, for long periods of Australian history the common view was that it was impossible for its society to become multiracial, perhaps not surprising when a whites-only policy dominated society from 1880 to the 1970s. Jupp identifies that politically and socially it was European 'settlers', most notably the Greek community, who became politically and socially influential and that Australian identity was strongly influenced by holding out 'to not being Asian':

> The dilemma that emerges is that Australia has traditionally defined itself as not being Asian and desirably insulated from Asian influences. Yet it now finds itself economically dependent on Asian trade, tourism and investment to a degree unpredicted at the end of World War II.
>
> (Jupp, 1994, p. 80)

Jupp argues that Australia became a multicultural nation in the early 1970s, influenced somewhat by the long-acknowledged injustices wrought on the indigenous population by white Australia and the repeated cultural references, relating the white settler back to their ethnic English and European identities. The following description of the Aranda people illustrates their almost ludicrous juxtaposition with the physique and even language/dialects of the English:

> The Aranda people are quite unlike other Australian Aborigines in appearance. Most of them are rather thin, with long, spindly legs, and are about the same height as Englishmen. The children quite commonly have fair hair, but as they grow older this colour steadily deepens to black, although it usually remains wavy. Their skin is usually chocolate brown in colour, not black, and their noses are broad and flat while their foreheads recede rapidly to leave the eyebrow ridges standing out prominently. In the various parts of the Aranda territory the language is spoken in different ways, just as the regional accents and dialects of England vary.
>
> (Rose, 1959, p. 9)

Considering the frame of reference and sense of superiority, it is unsurprising that indigenous Australians should be compared with Europeans and the English. Sir Robert Gordon Menzies, Australian prime minister for over 18 years between 1939 and 1966, idealized English and European culture, imaging an Australia that constantly used Europe and particularly England to define the notion of Australianness.

Literature on Australia refers to multiple conflicting notions in the formation of identity. The notion of tradition has been strongly espoused; likewise, the need for diverse cultures to recognize and embrace it. Regarding the question of Australia, notions of whiteness and 'Australianness' and the need for diverse cultures to integrate into white culture have

also been deeply engrained, even when nation builders have attempted to adopt a multiperspective approach, with considerations of social class and gender – the stereotype of the so-called Australian common man railing against English upper-class domination has long perpetuated the dominant notion of 'whiteness'. Jupp (1994) highlights that complex considerations of 'race' and cultural identity dominated Australian society for decades, being manifest in questions regarding state sensitivity to culture and its integration of multicultural viewpoints and histories. British inheritance and cultural imperialism continued to be dominant aspects of how Australian society was viewed in the 1960s, with a nostalgia for British culture pervading society.

8.5 The Creation of National Fictions

Politically, Australia established an Office of Multicultural Affairs in 1987, with social justice objectives. It was this organization that coined the phrase in the 1980s: 'multiculturalism is for all Australians' (Jupp, 1994, p. 86). However, the government brand of multiculturalism was dominated by

> an attempt to integrate immigrants (and their children) into an effectively harmonious society without alienating them by assimilationist expectations.
>
> (1994, p. 86)

For Jupp this new administrative office was not sufficiently strong to overcome the hangover of a whites-only policy, and as such there remained a black/white divide within Australian society. Clark agrees with this and argues that 'So far there have been two cultures in Australia – one aboriginal and the other European' (1980, p. 13). In exploring this duality, Meadows (1990) asked the question as to whether the portrayal of Aboriginal Australians is reporting or racism. He quotes how

> In April 1986, an article appeared in People magazine quoting at length a senior sergeant of police at Cairns police station. In the article, Senior Sargeant Vern Tim described Aborigines as 'coons', 'boongs', 'black bastards' and 'dingoes'. He continued, 'You know, I'd like to build a fence around this whole place and say

(to the Aborigines) right you bastards! Step through that fence and you're dead!'

(1990, p. 89)

Meadows reports how the police officer received an admonishment but did not lose his job and that indeed at that time this grotesque characterization of Aboriginal Australians and other ethnic groups would be the dominant image that emerged in the media. This outrageous outburst of racism has outwardly been replaced by a sensitivity of past injustices. Outwardly, within Australian society this is contrasted in 2008 with the Australian government again attempting to 'say sorry' for the injustices inflicted by white Australia on Aboriginal Australians. The then premier Kevin Rudd stated that the time had come for the nation to 'right the wrongs' on a 'stolen generation'.

8.6 Inescapable Cultural Geographies and Representations of Australian Society

If, as Mackay (1993) states, a nation is defined by its geography (both physical and human), the inescapable fact of Australia's geography is that its location is essentially Asian, and as such it should embrace this cultural certainty. Those certainties were not always prevalent, and indeed in the 1980s Australia returned to its rural nostalgia and the 'common Australian' through the film *Crocodile Dundee*. O'Regan noted:

> In sheer monetary terms and international recognition value, Crocodile Dundee represents a highpoint in Australian cinema output. In its first week of release in Australia it made 2 million (Aus dollars). By its eleventh week it had surpassed ET as the most successful Australian release ever.
>
> (1998, p. 156)

The film was viewed as the embodiment of populist, Australian masculinity, and indeed 'Australianness'. O'Regan, in examining the discourse around the film, notes

> a recurring feature of the public discussion of the film in Australia and overseas was at times, trenchant and inevitably 'intellectual' criticism of it for the kind of image of Australia and

Australians it furthered. This outlook was encapsulated in the question 'but is this the kind of thing we should be showing to Americans (and to the world) about us?' These critics were offended by backwardness, and 'outbackness' when they would rather have had an affirmation of Australia as a modern urban society.

> (1998, p. 167)

In 2008 the M&C Saatchi promotional campaign for Tourism Australia used a key theme, redolent of some of the values of 'Australianness' that were espoused in the *Crocodile Dundee* movie. These values were embodied in the 'So Where the Bloody Hell Are You?' marketing campaign and strap-line (Sweney, 2008). The then Minister for Tourism turned on critics of the campaign, claiming that they did not have a sense of humour. In contrast to his view, the fact that one of the campaign films featured a bikini-clad woman was viewed by critics as being an anachronistic view of a male-dominated and sexist society. However, it also was the bluntness of the language that accompanied the image below that external audiences found overly frank and offensive (see Fig. 8.1).

The campaign was later replaced by a video offshoot of the movie *Australia* directed by the Australian film director Baz Luhrmann. In the video Luhrmann uses a young Aboriginal boy to bring tired city workers on 'walkabout' into the Australian outback and in the process discover the authentic Australian natural environment. Symbolically more than that, tourists were encouraged to be guided by an Aboriginal boy to see the 'real' Australia, through the eyes of an empowered Aboriginal Australian (see Fig. 8.2).

In cultural tourism terms, Hall highlighted how

> culture has been shown to be a major determinant in the attractiveness of a destination for tourists and may provide an opportunity for marginal communities, such as Aboriginal groups to develop a strong economic base. However, it is possible that undesirable social and cultural change may result from the commoditisation of cultural artefacts, identity and performances, including the issue of the perceived authenticity of the tourist experience and the role that tourism plays in altering a sense of place.
>
> (1991, p. 155)

Fig. 8.1. Image of 'So Where the Bloody Hell Are You?' (From http://theinspirationroom.com/daily/2006/ tourism-australia/)

Fig. 8.2. Image of Baz Luhrmann's indigeous Australian boy. (From screen capture from *Australia*.)

Clearly, there are different potential interpretations of the Baz Luhrmann video and the tensions between the so-called authenticity of cultural tourism and the potential over-commoditization of Aboriginal culture as a key selling point for Australia. Within a UK context there is also an attempt to revisit past notions of cultural identity, and in this instance the notion being explored is the Great in Britain, which is heavily imbued with colonial overtones.

8.7   Great Britain in 2012

Examining the London 2012 Olympics suggests that blending sport and the five London boroughs wherein the Olympics were hosted provides an opportunity for multicultural identity to be celebrated and become integrated or even assimilated into so-called 'British culture'. From the outset the Olympic Delivery Authority highlighted the importance of diversity in the planning, implementation and legacy considerations of the London 2012 Games. This is exemplified in a multi-racial group of children who accompanied Lord Coe to hear the decision of the International Olympic Committee Bid Outcome in Singapore in 2005 for 2012. There is a rich cultural diversity in the five London boroughs to the east of London, surrounding the Lea Valley where the major Olympic facilities were based: Newham (East), Tower Hamlets (West), Greenwich (South), Hackney (North West) and Waltham Forest, reflecting a snapshot of the UK's multicultural society. Multiculturalism as a concept incorporates the notion of contested racialized spaces, identified earlier in the chapter; however, the Great British tourism marketing campaign and subsequent images are redolent of Morgan and Pritchard's (1999) notion that tourism marketing creates identities that represent certain realities, however stereotypical. While attractive, these images (see Fig. 8.3) have missed a real opportunity to move British culture in a more multicultural direction.

How then were these racialized spaces contained within the marketing of Britain in 2012, for both London 2012 and the cultural Olympiad? Were the residents of the London boroughs invisible within the marketing of the Great British Isles? The campaign not only received criticism because it encouraged people in Britain to stay at home rather than go abroad during London 2012 and the Jubilee celebrations, but also for the symbolism and colonial overtones of a Great Britain. The images in Fig. 8.3 were designed to promote Great British music, culture and identity, but largely ignored the rich tradition within the UK of non-white musicians, performers, artists and culture.

Within a UK context, consideration has also been made by marketers of the capacity UK cities have for forming a distinctive multicultural identity. This emerged during the shortlisting of UK cities for the European City of Culture bidding process, which was won by Liverpool in 2008. Bradford was also a bidding city prominently using its image as a British multicultural city in the bidding process (Williams, 2010). However, as was seen during the summer riots of 2011, UK political leaders have an uncertain and uneasy understanding of the social and cultural ecology of cities. There

is tension between the capacity of so-called multicultural cities to be promoted as a focus for tourism through festivals, carnivals and Mela, yet at the same time parts of these cities are viewed negatively because of intercultural tensions. The so-called legacy promises of the London 2012 Olympics will determine to what extent multicultural communities in the five London boroughs will benefit from infrastructural 'improvements' and international tourist visitation.

8.8   Summary

This chapter, in looking at two multicultural societies, has revealed contradictions in promoting multiculturalism as a product for tourism. Despite the perennial questioning of national and cultural identity, arguably Australia can lay claim to becoming a multicultural nation (perhaps more by accident), albeit a multicultural nation with insoluble contradictions it would seem. As such, Australia has had to absorb the moniker of a 'backward' nation and an immigrant society (Jupp, 1994). This has implications beyond the narrowing activities of 'marketing a nation', to fundamental questions of whether certain cultures enjoy hegemonic preferences in their place in society and the way that the world sees and consumes that nation.

With regard to established literature on cultural tourism, there is a traditional narrative of the Western tourist engaging with and defining cultures to be consumed. The complexity of multicultural discourses does not always emerge in these discussions, as tourism often seeks a simple and easy-to-consume narrative. This chapter has attempted to address the imbalance in academic discourse by using multiculturalism as the prism for considerations of cultural tourism engagement within both a British and Australian context.

In June 2012 Ed Miliband, leader of the UK Labour Party, proved that this struggle to grasp the concept of multicultural identity is still alive, when in a speech he reopened the debate about what it means to be British. This was a serendipitous reminder for a nation steeped in Jubilee fervour but at the same time trying to determine its national identity (Miliband, 2012).

Fig. 8.3. Great British Marketing Campaign. (From various links on the www.republikkreatif.com website – particularly http://www.republikkreatif.com/tourism-advertising-and-marketing-poster-design-of-great-britain-brand-campaign-uk/)

In a similar respect, Mackay (1993, p. 154) talks of an 'Age of Redefinition' for Australia. It could be argued that Australia has always been in a state of flux, not just in terms of redefinition but in trying to define what it means to be Australian. Likewise, the UK, despite its bold marketing campaign trying to put the Great back in Britain, is still in search of a national identity, communicating uncertain and tentative claims of a national harmonious identity within discourses of multiculturalism.

8.9   Discussion Questions

*   Can cultural tourism be a vehicle for expressions of national identity?
*   Should tourism image-making for cultural tourism incorporate images of cultural diversity?
*   Will tourism visitation to the London 2012 Olympics provide a lasting cultural legacy for the residents of the five London Olympic boroughs?

References

BBC News (2004) 'So what exactly is multiculturalism?' BBC News, 5 April. http://news.bbc.co.uk/mpapps/pagetools/print/news.bbc.co.uk/1/hi/uk/3600791.stm (accessed 1 February 2008).

Berger, P., Douglas, M., Foucault, M. and Habermas, J. (1984) *Cultural Analysis*. Routledge, Boston, Massachusetts.

Clark, M. (1980) *A Short History of Australia*. Mentor, USA.

Cohen, E. (1988) Authenticity and commoditisation in tourism. *Annals of Tourism Research* 3, 371–386.

Cooper, C. (2009) *Community, Conflict and the State: Rethinking Notions of 'Safety', 'Cohesion' and 'Well-being'*. Palgrave, London.

Galbally Report (1978) *Review of Post Arrival Programs and Services for Migrants*. Australian Government Publishing Services, Canberra.

Guardian (2012) Editorial. Britishness: identity parade. *Guardian* 8 June.

Hall, C.M. (1991) *Tourism in Australia: Impacts, Planning and Development*. Longman, Melbourne, Australia.

Hill, C.P. (1975) *British Economic and Social History 1700–1964*. Western Printing Services, Bristol, UK.

Hylton, K. (2009) *'Race' and Sport: Critical Race Theory*. Routledge, London.

Jupp, J. (1994) 'Identity'. In: Nile, R. (ed.) *Australian Civilisation*. Oxford University Press, Melbourne, Australia, pp. 74–92.

Levey, G.B. (ed.) (2008) *Political Theory and Australian Multiculturalism*. Berghann Books, New York.

MacCannell, D. (1976) *The Tourist: A New Theory of the Leisure Class*. Schoclen Books, New York.

Mackay, H. (1993) *Reinventing Australia: The Mind and Mood of Australia in the 90s*. Angus and Robertson, Sydney, Australia.

Meadows, M. (1990) Portryal of Aboriginal Australians: reporting or racism? In: Henningham, J. (ed.) *Issues in Australian Journalism*. Longman, Melbourne, Australia, pp. 89–98.

Meer, N. and Modood, T. (2012) How does interculturalism contrast with multiculturalism? *Journal of Intercultural Studies* 33, 175–196.

Miliband, E. (2012) 'Ed Miliband Speech – Defending the Union in England'. http://www.labour.org.uk/ed-miliband-speech-defending-the-union-in-england (accessed 7 June 2012).

Morgan, N. and Pritchard, A. (1999) *Tourism Promotion and Power: Creating Images, Creating Identities*. Wiley, Chichester, UK.

Nanton, P. (1989) The new orthodoxy: racial categories and equal opportunity policy. *Journal of Ethnic and Migration Studies* 15, 549–564.

Nuryanti, W. (1996) Redefining cultural heritage through post-modern tourism. In: Robinson, M., Evans, N. and Callaghan, P. (eds) *Managing Cultural Resources for the Tourist*. Athanaeum Press, Gateshead, UK, pp. 335–348.

O'Regan, T. (1988) Fair dinkum fillums': The Crocodile Dundee phenomenon. In: Dermody, S. and Jacka, E. (eds) *The Imaginary Industry*. AFTRS, Sydney, Australia.

Rose, A.J. (1959) *How People Live in Australia*. The Educational Supply Association Ltd, London.

Storry, M. and Childs, P. (1997) *British Cultural Identities*. Routledge, London.

Sweney, M. (2008) Tourism Australia drops M+C Saatchi. http://www.guardian.co.uk/media/2008/may/08/advertising.marketingandpr (accessed 11 June 2012).

Urry, J. (1990) *The Tourist Gaze: Leisure and Travel in Contemporary Societies*. Sage, London.

Vertovec, S. (1999) Minority associations, networks and public policies: re-assessing relationships. *Journal of Ethnic and Migration Studies* 25, 21–42.

Vertovec, S. (2007) Super-diversity and its implications. *Ethnic and Racial Studies* 30, 1024–1054.

Walker, M. (1977) *The National Front*. Fontana, Glasgow, Scotland.

Watson, G.L. and Kopachevsky, J.P. (1996) Interpretations of tourism as commodity. In: Apostlopaulos, Y., Leivadi, S. and Yiannakis, A. (eds) *The Sociology of Tourism: Theoretical and Empirical Investigation*. Routledge, Oxford, pp. 281–296.

Williams, P. (2010) Cultural Tourism and the UK City of Culture. April. http://www.insights.org.uk (accessed 11 June 2012).

9 Case Study 1: Irish Cultural Tourism – Case Study of Policy Development

Catherine Gorman

Dublin Institute of Technology, Dublin, Ireland

This chapter will discuss and analyse gardens and historic houses in the context of cultural tourism. This exploration will be placed within the context of policy development reflecting on the various policies. The chapter will further clarify the commodification of culture in order to provide a resource for tourism consumption and is an area that has attracted much debate. Provision of a tourist attraction is complex and involves many different levels such as the visitor, place/product development (tangible/intangible) and marketing. The tension between these pillars of provision requires constant rebalancing: provider and market needs are dynamic and a state of equilibrium is required to ensure that all involved will benefit.

9.1 Introduction

> Tourism can be seen as a more static spatial semiosis marking out places and objects for special attention, defining sites to be seen and making sights out of sites.
>
> (Crang, 1999, p. 240)

Gardens and historic houses have always been a source of interest and fascination to people. Outside the plant life and floral displays, structured or unstructured landscaping becomes a place of leisure and recreation, of relaxation and reflection. 'In a garden, physical work, mental reasoning and spiritual appreciation are synthesised' (Cox, 1990, p. 25).

Gardens are considered part of the cultural landscape – landscapes designed and created intentionally by humans. In Ireland there are over 300 gardens and historic houses open to the public (see http://www.garden.ie or http://www.discoverireland.ie). The use of gardens and historic houses as part of the tourism resource spans continents from the formal gardens and houses of England, France and Italy, to the religious gardens of India and Japan. However, in commodifying a garden or a historic house to become a tourist attraction there is a change in emphasis from resource provision to visitor consumption.

9.2 Gardens and Historic Houses in the Context of Cultural Tourism

The commodification of culture in order to provide a resource for tourism consumption is an area that has attracted much debate. According to the National Trust in the UK, cultural tourism can be defined as visiting and participating in living cultures, often in urban areas, and tends to be less place-bound than heritage tourism. Heritage tourism is often viewed as antiquated relics, often in rural areas and is more place-bound than cultural tourism. The content or resource is often the same, but the context is different. Rypkema and Cheong (2011), in measuring economic impacts of historic preservation in the US, reported that there is no clear definition of heritage tourism and it is difficult therefore to assess either its growth or decline.

It is increasingly evident that the ambiguous nature of intangibility contributes to cultural tourism. It can be a set of descriptors of a traditional way of living, associated with times past, or it can refer to present-day lifestyles.

> Culture should be regarded as the set of distinctive spiritual, material, intellectual, and emotional features of society or a society group that encompasses it in addition to art and literature, lifestyles, ways of living together, traditions, value systems and belief.
> (UNESCO, 2001)

However, where do gardens and heritage houses in Ireland fit within these definitions? Fáilte Ireland (the National Tourism Development Authority for Ireland), as part of their cultural tourism strategy, have a wide definition of cultural tourism, listing 28 different elements, including gardens and castles and historic properties. The tourist board visitor website (http://www.discoverireland.ie) lists information on 221 gardens and 282 castles and historic houses. Both feature highly in the activities pursued by overseas visitors to the country, as can be seen by the figures in Table 9.1.

9.3 Aspects of Policy in Ireland Relating to Gardens and Historic Houses

Policy in relation to culture and heritage provision in Irish tourism is complex in its formulation and implementation. Kelly (2006, p. 40) set out the background of policy provision in Ireland; however, since then political change has led to changes in responsibilities and

Table 9.1. Summary of overseas visitors engaging in historical/cultural activities (houses/castles and gardens) in 2010. (Fáilte Ireland, 2010a.)

	All activities	Houses/castles	Gardens
No. engaging (000s)	2752	2349	1255
Share by market %			
Britain	27	24	23
North Europe	43	44	47
France	7	7	8
Germany	9	10	8
Italy	6	6	6
North America	22	24	21
Other long haul	8	8	9

remits. At a national level, in 2012 there are four government departments that impact on policy in relation to gardens and historic houses. Changes in government or their reorganization, while inherently sympathetic to the conservation of gardens and historic houses, contributes to short periods of stability in relation to their provision and management. There are also a number of other bodies that have an interest in gardens and historic houses. Table 9.2 attempts to clarify the present (2012) situation.

In the public domain, local authorities own a number of the gardens and historic houses and these operate under the aegis of the Department of the Environment, Community and Local Government (http://www.environ.ie). Examples include Belvedere House and Demesne, County Westmeath and the Vandaleur Gardens in County Clare.

The Office of Public Works is located within the Department of Public Expenditure and Reform. Its remit is to manage and maintain the state property portfolio. This consists of 65 sites dispersed throughout the country, which attract over 2.5 million fee-paying visitors, including 20 historic properties with significant gardens, such as Emo Court and Heywood Gardens, both located in County Laois.

Table 9.2. Policy organizations and context.

Departments/bodies	Agency and responsibility	Garden and historic house context
Department of Environment, Community and Local Government (DECLG) http://www.environ.ie	Local Authorities	Publically owned spaces and places (e.g. Belvedere House and Garden, County Westmeath, Talbot Gardens, County Dublin)
Department of Public Expenditure and Reform (DPER)	Office of Public Work http://www.opw.ie http://www.heritageireland.ie	Twenty historic properties (e.g. Emo Court, County Laois, Muckross House and Gardens, County Kerry)
Department of Arts, Heritage and the Gaeltacht (DAHG) http://www.ahg.gov.ie	National Inventory of Architectural Heritage (NIAH) http://www.buildingsofIreland.ie	Survey and information on all gardens and houses of historic interest in both public and private ownership
	The Heritage Council http://www.heritagecouncil.ie	Remit on built and natural heritage, including gardens and heritage houses
Department of Transport, Tourism and Sport (DTTS) http://www.transport.ie	Tourism Ireland Limited http://www.til.ie	The marketing of the island of Ireland (north and south)
	Shannon Development http://www.shannondevelopment.ie	Support and marketing of gardens and historic houses in the mid-west region
	Fáilte Ireland http://www.Fáilte ireland.ie	Support and marketing of gardens and historic houses in the Republic of Ireland
Other bodies	ICOMOS Ireland http://www.icomos.ie	International Council on Monuments and Sites in Ireland
	An Taisce/Irish National Trust http://www.antaisce.ie	Independent monitoring body focusing mainly on planning issues
	Irish Historic House Association http://www.ihh.ie	Owners of private historic houses who hold events and seminars on topics such as sustainability and energy conservation
	Irish Georgian Society http://www.igs.ie	Specific interest in the conservation and use of Irish historic buildings

The Department of Arts, Heritage and the Gaeltacht (DAHG) has responsibility for national parks and wildlife, national monuments and built heritage, and architectural policy. The National Inventory of Architectural Heritage (NIAH) is located under the DAHG and includes both architectural and garden heritage. Research to identify historic gardens of note revealed that 6000 gardens existed at the time of the First Ordnance Survey in the mid-19th century. Phase 1 and 2 of this research are complete. Phase 3 will assess the heritage merit, and phase 4 will include designation, policy provision, planning and protection. The inventory of historic gardens and designed landscapes won a Europa Nostra Award in 2009, recognizing its important contribution to knowledge of the national cultural and heritage resource. Although many of the gardens are in private ownership, this inventory will help to direct future appropriate utilization within the tourism sector.

The DAHG also oversees the Heritage Council, which was set up under the Heritage Act 1995 with the objective of promoting public interest, knowledge, appreciation and protection of both the built and natural heritage of Ireland. Their remit includes heritage buildings of intrinsic architectural significance, heritage objects (over 25 years old) and heritage gardens and parks (collections and designs of significant botanical/historic interest).

Responsibility for supporting and marketing culture and heritage within the tourism sector lies within the Department of Transport, Tourism and Sport (DTTS). Its remit is

> to support the growth of a competitive and sustainable tourism industry, enhancing its contribution to national economic and social goals, through the development, implementation and influence of a range of policy actions and programmes by the Department, its Agencies and other Government Departments, in consultation with industry partners.
>
> (DTTS, 2012a)

There are three agencies directly involved with the provision, support and marketing of tourism: Tourism Ireland Limited (TIL) is an all-Ireland body that was set up under the Good Friday Agreement and has the remit of overseas marketing; Fáilte Ireland has responsibility for destination and product development, with an emphasis on partnerships and networks, domestic marketing and all aspects of support for the industry; and Shannon Development hold this latter remit for the mid-west of the country.

One of the main issues in Irish tourism cited by the DTTS when establishing a new tourism authority in 2002 was the 'development and appropriate management of a range of cultural and heritage activities capable of being marketed overseas' (DTTS, 2012b). Many of the resources that contribute to these activities, whether they are passive or more experiential, lie in the gardens and historic houses of the country. Within the tourism sector, Fáilte Ireland/Shannon Development have the most impact in terms of policy implementation.

In the mid-1980s an initiative involving horizontal cooperation between tourism suppliers was facilitated by the national tourism development authority Bord Fáilte (now Fáilte Ireland/Tourism Ireland Limited). Bord Fáilte invited a number of the more successful gardens to become members of a group using the name 'Only the Best'. It was this group that formed the original membership of the Houses, Castles and Gardens of Ireland. This segmentation of the tourism industry into different activities identified the need to cater for the specific needs of visitors within these segments, creating a capacity of product that could act as a referral system for visitors. It also brought together people who, in operating and offering a related tourism product, had to deal with similar issues. Another objective of the groups was to create better efficiencies in dealing with the support systems in place.

The need to invest in gardens rather than houses, and their importance as a tourism resource, was recognized in the early 1990s. Through implementation of the Operational Programme for Tourism 1994–1999 (Bord Fáilte, 1994) many of the gardens availed of substantial funding via the Great Gardens of Ireland Restoration Scheme (GGRS), which was administered as part of the programme between 1996 and 2001 (Gorman and Reid, 2000). A dedicated manager was responsible for the management of the scheme and during this time some 26 gardens availed of the funding. Houses could also be facilitated through the Operational Programme if they were prepared to become a tourist attraction or provide accommodation in the form of a hotel.

Then, because of its enhanced economy, Ireland lost European Objective 1 status and there has been a sharp decline in grant aid available for the development of products within the tourism sector. However, under the Regional Aid (Tourism) Scheme 2007–2013 (Commission ref. XR 18/2008), up to €6 million was made available for investment in historic or 'Great Gardens' (Fáilte Ireland, 2008a). As well as upgrading of other gardens that had been previously funded, new ornamental gardens of international merit are also considered. Historic houses are not considered unless they are part of a flagship attraction.

In addition to implementing policy through the allocation of funding, provision of support and marketing, Fáilte Ireland in conjunction with the Revenue Commissioners publishes a list of properties of significant historic interest that open their doors to the public for not less than 60 days a year. This opening of the properties is to facilitate a tax exemption scheme (Section 482, Taxes Consolidation Act, 1997), which allows tax relief on repair, maintenance and restoration of buildings and gardens considered to be of intrinsic significance from a cultural and heritage perspective (Fáilte Ireland, 2008b).

A cultural tourism strategy was developed by Fáilte Ireland (2006). The definition given to cultural tourism by Fáilte Ireland in this document is based on that developed by the Commonwealth of Australia Creative Nation 1994, which seeks to encapsulate lifestyles, heritage, the arts and the people that make a destination different. There is a need to develop experiences that can be delivered to visitors and, mindful of this need, the strategy identifies the holistic nature of cultural tourism that is part of a visitor's experience in terms of demand, and recognizes that access and interpretation is essential in order for it to be utilized by the visitor (Fáilte Ireland, 2006). A priority of this programme is improvement of the cultural assets on a sustainable basis, thereby optimizing their value.

There are several other bodies within Ireland that have interest in gardens and historic houses as part of the cultural tourism resource. These may be independent or of a charitable status and include ICOMOS Ireland, An Taisce (Ireland's National Trust), the Irish Historic House Association (IHH) and the Irish Georgian Society (IGS). ICOMOS Ireland is the Irish arm of the International Council on Monuments and Sites. The structure of the organization includes a number of national scientific committees (NSC) that feature gardens and historic houses as part of their remit. These include the NSC for cultural landscapes, cultural tourism and vernacular architecture. An Taisce/the National Trust focuses mainly on planning issues and is an independent monitoring body. The Irish Historic House Association is the most recently formed of these organizations (2008) and at present (2012) has 49 members. It has been formed to address issues commonly affecting these types of properties. The Irish Georgian Society was founded in 1958 by the Hon. Desmond Guinness. It attracts both funding and support from all over the world and is concerned with the promotion and protection of Ireland's architectural heritage.

9.4   Gardens and Historic Houses in Ireland

Gardens are ephemeral because they are created, change and disappear over time, so often it may be a reference in a book or document or even oral history that allows them to live on, or to be restored. Historic houses have more durable structures however, but also require care and maintenance. According to Fox and Edwards (2008), gardens open to the public have developed in five different ways (see Fig. 9.1).

Bowe and Nelson (1988) in conjunction with ICOMOS identified 47 gardens and parks of international significance and a further 23 of national importance in the Republic of Ireland. This work was undertaken with a view to conservation of the identified parks and gardens and has provided the rationale for funding some of these gardens in terms of restoration.

Fig. 9.1. Five ways gardens open to the public have developed. (From Fox and Edwards, 2008.)

However, some have been lost through sale, change of ownership or use.

In Ireland the art of gardening arrived with Christianity (about AD 500) and the Roman-educated Christians brought knowledge and skills from abroad to both Great Britain and Ireland:

> Ecclesiastics were not only the rulers and the lawyers, the arbiters, the almoners, the architects, musicians, painters of the nation; they were the farmers and the gardeners also. They dug and drained, they planted and sowed, they made the desert smile.
>
> (Hole, 1899, p. 39)

The history of gardening in Ireland has been documented by several authors, including Pim (1979) and Lamb and Bowe (1995). The use of plants in medicines and as cures was commonplace over the following centuries. *A Treatise of Medicine and Botany* was written in 1432 by Donal Og O'Herlihy. A copy of this can be viewed in the Royal Irish Academy in Dublin. The interest in medicinal plants, herbs and flowers was embraced by the Christian Church around the world and included the Abbey of Cassino, which was created in Italy in AD 1070. This was viewed by many as a piece of paradise influenced by Roman fashion. A mix of vegetables for culinary use and flowers for pleasure were cultivated alongside each other in this abbey garden, and this approach to mixed gardening, now termed 'potager', was echoed in many monasteries throughout Europe.

One of the first books (1485) that addressed garden design was written by Leon Battista Alberti, *De re aedificatoria*, which, although it was considered a classical architectural treatise, viewed ornament and garden design as a part of design and building. The theory of propagation and geometry was a prelude to garden design and very much linked to the influence of the Italian renaissance villas that were built by the de Medici family in Italy. Of note are Villa Cassello (1537) and Boboli gardens (1550).

A number of factors influence the 'art of gardening' in Ireland. Countries with the greatest diversity of climate, such as France, are home to 4000 species and the range of climate allows the growth of thousands of exotics (Taylor, 1998). Ireland, which has less climatic range, is separated from mainland Europe and is far smaller (83,000 km^2), is home to only 1309 vascular plant species. During the 18th century, the landscapes of France were an influence on gardens in Ireland (and Great Britain) and a more formal approach to gardening was adopted. Two different traditions emerged – the 17th-century baroque gardens and the municipal gardens. This 17th-century French influence can be seen at Killruddery in County Wicklow, which is one of the most intact early gardens in Ireland. In the late 18th century, an increasing Anglo-Italianate influence in France saw huge increase in the number of public parks. This Italian and English influence also impacted on trends in gardening throughout the rest of Europe, including Ireland.

The first recorded example of a formal garden in Ireland is that of the Great Earl of Cork, The College, Youghal in Co. Cork, and this was described in 1681. The garden was created in 1620 and this is the only Jacobean Garden to survive in its original form today. Also during this period, in 1682, Lord Granard of Castleforbes in County Longford created one of the first documented gardens. This garden and demesne are still in the family, though are not open to the public.

The British landscape movement (1700s) introduced a new formal approach to garden design. It was in the mid-18th century that Capability Brown, and later his successor Humphrey Repton, introduced picturesque elements and flowerbeds to gardens. However, in the mid-19th century, the tide and fashion again changed, from a more formal approach of planting to one that respected the natural habitats of plants.

The Georgian era of the 18th century was a period of significance that has contributed some of the finest historic buildings of tourism interest. These include Castletown House and Carton House in County Kildare (see Fig. 9.2). Large rooms, ornate ceilings and interior plasterwork, often undertaken by Italian plaster workers brought to Ireland by the wealthy, typify this era (Dargan, 2008). The ornate stucco and rococo interior plasterwork that is associated with Georgian architecture, along with the Georgian doorway, is a familiar tourism image used to promote Dublin abroad. There is more Georgian architecture in Dublin than in any other city in the world.

The National Botanic Gardens in Dublin, Ireland, was founded in 1795. The Belfast Botanic Garden was founded in 1828 by Thomas Drummond. The glass house there was built by Turner, who is also responsible for the curvilinear glasshouse range in the National Botanic Gardens, Dublin. The glasshouse was used to house the exotic collections of plants that had been collected from throughout the New World and required humid and often tropical climates to survive.

In 1870 in Britain the Irish landscape gardener William Robinson published the *Wild Garden* and pioneered a more ecological approach to gardening, which up until then had been quite formal in both planting and appearance. The sweep of planting and the wildness of native habitats were allowed to make an appearance and this characterizes many of the gardens open to the public in Ireland today, such as Mount Usher in County Wicklow (see Fig. 9.3).

Exploration and plant hunting in China, such as that undertaken by Augustine Henry in the late 19th and early 20th centuries, led to the introduction of many species, some of which are named after the western plant hunters, for example *Parthenocissus henryii* (after Augustine Henry) and *Rhododendron maddenii*, which is named after an officer in the Bengali army whose family came from Kilkenny (Nelson and McCracken, 1987). The search for the exotic and unusual meant that plants of

Fig. 9.2. Carton House, Co. Kildare, Ireland. (From Author.)

Fig. 9.3. View of Mount Usher in about 1902. (From Walpole n.d.)

note were plundered during the Victorian times. In Ireland, the Killarney Fern (*Trichomanes speciosum*) was often taken from the wild for fern gardens, a speciality of the time. The Irish climate is benign and dictated by a south-westerly influence, humid temperate conditions and the warming effect of the North Atlantic Drift. This has allowed many of these exotic/non-native plants to thrive in Irish gardens and indeed at times become alien invasives, for example *Rhododendron ponticum* (in Kerry) and *Gunnera tinctoria* (on Clare Island).

During the 19th and early 20th centuries historical events (two Acts of Law, the Great Irish Famine and civil unrest) had direct impacts on both Irish gardens and historic houses. As the properties were primarily owned by the Anglo-Irish aristocracy and some of the owners were absent for much of the year, through political negotiation the Encumbered Estates Act of 1849 was passed, which encouraged tenants to buy out their farms and over 5 million hectares changed ownership. The exodus from Ireland during the famine, especially of the tenant classes, meant that cheap labour was less available to work on the estate gardens and in the large demesne houses. In the early 20th century, the Land Acts (1923), which was legislated a year after Ireland achieved independence, empowered an organization called the Land Commission to purchase land by compulsory order, and over 120,000 hectares were purchased and sub-divided among farmers. These various events, in addition to the burning of

some of the large houses during this time due to civil unrest (Johnson, 1996), meant that by the mid-20th century the stock of Irish houses and gardens was much diminished in numbers, and those that survived were ridden with a lack of resources to maintain and manage their existence.

During the early 20th century a partnership between Gertrude Jekyll and Edward Lutyens set a trend in terms of both architectural and planting style, and their use of compartments within a garden had an influence on garden design in Ireland. Examples of these can be seen in Heywood Gardens, County Laois and at the Memorial gardens, Islandbridge in Dublin. Dating from this period, and typical of its time, Mount Stewart in County Down is set on 32.4 ha (80 acres) and the lime-free soil makes it suitable for ericaceous plants such as heathers and rhododendrons.

Located in Britain and regarded as an iconic garden of the 20th century, Vita Sackville-West created Sissinghurst in 1932. This garden has had lasting influence on the design of many more recent gardens in Ireland, such as Butterstream, located in Trim, County Meath. However, the late 20th century has seen modernist designers with no one specific style. A mix of formal, cottage (informal) (Ram House, County Wicklow) and modern may exist together. The increase in close-proximity housing with small urban gardens, less time due to work commitments and post-modern influences have led to the demand for 'instant' low-maintenance gardens and the use of hard structure such as decking, paths and pergolas vying for importance in the garden space. There is an emphasis in bringing the indoors outside and creating an 'outside' room. Gardens have become an extension of the house and part of lifestyle living (Taylor, 2002).

The emphasis on instant gardens, created within a day/weekend, is very much the theme on which a number of television garden programmes has been based, for example 'Home Front' and 'Ground Force', 'where the promise is to have paradise without the hassle of exerting physical energy' (Hewer, 2003, p. 330). However, since 2007 there has been a reversion back to a more traditional approach to gardening and this is becoming more evident through the increased emphasis on 'growing your own' (vegetables) and eco- and nature-oriented media programmes. While there has always been a plethora of gardening magazines in Great Britain, there is also an increased number of Irish magazines devoted to gardening, with *An Irish Garden* and *Garden Heaven* holding their own within the marketplace. Books on both gardening and gardens are published in increasing numbers, many with large, glossy pictures and emphasis on the beauty rather than the reality of gardens and gardening.

9.5   Consuming Gardens and Historic Houses as a Tourism Experience

Gardens and historic houses are considered part of the built and managed heritage. Market segments attracted to these places vary: visitors from the local community; day attraction visitors seeking a 'something to do' experience; tourists visiting the area; and individuals and groups with a specialized interest such as plant people, architects and historians whose motivation to visit the garden or historic houses is central to the decision-making process. The pull–push factors vary from one segment to another. Ease of access and location, unique features, available interpretation and information all contribute to motivation to visit.

According to Connell (2005), visiting country houses and gardens in Great Britain has been documented by several authors (Girouard, 1987; Hoskins, 1988; Towner, 1996; Mandler, 1997). Fox and Edwards (2008) more recently have evaluated visitors to a number of gardens in southern England in the context of gardens providing social and natural spaces. The visiting of gardens became particularly important in the Victorian era when motivation was driven by the growth in leisure pursuits and was stimulated by transport improvements, the desire to escape urban life, more disposable income, an increase in leisure time and changing attitudes to rural life (Connell, 2005). Johnson (2007) remarks on a lady named Anne Plumptre who visited Ireland a little earlier than this, in 1814, and noted that Irish gardens were larger than expected and well laid out, though the collections of exotics and conservatories were not as good as those

seen at Kew in London. However, in Victorian times, because Ireland had much smaller middle- and upper-class societies than in Great Britain, garden and country house visiting were not as prevalent. Those involved with botany, however, did visit each other's gardens. Up until the 1990s, when the Office of Public Works took over its management from the Department of Agriculture, the National Botanic Gardens in Dublin were not considered specifically a tourist attraction, whereas its counterpart in Kew, London, has been attracting visitors for over two centuries.

Groups such as the Royal Horticultural Society (RHS) in Great Britain, founded in 1804, the Royal Horticultural Society of Ireland (RHSI), founded in 1816, the International Dendrological Society (IDS), founded in 1952, and the Irish Garden Plant Society (IGPS), founded in 1983, as well as many local groups, have encouraged an interest in plants, gardens and garden visiting. This interest is still active to the present day – but why visit a garden or historic house? 'Gardens are widely regarded as sources of freedom and play, havens of pleasure away from the world of control and constraint' (Bale, 1999, p. 56). Originally a raw physical environment, a garden is a space that has been developed for the purposes of consumption, 'not primarily for production, but for appropriation' (Urry, 1999, p. 35). The three other ways, according to Urry (1999), in which society may interact with a physical environment are through stewardship (caring for), exploitation and scientization. Garden and historic house tourism can be viewed as a mix of these and in striving to be sustainable it creates equilibrium between provider, visitor and nature (environment).

It is noted in the Republic of Ireland that there has been a significant increase (over 200%) in visitors to gardens between 2005 and 2010, with an increase of 21% to historic houses over the same period. Statistics within the sector are difficult to extract because definitional contexts of gardens and historic houses have changed over the period. However, they do demonstrate an increase in demand. (see Table 9.3).

From the late 1980s to the late 1990s gardens open to the public in Ireland were considered a separate tourism product. In 1997

Table 9.3. Overseas visitor numbers to gardens and historic houses in Ireland 2005 and 2010. (From Fáilte Ireland (2010b) and Gorman (2010).)

Year	Overseas visitors (000s)	
	Gardens	Historic houses
2005	419	1989
2010	1290	2414

gardens became integrated as part of the heritage product and joined forces with the 'Big House', due to the similarity of the markets that were attracted to them. Dooley (2003) found that in 'real terms', when researching historic houses, tourist numbers had declined to these attractions. One of the reasons was the fact that Ireland does not have the indigenous population to support such attractions and an increase in the number of properties open to the public has spread the demand. The government subsequently commissioned a report by Indecon (2004), and this resulted in the formation of the Irish Heritage Trust in 2006 by the then Department of Environment, Heritage and Local Government (http://www.irishheritagetrust.ie). Tax relief for donations to the trust are allowed under Section 1003 of the Taxes Consolidation Act 1997. Since that time, they have only acquired one property (Fota, County Cork); however, this garden and demesne attracted 377,004 visitors in 2010.

Some regard that many of the gardens may benefit from their association with a 'Big House'. Increasingly, integrated tourism development has been the path taken by some of the larger houses and estates, for example Ballyfin in County Laois (5* hotel), Lissadell House in Sligo (in new private ownership), Farnham Castle in Cavan (hotel and golf club), and Powerscourt House and Gardens in County Wicklow (shopping, golf and accommodation – attracting over 200,000 visitors in 2010). However, some people and organizations (e.g. An Taisce/National Trust) are unhappy with the change in use of some of the houses and gardens (Lumley, 2007), considering this change inappropriate. Dooley (2003) takes recommendations from Owen in 2002, who assessed the sustainable tourism potential of historic properties under the management of

An Taisce and advocated a trust approach to ownership rather than a government approach. It was hoped that the establishment of the Irish Heritage Trust would give support to some of these estates and gardens, restoring them to a more appropriate use. However, this has yet to take place.

9.6   Issues Facing Gardens and Historic Houses

A number of issues face gardens and historic houses in Ireland. There is increasing pressure and costs associated with their development and maintenance. Land, especially in the Dublin area, increased in value exponentially from the early 1990s and this resulted in the demise or uncertain future of some gardens. Examples of those places sold include Fernhill, Sandyford and Kensington Lodge, both in Dublin, and Carigglas Manor (stables designed by Gandon) in County Longford. Dooley (2003), evaluating 50 historic houses in Ireland, identified that privately owned houses in particular were of specific importance to visitors as they were largely unaltered. These houses (and gardens) faced huge costs while lacking funding and resources to keep them operational. Increasingly, many of the gardens have looked towards cultural and heritage tourism as having potential to generate revenue and contribute towards the cost of upkeep. Local authorities have broadened their remit and acquired gardens and historic houses. The walled gardens and Georgian pleasure grounds at Duckett's Grove, County Carlow (see Fig. 9.4), and the gardens at Marley Park, Dublin, have been restored through their local authorities. However, in a time of recession and competition for ever-shrinking funds, these gardens will have to deal with a smaller pool of resources for maintenance.

Prideaux (2003) identified four factors critical to the success of attractions in peripheral areas. These are illustrated in Fig. 9.5.

Due to the transient nature of gardens and their reliance on good weather, their development and maintenance are fraught with barriers to the creation of a tourism product that can sustain itself. The climatic conditions and indeed the global location of Ireland contribute

Fig. 9.4. Duckett's Grove, County Carlow, September 2007. (© Finola Reid)

Access and location.

Community support.

The economics of the operation.

Supporting tourism infrastructure.

Fig. 9.5. Four factors critical to the success of attractions in peripheral areas. (From Prideaux, 2003.)

to the very seasonal nature of the product and its potential viability. Some gardens are linked to other facilities and attractions, which can include accommodation, conference facilities, events, exhibition areas, coffee shops and play areas. The provision of these seeks to increase the attractiveness of the garden by developing facilities that appeal to a wider range of markets. However, some of the older and privately-owned

gardens and historic houses are reluctant to follow this route and many are operating at a loss. Some private individuals have had the recent ability to restore gardens and houses, either as sole provider of the financial resources required or with the help of funding. Ballinlough Castle and walled gardens, County Westmeath, is a historic property and garden that has been restored by its owners, as is Lough Crew Gardens, County Meath, which has diversified into offering an adventure playground.

9.7 The Real Economic Impact of Gardens and Historic Houses

Tourism has acted as a catalyst in the recognition of gardens and historic houses as an important resource to both local people and visitors alike. However, they may be seen by many as a loss-making resource and, therefore, a burden rather than a bonus to the tourist destination. Sharpley (2007), on examining the success of Alnwick Gardens in the UK, identified a number of contributing factors. These included the differentiated nature of the attraction and its potential to attract a broad market, embeddedness in the context of the regional tourism experience, its contribution to a critical mass of attractions and development within the existing resource capability, together with a need for integrated planning and control. It also certainly helped that it was the site of 'Hogwarts' for the first two Harry Potter films. Warwick Castle (also in the UK) is also a successful attraction; however, in ensuring continued 'pull' it has taken the route of diversifying into spheres unrelated to the place and space of the castle and a 'best price guarantee'.

Recently, there has been an increased focus on ascertaining the role and benefit of heritage as an economic driver of development. This comes at a time when many global economies are struggling and in recession. Heritage is providing an avenue of promise. Pereira Roders and van Oers (2011) argue that the role that the historic built environment plays in promoting economic growth is fully acknowledged. The 2011 International General Assembly of ICOMOS in Paris focused on heritage as a driver of development. Rypkema and Cheong (2011), in an attempt to quantify the economic impacts of historic preservation, use indicators (such as occupancy and revenue generated) to measure the tourism input. The Heritage Council of Ireland strongly supports the recognition of heritage as an economic driver for growth. Their strategic plan 2012–2016 supports heritage-based tourism through a number of objectives and recommendations. These include building visitor numbers, developing a community approach to heritage and event provision, and increased collaboration with Fáilte Ireland. In a recent study funded by them (Whitfield, 2011), and using figures provided by Fáilte Ireland, it was estimated that: direct tourism-related expenditure attributable to the historic environment in Ireland is equivalent to over €700 million; tourism-related effects in the area support some 17,000 full-time job equivalents; and the GVA (national income) contribution is equivalent to €645 million.

9.8 Authenticity versus Access

The balance between delivering authenticity while giving access to culture and heritage is one of the key challenges identified by Fáilte Ireland. Butcher (2006, p. 33) argues that cultural policy has, through a populist approach, adapted to criticism, that it has excluded alternative narratives and is elitist. Cultural attractions (such as gardens and historic houses), however, now reflect increased cultural diversity and therefore display a policy for greater open access. There is a question as to the type of packaging and commodification that should be undertaken in relation to these cultural and heritage resources. In order to achieve high levels of satisfaction (provider and consumer) and economic sustainability, either complex and layered packaging or focused packaging may be required, taking into account the relationship between cultural integrity (physical remains and conservation status) and the commercial factors associated with transforming a heritage place into a cultural heritage tourism attraction as identified by Du Cros (2001). Gardeners as media celebrities, festivals and events have changed the landscape both literally and metaphorically in many gardens and historic houses. Are these added values and links with related lifestyle products a way to create greater sustainability in garden tourism in the future? Or are the gardens losing sight of their core meaning? Finola Reid, Manager of the Great Gardens Restoration Scheme, calls for a rethink in the management policies for historic gardens and the requirement of some form of legislative protection for historic gardens (Reid, 2009). She cites Article 19 of the Florence Charter developed by ICOMOS in 1988:

> By reason of its nature and purpose, an historic garden is a peaceful place conducive to human contact, silence and awareness of nature.
>
> (ICOMOS charters)

Dooley (2003) recommends the introduction of legislation, tax incentives and grant availability, while also referring to the need for a more effective and coherent tourism marketing to be undertaken by all stakeholders involved with historic houses. He refers to the success of such places as Kylemore, County Galway, Belvedere, County Westmeath and Westport House and Gardens, County Mayo. Pavoni (2001) identifies the need to bear in mind the great potential narrative of historic houses, advocating a checklist of essential features using integrity based on historical accuracy. In response to a demand in changing consumer expectations and increased emphasis on economic sustainability – in many cases to the detriment of other forms of sustainability – there has been a change from passive (garden/historic house visiting) to active recreation such as events and activities, some of which are not associated with the nature of the garden/historic houses. This has an impact on the historic elements of the garden or site, with it being perceived as a space to consume rather than a place to experience and engage with the original concept.

9.9   Marketing

There are several groups that are involved in the development and marketing of gardens and historic houses. Ireland is a small country and there is a need for a unanimous vision for places of international, national and regional significance. The national group Houses, Castles and Gardens of Ireland (HCGI) provides a cooperative marketing body that focuses on both the international and domestic markets, mainly representing a mix of privately and publically owned gardens (http://www.hcgi.com). The Office of Public Works (OPW) also separately markets its own premises (http://www.heritageireland.ie). Heritage Island is a privately operated marketing body that has both private and public gardens and historic houses among its attractions (http://www.heritageisland.com). A number of tourist trails linking houses and gardens do exist, although these are often locally based and information for the tourist is available only once they are in the local/county area. There are 14 garden trails and festivals listed on http://www.garden.ie, including the West Cork Garden Trail, Carlow Floral Trail and the long-running Wicklow Gardens Festival that offers 33 gardens open to the public during the months of May to September each year. There are an increasing number of websites dedicated to garden blogs and messaging. Although a screen and picture is a poor substitute for a tourism product that requires all the senses, potential visitors can become familiar with a vast amount of information about a garden (much of it referral) prior to their visit.

Media influences the expectations of the visitor. This anticipation creates a pressure on both the garden and the owner/manager. The garden-owner strives to live up to this expected image, in deference to the seasonal and climatic changes that occur naturally in the horticultural world. In some cases, this may provide for a less than satisfying garden visit experience for some of the more amateur gardeners. Most recently social and personalized media, including the use of apps and other software, are providing voluminous information linked to a place. Ingenious Ireland, for example, serves the market with apps developed for the National Botanic Gardens and Trinity College Dublin (http://www.ingeniousireland.com).

9.10   An Emphasis on Creative Tourism

Although creativity in tourism has been part of the discussion and the cultural experience since the mid-2000s, it is now firmly on the tourism agenda in Ireland (H. O'Halloran, Fáilte Ireland, personal communication, March 2012). Cultural tourism can be considered as a passive approach to consumption, involving observation, educational and one-way narrative. Creative tourism, however, encourages a tripartite approach, linking the place, the people and media technologies (Smith, 2009).

> Creative tourism is travel directed toward an engaged and authentic experience, with participative learning in the arts, heritage, or special character of a place, and it provides a connection with those who reside in this place and create this living culture.
>
> (UNESCO, 2006, p. 3)

It links experience with authenticity and brings together both tangible and intangible cultural heritage. According to UNESCO (2009), intangible cultural heritage includes oral traditions, social practices such as rituals and festivals and events. This form of tourism is focused on a generation of visitors and their increased need to have choice and involvement in both their decision and experience. There is a link to local people and local histories. One way of doing this is collection of data and their use to enrich the experience.

There is a need to develop management tools for the collection and use of data at all levels. Management of the ever-growing bank of our information society is also required. Brine and Feather (2010) evaluated the information needs of historic houses in the UK and found a level of inadequacy in terms of information use, with one of the issues being the mix of ownership and approach. They recommended policy changes, education auditing, cooperation and technological improvement in order to improve the collection and use of information. There are many documents that guide cultural and heritage suppliers. The ICOMOS International Cultural Tourism Charter, as part of its principles and guidelines for managing places of cultural and heritage significance, focuses on the role of both public and local input and output in terms of benefits. Likewise, enriching the experience through innovation and cooperation is advocated by the World Tourism Organization (UNWTO) as part of their guideline document *Communicating Heritage* (UNWTO, 2011). However, in relation to gardens and historic houses, principles need to become practice in Ireland.

9.11   Summary

Because of its history, Ireland has a rich resource of both gardens and historic houses. These have been shaped by conflict and control, and the resultant fragmented nature of policy formulation and implementation does not provide a unifying and clear vision for this resource. In the future the balance between authenticity and access using information tools and marketing will inculcate a level of innovation and creativity, which in turn will further develop a level of experience and engagement for the visitor based on both tangible and intangible assets.

Over the next decades a generational change in the perception of gardens and historic houses in Ireland will result in one of several avenues being followed. They will be re-presented as their past history and narrative and serve a market knowledgeable and appreciative of their cultural and historic value; they will be reinvented primarily reflecting the changing needs of a post-neoliberal society that seeks to reconnect to a past time of economic boom; or they will be repudiated as a time past and forgotten.

The choice is ours.

> La forma general di paradiso
> già tutta mïo sguardo avea compresa,
> in nulla parte ancor fermato fiso.
> > (Dante, *Divina Commedia Paradiso*,
> > Canto XXXI, 52–54)

9.12   Discussion Questions

- Gardens and historic houses are embedded in local history. Discuss.
- Evaluate the benefits to both the local community and owners of opening a garden or historic house to visitors.
- Discuss the complex nature of cultural provision in terms of gardens and historic houses.
- Discuss the issues that require attention in commodification of a garden and/or historic house as a tourist attraction. How can balance be achieved between provision and consumption?

Acknowledgement

I wish to acknowledge Finola Reid for the photo of Duckett's Grove, County Carlow.

References

Bale, J. (1999) Parks and gardens: metaphors for the modern places of sport. In: Crouch, D. (ed.) *Leisure/Tourism Geographies: Practices and Geographical Knowledge*. Routledge, London, pp. 46–58.

Bord Fáilte (1994) *The Operational Programme for Tourism and Management for Sustainability 1994–1999*. Bord Fáilte, Dublin.

Bowe, P.T. and Nelson, E.C. (1988) A list of gardens and parks of international and national significance in the Republic of Ireland. *Moorea* 7 June.

Brine, A. and Feather, J. (2010) The information needs of UK historic houses: mapping the ground. *Journal of Documentation* 66, 28–45.

Butcher, J. (2006) Cultural politics, cultural policy and cultural tourism. In: Smith, M.K. and Robinson, M. (eds) *Cultural Tourism in a Changing World, Politics, Participation and [Re]presentation*. Channel View Publications, Bristol, UK, pp. 21–35.

Connell, J. (2005) Managing gardens for visitors in Great Britain: a story of continuity and change. *Tourism Management* 26, 185–201.

Cox, J. (1990) The garden as idea, place and action. In: Francis, M. and Hester, R. (eds) *The Meaning of Gardens: Ideas, Place and Actions*. MIT Press, Cambridge, Massachusetts, p. 25.

Crang, D. (1999) Knowing, tourism and vision. In: Crouch, D. (ed.) *Leisure/Tourism Geographies*. Routledge, London, pp. 238–256.

Dargan, P. (2008) *Exploring Georgian Dublin*. Nonsuch, Dublin.

Dooley, T. (2003) *A Future for Historic Houses? A Study of Fifty Houses*. A study commissioned by the Irish Georgian Society and the Department of Environment, Heritage and Local Government.

DTTS (2002) *Establishment of a New Tourism Development Authority*. Report of Implementation Group, April 2002, p. 4. www.transport.ie/tourism/pdfs/tda.pdf (accessed 12 September 2012).

DTTS (2012) www.transport.ie/tourismandsport.aspx (accessed 12 September 2012).

Du Cros, H. (2001) A new model to assist in planning for sustainable cultural heritage tourism. *International Journal of Tourism Research* 3, 165–171.

Fáilte Ireland (2006) *Cultural Tourism: Making It Work For You: A New Strategy for Cultural Tourism in Ireland*. Fáilte Ireland, Dublin.

Fáilte Ireland (2008a) *Operational Guidelines National Development Plan 2007–2013. Tourism Product Development Programme Annex 1*. Fáilte Ireland, Dublin.

Fáilte Ireland (2008b) *Properties of Significant Interest in Ireland*. Fáilte Ireland, Dublin.

Fáilte Ireland (2010a) *Summary of Overseas Visitors Engaging in Historical/Cultural Activities 2010*. Fáilte Ireland, Dublin.

Fáilte Ireland (2010b) www.failteireland.ie/FailteIreland/media/WebsiteStructure/Documents/3_Research_Insights/1_Sectoral_SurveysReports/Cultural-Activities-2010F.pdf?ext=.pdf (accessed 12 September 2012).

Fox, D. and Edwards, J. (2008) Managing gardens, ch 13. In: Fyall, A., Leask, A. and Garrod, B. (eds) *Managing Visitor Attractions: New Directions*. Butterworth-Heinemann, Oxford.

Girouard, M. (1978) *Life in the English Country House*. Yale University Press, New Haven, Connecticut.

Gorman, C. and Reid, F. (2000) Developing Ireland as a successful garden tourism destination. In: Ruddy, J. and Flanagan, S. (eds) *Tourism Destination Marketing: Gaining the Competitive Edge*. Dublin Institute of Technology, Tourism Research Centre, Dublin, pp. 437–443.

Gorman, C.E. (2010) Garden tourism in Ireland. An exploration of product group co-operation, links and relationships. Unpublished PhD thesis, Department of Geography, Trinity College, Dublin, Ireland.

Hewer, P.A. (2003) Consuming gardens: representation of paradise, nostalgia and postmodernism. *European Advances in Consumer Research* 6, 327–331.

Hole, S. (1899) *Reynolds Our Gardens*. J.M. Dent and Co. Aldine House, London.

Hoskins, W.G. (1988) *The Making of the English Landscape*. Hodder and Stoughton, London.

ICOMOS charters http://www.international.icomos.org/charters/charters.pdf (accessed 12 March 2012).

Indecon (2004) *Examination of the Issue of Trust Type Organisations to Manage Heritage Properties in Ireland*. Report commissioned by Department of the Environment, Heritage and Local Government. http://www.irishheritagetrust.ie/downloads/Indecon-Report-November-2004.pdf (accessed 12 March 2012).

Johnson, N. (1996) Where geography and history meets: heritage tourism and the big house in Ireland. *Annals of the Association of American Geographers* 86, 551–566.

Johnson, N. (2007) Grand design(er)s: David Moore, natural theology and the Royal Botanic Gardens in Glasnevin, Dublin, 1838–1879. *Cultural Geographies* 14, 29–55.

Kelly, C. (2006) Heritage tourism politics in Ireland. In: Smith, M.K. and Robinson, M. (eds) *Cultural Tourism in a Changing World, Politics, Participation and [Re]presentation*. Channel View Publications, Bristol, UK, pp. 36–55.

Lamb, J. and Bowe, P. (1995) *History of Gardening in Ireland*. Brunswick Press, Dublin.

Lumley, I. (2007) Parkland and gardens. *An Taisce* summer, 12–14.

Mandler, P. (1997) *The Fall and Rise of the Stately Home*. Yale University Press, New Haven, Connecticut.

Nelson, E.C. and McCracken, E.M. (1987) *The Brightest Jewel: A History of the National Botanic Gardens, Glasnevin, Dublin*. Boethius Press, Kilkenny, Ireland.

Owen, D. (2002) *An Assessment of the Sustainable Tourism Potential of the Properties Under An Taisce Management*. An Taisce, Dublin.

Pavoni, R. (2001) Towards a definition and typology of historic house museums. *Museum International No. 210* 53, 16–21.

Pereira Roders, A. and van Oers, R. (2011) Editorial: Bridging cultural heritage and sustainable development. *Journal of Cultural Heritage Management and Sustainable Development* 1, 9.

Pim, S. (1979) The history of gardening in Ireland. In: Nelson, C. and Brady, A. (eds) *Irish Gardening and Horticulture*. Royal Horticultural Society of Ireland, Dublin, pp. 45–70.

Prideaux, B. (2003) Creating visitor attractions in peripheral areas. In: Fyall, A., Garrod, B., Leask, A. and Wanhill, S. (eds) *Managing Visitor Attractions: New Direction*. Butterworth-Heinemann, Oxford, pp. 80–94.

Reid, F. (2009) *Outlook Winter 2008/Spring 2009*. Heritage Council, Kilkenny, Ireland.

Rypkema, D. and Cheong, C. (2011) Measuring economic impacts of historic preservation. A report to the advisory council on historic preservation. http://www.achp.gov/docs/economic-impacts-of-historic-preservation-study.pdf (accessed 12 January 2012).

Sharpley, R. (2007) Flagship attractions and sustainable development: the case of Alnwick Castle, England. *Journal of Sustainable Tourism* 15, 125–143.

Smith, M.K. (2009) *Issues in Cultural Tourism*, 2nd edn. Routledge, London.

Taylor, L. (2002) From ways of life to lifestyle: the ordinari-ization of British gardening lifestyle television. *European Journal of Communication* 17, 479–493.

Taylor, P. (1998) *Gardens of France*. Mitchell Beazley, London.

Towner, J. (1996) *A Historical Geography of Recreation and Tourism in the Western World 1540–1940*. Wiley, Chichester, UK.

UNESCO (2006) Towards creative strategies for sustainable tourism. Discussion report of the planning meeting for 2008 International Conference on Creative Tourism, p. 3. Santa Fe, New Mexico, USA, 25–27 October 2006. http://unesdoc.unesco.org/images/0015/001598/159811e.pdf (accessed 12 March 2012).

UNESCO (2009) What is intangible cultural heritage? http://www.unesco.org/culture/ich/doc/src/01851-EN.pdf (accessed 12 March 2012).

UNWTO (2011) *Communicating Heritage: A Handbook for the Tourism Sector*. World Tourism Organisation, Madrid.

Urry, J. (1999) Sensing leisure spaces. In: Crouch, D. (ed.) *Leisure/Tourism Geographies: Practices and Geographical Knowledge*. Routledge, London, pp. 34–45.

Walpole, E.H. (nd) *Mount Usher 1868–1928: A Short History*. Walpole Brothers Ltd, Dublin.

Whitfield, C. (2011) *The Economic Value of Ireland's Historic Environment*. http://www.heritagecouncil.ie/fileadmin/user_upload/Events/Place_As_Resource/Presentations/3_C_Whitfield_Presentation.pdf (accessed 12 January 2012).

10 Case Study 2: Archaeotourism – The Past is Our Future?

Frances McGettigan[1] and Agnieszka Rozenkiewicz[2]
[1]*Athlone Institute of Technology, Athlone, Ireland;*
[2]*University of Wrocław, Wrocław, Poland*

The fundamental aim of this chapter is to address the question of archaeotourism as a recent tourism phenomenon and a possible niche for further specialization of Ireland as a tourist destination. As has been suggested by Baram (2008), archaeotourism is focused on the promotion of passion and conservation of historical-archaeological sites. Detailed insight into the target issue is provided in the theoretical framework for subsequent empirical investigations.

The chapter then concentrates on the characteristics and importance of the tourist experience and the critical factors influencing tourists' satisfaction. The final key concepts discussed are the ones of authenticity and interpretation, insofar as they are the defining elements of visitor experience and understanding of the archaeological sites as tourist attractions. Therefore, the chapter attempts to bridge the gap in the academic literature between archaeology and tourism, particularly with reference to the measurement of visitor experience at archaeological sites.

10.1 Introduction

In touristic terms, enormous qualitative and quantitative potential, uniqueness and authenticity are beyond doubt the fundamental features that describe the archaeological heritage of Ireland. Numerous archaeological sites in the country are accessible to the public and have become widely recognized as tourist attractions. Nonetheless, the phenomenon of archaeotourism in the Irish context remains largely unresearched. Hence, this chapter draws attention to the relationship between the domains of tourism and archaeology, particularly with reference to investigating the visitor experience at archaeological sites, using the example of Newgrange. Newgrange is an integral element of the archaeological ensemble of the Bend of the Boyne, in the eastern region of Ireland (see Fig. 10.1), and was chosen as the case study for this chapter because it constitutes the most recognized tourist attraction of this type in Ireland (see Fig. 10.2). At the same time it is very well adjusted to the needs of tourism. The key aim of this chapter is achieved through two objectives, which are to identify motivations behind visits to Newgrange and to examine visitor perception of archaeological sites as tourist attractions based on the example of Newgrange.

The case study site under investigation in this chapter is Ireland's premier prehistoric/archaeological visitor attraction, which receives over 200,000 visitors per year. Newgrange is a Neolithic passage tomb, located in Brú na Bóinne – an archaeological ensemble of outstanding cultural heritage that has been designated as a World Heritage Site since 1993 (Smyth, 2009).

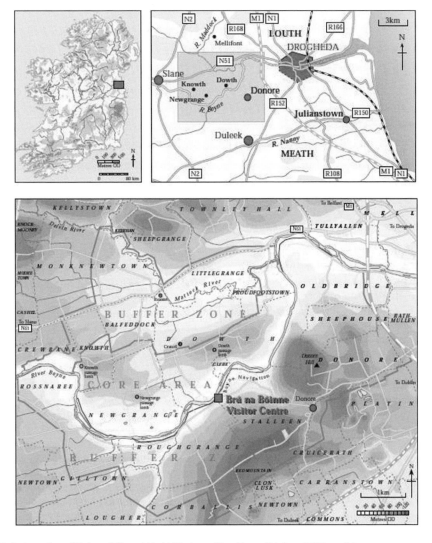

Fig. 10.1. Location of Brú na Bóinne World Heritage Site. (From Dúchas, 2002, p. 8.)

Fig. 10.2. Passage tombs of Newgrange (A), Knowth (B) and Dowth (C). (Photographs: A & B: A. Rozenkiewicz, 2011; C: Knowth.com, 2011a.)

10.2 Culture, Heritage and Archaeology – Definitional Considerations

It is widely acknowledged in academic literature that the notions of culture, heritage and tourism are inextricably linked (Richards, 1996; McManus, 1997; Leslie and Sigala, 2005; Goeldner and Ritchie, 2009). Understanding the place where these terms are interrelated with archaeology as the subject of tourists' interests requires an in-depth analysis of the available conceptual definitions.

Baram (2008) seeks to clarify the term archaeotourism, stating that it is focused on the promotion of passion and conservation of historical-archaeological sites. Prentice (1994, cited in McManus, 1997) explores the question of heritage from the tourism perspective, stressing its commercial dimension. He notices that not only does it comprise the elements

traditionally indicated in various definitional approaches, such as landscapes, buildings, traditions, etc., but it also refers to every aspect of heritage that can be promoted as a commodity. In the era of globalization and mass tourism development, the case is similar in relation to broadly understood culture (Reisinger, 2009) and archaeology (Baram and Rowan, 2004). Yet, as has been noted by Alzua et al. (1998), there are no standardized and generally accepted definitions of cultural and heritage tourism, and thus, an exhaustive assessment of the relationship between these phenomena poses a challenge.

In his attempts at defining the concepts, Richards (2001) looks to the theme of cultural tourism, reporting that a learning function is the basic element that differentiates this from other forms of tourism. He also observes the existence of a distinct dichotomy of cultural tourism that stems from the complex notion of culture itself. Firstly, cultural tourism consists of consuming the past in the form of the cultural products created by previous generations. On such understanding of the term, it can be equated with heritage tourism. On the other hand, Richards declares, cultural tourism is also interdependent with the second constituent of culture, namely contemporary cultural production, which can be defined as arts tourism. Similar results in defining cultural tourism emerged from a study by Zeppel and Hall (1991). Richards (1996, p. 24) presents two definitions of cultural tourism that were accepted by the Association for Tourism and Leisure Education (ATLAS). According to the conceptual definition, the term can be defined as the movement of persons to cultural attractions away from their normal place of residence, with the intention to gather new information and experiences to satisfy their needs. Under the technical definition, cultural tourism can be understood as all movements of persons to specific cultural attractions, such heritage sites, artistic and cultural manifestations, arts and drama outside their normal place of residence.

In the general typology of cultural tourism resources, Munsters (1994, cited in Munsters, 1996) distinguishes two major groups, namely attractions and events. The first one, aside from museums, routes and theme parks, comprises monuments, with archaeological sites and industrial-archaeological buildings being a subgroup of this component. Orbaşli and Woodward (2009) explain that archaeological sites are an essential constituent of the cultural built heritage and, as such, manifest the achievements of past generations. Smith (2003) presents a comprehensive typology of cultural tourism based on activities and places of tourist interests, placing archaeological sites in the category of heritage sites. Consequently, when it comes to the typology of cultural tourists, the person who visits archaeological sites is called a heritage tourist.

With reference to locating archaeotourism in the broad interests of cultural tourism, Buczkowska (2008) proposes the division of the latter into cultural heritage tourism and contemporary cultural tourism that, incidentally, is fully applicable to the dual characteristics of culture that were previously discussed. In her study, the author further subcategorizes

cultural heritage tourism into five subgroups, one of which is protected heritage tourism comprising, among other things, the notion of archaeotourism or archaeological tourism.

Summarizing the above-mentioned findings, archaeological tourism and its components are a niche tourism category subsumed into heritage tourism that, because of the tourists' interests and typology, is a constituent of a wider term – cultural tourism.

10.3   Tourist Motivations and Archaeotourism

Following suggestions from Richards (2007), the predominant motivations of cultural tourists are seen as a synthesis of atmosphere, culture and history of the visited place. Taking into account the interest in cultural attractions and activities, tourists can be labelled as culture-core or culture-peripheral (Hughes, 2002, p. 170). The first term applies to tourists for whom culture constitutes the main reason for the visit, the decision to engage actively with culture was made before arrival, whereas culture-peripheral tourists visit cultural destinations for different reasons, e.g. business, VFR (Visiting Family or Friends) or other. Following assumptions made by Hughes (2002) and Al-Busaidi (2008, p. 53) suggests that archaeological tourism can be defined as a form of heritage-based tourism in which the archaeological landscape represents a core motivation or peripheral motivation for on-site visits and/or off-site experience, e.g. museums, travelling exhibitions. It also includes all structural aspects (e.g. organizations and policies) as well as operational processes (e.g. marketing and tour guiding) that are relative to archaeological heritage in a particular area.

10.4   Visitor/Tourist Experience

The rationale behind this investigation of archaeotourism among other things can be justified by the findings that measuring the tourist experience has been vastly neglected in the realm of destination management studies (Vittersø et al., 2000; Munsters, 2010). This is all the more surprising when one realizes, as

Munsters (2010) emphasizes, that there is a direct correlation between the visitor experience and the possibility of returning to a destination.

Page and Connell (2009) note that tourist experience is composed of subjective and objective variables that determine the level of satisfaction with the visit. Regarding the archaeological heritage of Ireland, Costa (2004) claims that visitor experiences at the ancient sites is affected equally by the core heritage and the tourist facilities available on-site. As has been argued by Laws (1995), tourists can be compared with consumers whose contentment is strongly dependent on the quality of services they purchase. Furthermore, in order to ensure a high level of tourist experience, it is crucial to remember that experience is a complex process that begins with the intention of visiting a destination, followed by the on-site reception of the attraction and services, finally ending with the memories retained after the visit.

Among the major determinants that make up the visitor experience, Shackley (2001, cited in Griffin, 2010, p. 45) presents a list of elements (Fig. 10.3).

10.5 Authenticity and Interpretation of Archaeological Sites as Tourist Attractions

The authenticity of archaeological heritage presented *in situ*, especially in relation to the quality and quantity of tangible architectural

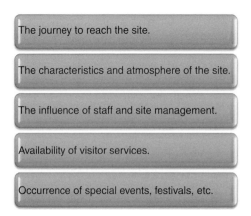

Fig. 10.3. Determinants of visitor experience. (From Authors.)

traces of prehistory in Ireland, is unquestionable. The matter of reliability and true experience of the past occurs when the heritage undergoes tourist interpretation. The authenticity of the heritage itself, which is in fact the major attracting force to certain destinations, is often perceived as different from the visitors' perception, but it is in fact the latter that is the predominant factor that shapes the authenticity of the tourist experience (Ivanovic, 2008). Due to this discrepancy, as pointed out by Hall and McArthur (1993, cited in Moscardo, 1996), visitor experience should play a pivotal role in the process of heritage management. Gazin-Schwartz (2004) delves into this subject and makes the point that interpretation of authentic archaeological heritage is facilitated by various modern marketing processes. For instance, by promotion or availability of tourist facilities such as gift shops, the heritage of the past that is consumed seems to become more familiar and recognizable for the visitors. Lastly, Little (2004) highlights the fact that the role of archaeologists in communicating the past to the public is invaluable. They are seen to be the main facilitators for the interpretation of the message that is conveyed by the relics of the past.

10.6 An Investigation into the Visitor Experience at Archaeological Sites – the Case of Newgrange

This chapter presents a range of findings in relation to visitor experience at Newgrange. The findings are derived from various sources. Firstly, Delany (2004) undertook an investigation of tourist motivations to visit the Irish County of Meath (within which Newgrange is located) in the off-peak season. The research findings from that study were derived from 100 questionnaires distributed among visitors at the Brú Na Bóinne Visitor Centre (which acts as the 'reception' area for Newgrange and a range of other Neolithic sites). The analysis comprises the following areas: a socio-demographic profile of respondents, specification of travel planning processes, the sources of information used before and during the visit, and finally the dominant motivations behind the visit.

The results of Delany's examination, where applicable, are set against the outcomes of the present study in the discussion section.

Specifically regarding the visitor experience at Brú na Bóinne, the general findings of two state-sponsored studies, namely the Visitor Satisfaction at Brú na Bóinne Survey by Fáilte Ireland (2003) and the Survey of Visitors to Brú na Bóinne carried out on behalf of Dúchas by Tourism Development International in 2000, prove a high level of visitor satisfaction with the archaeological park and are compared with the findings of the present research in the discussion of the results.

Finally, an interesting study into interpretation evaluation at Brú na Bóinne was carried out by Fitzgerald (2006), who provides an insight into various facilities and services that enable interpretation. In this context, interpretation is understood as communication with the visitor, and Fitzgerald presents its assessment from the tourist perspective. Again, these findings are related to the results of the present research.

The original empirical data for this chapter derives from quantitative research by the authors that formed part of an undergraduate degree in Tourism and Hospitality Management at Athlone Institute of Technology. Because of institutional directives, the primary work for such a project is limited to 50 surveys, which were administered to Newgrange visitors to explore their experience at the site. Research was conducted at Brú na Bóinne Visitor Centre in February 2011.

As a background for the discussion it is useful to examine briefly a profile of the visitors surveyed. Regarding gender the group was equally balanced, and the largest age groups representative were the 25–34 age bracket (40%) and the 35–44 age bracket (34%). As regards nationality, the survey predominantly represents Europeans and Americans. Four nationalities stood out, namely Irish (26%), Americans (18%), Germans (18%) and Poles (16%). An interesting finding is the division of the visitors according to nationality and their place of residence – as many as 27% of Irish visitors were of Polish nationality, 13% were Germans and 7% were Czechs. The rest were Americans and Italians. These results correspond with the changing situation in Ireland

concerning immigrants and suggest that the growing numbers of international residents in Ireland display an active interest in the heritage of the country. Hence, they are becoming a substantial target groups for domestic tourism in Ireland. Regarding county of residence, domestic visitors to Newgrange were either local residents from the County of Meath or from the neighbouring County of Dublin, who together accounted for nearly two-thirds of the visitors. The majority of overseas visitors came from the USA (40%), with other groups including Germany (25%), Great Britain (15%), France (10%), Slovenia (5%) and Finland (5%).

Nearly three-quarters of visitors to the site possess a third-level qualification, with as many as 36% holding a Bachelor degree, 28% having a Master's qualification and 10% with PhDs. The remaining 26% of visitors have primary, secondary or vocational education. The high level of education is also reflected by their present or previous occupation. A substantial number of visitors were 'student', and other substantial groups included doctors, lawyers, teachers (18%), service or sales workers (16%) as well as clerical/administrative workers (14%), and directors/managers (14%). Only four of the 50 visitors surveyed were manual workers.

One of the key aims of the 2011 survey was to identify motivations behind individuals' visits to Newgrange. To establish this participants were asked a number of questions. The first of these examined the sources of information that prompted them to visit the site (Fig. 10.4). As expected in the global era of exchanging information at a click of a button, the Internet received the biggest number of answers (38%); perhaps this can be linked with the main age group of visitors (25–34). Almost equally significant (36%) were recommendations from family and friends. This corresponds with the results achieved by Delany (2004), where information from family and friends combined with word of mouth accounted for 28% of responses. Guidebooks also remain an important source of information, consulted by 30% of respondents before their visit.

Secondly, the visitors were asked to choose their main motivation in undertaking the trip, and the overwhelming majority (82%) came to visit the archaeological site. This is understandable, taking into account the out-standing features of the place (Fig. 10.5), the most appealing of which were its historical significance (70%), uniqueness (50%), authenticity (28%) and the natural environment (28%). Similar motivations were revealed in the research by Fitzgerald (2006, p. 17). Surprisingly, status as a UNESCO World Heritage Site was not a motivating factor for most of the survey participants (64%), yet the

visitors seem to be well informed in this regard, considering as many as 58% have visited at least one other archaeological site within the last year, including sites such as the Rock of Cashel, the Burren and the Hill of Tara. The research also revealed that 64% of the surveyed visitors consider themselves to be archaeological tourists. However, an interesting finding, which somewhat refutes this concept of 'archaeotourism', is that one in two

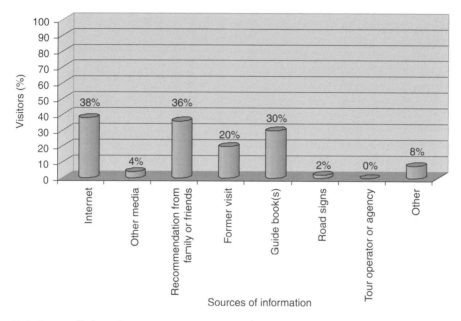

Fig. 10.4. Source of information prompting visit. (From Authors.)

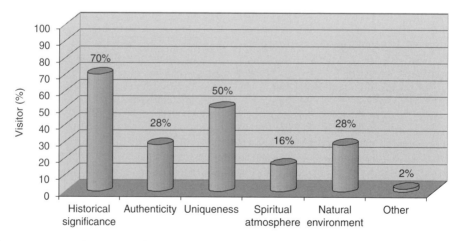

Fig. 10.5. Features of Newgrange that encouraged the visit. (From Authors.)

tourists who do not consider themselves to be archaeological also visited at least one other Irish archaeological site, but presumably they are motivated by other reasons than willingness to see an archaeological attraction.

By virtue of the fact that nearly two-thirds of visitors to Newgrange considered themselves to be archaeotourists, the authors explored the visitor profile of this particular group. With reference to the gender ratio of archaeological tourists, males (62%) outnumbered females (38%). The most prominent age group was 25–34, with 47% of respondents belonging to this category, and people between 35 and 44 years of age accounted for a further 28% of archaeotourists. Considering nationality, a quarter of archaeotourists were Americans and other prominent groups comprised Germans (22%) and Poles (19%), with the Irish visitors accounting for 13%. The most prominent domestic archaeotourists were Poles (35%), Irish (24%), Germans (18%) and Czechs (12%). The survey results demonstrate that archaeotourists are even better educated than the general visitor to Newgrange, 78% having a higher education qualification. As far as occupation of archaeotourists is concerned, nearly a quarter of respondents were students. The second biggest group were directors/managers and doctors, lawyers or teachers, with 19% of archaeotourists falling into each category.

The next theme to be explored relates to visitor perception of archaeological sites as tourist attractions, based on the example of Newgrange. With reference to access the site fares poorly, with only 8% of visitors using public transportation. In general however, access did not pose any difficulties for those interviewed, with some tourists finding access very easy (with the use of navigation systems). However, 12% of visitors reported problems reaching the site due to inadequate signage. This shows an improvement over the Survey of Visitors to Brú na Bóinne findings in 2000, where the necessity to improve signposting was mentioned in additional suggestions by 18% of visitors.

Regarding the time that visitors reported to spend visiting the site and its surroundings, 62% spent less than 2 hours, 8% needed between 2 to 3 hours to visit and for 30% the visiting time ranged from 3 to 5 hours. It is crucial to add that the length of stay was undoubtedly related to the weather, which was very nice and sunny when the research was being conducted, and also the site has a modern high-quality catering facility (in addition to other facilities such as tourist office – see Fig. 10.6). Some visitors suggested creating walking routes through the World Heritage Site and a walkway along the river with places for picnics and barbeques; this would be an interesting idea for increasing the length of time spent visiting the site.

The overall level of visitor satisfaction with tourist facilities and services in Newgrange was very high (see Fig. 10.7); this is consistent with the 2000 Survey of Visitors to Brú na Bóinne. In the present study the visitor centre was rated mainly as 'very satisfactory', 64%, and 'satisfactory', 36%, and guide services were evaluated as 'very satisfactory' by 70% of visitors, which was the highest score among all elements being

Fig. 10.6. Brú na Bóinne tea room (A) and tourist office (B). (Photograph: A. Rozenkiewicz, 2011.)

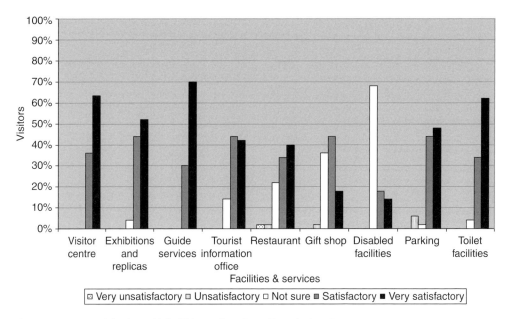

Fig. 10.7. Visitor satisfaction with facilities and services. (From Authors.)

rated. This is comparable with findings by Fitzgerald (2006), who states that guided tours were liked 'a lot' by 67% of visitors. The only site elements to receive negative comments were the gift shop, restaurant and parking; however, these were only 2%, 4% and 6% of responses respectively.

Regarding the provision of interpretation facilities, 44% of visitors prefer visiting archaeological sites with a guide and 48% like only part of the experience to involve a guide, while only 8% favour visiting archaeological sites on their own. Reflecting on the importance of various elements of archaeological sites, guide services were identified by 70% of respondents as facilitating understanding and interpretation, while 56% state that they require at least some time for individual sightseeing. Fortunately, the experience at Brú na Bóinne combines both. Visiting the interior of Newgrange passage tomb is exclusively facilitated in the company of a guide, while the tomb's surroundings and the visitor centre can be appreciated individually.

Touching on the dominating role of archaeological sites, over half of visitors (56%) highlighted their educational value, for 34% cultural values were the most important, whereas recreational roles were present in 10% of the answers. Linked to this, tourists were asked about their attitude to the protection of

archaeological sites and the provision of access for the general public. Over half of the visitors (56%) perceive the present situation to be at an acceptable level. For the rest opinions were split between contrasting views, with 22% believing that 'protection of archaeological sites in Ireland should be increased and direct access for tourists reduced', while the same number (22%) stated that 'more tourists should gain direct access to archaeological sites in Ireland'.

The visitor reaction to Newgrange was highly positive for as many as 98% of respondents, with 66% classifying the experience as 'excellent' and 32% as 'good'. Only one person assessed the visitor experience as 'fair'. These findings concur with the Visitor Satisfaction at Brú na Bóinne Survey by Fáilte Ireland in 2003, which revealed that 93% of visitors would recommend this attraction to a friend.

10.7   Summary

This study addresses the issue of visitor experience at archaeological sites based on a case study investigation of Newgrange. Regarding the identification of motivations behind their visit, the survey participants were prompted primarily by a vast array of information sources, with the Internet and recommendation from family and friends being the dominating ones. The most important feature of the visit to the archaeological site is its historical significance, which was the chief reason for undertaking the trip for the vast majority of respondents. In contradiction to initial expectations, the fact that Newgrange is a World Heritage Site was not a criterion of value or a motivating factor for the vast number of visitors. One of the most interesting findings was that nearly two-thirds of the survey participants consider themselves to be archaeological tourists, which confirms that archaeotourism should be considered as a separate and significant subcategory of tourism.

As to the perception of archaeological sites as tourist attractions, based on the example of Newgrange, a very positive visitor experience at the site results from the unique values of the archaeological site itself, being easily accessible, the natural environment of its surroundings, friendly personnel, generally good management of the site, and finally very satisfactory and modern tourist facilities, in particular the visitor centre includes all the necessary elements to facilitate understanding of the archaeological heritage of the Bend of the Boyne.

To sum up, this research results in deepening the understanding of the phenomenon of archaeotourism, which, due to its multidimensional character, can be recognized as a distinct category of tourists' interests. The high potential and outstanding features of Ireland's archaeological heritage may play a pivotal role in attracting future visitors, and hence further research, including a detailed profile of archaeological tourists, in particular their needs and expectations towards the Irish archaeological sites as tourist attractions, should be undertaken. The authors also especially believe that overseas tourists' awareness of Ireland as an archaeological tourist destination is limited. Therefore, the existence of exceptionally well-preserved and well-presented archaeological attractions, that in many cases provide high-class tourist facilities, should be promoted. 'Smart' marketing campaigns raising the visitors' awareness of this angle of the Irish tourism potential can be seen as one of the routes to the recovery of the tourism industry in Ireland.

10.8   Discussion Questions

•   What are the main motivations of individuals who visit archaeological sites such as Newgrange?
•   Do you think archaeotourism is a viable niche market/product proposition?
•   What are the main factors influencing the visitor experience at an archaeological site?

References

Al-Busaidi, Y.S.A. (2008) Public interpretation of archaeological heritage and archaeotourism in the Sultanate of Oman. PhD, Cardiff School of Management, Cardiff, UK.

Alzua, A., O'Leary, J. and Morrison, A. (1998) Cultural and heritage tourism: identifying niches for international travellers. *Journal of Tourism Studies* 9, 2–13.

Baram, U. (2008) Tourism and archaeology. In: Pearsall, D.M. (ed.) *Encyclopedia of Archaeology*, vol. 3. Amsterdam/London: Elsevier/Academic Press, pp. 2131–2134.

Baram, U. and Rowan, Y. (2004) Archaeology after nationalism: globalization and the consumption of the past. In: Rowan, Y. and Baram, U. (eds) *Marketing Heritage: Archaeology and the Consumption of the Past*. AltaMira Press, Oxford, pp. 3–23.

Buczkowska, K. (2008) *Turystyka Kulturowa: Przewodnik Metodyczny*. Akademia Wychowania Fizycznego im. Eugeniusza Piaseckiego w Poznaniu, Poznań, Poland.

Costa, K.A. (2004) Conflating past and present: marketing archaeological heritage sites in Ireland. In: Rowan, Y. and Baram, U. (eds) *Marketing Heritage: Archaeology and the Consumption of the Past*. AltaMira Press, Oxford, pp. 69–91.

Delany, C. (2004) A study into motivational issues of tourists visiting County Meath in the off-peak season. MBS, University College Dublin, Dublin.

Dúchas (2002) *Brú na Bóinne World Heritage Site Management Plan*. Dúchas the Heritage Service and Department of the Environment and Local Government, Dublin.

Fáilte Ireland (2003) Hospitality study – visitor satisfaction at Brú na Bóinne. Unpublished report. Fáilte Ireland, Dublin.

Fitzgerald, A. (2006) Interpretation evaluation at Brú na Bóinne. MBS, University College Dublin, Dublin.

Gazin-Schwartz, A. (2004) Mementos of the past: material culture of tourism at Stonehenge and Avebury. In: Rowan, Y. and Baram, U. (eds) *Marketing Heritage: Archaeology and the Consumption of the Past*. AltaMira Press, Oxford, pp. 93–102.

Goeldner, C.R. and Ritchie, J.R.B. (2009) *Tourism: Principles, Practices, Philosophies*, 11th edn. John Wiley and Sons, Hoboken, New Jersey.

Griffin, C. (2010) A case study to explore the nature of the visitor experience at religious sites in Ireland. MA, Athlone Institute of Technology, Athlone, Ireland.

Hughes, H. (2002) Culture and tourism: a framework for further analysis. *Managing Leisure* 7, 164–175.

Ivanovic, M. (2008) *Cultural Tourism*. Google Books. http://books.google.com/books?id=fZ6Wb8AptvYC&printsec=frontcover&dq=cultural+tourism+ivanovic&hl=en&ei=AZFUTYSGDIaZOo_X4b0F&sa=X&oi=book_result&ct=result&resnum=1&ved=0CC4Q6AEwAA#v=onepage&q&f=false (accessed 7 February 2011).

Laws, E. (1995) *Tourist Destination Management: Issues, Analysis and Policies*. Routledge, London.

Leslie, D. and Sigala, M. (2005) *International Cultural Tourism: Management, Implications and Cases*. Google Books. http://books.google.com/books?id=bOWYKdlyJ8IC&printsec=frontcover&dq=leslie+sigala&hl=en&ei=J2NUTe3lMs6WOpirlO0E&sa=X&oi=book_result&ct=result&resnum=1&ved=0CCYQ6AEwAA#v=onepage&q&f=false (accessed 30 January 2011).

Little, B. (2004) Is the medium the message? The art of interpreting archaeology in US national parks. In: Rowan, Y. and Baram, U. (eds) *Marketing Heritage: Archaeology and the Consumption of the Past*. AltaMira Press, Oxford, pp. 269–286.

McManus, R. (1997) Heritage and tourism in Ireland – an unholy alliance? *Irish Geography* 30, 90–98.

Moscardo, G. (1996) Mindful visitors: heritage and tourism. *Annals of Tourism Research* 23, 376–397.

Munsters, W. (1996) Cultural tourism in Belgium. In: Richards, G. (ed.) *Cultural Tourism in Europe*. CAB International, Wallingford, UK (re-issued in 2005 in electronic format by ATLAS), pp. 80–92.

Munsters, W. (2010) The cultural destination experience audit applied to the tourist-historic city. In: Richards, G. and Munsters, W. (eds) *Cultural Tourism Research Methods*. CAB International, Wallingford, UK, pp. 52–60.

Orbaşli, A. and Woodward, S. (2009) Tourism and heritage conservation. In: Jamal, T. and Robinson, M. (eds) *The SAGE Handbook of Tourism Studies*. SAGE, London, pp. 314–332.

Page, S.J. and Connell, J. (2009) *Tourism: A Modern Synthesis*, 3rd edn. Cengage Learning EMEA, Andover, UK.

Reisinger, Y. (2009) *Tourism: Cultures and Behavior*. Google Books. http://books.google.com/books?id=_Jz4ZJsoaMgC&printsec=frontcover&dq=international+tourism+cultures+and+behavior&hl=en&src=bmrr&ei=yWVUTbOOE4Gb8QPwyMnuBw&sa=X&oi=book_result&ct=result&resnum=1&ved=0CC8Q6AEwAA#v=onepage&q&f=false (accessed 1 February 2011).

Richards, G. (1996) The scope and significance of cultural tourism. In: Richards, G. (ed.) *Cultural Tourism in Europe*. CAB International, Wallingford, UK (Re-issued in 2005 in electronic format by ATLAS), pp. 21–38.

Richards, G. (2001) The development of cultural tourism in Europe. In: Richards, G. (ed.) *Cultural Attractions and European Tourism*. CAB International, Wallingford, UK, pp. 3–29.

Richards, G. (2007) Introduction: global trends in cultural tourism. In: Richards, G. (ed.) *Cultural Tourism: Global and Local Perspectives*. The Haworth Press, New York, pp. 1–24.

Smith, M.K. (2003) *Issues in Cultural Tourism Studies*. Routledge, London.

Smyth, J. (2009) *Brú na Bóinne World Heritage Site: Research Framework*. The Heritage Council of Ireland, Kilkenny, Ireland.

Tourism Development International on behalf of Dúchas (2000) Survey of visitors to Brú na Bóinne, unpublished report. Tourism Development International on behalf of Dúchas, Dublin.

Vitterssø, J., Vorkinn, M., Vistad, O.I. and Vaagland, J. (2000) Tourist experiences and attractions. *Annals of Tourism Research* 27, 432–450.

Zeppel, H. and Hall, C.M. (1991) Selling art and history: cultural heritage and tourism. *Journal of Tourism Studies* 2, 29–45.

11 Case Study 3: Urban Regeneration and Culture: Maltese Example

Vincent Zammit

Institute of Tourism Studies, St Julian's, Malta

This chapter presents a case study of urban regeneration and culture in Malta, identifying the key motivations for engaging in urban regeneration and the logic behind intrinsically linking (re)developments to the encouragement of local engagement with Maltese culture. It is posited that the engagement of locals is paramount to the success of urban cultural developments, and while cultural tourism is the most immediate driving force behind progressing such investment, the local meaning and ownership of such advancements must be central to the entire process.

11.1 Introduction

With tourism being one of the most important economic activities for the islands of Malta it stands to reason that there should be a lot of effort to make sure that what is on offer always matches the expectations of the modern visitor. This chapter outlines some of the attempts that have been made to ensure an increase in appreciation for the cultural heritage of the islands. Government authorities have published more than one Cultural Policy Paper in order to promote this aspect of Malta. One approach to cultural development via tourism has been an increased interest in historical re-enactments; however, this has not been a free-standing development. These activities go hand-in-hand with a regeneration of the city and/or locality where the activity is held. After the first such activity held in Mdina (the ancient capital of Malta) there has been an increased interest by other localities. New ideas have been introduced and more of these activities have been organized. The central authorities, together with the local councils, have realized the need to upgrade the cities and villages where these cultural activities are taking place, thus a lot of

Fig. 11.1. Maltese locals taking part in a re-enactment pageant. (Photo, V. Zammit.)

work has been carried out, resulting in a programme of regeneration all over the islands. Utilizing this improved physical environment, there have been a variety of cultural activities held, which have helped regenerate various cultural manifestations (see Fig. 11.1).

11.2   Development of Maltese Tourism Market

The Maltese islands obtained independence from Britain in 1964. This resulted in the need to build a local economy that would eventually substitute economic dependence based on the British military presence. Subsequent years led to an increase in industrialization, wherein a number of industrial estates were established. Foreign companies were encouraged to set up factories in Malta, and this helped to provide work for the local population.

Tourism was also earmarked as an important source of revenue. In 1958 the Malta Government Tourist Board was set up with the sole aim of attracting tourists to Malta and to establish a young but stable industry (Spiteri, 2002). The increase in tourists, and subsequent income, to Malta over the years convinced the authorities to continue supporting and investing in this industry. Diversification in tourism meant the building of hotels and ancillary services, adding more facilities to the only airport and starting a yacht marina sector. Today the industry has progressed and, for more than a decade, each year more than a million tourists have visited Malta. The industry provides €840 million to the local economy (NCHE, 2009), emphasizing the importance of the industry.

All of this development took place within specific areas. The new hotels were built in non-developed areas, and although the main cultural and heritage attractions continued to be crowd-pullers when the attractions closed for the day the historical cities became dead. Diversification took place and economic activity was dispersed to other less-developed areas of Malta. This helped in tackling areas that were still in need of modernization, in terms of both fabric and infrastructure. Combined with the policies of diversification and others, these old urban centres started to lose their attraction as residential areas. Given the fact that dwellings were usually old fashioned and not very comfortable, people started to move away and opted to live in the new housing estates that were developed. This continued the gradual population decline of central urban areas, particularly the evacuation of people living in the historical centres. This phenomenon was to be noticed in various parts of the islands.

In the recent past a new trend has developed. It has become fashionable to return back to the old historic cities and centres, renovate old buildings and start living there. While in the past there was a tendency that evening activities were concentrated in the newer parts of the island, there is a trend wherein new eateries and other leisure-related places are opening up for business in the old historic centres. The local authorities have encouraged this trend by providing the necessary permits and are helping to organize cultural events so that more people discover these places.

The development of tourism is not without its detractors however, and not for the first time certain media have been reporting in recent years about the over-development of particular areas, at the same time noting the abandonment of others. Thus, there has been an impression given regarding an inequality of economic distribution generated by the tourism

industry. This poor image of tourism as an economic driver seems to be tackled somewhat successfully by the authorities as more establishments are set up, aimed at improving and professionalizing the tourism industry. Not least of these positive developments is the upgrading of numerous historic centres/cores by creating heritage trails and making sure that the upgrading being carried out is taken care of in the long term. A specific example of this type of development was recently reported when the Minister of Tourism and Culture, together with the Minister of Dialogue, visited the village of Balzan and were shown around the embellishments that were being carried out in the historic centre (see Fig. 11.2). A sum of €500,000 has been provided for these improvements with the aim of attracting tourists to this small village, which has never before benefited from this industry (Caruana, 2012).

11.3 Culture as a Tool for Urban Regeneration

Culture and heritage have always been considered an integral part in any regeneration process, because they will positively affect the economy and the nature of the urban centre (Galdini, 2007). It has been stated that 'culture

Fig. 11.2. Recent renovations in Balzan. (Photo, V. Zammit.)

has become a major driver of tourism demand' (Sigala and Leslie, 2006, p. xii), and that there has been a rapid growth in cultural tourism due to the increased interest in art, culture and history (Munsters and Freund de Klumbis, 2006). The World Tourism Organization (UNWTO) states that cultural tourism represents more than a third of global tourism (Munsters, 2004). It has also been noted that as more senior tourists are travelling cultural and heritage sites tend to become more frequented, because these travellers are the ones who opt for a cultural visit. It is therefore understandable why authorities want to enhance their cultural resources in order to attract more tourists interested in local heritage (McIntosh et al., 1995).

Meanwhile, it has been recognized that the involvement of the local community in any development would enhance the final product and be a valuable element in the same tourist development (Leslie, 2006). One needs to have the local community take on board any development in order for success to be guaranteed because they are a key component of any development taking place within their environment (Galdini, 2007). There has been a consistent increase in cultural activities throughout Malta, yet there is a need for variety in such activities, events and approaches, in order to sustain the activities and the development. As more people travel, with a wider variety of interests, there is a need to keep providing different activities and cultural events. At the same time, these activities need to be accepted by the local population (Sepe and Di Trapani, 2010), because otherwise there might not be the necessary local support.

11.4   Cultural Expression in Malta

Public cultural manifestations are an everyday occurrence in Malta. Anything that needs to be celebrated is usually done so in public. Whether it is sporting, political or religious, in most cases manifestations are held for public consumption. Yet, in the majority of cases, they are locally based and meant for the immediate locality. In the main, the large manifestations of culture that are organized are connected with the religious aspect of each parish. Some of these can be seen as national expressions of culture, as well as having local meaning and depth (see Fig. 11.3).

In the last decade or so the Maltese authorities have been looking at how to enhance the tourist product. Successive administrations have increasingly recognized the need to harness the extant cultural product and also to increase the offering. The latest launching of the National Cultural Policy is a case in point. In its introduction, the Prime Minister of Malta wrote:

Fig. 11.3. Fiesta St Paul Valletta. (Courtesy of Daniel Cilia.)

Government perseveres in the creation of an environment that encourages cultural development as a main sector in our educational, social and economic development, and also as a sector that keeps our identity alive and regenerates it, for us and for the tourists who visit us both physically and virtually, and for our future generations.

(Parliamentary Secretariat for Tourism, 2011, p. 5)

11.5 First Cultural/Historical Mega Event in Malta

With this type of philosophy in mind, a completely different cultural event was organized in 1993. The Ministry of Tourism decided that they would organize the first cultural/historical mega event in Malta. It was to be the start of a trend that has become extremely popular. There had never been anything like the event before, and it acted as a catalyst for future and present activities. This was a unique event in all aspects. The historical re-enactment was spectacular, as more than 300 participants were gathered, all with period costume, recreating an event that was only known through history books. The event commemorated was a ceremony that used to be held whenever a new Grand Master was chosen to head the Order of the Knights of

St John, then rulers of Malta. Soon after the election the Grand Master would be invited to visit the old capital city of Malta, Mdina, in order to take possession of the city. There were a number of rituals and ceremonies that needed to be carried out, before the Grand Master was given the keys of the city and the gates of the fortified city were opened. After the formal ceremonies festivities would be held in the streets of the city and in its immediate area. This historical event was the idea behind this first Mdina Festival – a re-creation of this day-long inauguration event. Besides the particular ceremony, a number of small acts were offered as part of a street theatre performance in which the everyday life of the time was recreated.

When the decision was taken to organize this first event Mdina was the logical choice of location. The city (see Fig. 11.4), popularly referred to as 'The Silent City', has a population of only about 300 inhabitants. Most of these are elderly, and there is very little human interaction between the elderly local population and visitors. The city is well marketed, however, by the tourism authorities, and large numbers of tourists visit it every day. The activity of this cultural event took 2 years in the planning and involved historical research, the manufacture of costumes, arms and armour, as well as planning the street decorations. This first festival was spread over 7 days, and it proved

Fig. 11.4. Aerial photo of Mdina 'The Silent City'. (Courtesy of Daniel Cilia.)

to be a marathon not to be repeated. All future events have been organized over a maximum 3-day period, thus minimizing the inconvenience that was experienced by the residents. Complaints by the local population after this first event tended to be very strong and vociferous. It was felt, and immediately agreed, that any future activities would try and minimize the disturbance and the inconvenience that was created by thousands of people visiting the small medieval city.

Following the success of the first activity the authorities gave the go-ahead to have it repeated the following year. This created an interest by other cities and villages, wherein they felt that such an event could also be organized within their territory. Eventually these cultural activities were spread to other cities and localities. It has been the policy that while the national authorities have supported these activities, there has been a drive to try and diversify the product as well. Different themes are being suggested, in particular activities connected specifically with the local area where the festivals are organized. Since this first festival a variety of thematic festivals were eventually organized: commemoration of historical events, agricultural festivals, extolling the local gastronomic culture (wine, strawberries, chocolate, agricultural produce, ricotta, pumpkin, bread, olive oil, honey, etc.), maritime activities, and others (see Fig. 11.5).

Maritime Festival

Farmers' Festival

Music Festival

Arts Festival

Chocolate Festival

Fireworks Festival

Fig. 11.5. Selection of Maltese festival posters. Clockwise from left: Senglea Maritime Festival (www.lc. gov.mt); Burmarrad Farmers' Festival (www.manicmalta.blogspot.com); Music Festival (www.vfimf.com); Malta Fireworks (Dominatorfireworks.com); Chocolate Festival (www.its.edu.mt); Arts Festival (www. maltaartsfestival.com).

The effects of these festivals and cultural activities have created a sense of belonging, although some would claim it as parochialism. The various entities started to realize that they can organize similar events within their localities and start to attract tourists as well. The first activities immediately set a train in motion. Various groups were created – some to organize the actual activities and to supervise the whole event. A number of re-enactment groups started to be formed, all interested in recreating life from different historical eras. Others felt the need to increase interest in the gastronomic heritage, giving the chance for old recipes to be rediscovered and presented once more to the public, locals and tourists alike.

These activities necessitated the upgrading of various areas where they were to be held. The popularity of these events highlighted the lack of various facilities and upgrading that was needed. Various local councils took the initiative to upgrade the areas where the actual festivals were to be held. New street lighting, paving and even street furniture were installed.

Notwithstanding the material improvements, the most important aspect of regeneration in the various urban centres came from the local population. There has been a drive towards increasing the participation of local people, and the locals in most instances have answered by helping out, volunteering and even making sure that their locality is well presented for the occasion.

11.6   The Vittoriosa Historical Festival

Vittoriosa is one of the cities that has witnessed such regeneration. The Vittoriosa Historical Festival was first organized in the summer of 1995. Many local societies set up shops offering all kinds of food, drinks and other items. The same associations made sure that they also set up exhibitions of all kinds within their premises. All of this necessitated the restoration, repainting and rehabilitation of many of these places. The local council also encouraged the locals to put flower pots on their window sills. The last suggestion was well accepted, as

today, 18 years later, the city of Vittoriosa is still decorated with large pots along its narrow and medieval streets.

The amount of restoration that is going on throughout the main cultural sites of Malta is impressive. Valletta, as the European Capital of Culture for 2018, has seen an upsurge in restoration – the city has already been given new paving along the two main streets of the city and a good part of the same streets has been pedestrianized, for the benefit of the locals and tourists alike. It must be remembered that Valletta is already a well-established cultural centre in its own right. The city was built in the 16th century and is adorned with lush baroque palaces, churches (see Fig. 11.6) and other buildings constructed in the later centuries.

Valletta survived the ravages of the Second World War and was inscribed on the UNESCO World Heritage List in 1980. However, the social fabric of Valletta has deteriorated in recent decades, and the population

Fig. 11.6. Rich Baroque decoration – restored arch in Chapel of Aragon. (Courtesy of Daniel Cilia.)

has continued to decrease. In recent years there has been an increased interest by foreign residents and locals in returning to Valletta, rehabilitating residences and infusing a new life in the capital city. Figure 11.7 illustrates parts of the 16th-century fortifications of Valletta, which are being restored as part of a drive to restore the fortifications and at the same time prepare for when Valletta is to be the European Cultural Capital 2018. Much of the motivation for renovating such historical structures comes from the local pride in historical culture, which may be derived from the increased importance being placed on culture and heritage within Malta.

Recently the central authorities have declared that the National Museum of Fine Arts, located in one of the 18th-century palaces, will be relocated to a more central location, and within another important 17th-century building. The move is seen as a positive one, as the new venue for the Museum would be restored, upgraded and the general public will be able to enjoy the palace in its entirety. With more space being made available within the new venue more exhibits will be placed on display. A further recent development is a suggestion

that the old covered market, built in the middle of the 19th century, should be turned into a Contemporary Art Museum. This is a relatively new idea, and, as is common in Malta, it has created a lot of debate. The building is considered to be one of the iconic 19th-century buildings in Malta, which introduced the concept of making use of metal in buildings (Baldacchino, 2012).

Another aspect of urban regeneration is using past industrial complexes, which are usually derelict, for modern cultural and leisure centres (Smith *et al.*, 2010). In recent years, as more space became available around Valletta Grand Harbour, a number of projects were initiated with the aim of regenerating economic activity in that area. One of the most successful projects has been the Valletta Waterfront (see Fig. 11.8). The area comprises old warehouses built in the middle of the 18th century, the first power house in Malta, and other storage places that were built throughout the centuries, as well as the historic quay with its centuries-old landing places. The restoration work concentrated on the rehabilitation of the structures and restoration of the historic places. Offices, shops and eateries have been set up, and this

Fig. 11.7. Renovation of 16th-century fortifications of Valletta. (Photo, V. Zammit.)

Fig. 11.8. Valletta waterfront and a visiting cruise liner. (Courtesy of Daniel Cilia.)

place has become one of the most sought-after locations for entertainment in Malta. Yet, the most important activity is as a cruise terminal, where more than half a million tourists a year visit Malta on the many cruise ships that ply the Mediterranean. A small church, dating from the 18th century, has also been restored, and classical and baroque concerts are held here for the benefit of locals and tourists alike.

11.7   Maltese Carnival

Another added cultural attraction is planned for the very near future – a Museum of Carnival. The annual carnival event (see Fig. 11.9) has been organized in Malta for centuries. Originally a religious feast, established in the 16th century, carnival has taken on a different aspect with popular participation, similar to that which happens in various other parts of the world. Although this is a very popular annual activity in Malta, it has never been represented in a museum. This museum aims to present cultural mementoes from past carnivals, as well as parts of previous carnival floats. The organizers are planning to have this museum as part of an on-going regeneration of the Valletta Waterfront area, an added attraction, and at the same time offering, especially the cruise passengers, an inkling of what carnival in Malta is all about.

The Valletta Waterfront is always teeming with visitors, and this can be considered one of the most successful urban regeneration projects ever carried out in Malta. A myriad of activities have been held here, from rock concerts to

Fig. 11.9. Maltese carnival. (Courtesy of Daniel Cilia.)

evenings of classical music, classic car exhibitions and many other activities for all the family.

Yet, the main works that are transforming Valletta into a 21st-century city are concentrated in and around City Gate. The whole project has been entrusted to the internationally renowned architect Renzo Piano. The regeneration of this area is more than rehabilitation of a number of buildings. There is the pulling down of the

1960s City Gate structure, the narrowing of the entrance bridge to its original size, the building of a new Parliament House on entering the city and the rehabilitation of the ruins of the Royal Opera House. The main emphasis of the whole project, however, is not on architecture but on cultural regeneration. During a speech in 2010 Prime Minister Dr L. Gonzi stated: 'whilst preserving the heritage Valletta is endowed with, we want to project a modern, cosmopolitan and attractive cultural identity' (Gonzi, 2010).

11.8   Summary

Urban regeneration through culture has become widespread. Instead of simply renovating abandoned buildings and areas for the sake of economic revival, it has been realized that there needs to be a deeper commitment. This has led to realization that a full package of development needs to be employed: restructuring the urban fabric, renewing the urban economy and involving the local population in the whole process. The examples from Malta have been planned taking into account this holistic concept.

Urban regeneration tends to be more of a physical activity than anything else. Yet, throughout the whole process, there is always the need to involve local people, because they need to make the changes their own. In generating such interest, the regeneration of an area, or even of a city, will ensure participation and eventual success. This activity also gives rise to an increased cultural awareness of the local population. The debates that are generated because of the regeneration programmes will also lead to engagement of a wider audience. One way or another the local population will become involved, and this helps in generating more interest.

The tourist still remains the main client. In studies conducted by the Malta Tourism Authority, history and culture has been the third most popular reason why tourists travelled to the islands (Malta Tourism Authority, 2010, personal communication). More than 19% of tourists would recommend Malta to their friends and families for the history, culture and architecture that can be experienced while visiting. The same terms of history and culture have been noted as being among the most noted ideas and concepts connected with Malta by those visiting the islands. It is no surprise therefore that the local authorities are using culture as a marketing tool and regenerating historical cores in order to continue to provide a more authentic experience for the discerning traveller.

Many locations have experienced difficulties in attracting tourism, even though regeneration of their city has taken place. Smith *et al.* (2010) suggest that this occurs when there is not enough cultural activity going on. Furthermore, the type of cultural activity needs to be taken into consideration in order to make sure that this will attract the right amount of visitors (local and tourist alike). It has been pointed out that usually it is a small minority of tourists who are truly interested in the real culture that a place can offer (Craik, 1997). The vast majority of tourists are not looking for anything exotic (Robinson and Smith, 2006) but rather for something that is combined with relaxation and helps to foster the holiday mood.

11.9   Discussion Questions

• How have the authorities in Malta encouraged the local population to become involved and take ownership of their culture and heritage?
• What events are the key catalysts for the regeneration of Maltese culture and heritage?
• What are the main motivations for the regeneration of Valletta?

References

Baldacchino, L.G. (2012) An appetite for art. *Times of Malta* 31 March.
Caruana, B. (2012) Embellishment of Balzan Centre to attract tourism – Mario de Marco. *Malta Today*. http://www.maltatoday.com.mt/en/newsdetails/news/national/Embellishment-of-Balzan-centre-to-attract-tourism-Mario-de-Marco-20120321 (accessed 21 March 2012).

Craik, J. (1997) The culture of tourism. In: Rojek, C. and Urry, J. (eds) *Touring Cultures: Transformations of Travel and Theory*. Routledge, London, pp. 113–136.

Galdini, R. (2007) Tourism and the city: opportunity for regeneration. *Tourismos: An International Multidisciplinary Journal of Tourism* 2, 95–111.

Gonzi, L. (2010) Speech by the prime minister, the Hon. Lawrence Gonzi during the Valletta Alive seminar 'Valletta the people's capital: a cultural perspective'. 6 November 2010. https://opm.gov.mt/vallettaalive?l=2 (accessed 28 March 2012).

Leslie, D. (2006) Effective community involvement in the development and sustainability of cultural tourism: an exploration in the case of New Lanark. In: Sigala, M. and Leslie, D. (eds) *International Cultural Tourism: Management, Implications and Cases*. Elsevier, Oxford, pp. 122–136.

McIntosh, R.W., Goeldner, C.R. and Brent Ritchie, J.R. (1995) *Tourism – Principles, Practices, Philosophies*, 7th edn. John Wiley & Sons, New York.

Munsters, W. (2004) Culture × tourism: merely a marriage of convenience? Inaugural speech in the Centre of Expertise for Cultural Tourism, Zuyd University, Maastricht, the Netherlands.

Munsters, W. and Freund de Klumbis, D. (2006) Culture as a component of the hospitality record. In: Sigala, M. and Leslie, D. (eds) *International Cultural Tourism: Management, Implications and Cases*. Elsevier, Oxford, pp. 26–39.

NCHE (2009) *Report on Skills for the Future*. National Commission for Higher Education, Valletta.

Parliamentary Secretariat for Tourism (2011) *National Cultural Policy – Malta*, 1st edn. Parliamentary Secretary for Tourism, the Environment and Culture, Valletta.

Robinson, M. and Smith, M. (2006) Politics, power and play: the shifting contexts of cultural tourism. In: Smith, M. and Robinson, M. (eds) *Cultural Tourism in a Changing World: Politics, Participation and (Re)presentation*. Channel View Publications, Bristol, UK, pp. 1–18.

Sepe, M. and Di Trapani, G. (2010) Cultural tourism and creative regeneration: two case studies. *International Journal of Culture, Tourism and Hospitality Research* 4, 214–227.

Sigala, M. and Leslie, D. (2006) Introduction. In: Sigala, M. and Leslie, D. (eds) *International Cultural Tourism: Management, Implications and Cases*. Elsevier, Oxford, pp. xii–xix.

Smith, M., MacLeod, N. and Hart Robertson, M. (2010) *Key Concepts in Tourist Studies*, 1st edn. SAGE, London.

Spiteri, E.J. (2002) *Malta – From Colonial Dependency to Economic Viability (Maltese Economic History 1800–2000)*, 1st edn. Publishers Enterprises Group, San Gwann, Malta.

12 Case Study 4: The Cultural Tourism Sustainability Mix Applied to the Development of Contemplative Tourism in Limburg, the Netherlands

Wil Munsters and Manon Niesten

Zuyd University of Applied Sciences, Maastricht, the Netherlands

---

This chapter explores the challenges of dealing with a particular cultural tourism resource in the province of Limburg in the Netherlands. This region has a long Roman Catholic tradition but, due to secularization, a lot of religious buildings are losing their function and become vacant. There are several monasteries still active, but the numbers of fathers and sisters is shrinking, and they have to deal with declining revenues from their regular activities and from donations by the faithful. Therefore, increasingly, administrators are looking for ways to generate income by opening up the monasteries to the public with new activities and by taking advantage of the rise of contemplative tourism as a promising niche market.

12.1 Introduction

As this chapter will illustrate, there is always a tension between exploiting monasteries for commercial activities and the practising of faith. The symbiosis between religion and tourism is complex and not self-evident, because in the first instance religious buildings and rituals have not been created to serve as tourist attractions. The preservation of religious heritage and traditions and their commercialization by way of tourism product development appear to be contradictory and incompatible objectives. What may be good for tourism is not necessarily good for religion and vice versa. How to find a sustainable balance? The application of the so-called cultural tourism sustainability mix to the policy of the Wittem Monastery in South Limburg illustrates very well the challenges the suppliers of contemplative tourism products and services are dealing with.

12.2 Contemplative Tourism as a Niche Market Opportunity

Limburg is a province in the southern part of the Netherlands, located in the so-called Euregion between Belgium and Germany. Tourism and leisure are well developed and are considered a top priority in the regional policy in order to achieve long-term growth, employment and prosperity. Contemplative tourism is one of the spearheads in the regional tourism policy. In the framework of the development plan for contemplative tourism in Limburg, the Chamber of Commerce as the initiator and leader of the project has defined this form of cultural tourism as an experiential tourist activity that leads to inner peace and balance, and that is linked to giving meaning to life.

An overall analysis of the strengths, weaknesses, opportunities and threats for the region of Limburg provides the following outcomes (Fig. 12.1).

Contemplative tourism is rapidly growing in the province of Limburg thanks to the internal strengths of the region and the favourable external developments analysed above. The suppliers of contemplative tourism products and services in Limburg's countryside can benefit from the need for authentic personal experiences and the desire to escape from the busy everyday life in order to contemplate in peace and quiet. In rural Limburg the contemplative tourist finds the beauty and the stillness of the landscape they are searching for. Furthermore, Limburg has another important asset that meets the needs of this tourist: the Catholic faith has a long tradition in this region but, because of the secularization process, buildings like churches and monasteries are losing their religious function, becoming vacant and even abandoned. The provincial government of Limburg wants to preserve this built heritage by creating new functions for it, such as exploitation for tourism purposes. Another factor worth mentioning that stimulates the growth of

contemplative tourism is the ageing of Western Europe's population. Senior citizens (50+) have much time and money to spend and seek culture, nature and rest during their holiday (Munsters, 2007).

The contemplative tourism market in Limburg can be divided into three submarkets: religious tourism, spiritual tourism and wellness tourism. For the latter there should also be a link with spirituality. The yearly revenue of contemplative tourism for Limburg is estimated to reach €11–16 million in the near future (ZKA Consultants & Planners, 2008). This rise of contemplative tourism in Limburg can also be seen in an international perspective as it illustrates the world-wide growth of religious and spiritual tourism. This is one of the major niches emerging from postmodern fragmentation of the cultural tourism market caused by the proliferation of cultural motives for travel.

The World Tourism Organization (UNWTO) identified the spiritual tourism sector as one of the fastest growing areas within tourism and travel in 2007. Concerning religious tourism, it is estimated that over 250 million pilgrimages are undertaken per year. At the same time purely religious motives are becoming more and more combined with secular motives (Richards, 2011). A similar mix of motives can be observed in the province of Limburg, where two types of contemplative tourists have been identified. To the first category belong those who actively seek an offer related to contemplation; in other words their primary visit motive is the search for reflection and spirituality. The second group of tourists are those who visit Limburg for motives other than contemplation. This accidental tourist comes to the region because of the landscape or the cultural sites. When passing by the contemplative offer he or she will visit it (ZKA Consultants & Planners, 2008). Figure 12.2 shows how this type of tourist can be integrated in the continuum of religion-oriented visit motives that Smith has described in the so-called pilgrim–tourist motive path (Smith, 1992). The pilgrims with a pure religious motive are on one end of the continuum and on the other end one can find the secular tourist. When linking the previously mentioned typology of contemplative tourists to this continuum, the active seeker, being driven primarily by sacred and profane rather than secular motives,

Product element	Strengths	Weaknesses
Tourism supply	Various offers: landscape, history, religious built heritage and traditions	Necessity of quality improvement
Tourism image	Strong image based on landscape, culture, hospitality, gastronomy and atmosphere	
Situation	Central location in the Euregion Meuse-Rhine between Belgium and Germany	
Competitiveness and entrepreneurship	Second position in the national holiday market Highest average expenses per tourist compared to the other Dutch provinces Passionate entrepreneurs	Many small (family) businesses characterized by a: - lack of entrepreneurial competencies - lack of innovation - lack of cooperation, coordination and networking between entrepreneurs The mass of initiatives in tourism makes it difficult for entrepreneurs to get the right information at the right place and at the right time

Field	Opportunities	Threats
Market supply side	Rise of niche markets, like contemplative tourism	Heavy competition with other regional destinations
Market demand side	Experience economy: consumers are willing to spend more time and money in order to get memorable holiday experiences Tourists are looking for authentic values: truthfulness of origins, intentions and behaviour, especially related to hospitality Localization as a reaction to cultural globalization Need to get away from the hectic every-day life	Economic crisis causing a decrease of tourist expenses and of holiday frequency

Fig. 12.1. SWOT-analysis of the Limburg region as a tourism product. (From Authors.)

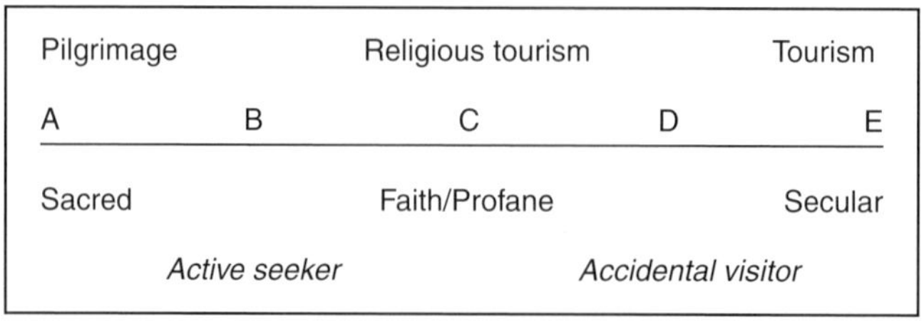

Pilgrimage		Religious tourism		Tourism
A	B	C	D	E
Sacred		Faith/Profane		Secular
	Active seeker		Accidental visitor	

Fig. 12.2. The pilgrim–tourist motive path. (Adapted from Smith,1992.) A = Pious pilgrim; B = Pilgrim > tourist; C = Pilgrim = tourist; D = Pilgrim < tourist; E = Secular tourist.

can be positioned at the left side of the continuum, and the accidental visitor at the right side of the continuum, since his/her motives to visit are more secular.

12.3 The Cultural Tourism Sustainability Mix

Contemplative tourism excludes by definition mass tourism. With the development of contemplative tourism quality needs to take precedence over quantity. Care for the quality of supply determines the attractiveness of the contemplative tourism product and has to keep pace with the ever-increasing requirements of the modern, critical, widely travelled tourist/consumer. In order to achieve the required quality level contemplative tourism has to develop in the direction of sustainable tourism. More than that, because of its respect for the integrity of man, nature and culture, contemplative tourism can only be genuine if it is sustainable.

In its broad sense, sustainability takes full account of environmental, socio-cultural and economic aspects of tourism development. According to the definition of the World Tourism Organization (UNEP & WTO, 2005), sustainable tourism should make optimal use of environmental resources, respect the tangible and intangible culture of host communities, and ensure long-term economic benefits to all stakeholders. At the same time, sustainable tourism should provide a high level of satisfaction and experience to the tourists while raising their awareness about sustainability issues. Sustainable tourism implies that the interests of all these stakeholders are guaranteed in the long run.

However, the comprehensive approach of sustainability as expressed by the WTO definition is seldom realized in practice. In fact, the principles of sustainability have so far been applied almost exclusively to the environmental aspects of tourism policy and development. Companies and destinations that adhere to the slogan 'people, planet, profit' mostly lay the emphasis on the second element, which has led to stimulating nature-friendly types of tourism, such as ecotourism. As a reflection of this reality, the vast majority of studies within this research area focus on the ecological aspects

of sustainable tourism (see Page and Connel, 2006, chapter 20, and Rotherham's chapter in this volume). Although the research interest in cultural sustainability has risen in recent years (Lu and Nepal, 2009), systematic strategic thinking about sustainable cultural tourism has scarcely received any attention up to now. There are some reports dealing with the strategic aspects of sustainable cultural tourism, especially related to museums and historic towns (ICOM, 2000, 2007; EAHTR, 2006), but these are rather broad and so few in number that one could be allowed to speak of an 'as good as virgin' field of research. What can be inferred from the existing studies is that the principles of sustainable environmental tourism are *mutatis mutandis* just as much applicable to the tangible and intangible cultural supply, which, when exposed to negative impacts from tourism, can be just as vulnerable as certain eco-systems. Following this line of reasoning, sustainable cultural tourism should aim at finding a balance between the various interests and objectives of the different stakeholders within an integral approach that takes into account the overlapping and the interplay of their fields of action. By embroidering on the elements of the slogan 'people, planet, profit' and the P-alliteration, we can distinguish with regard to cultural tourism the key actors and the respective objectives that each of them pursues (see Fig. 12.3; cf. Munsters, 2005).

If well geared to one another in their realization, the objectives of the various stakeholders form the basis for the so-called cultural tourism sustainability mix, a conceptual model that can serve as a general policy framework (Fig. 12.4).

For the realization of these strategic objectives there is a range of possible tactical and operational measures in the field of product development, planning, organization, finance, promotion and education described in reports and studies on this subject (ICOM, 2000, 2007; Schouten et al., 2005; EAHTR, 2006; Munsters, 2007). With regard to preservation, for instance, the choice of measures depends on the type of cultural supply and the level of visitor pressure on the area. As part of visitor management one can apply soft measures, such as advice and information, when the number of visitors or their behaviour does not

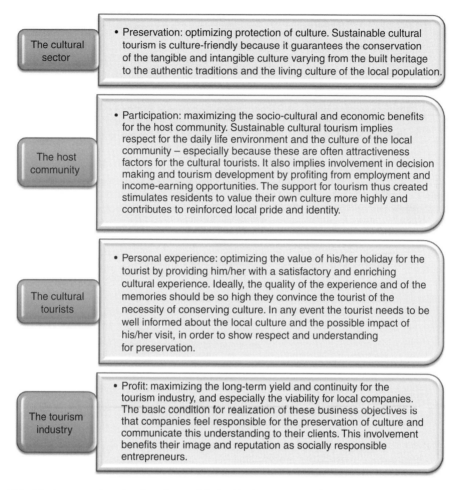

Fig. 12.3. The key actors in cultural tourism and their objectives. (From Authors.)

give any cause for serious concern. Hard measures, such as severe visiting regulation and deflecting demand, are required when tourist pressure damages the local culture, be it the built heritage or living traditions, and devalues the quality of the visitor experience. In order to ensure a meaningful holiday experience for the tourist, social media can play a crucial role as a promotion and communication instrument because it gives the opportunity for visitors to share information and experiences by means of user-generated content. Worth mentioning is the field research carried out by Lynch *et al.* (2010) on the Mi'kmaw aboriginals living in Nova Scotia, Canada. This case study provides and interprets empirical data expressing the tourists' and locals' perspectives and presents practical recommendations for sustainable cultural tourism development in Canadian aboriginal communities, such as in-house marketing in order to ensure authenticity and promote Mi'kmaw ownership. But the most critical success factor for the implementation of the cultural tourism sustainability mix is cooperation based on informed participation of the different stakeholders, shared interests and mutual understanding (McKercher and du Cros, 2002; Castellani and Sala, 2010). The cultural tourism product benefits strongly from cooperation because it contributes to its cohesion and quality (cf. Robinson and Picard, 2006).

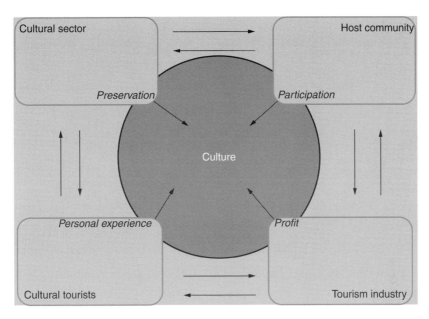

Fig. 12.4. The cultural tourism sustainability mix: the key actors and their strategic objectives. (From Authors.)

12.4 Contemplative Tourism as a Form of Sustainable Cultural Tourism: the Case of the Wittem Monastery – From Policy to Practice

Sustainable tourism is often criticized as a utopian dream that will never come true because of obstacles varying from lack of stakeholder involvement to priority of economics (Dodds and Butler, 2010). However, there are good practices showing that sustainable cultural tourism can be a feasible option, as witnessed in successful restoration of the historic Saint Gerlachus country estate in South Limburg (Munsters, 2005). The case of the Wittem Monastery situated in the same region is also an example of evidence to the contrary (Fig. 12.5a and b).

Founded in 1732, the Wittem Monastery became derelict after the French Revolution until 1836 when the Redemptorist Order moved into the building. After the canonization of the Italian Redemptorist Gerardus Majella in 1904 Wittem grew into a popular place of pilgrimage among Dutch Catholics and nowadays attracts between 150,000 and 180,000 visitors per year. Because of secularization the number of visitors is dropping,

as also is the number of fathers: not more than 12 of them are still living in this huge complex. At the same time the costs of the building are rising, while revenue from the regular services and donations are sharply decreasing. In spite of all this the Redemptio foundation, which is responsible for exploitation of the complex, is convinced that today there is still a need for places where people can reflect on the fundamental questions concerning faith, religion, spirituality and life they are facing. In order to preserve the monastery for the future the Redemptio foundation has set up a master plan. When analysing the foundation's policy expressed in the master plan and putting it to the test against the objectives of sustainable cultural tourism, it appears that in practice it is quite possible to find a balance between the diversity of objectives and interests represented by the Ps of the cultural tourism sustainability mix.

12.5 Preservation of the Monastery and the Redemptorist Tradition

The Redemptio foundation is responsible for the development of sites belonging to the

(a)   (b)

Fig. 12.5. Wittem Monastery: (a) view from the garden; and (b) the library. (From Authors.)

Redemptorists, in line with the pastoral and contemplative tradition of the congregation, as well as for the conservation and the exploitation of the buildings by combining the functions of living, working and visiting. In other words, the objectives of the foundation address the preservation of both the intangible and the material cultural heritage of the order (see Fig. 12.6, which illustrates the implementation of the three other Ps of the cultural tourism sustainability mix).

12.6 Future Development of the Monastery as a Contemplative Tourism Product

An analysis of the Wittem Monastery as a cultural tourism product on the basis of the model developed by Munsters (2010) shows that the existing supply consists of guided tours through the buildings and the garden, and cultural events, like lectures, concerts and exhibitions of paintings in the monumental monastery library. With regard to the general tourist services, food and beverage facilities can be made use of in the refectory, and the monastery book shop presents a large assortment of religious literature. The transport infrastructure is up to standard, especially thanks to the capacious and free car parking across the complex.

In order to realize the main objectives of the master plan management wants to go ahead with the development of the monastery as a contemplative tourism product, guided by cultural sustainability as a leading principle. Plans for the future focus on the points outlined in Fig. 12.7.

Central to these plans is the development of the monastery as a contemplative tourism product. Figure 12.8 illustrates the various layers of product required to attain this goal.

All of these plans meet the increasing demand for stays and retreats in an authentic setting with a high experience value, a personal hospitality touch and regional gastronomy. Evidence suggests that these needs are especially present among the well-to-do and highly-educated cultural tourists (Munsters and Freund de Klumbis, 2005). An important challenge for the future will be to set up a visitor management policy that will make both the faithful and the unbelievers feel equally at home, in the knowledge that the religious visitor doesn't want to be exposed to commercial tourism activities, whereas the secular tourist doesn't mind as long as these don't devalue the authenticity of his or her experience (Niesten and Munsters, 2011).

12.7 Towards a Vital Cultural Tourism

The cultural tourism sustainability mix has not been applied knowingly by the foundation and

Profit as a means to preservation	• In order to guarantee the preservation and maintenance of the complex, the foundation has to look for new ways to generate revenue. That is why the first objective of the master plan is fleshing out and developing contemplative tourism as a new 'product' to attract visitors. In accordance with this objective, the foundation has decided to participate in the regional pilot project for contemplative tourism and to appoint a programme director entrusted with the development of a special supply. Thus, the monastery has become one of the regional supply figureheads in the fast-growing niche market of contemplative tourism.
Personal experience for each type of visitor	• Another main objective mentioned by the master plan is the improvement of accessibility to the religious and cultural-historic heritage of the monastery by opening up a substantial part of the site to visitors, varying from pilgrims with a pure religious motive to secular tourists driven by cultural interest.
Participation of the host community	• The monastery employs 30 people, most of them coming from the surrounding villages and towns (as do the many volunteers, without whom the monastery could not subsist since they contribute to the whole range of its activities, be it as singers in the church, hosts in the refectory or assistants in the book shop). Worth mentioning is the social inclusion project enabling reintegrants to gain work experience by redesigning the monastery garden. Thanks to this policy, public support for the Wittem Monastery has been firmly secured within the local and regional community.

Fig. 12.6. The cultural tourism sustainability mix applied to the development of Wittem Monastery (From Authors.)

the management of the Wittem Monastery. In the framework of this case study, it has been used as a method to scan and analyse the existing situation. But, the cultural tourism sustainability mix is much more than an analysis instrument since it can also serve as a strategic framework and a practical guideline for development (e.g. the future product development of the Wittem Monastery mentioned above), implementation, monitoring and evaluation of a sustainable cultural tourism policy. Therefore, general objectives have to be translated into specific and measurable goals for each field of action. These goals can be either quantitative (numbers of tourists, profit margin) or qualitative (state of the historical building, level of visitor satisfaction). Innovative measurement and evaluation instruments like the sustainable performance index for local development and the tourist experience audit are available in order to collect and analyse the necessary data and to monitor policy impacts as a basis for possible preventive and/or corrective measures (Castellani and Sala, 2010; Munsters, 2010). When passing through the successive stages of this plan–do–check–act cycle, one should always bear in mind that sustainable cultural tourism can only be VITAL (an acronym including the different stakeholders: volunteers – industry – tourists – administrators – locals) if at each step these key actors are involved and their interests are taken into account. Consensus building and strategic partnerships are the foundations of a healthy symbiosis between culture and tourism.

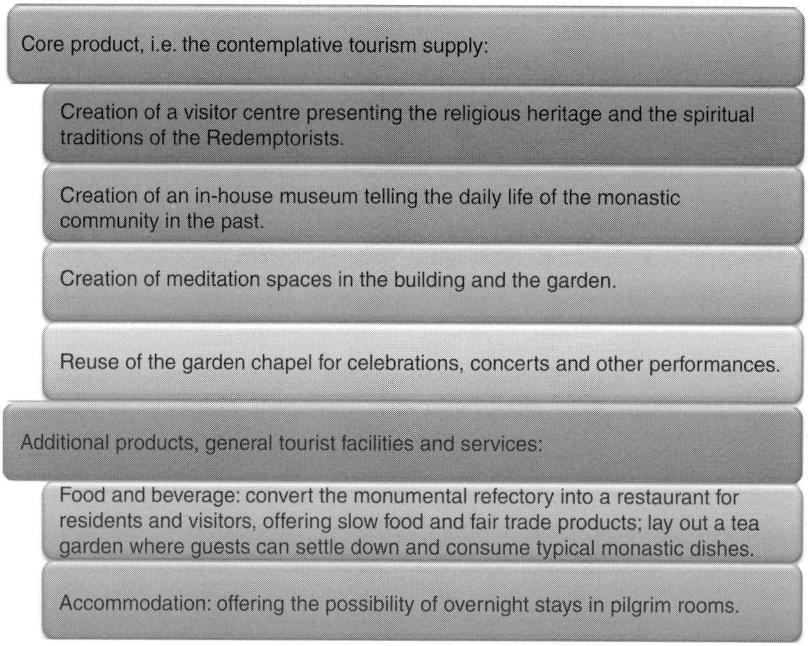

Core product, i.e. the contemplative tourism supply:
Creation of a visitor centre presenting the religious heritage and the spiritual traditions of the Redemptorists.
Creation of an in-house museum telling the daily life of the monastic community in the past.
Creation of meditation spaces in the building and the garden.
Reuse of the garden chapel for celebrations, concerts and other performances.
Additional products, general tourist facilities and services:
Food and beverage: convert the monumental refectory into a restaurant for residents and visitors, offering slow food and fair trade products; lay out a tea garden where guests can settle down and consume typical monastic dishes.
Accommodation: offering the possibility of overnight stays in pilgrim rooms.

Fig. 12.7. Main focal points for future plans at Wittem Monastery. (From Authors.)

transportation infrastructure
facilities & services
accessibility
car
contemplative tourism supply
tourist promotion
refectory restaurant
signposting
guided tours
cultural events
tea garden
coach
visitor centre
museum
meditation spaces
garden chapel
book shop
pilgrim rooms
regional bus
parking facilities
taxi

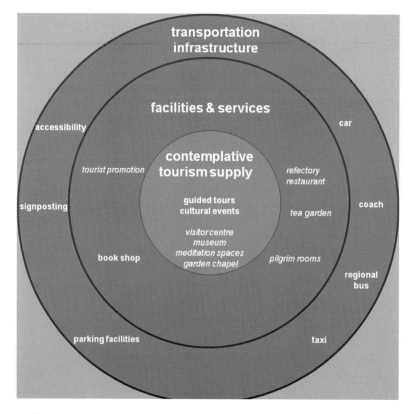

Fig. 12.8 The Wittem Monastery as a contemplative tourism product. The existing supply is in bold, the not yet realized product elements are in italics. (From Authors.)

12.8 Summary

Limburg is a province located in the southern part of the Netherlands where tourism plays a key role in the regional economy. One of the spearheads of the regional tourism policy is the development of contemplative tourism, a cultural tourism niche market defined as a tourist experiential activity that leads to inner peace and balance, and that is linked to the meaning of life.

The Catholic faith has a long tradition in this region but, because of the secularization process, buildings like churches and monasteries are losing their religious function and becoming vacant. The provincial government of Limburg wants to preserve this built heritage by creating new functions for it, such as exploitation for tourism purposes. At the same time more and more administrators of religious heritage are looking for ways to generate income by taking advantage of the rise of contemplative tourism as a promising niche market. This is a complex process because religious buildings and rituals have not been created to serve as tourist attractions. The preservation of religious heritage and traditions and their commercialization by way of tourism product development appear to be contradictory objectives. How to find a sustainable balance? The application of the so-called cultural tourism sustainability mix to the policy of the Wittem Monastery in South Limburg illustrates very well the issues and the problems the suppliers of contemplative tourism products and services have to face.

In our research the cultural tourism sustainability mix has been used to analyse the existing situation of Wittem Monastery. But the cultural tourism sustainability mix is much more than an analysis instrument since it can also serve as a strategic framework and a tactical guideline for the implementation, monitoring and evaluation of a sustainable religious tourism policy. Sustainable religious tourism can only be VITAL (an acronym including the different stakeholders: volunteers – industry – tourists – administrators – locals) if at each step these key actors are involved and their interests and objectives taken into account. Consensus building and strategic partnerships are the foundations of a sound symbiosis between religion and tourism.

12.9 Discussion Questions

- Explain why the preservation of religious heritage and its exploitation for tourism purposes can be contradictory objectives.
- Identify the internal assets and the external factors that stimulate the growth of contemplative tourism.
- The cultural tourism sustainability mix: who are the key actors and what are their objectives?
- Apply the model of the cultural tourism product developed by Munsters to a contemplative tourist attraction you have visited.
- What are the different purposes the cultural tourism sustainability mix can serve?

References

Castellani, V. and Sala, S. (2010) Sustainable performance index for tourism policy development. *Tourism Management* 31, 871–880.

Dodds, R. and Butler, R. (2010) Barriers to implementing sustainable tourism policy in mass tourism destinations. *Tourismos: An International Multidisciplinary Journal of Tourism* 5, 35–53.

EAHTR (2006) *Sustainable Cultural Tourism in Historic Towns and Cities*. Council of Europe Publishing, Strasbourg, France.

ICOM (2000) Cultural tourism. http://icom.museum/what-we-do/programmes/cultural-tourism.html (accessed 10 January 2012).

ICOM (2007) Sustainable cultural tourism. http://archives.icom.museum/declaration_tourism_eng.html (accessed 10 January 2012).

Lu, J. and Nepal, S.K. (2009) Sustainable tourism research: an analysis of papers published in the *Journal of Sustainable Tourism*. *Journal of Sustainable Tourism* 17, 5–16.

Lynch, M.-F., Duinker, P., Sheehan, L. and Chute, J. (2010) Sustainable Mi'kmaw cultural tourism development in Nova Scotia, Canada: examining cultural tourist and Mi'kmaw perspectives. *Journal of Sustainable Tourism* 18, 539–556.

McKercher, B. and du Cros, H. (2002) *Cultural Tourism: The Partnership Between Tourism and Cultural Heritage Management*. Hayworth Hospitality Press, New York.

Munsters, W. (2005) Culture and tourism: from antagonism to synergism. *ATLAS Reflections 2005: Tourism, Creativity and Development*, 41–50.

Munsters, W. (2007) *Cultuurtoerisme*, 4th edn. Garant, Antwerp-Apeldoorn.

Munsters, W. (2010) The cultural destination experience audit applied to the tourist-historic city. In: Richards, G. and Munsters, W. (eds) *Cultural Tourism Research Methods*. CAB International, Wallingford, UK, pp. 52–60.

Munsters, W. and Freund de Klumbis, D. (2005) Culture as a component of the hospitality product. In: Sigala, M. and Leslie, D. (eds) *International Cultural Tourism: Management, Implications and Cases*. Elsevier/Butterworth-Heinemann, Oxford, pp. 26–39.

Niesten, M. and Munsters, W. (2011) Attracting contemplative tourists to religious sites. Practices and experiences in the province of Limburg, the Netherlands. Paper presented at the ATLAS Religious Tourism and Pilgrimage Conference 2011 'Enhancing the Religious Tourism Experience', New Norcia, 20–25 June 2011.

Page, S.J. and Connel, J. (2006) *Tourism: A Modern Synthesis*, 2nd edn. Thomson Learning, London.

Richards, G. (2011) Cultural tourism trends in Europe: a context for the development of cultural routes. In: Khovanova-Rubicondo, K. (ed.) *Impact of European Cultural Routes on SMEs' Innovation and Competitiveness*. Council of Europe Publishing, Strasbourg, France, pp. 21–39.

Robinson, M. and Picard, D. (2006) *Tourism, Culture and Sustainable Development*. UNESCO, Paris.

Schouten, F., Beunders, N., Landré, M. and Barten, C. (2005) *Managing Visitors: Helping the Frail to Prevail*. NHTV Academic Studies 1, Breda, the Netherlands.

Smith, V. (1992) Introduction: The quest in guest. *Annals of Tourism Research* 19, 1–17.

UNEP & WTO (2005) *Making Tourism More Sustainable: A Guide for Policy Makers*. UNEP/WTO, Paris/Madrid. http://www.unep.fr/shared/publications/pdf/DTIx0592xPA-TourismPolicyEN.pdf (accessed 21 December 2011).

ZKA Consultants & Planners (2008) *Bezinningstoerisme in Limburg: kansen, concepten en voorwaarden*. ZKA Consultants & Planners, Breda, the Netherlands.

13 Case Study 5: Network of Hungarian Rural Heritage Farmhouses

Lia Bassa

Foundation for Information Society, Budapest, Hungary

This chapter explores the use and networking of cultural houses, this time in Hungary. A difference, however, is that in this instance the chapter focuses on indigenous dwellings, which are referred to as 'rural heritage houses'. Rural heritage houses comprise all features of heritage – built, natural, tangible, intangible – therefore they are a good example through which the presentation of cultural heritage and tourism can be linked. The buildings themselves, in addition to their related objects, natural formations, language, national customs, music and dance, are constantly changing; the basic aim of the researchers who are examining these properties is to record their current status so that managers can maintain them, their protection can be professional and to acquaint people with the values surrounding them, so that they are appreciated and transferred to future generations.

The collected and systematically arranged data on the houses can be useful for tourism, with the help of modern technologies, to communicate about these heritage sites, e.g. by cell phone, audio-guides or other new ways of information provision. At the same time, these data assist caretakers to prepare for the requirements of visitors of various ages and interest groups, and assist decision makers, professional bodies and authorities to select the relevant data for their own purpose.

13.1 Introduction

There is a complex branch of economic life: tourism. It includes and makes use of many branches of economic and cultural life as well as contributing to international relations. Therefore, it is very difficult to define its right place in the administrative structure of a country: sometimes it is attached to foreign or inner affairs, at the highest political level or sometimes subordinated to the economic or cultural administration. Nowadays it has become a rightful means of international relations, as a theme for international conferences, as part of intercultural relations and, because of the amount of visiting students and teachers, part of the education landscape as well. Taking into consideration these manyfold motivations, visitors have very different, numerous and specific aims and requirements. In order to meet them all, both the investigated sites and local technical conditions of reception have to be made available according to international standards, using the most recent developments.

There is a connection between tourism, its overall and sustainable development – through technological tools – and heritage management. This area belongs to both culture, namely to conservation and heritage management processes, and to the state of the art economy. One of the outcomes of examining the interplay between tourism and heritage has been the development of a tool for network management via heritage digitization and preservation. In the course of our investigation, we have found a case study example that incorporates many issues in this field of study – incorporating built, natural, tangible and intangible cultural heritage including the indispensable contribution of tourism (visits, events, festivals, shows). This is the process by which the so-called 'rural heritage houses' have become the main target of our research.

Our project began in 2005, when the World Heritage Research Team in the Department of Information and Knowledge Management at Budapest University of Technology and Economics started to assess the Rural Heritage Farmhouses of Hungary. In the following years, within the framework of the Foundation for Information Society, the same team began to apply its digitization techniques to the case of these houses, making this a complete pilot study. We are now at the end of an extensive investigation, whereby we have undertaken a full country investigation with questionnaires for the managers or owners of the houses. In addition to the data collection and evaluation work regarding the houses, in

parallel the gathering of local crafts practised has also become part of our work, and all of these in addition to their digital recording, especially of unique and vanishing elements, in an attempt to preserve and teach these skills for the future.

The purpose of our examination is to document the methods of this data-recording process, to enable all users to utilize the database with ease. The process can be qualified as a conservation job because it provides assistance regarding the scientific records and access to them for market value purposes. Our intention in this chapter is to present a description of the network of Hungarian rural heritage houses (being part of the national list of heritage properties), which is a network system of complex cultural heritage, as well as the establishment of a special information management system of their data complying with the Operational Guidelines of UNESCO's World Heritage Convention and with the later established Convention for the Safeguarding of Intangible Cultural Heritage.

13.2 Hungarian Rural Heritage Houses

In Hungary these rural heritage houses are very specific museum-like buildings and there are approximately 400 examples scattered all around the country (see Figs 13.1 and 13.2). These country, farm or village houses nowadays function as museums, with the tools of past industries collected and presented, the rooms furnished according to their old function and tourists visiting them to learn about past ways of living. Sometimes there are tools shown in their historic functions illustrating the origins of industry or agriculture of former periods. Additionally, each region has its own folklore tradition, including textual, poetic, musical and dancing conventions. The value of these houses lies, therefore, in the combined information and knowledge management techniques being utilized, and many are making profit out of their achievements – even if the original target of the examination has not been anything else but to see a building representing the past life of its inhabitants.

Fig. 13.1. Example of rural heritage house: Létavértes (North Plain), farm house with vinery tools. (From Author.)

Fig. 13.2. Example of rural heritage house: rich Hungarian rural heritage farm house (late 19th century). (From Author.)

13.3   The Rural Heritage Development

The primary objective of our 'rural heritage' programme has been to find a tool that captures the attention of visitors arriving from another part of the country or from abroad, from any social or cultural level, to make their acquaintance with rural life in its original surroundings. This experience provides them with information and knowledge, develops their cultural awareness and, last but not least, their visit is a financial resource for the site. In Hungary tourism is the main way of funding preservation and presentation of the past; however, it is important to note that heritage can be an attracting feature only when it meets all the requirements set up by those engaged in up-to-date information management.

Our work has included information procurement about the access, environment, history, inner and outer structures (tangible culture) of the houses, as well as description and presentation of the objects within the house – covering the intangible heritage relations (traditions, folk art, songs, music, craftsmanship, etc.). The collected data are recorded in line with the national conservational, museological and ethnological rules and standards.

The resultant information package can be made available and used (with regulated access) by local authorities and site managers as well as by researchers, the general public and tourists. Moreover, any special request for information characteristics can be added to satisfy the special needs of the 'client' to assist their work. Other applications of the dataset of built, natural, movable and intangible heritage can be used locally, regionally, nationally and internationally for teaching purposes.

The buildings, objects, natural formations, language, national customs, music and dances all change over the course of time. Our aim could only be to record their current status so that managers can maintain their continuation. Consequently their protection must be professional and with the purpose of making people acquainted with the values surrounding them, in order to appreciate and transfer them to the next generations. The recording and description of the values is a milestone in the permanent maintenance work, which consumes both time and money, but a long-term return on investment can be realized with the cooperation of numerous experts and organizations.

The digital presentation of a site includes data collection and retrieval as well as information provision for authorities, researchers, the public and tourists. All information is collected with a view towards site management, and in addition, monitoring has become necessary. This can be commenced when the prioritization of activities to be carried out at the site are identified as a conclusion of the data collection process. The methods of data mining can contribute to the relevance of the assembled and systematically arranged data, and its related translation and presentation as a tourism resource for use by modern technologies (e.g. internet or mobile guides in up-to-date information provision). At the same time that data assists caretakers to be prepared for the requirements of visitors of various ages and interest groups, and helps decision makers, professional bodies and authorities to possess a full set of data and select the relevant data for their own purposes.

13.4   Site Management and Development of Heritage Sites

The first stage of the research was a complete digital presentation pilot programme, which has been prepared out of the network of more than 400 buildings, including all information on the access, environment, history, inner and outer structure of the house as well as a description and presentation of the objects within the house (see Fig. 13.3), also covering intangibles (environment, folk art, songs, music, etc.). Later, we have extended the process with special local requests, e.g. the description of the neighbouring local cemetery and restoration of objects so that they could be put on show in their original place.

In the course of data processing, various sorts of data collection, registration, archiving and retrieval methods have been applied. The information gained is put together to establish proper management models for the maintenance and presentation of the site under investigation. One of our conclusions has been that any heritage site management project must make – among others – an attempt to undertake the various tasks outlined in Fig. 13.4.

At the beginning of the process, the first step is the search for values, their systematic arrangement and the establishment of the database. This can be done by taking into account the contribution of both heritage conservators, including folklore experts, and IT personnel. This is not a one-time job but involves continuous research, system building and updating. Next, the state of conservation

Fig. 13.3. Dining room with associated material objects. (From Author.)

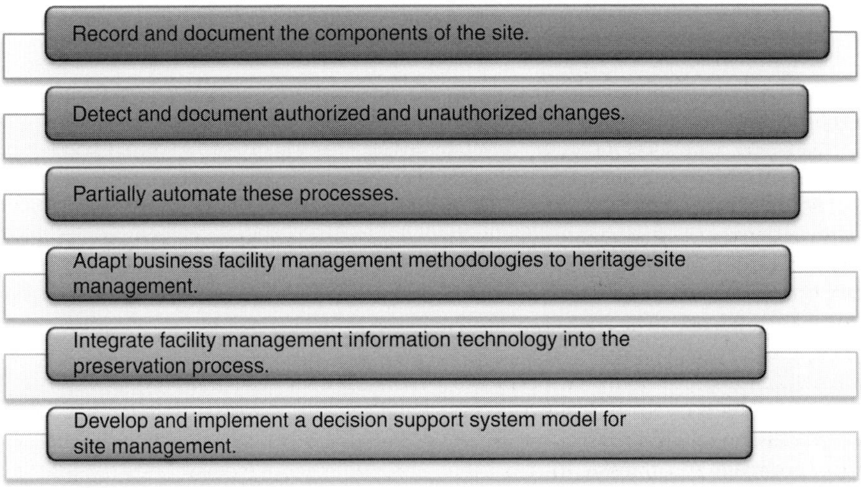

- Record and document the components of the site.
- Detect and document authorized and unauthorized changes.
- Partially automate these processes.
- Adapt business facility management methodologies to heritage-site management.
- Integrate facility management information technology into the preservation process.
- Develop and implement a decision support system model for site management.

Fig. 13.4. Site management goals for heritage sites. (From Author.)

has to be recorded and decisions must be made about the restoration or just the 'preservation' of the objects. The tracking of this, the monitoring activity, also requires organization and decision making.

The regularity/frequency of data updating for the entire network must also be identified and undertaken via a change management form, which is to be filled in and dispatched, collected, processed and classified. The areas involved in this procedure include entrance fees, reporting of executed repairs, modifications in the number of visitors and existing publications. For the sites it should be made mandatory (or preferably automatic or evident) to report changes, especially changes of address, owners, caretakers, including their availability. Central coordination is appreciated in many cases as these houses are scattered all around the country far from central monument preservation organizations. Currently regional management structures are governing the overall network, therefore local interests prevail.

Monitoring can be correctly undertaken when the prioritization of activities to be carried out is based on conclusions from the data collection process. This also entails taking into consideration other view points. In Hungary professional training is of a high level; therefore, the number of available experts is sufficient. The crucial problem for heritage protection is the lack of resources for the owners (organizations, private persons, local governments). The solution applied in most cases for the establishment of maintenance, renovation, development, even archiving, is to submit various applications to the EU and other funding organizations. The database created by our work can be used as a good source for these funding claims. It can be used not only by the writers of the bid, but it can give a full picture for the evaluators to enable them to make a sound judgement. In the course of the evaluation process what is mostly needed becomes clear, as does the procedure to assure a correct operation of the heritage site. At the same time it clearly reveals how investment can be made profitable and what are the most successful means for obtaining return on investment.

New information processing and IT methods must be applied because the increased volumes of data impede their access and retrieval, and these collections are hard if not impossible to handle by traditional technical tools. Established special methodologies and processes aim at a sort of 'informational treasure hunting'. The hidden point, correlations and regularities of the databases can be disclosed by this method. Data mining can contribute to the application of the collected and systematically arranged data into three directions, as illustrated in Fig. 13.5.

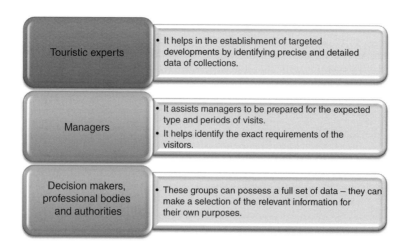

Fig. 13.5. Users and uses of data. (From Author.)

Access to the database enables managers, authorities and owners to extract statistics concerning the collection. Other statistical data on visitors can also be used for decisions concerning infrastructural investments. For instance, it is proved that when selecting a hotel via the internet the amount and quality of information about the surrounding points of interest can have a very powerful impact on the choice of the tourist. In the long run (after some years) data processing will be able to produce and show internal relations and it will also enable researchers and experts to draw relevant conclusions regarding protection and utilization of the various properties.

In consequence of these data-based management achievements, both the invested work and publicity fees can be reduced, thus allocating more revenue for preservation of value, maintenance, research and renewal. The awareness of and interest in the site can be grown, effecting an increase in the number of visitors and generating more income that can be invested in further development.

13.5 Heritage Preservation and Education

In our process of heritage preservation, stories become legends and disseminate the local culture: think of the Arthur legend, where there is no extant evidence of Camelot – if there ever was such a place – but, through stories, the way of life in that historic period is common knowledge throughout Europe.

In our case, in the small settlements, these stories preserve the memory and way of living of the ancestors. They determine the life of current inhabitants, and if this knowledge is transmitted future people will really have a clear identity, which is crucial in this time of globalization. In the course of our work it has become clear for us what we would like to hand over to people of the present: the continuity of history. This must be safeguarded; no civilizations, none of their constructions physical or spiritual can be allowed to disappear any more, because they can have a strong influence on the economic and financial position of a given area. People educated and living in an area must be made

conscious of their shared legacy, of their common heritage. In order to enable them to keep and convey it, their identity has to be defined and preserved deliberately by the setting up of systematic and comprehensive educational projects. Both the people and the historical record combine in contributing to community building and knowledge transfer that can and has to be successfully implemented.

Even a small country such as Hungary has a great variety of culture and heritage: tangible, intangible, historic, folkloric, built and natural, of local importance or international, such as that which is inscribed on the World Heritage or Tentative Lists. These can survive only by the help of education and awareness building, based on the most useful and innovative techniques. We have set up a structure by combining research and training to develop a programme in close connection with our new IT recording process of preservation and presentation technologies, together with information and knowledge management tools. This new structure is very complex and must also include all aspects of heritage.

13.6 Tangible–Intangible Heritage Presentation

Industrialization, urbanization, migration, environmental deterioration and mass tourism: all of these tokens of modernity are a threat to the transmission of human know-how and creativity. International communities are consequently making determined moves to prevent any risk of cultural uniformity and loss of collective memory. A first step was taken in 2003 with the adoption of the Convention for the Safeguarding of the Intangible Cultural Heritage. On 25 November 2005 UNESCO organized the Third Proclamation of Masterpieces of the Oral and Intangible Heritage of Humanity, which aims to celebrate and safeguard selected elements of the intangible cultural heritage. The convention concerning the protection of World Cultural and Natural Heritage adopted in 1972 exclusively protects tangible heritage. UNESCO wished, in this new convention, to extend protection to intangible cultural heritage, fragile and perishable but essential for communities' cultural identity. Creating this new international distinction was a means for UNESCO to alert the international community to the importance of considering this heritage and safeguarding it. UNESCO has four major programmes in the field of intangible cultural heritage, as identified in Fig. 13.6.

Masterpieces of Oral and Intangible Heritage have been recorded since 2008 and comprise two different lists – one recording practices and expressions that demonstrate the diversity of cultural heritage and the other recording intangible heritage that is in urgent need of safeguarding. This programme documents a broad range of cultural heritage, including foods, forms of theatre and music, festivals, events, rituals, and the manufacture of ethnically significant products, clothing and objects.

Living Human Treasures are persons who possess to a very high degree the knowledge and skills required for performing or creating specific elements of the intangible cultural heritage that the Member States have selected as a testimony to their living cultural traditions and to the creative genius of groups, communities and individuals present in their territory.

Languages are not only extremely important tools of communication, they also reflect a view of the world. They are vehicles of value systems and of cultural expressions and they constitute a determining factor in the identity of groups and individuals. Endangered languages and linguistic diversity are to be safeguarded as an essential part of the living heritage of humanity. There is a lot to do in this territory that can be seen from the figures below:

Fig. 13.6. Four major UNESCO programmes in the field of intangible heritage. (From Author.)

- over 50% of the world's 6000 languages are endangered;
- 96% of the world's 6000 languages are spoken by 4% of the world's population;
- 90% of the world's languages are not represented on the Internet;
- one language disappears on average every two weeks; and
- 80% of the African languages have no orthography.

Traditional music of the world developed from the very beginning of human existence and always reflects the status of people, their state of mind and their thoughts. This is different from language, as it can communicate without borders and limitations and link with movements, gestures and motions.

In the course of history, because of the materials used for knowledge transmission and because of history being too violent to save them, a lot of the knowledge from the past has been destroyed. If at last we have come to a point of awareness regarding what we have to do, if social, technical and economic conditions can provide us with the necessary means to execute it, it is our imperative task to join forces and, with the assistance of the above-mentioned structures, other similar conventions and international organizations, save the objects of our past for our children. Developing action plans for the preservation of cultural heritage, both tangible and intangible, provides concrete activities such as reinforcing research and documentation, identifying and census-taking of the knowledge bearers, providing support to measures ensuring transmission of knowledge and know-how to future generations, raising awareness at local and international levels through festivals and conferences, adopting protective legal measures, introducing specialized teaching in school and university curricula, etc.

13.7   The Value of Heritage

Heritage is entrusted to us by our ancestors, and our responsibility is to preserve it for future generations. The means of conservation and transmission have been changing a lot in recent times. Our cultural heritage protection projects have the duty to connect the values to be protected with the up-to-date technical potentials. Through the application of them, new ways of value protection, presentation and popularization come into use to promote the human track of globalization by connecting people with different backgrounds. Besides producing theoretical, aesthetic and cultural profit, business value is also being generated. Adjacent to increasing touristic income, it contributes to enrich the image formed of the given country.

By working with complex folk heritage sites, strongly rooted in local history and traditions, it has become clear to us that these processes and resultant data need to be disseminated, to be taught, to be transmitted to as many people as possible, both within the nation and beyond its borders. The continuity of history must be safeguarded; no civilizations, none of their construction, physical or spiritual product, may disappear any more, because it can also have a strong influence on the economic and financial position of a given area. People educated and living among such circumstances are to be aware of the shared legacy of their common heritage. In order to

enable them to keep this heritage and convey it, their identity has to be defined and preserved deliberately by the setting up of systematic and comprehensive educational projects. All of this contributes to community building and knowledge transfer that can and has to be successfully implemented.

Heritage has value and raising awareness of it in the 21st century must still be an objective. It does not only mean the protection of the environment and human creations, but the validation of these universal values. The work of UNESCO for cultural heritage principles can orient future generations by enabling them to separate good from bad, right from wrong, true from false, genuine from fake (Figs 13.7 and 13.8 illustrate attempts at representing genuine elements of cultural heritage in Hungarian rural houses). Moreover, they will be able to understand their roots and their identity. The end result will be a facilitated increase in tourism, based on the incredible options that people have to travel around the world, and linking this to inexhaustible sources of knowledge that can be useful if it is complemented by a well-managed cultural background network.

Fig. 13.7. Inner stove. (From Author.)

The basic aim of our cultural heritage projects (both tangible and intangible) is to set up a connection between value preservation by the conservator, the most recent technological advancements and the economic value of these heritage objects, as well as their realization. The main stages of investigation are outlined in Fig. 13.9.

Fig. 13.8. Wedding costumes and a cradle. (From Author.)

The use and knowledge of management techniques is important. The management of heritage sites is very particular and complex, therefore new methodologies are required in the areas of supervision, administration, organization, planning, control and marketing. Our investigations have proved that the majority of these tasks have never been dealt with before and such management activities have never been put into practice in Hungary. To achieve our goals the work of several different institutional communities will have to be harmonized, and ideally this can be implemented by using our database and information management system.

13.8   Summary

Cultural heritage, technological development and tourism are interrelated. To ensure an accurate description of a heritage site and its state-of-conservation, as well as monitoring by technical means, a depth of data collection is required. The approach taken in this project, which focuses on traditional rural housing in Hungary, is to connect the values to be protected with up-to-date technical methodologies. An important element of the project is to analyse the data in order to identify the most appropriate direction for these sites from the perspectives of their aesthetic, cultural and business future. While economic goals are important, to maintain this network of heritage

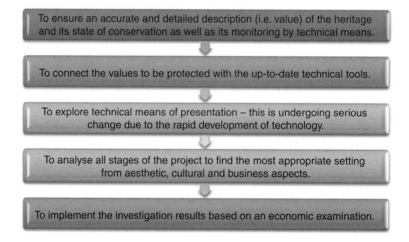

Fig. 13.9. The main stages of a cultural heritage investigation. (From Author.)

sites, any and all future development is predicated upon sound principles of conservation and preservation of identity.

A key purpose of our work is to establish a strategic plan taking into account the methods and depth of our research into history, cultural elements, local stories, legends, music, handicraft and other artistic values. It is also important to note how these results can contribute to preserve cultural heritage traditions by utilizing technological developments and by being closely linked to tourism.

The various means of information transfer have undergone serious changes in the recent period: beside the traditional leaflets, tourist agencies, so called word-of-mouth, there is an increasing influence of the internet. It is the most popular tool for information provision and procurement in the majority of the world, and the tools by which it can be accessed are also rapidly spreading thanks to falling prices. It has also to be noted here that Information Technology is the best way to involve young people in the knowledge procurement process. Furthermore, technological development also has the potential to transform payment methods, which can positively affect both sellers and buyers of touristic products. Electronic payment can be used for buying entrance tickets and for booking transport, hotels and trips. The new technologies can also influence the visits to museums and exhibitions, i.e. utilizing films or providing much more detail about the objects on view. Such tools can function on-site in an interactive way, raising interest and providing possibilities for the visitors to attempt something they have never encountered before. These methods can facilitate learning about a given folkloric custom or activity from an era long past.

Here we come to the point of how to finance cultural heritage education and maintenance, because in most territories it is not the most immediate priority. In the majority of countries culture (and also its education) has to produce sources for its own purposes. In order to achieve this all documents, research achievements, publications and books have to be collected, registered and processed. As part of the next step, our project will analyse the kind of methods and tools useful for raising touristic interest and for attracting people. At the same time the complete touristic value chain will be examined, where this special value can produce extra income. The potential advantage of increased visits is that income can be generated from which maintenance, new procurements, publication materials, etc. can be financed. An increase in the number of tourists affects other branches of the economy as described above: hotels, restaurants, other monuments and any commercial objects in the proximity of the presentation. Science and economy are also interrelated, as is conservation and tourism. They can cooperate for promoting each other, they can use each other's achievements, for the benefit of the entire cultural heritage landscape.

13.9   Discussion Questions

- Why are rural heritage farm houses appropriate for the investigation of cultural heritage?
- What kind of international conventions support the preservation of cultural heritage, and in particular intangible elements of cultural heritage?
- How can data collection be useful for management purposes?
- Why is heritage education essential?
- What is the role of technological development and tourism in the preservation process?

References

Bold, J. (1990) Patrimoine architectural: cooperation de centres de documentation. In: *Villes, Architectures, Metiers: Banques de Données des Savoir-Faire*. Atelier du Patrimoine, Marseille, pp. 4–7.

Canadian Heritage Information Network (1993) *Humanities Data Dictionary of the Canadian Heritage Information Network*. Canadian Heritage Information Network, Ottawa, Canada.

Council of Europe (1993) *Architectural Heritage: Inventory and Documentation Methods in Europe*. Proceedings of a European colloquy organized by the Council of Europe and the French Ministry for Education and Culture Direction du Patrimoine, Nantes, 28–31 October 1992. Council of Europe, Strasbourg, France.

Council of Europe (1995) Core data index to historic buildings and monuments of the architectural heritage. Recommendation R (95) 3 of the Committee of Ministers of the Council of Europe to member states on co-ordinating documentation methods and systems related to historic buildings and monuments of the architectural heritage. Council of Europe, Strasbourg, France.

Council of Europe (1996) Compendium of Basic Texts of the Council of Europe in the Field of Cultural Heritage, CC-PAT (96) 58, provisional version. Convention for the Protection of the Architectural Heritage of Europe, Granada, 3.X.1985, Council of Europe Treaties ETS No. 121. Council of Europe, Strasbourg, France.

Getty Art History Information Program and International Council of Museums International Documentation Committee (1993) *Developments in International Museum and Cultural Heritage Information Standards*. Getty Art History Information Program, Santa Monica, California (updated July 1995).

Harrison, R. (ed.) (1994) *Manual of Heritage Management*. Oxford University Press, Oxford.

International Council of Museums (1994) *Minimum Categories for Museum Objects: Proposed Guidelines for an International Standard*. International Council of Museums, Paris.

International Council of Museums (1995) *International Guidelines for Museum Object Information: The CIDOC Information Categories*. International Council of Museums, Paris.

International Organisation for Standardisation (1988) *Specification for Representation of Dates and Times in Information Interchange* (ISO 8601: 198S/ES EN 28601: 1992). International Organisation for Standardisation, Geneva.

Roberts, D.A. (ed.) (1993) *European Museum Documentation Strategies and Standards*. The Museum Documentation Association, Cambridge, UK.

Royal Commission on the Historical Monuments of England and the Association of County Archaeological Officers (1993) *Recording England's Past: A Data Standard for the Extended National Archaeological Record*. RCHME, London.

Thornes, R. (1995) *Protecting Cultural Objects through International Documentation Standards: A Preliminary Survey*. Getty Art History Information Program, Santa Monica, California.

Thornes, R. (1997) *Protecting Cultural Objects in the Global Information Society: The Making of Object ID*. Getty Information Institute, Santa Monica, California.

14 Case Study 6: Managing Heritage and Cultural Tourism Resources in Dubrovnik

Ivana Pavlic and Ivona Vrdoljak Raguž

University of Dubrovnik, Dubrovnik, Croatia

This chapter determines a model to manage the development of cultural tourism in Dubrovnik in accordance with sustainable development. Dubrovnik requires better organization of cultural tourism, better cooperation of everyone who is directly or indirectly involved with culture and the formation of an authority that will manage the cultural tourism product. The chapter will also look at cultural-historical heritage in Dubrovnik: the most important segment of Dubrovnik's tourism supply is without doubt its priceless cultural-historical heritage. The case study will provide in-depth analysis of the city of Dubrovnik, with its numerous historical buildings and monuments within centuries-old city walls. Apart from material movable and immovable monuments, Dubrovnik's heritage is rich with cultural manifestations, traditional customs, folklore performances and many other elements belonging to the immaterial cultural heritage of the region.

14.1 Introduction

An important determinant of each nation is culture, which is represented with the universality of the knowledge, beliefs, behaviours and actions of the local communities. Cultural heritage as a main concept of culture is an integral part of cultural identity. As an anthropogenic resource, cultural heritage is often valorized in tourism, regardless of the form it takes.

Correlation between cultural heritage and tourism has benefits for both sides and for the local community. Cultural heritage enriches the tourism product and improves the quality of the tourism destination. Tourism with adequate management revitalizes cultural heritage and contributes to its efficient protection and preservation.

Segmentation of the tourism market caused the development of specific tourism

products. One such specific product is certainly cultural tourism, the development of
which was based on cultural heritage.
Culture, cultural heritage and tourism are
increasingly being used to promote tourism
destinations and enhance their attractiveness and competitiveness. In addition, tourism and cultural heritage became a very
interesting area for many researchers who
tried to analyse the best model of correlation
between these mentioned elements. An
example of the intense tourism valorization
of cultural heritage is certainly the city of
Dubrovnik, which is known as a UNESCO
World Heritage City.

From the very beginning of tourism
development in Dubrovnik culture and cultural heritage were the most important segments of the overall tourist supply. Dubrovnik
has recently turned to the more intensive
development of specific tourism products and
cultural tourism with all its tangible and intangible assets is certainly one of the most
important destination products. An appropriate development of the tourism product,
which includes managing and valorization of
the cultural-historical heritage, will contribute
not only to the cultural and tourism sectors
but also in a substantial way to the local
community.

14.2   Culture and Tourism

Modern tourism market is extremely competitive and every destination is facing the challenge of having to improve the quality of its
supply on a daily basis. For these purposes
there are a number of resources at their dis-
posal, representing the basis of the tourism
product being offered to the potential consumers – tourists. Besides the stereotypical tourism supply elements (sun and sea, catering
facilities, etc.), destinations have been introducing an array of other resources to diversify
the supply and offer something unique that
would give them a competitive edge in the
market. Cultural heritage is among these
resources.

Culture (lat. *cultura* = cultivation) is a meta-
phor for the development of human localities

in society: the way of living, thinking, feeling,
organizing, celebrating and collective behaviour of a group of people (Mišić, 2000). If economic criteria are applied to analyse culture
the term would mean all created and inherited
material and spiritual goods and values (Geić,
2002).

Culture, however, is much more than an
economic concept: it represents a set of values, beliefs, behaviour, symbols and forms
of learned behaviour of a local community.
It can be defined as the 'way of living' within
a society, passed on from generation to generation and considered to be typical of a
social group (Jelinčić, 2008). Heritage
means the inheritance left by ancestors to
their descendants. It covers a wide range of
inherited cultural heritage left by ancestors
in language, literature, architecture, art,
music, theatre, film, science and other areas
that form a culture (Marasović, 2001). The
term cultural heritage is of particular importance because of its multiple meanings on
various levels, as outlined in Fig. 14.1
(Jelinčić, 2010).

According to the definition given by
UNESCO in 1972, the following are considered as cultural heritage: monuments, groups
of buildings and sites of historical, aesthetic,
ethnological   or   anthropological   value
(UNESCO, 1972). This definition has the
disadvantage of referring to the material
dimension of cultural heritage only. However,
the omission was 'rectified' by the WTO in
1985, when the definition of a nation's heritage was specified as works of its artists,
architects, composers, writers and philosophers, works of unknown artists that have
become an integral part of the nation, as well
as the totality of values giving meaning to
life. Under the term 'works' it is to be understood the works of both material and immaterial origin show the creativity of a nation
(Gredičak, 2008). This means that cultural
heritage is manifested in verbal tradition,
expression and language, performing arts,
social practice, rituals and celebrations,
knowledge and practice of nature and the
universe, as well as traditional crafts (Fairchild
and Silverman, 2009). Among all of these
elements, the part of cultural heritage with
the   highest   representation   in   tourism

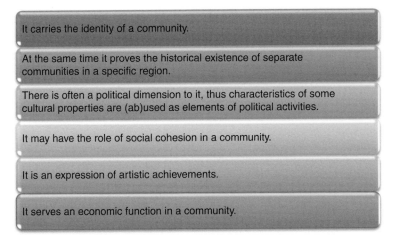

It carries the identity of a community.

At the same time it proves the historical existence of separate communities in a specific region.

There is often a political dimension to it, thus characteristics of some cultural properties are (ab)used as elements of political activities.

It may have the role of social cohesion in a community.

It is an expression of artistic achievements.

It serves an economic function in a community.

Fig. 14.1. Multiple meanings of cultural heritage. (Jelinčić, 2010.)

resources worldwide is architectural and artistic (visual) heritage (Marasović, 2001).

Within the process of globalization, cultural heritage is a key element in understanding and developing mutual respect among nations. Cultural heritage plays an important role in bringing individuals and groups together, regardless of their cultural, religious or ethnic background; it crosses national and linguistic borders and creates a tight bond between the past, the present and the future.

The complexity of defining culture itself makes it even more difficult to define cultural tourism, and so definitions abound. There are two basic approaches. The first approach is focused on areas and monuments; description of the choice of attractions visited by cultural tourists clearly referring to culture as a product. The second approach is more conceptual in character and cultural tourism is described with respect to motives and meanings linked to activities in cultural tourism comprising 'all aspects of travel during which tourists learn about history and heritage of other nations or their own modern way of life and thinking' (Ivanovic, 2008).

Deriving from these two roots, tourism definitions of culture can be considered in four groups: tourism-derived definitions, motivational definitions and experimental and operational definitions. Tourism-derived definitions view cultural tourism through a wide perspective of tourism and tourism management the-

ory, making cultural tourism clearly recognizable as a form of tourism, attracting tourists with special interest, in which culture is the basis having the purpose of either an attraction or motivation to travel. Fitting in with this, a definition by the European Association for Tourism and Leisure Education states that cultural tourism travels are 'all travels including visits to specific cultural attractions, from historical sites, artistic and cultural manifestations to visits to museums and theatres, made outside the place of residence' (Richards, 2005, p. 24). Motivational definitions consider purpose as the defining factor in categorizing cultural tourism rather than its actual manifestation into tourism (McKercher and DuCros, 2002).

The conclusion may be reached that definitions vary as much as the products and activities comprised in cultural tourism. Some of them focus on motivation and experience as elements of importance, and the others by pointing out activities within the cultural tourism sphere, endeavouring to give it the widest scope possible. Moreover, each sector, from tourism to economics or politics, adapts the definition of cultural tourism to itself and its goals. As a result, complexity in defining cultural tourism is obtained within the otherwise broad activities of tourism itself.

Culture and tourism are two extremely layered and significant phenomena reflecting progress and development of a human individual as well as humankind. Although we are talking about two separate spheres that can function individually, their interdependence and interactions are numerous and intertwined. Bringing culture to bear on tourism supply improves the economic results and gives a special social value to the tourism industry. Tourism, however, is a phenomenon resulting from the historical development of culture, and it is at the same time the most prominent promoter of culture and cultural activities (Jadrešić, 2001).

The choice of a destination is often influenced by cultural attractions, since they mostly serve as the means of advertising and creating an image of a tourist destination (Vrtiprah, 2006). A wide variety of cultural attractions, their originality and diversity, largely contributes to the quality and value of the total tourism supply of any destination. This also works the other way; consequently, there is a significant influence of tourism on culture and cultural heritage, which is valorized in the tourism industry (Pančić Kombol, 2006). Manifestations of impacts and relations between culture and tourism can be found in different areas and spheres, such as social-cultural manifestations, cultural-development manifestations, the link between cultural-historical heritage, nature and tourism, as well as creation of a cultural and cultural-tourism environment in a given area (Jadrešić, 2001). The role of tourism is of great significance in revitalizing and evaluating cultural elements and discovering new facts; therefore, from that point of view the elements of subjective and objective culture can be distinguished (Geić, 2002). Objective culture is one of the most important given and non-transferable elements in tourism supply (Alfier, 1994). Some of these objective cultural objects can be moved (books, paintings, theatrical performances), but the overall picture of cultural history and extant cultural creativity of an area or a nation contained in historical cities and individual independent objects can be best seen, fully experienced and thoroughly known in their original spatial and historical perspective.

As long as cultural heritage can supply tourism with content, it needs tourism and vice-versa (Gredičak, 2008). Tourism can provide cultural heritage with the funding necessary for preservation and protection, and cultural heritage provides tourists with an exceptional experience at a destination.

There are numerous negative aspects of the correlation between tourism and culture. The most commonly considered negative impacts of tourism concerning culture are all related to damaging the authenticity of the 'product' by the commercialization of culture, encouragement of fake authenticity, creating social conflict, creating cultural paradox, clashes of values, misunderstanding and creating stereotypes (Jelinčić, 2008). Tourism can exert many of these negative impacts, which can result in a direct physical impact on cultural heritage – particularly when tourists are searching for too authentic an experience, causing significant damage to the local population and sensitive cultural localities. One of the possible solutions to this problem could be creation of cultural forms and manifestations intended solely for tourists and their needs (Pančić Kombol, 2000).

Unfavourable effects from cultural tourism can best be limited by controlling the tourist experience. This is often done by standardization, modification and commodification of experience (Cooper, 2008), which is normally characteristic of mass tourism and is definitely not the best solution for selective forms of tourism created by moving towards uniform tourism supply in mass tourism. However, for some cultural-historical localities that approach is inevitable. Furthermore, all localities cannot become tourist attractions – the tourist potential should be tested first. If this is not done mistaken valorization and cultural resource management may lead to irreparable damage, even to a complete loss, which would ultimately result in a loss of identity for a community.

Cooper (2008) claims that many cultural products being offered to tourists nowadays do not originate from the history or culture of a local community, rather they are invented to make the destination more attractive. Introduction of cultural aspects into tourism supply makes the matter of authenticity extremely important. Although some groups of tourists seek an authentic interpretation of history/culture in a destination, the majority are not interested in the exact presentation of culture and tradition. Consequently, tourism workers are often known to 'adjust' facts and history to make it more appealing to a larger number of tourists. This can cause tension and conflicts with the local population, who might find their culture and tradition threatened by such actions. At a more extreme level, this 'adjustment' can result in so-called 'commodification of culture' (Vukonić and Čavlek, 2001).

14.3 Valorization of Resources as a Basis of Tourism Supply

From a tourism perspective resources are natural or anthropogenic assets that may be economically valorized. They are part of the overall development of a geographic area and there must be a high level of attractiveness so that a segment of tourism demand, i.e. people from a particular region or country, may be attracted by their properties and characteristics (Bilen and Bučar, 2001). Properties and characteristics of tourism resources can satisfy tourist needs, but in order to enable their use in tourism activities it is necessary to carry out an analysis consisting of 'inventorization' and systematization of chosen resources. Only after that can their utilization in tourism take place.

Resource 'inventorization' comprises learning about and listing of all natural and anthropogenic facilities appropriate for tourism valorization (Bilen and Bučar, 2001). The level of attractiveness in tourism valorization depends on many factors that are determined in accordance with the level of interest in tourism demand (Pirjevec, 1998). The process used for analysis of chosen resources and their qualitative properties is called tourism resource systematization (Bilen and Bučar, 2001).

The properties of attractiveness are recreation, curiousness or rareness, famousness or aesthetic property (Vukonić and Čavlek, 2001).

The new tourism product must be personalized and must involve more activities, be more authentic, and tourism as a whole must benefit from its inclusion as a cultural product (Valls, 1997). In this regard the terms cultural tourism and heritage tourism are often intertwined. Some authors consider heritage tourism to be a part of a wider category of cultural tourism (Richards, 1996). Other authors place both cultural and natural resources (Mikačić, 1992) within heritage tourism resources, which means that heritage tourism with its share of natural attractions surpasses the cultural tourism parameters if we assume that cultural tourism comprises all types of travel during which travellers learn about the ways of living and thinking of other people (McIntosh et al., 2009).

Cultural tourism resources therefore include sacral monuments, museums, routes, entertainment centres, cultural-historical events and artistic events (Richards, 1996). Cultural resources turn into tourism attractions through careful planning, and the process of interpretation turns them into a product, which includes selection and design or packaging. Cultural resources that are made available to the public by presentation and interpretation satisfy the cultural needs of people and therefore become economic resources or products, unlike cultural resources with artistic value but not available to the public (Pančić Kombol, 2000). For a high-quality development of cultural tourism four basic elements are required (Moulin, 1995). These are outlined in Fig. 14.2.

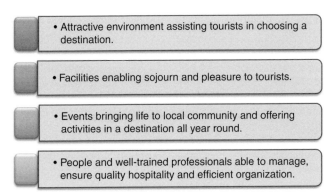

• Attractive environment assisting tourists in choosing a destination.

• Facilities enabling sojourn and pleasure to tourists.

• Events bringing life to local community and offering activities in a destination all year round.

• People and well-trained professionals able to manage, ensure quality hospitality and efficient organization.

Fig. 14.2. Basic elements for high-quality development of cultural tourism. (Moulin, 1995.)

14.4   Cultural-historical Heritage as Tourism Resource

As a tourism resource, cultural-historical heritage represents all preserved remains from past civilizations, their technological inventions, monuments and individual objects, urban complexes, artistic achievements in sculpting and painting, and other branches of art that tourists find attractive (Vukonić and Čavlek, 2001). Cultural heritage, or inheritance, together with daily cultural resources and tourism culture form a group of spiritual tourism resources satisfying specific cultural needs, and having an actual (material) and spiritual (immaterial) component.

In an analysis of resources according to their genetic origin, cultural-historical heritage falls within the group of anthropogenic tourism resources (Vukonić and Čavlek, 2001). Through valorization of culture and cultural heritage in tourism the cultural function of modern tourism is accomplished (Marković, 1989). This is a non-economic function with a direct impact on individual tourists, i.e. it satisfies their recreational needs. The realization of this function can be observed both from a closer and wider perspective. The basis for the cultural functioning of tourism are various events – from cultural entertainment to serious cultural events (visiting museums, listening to concerts, watching plays). This latter category is a more focused perspective through which the cultural function offers physical recreation of 'higher' cultural quality.

The concept of heritage consumption (Antolović, 1998) plays a special part in the touristic valorization of cultural-historical heritage. This cultural-historical heritage can be a part of tourism supply in any destination that chooses to offer such elements to potential visitors, as a primary attraction or a secondary one. The link between heritage and locality is shown on four different levels: global, national, local and personal (Jelinčić, 2010), and consumption of such resources, irrespective of level, can be indirect or direct. Indirect consumption is utilization of information on a locality through books, lectures, TV shows, etc., i.e. there is no direct contact between the consumer and the locality. Direct consumption of services offered by a heritage locality can be realized by visiting or observing. When directly utilizing historical heritage in tourism it is important that

consumers and carriers of cultural heritage are not required to engage with the 'product' to the same extent in each of its forms.

An even narrower term than cultural tourism is heritage tourism, which identifies or valorizes cultural-historical heritage as a central element of tourism supply for a destination (Jelinčić, 2010). There are numerous elements of cultural-historical heritage that are valorized in tourism. The only crucial difference is that they are either in a material or immaterial form. On the basis of that characteristic they are managed, interpreted and protected in different ways from the negative consequences arising from their exploitation in tourism.

14.5   Managing Cultural-historical Heritage in Tourism

Cultural resource management implies constant efforts in maintaining the cultural values of resources for present and future generations (Jelinčić, 2010). Cultural resource management is more complex than resource management in other forms of tourism because cultural resources are realized in an open system in which many elements pertain to the way of life or non-tourism functions of an area (Pančić Kombol, 2006). In cultural resource management it is necessary to coordinate the scope of demand with tourism product marketing, i.e. the number of visitors and duration of their visits in relation to resource capacity. Development of cultural resource management and cultural tourism development policy involve the need to understand and utilize culture in four different ways (see Fig. 14.3, based on Pančić Kombol, 2006).

Management of cultural-historical heritage is largely defined by its ownership, which can be public, private or civil (Jelinčić, 2010). Cultural resources in most countries are in public ownership and managed by governmental bodies. This form of ownership is the most represented form in transitional countries. Nowadays, with modern cultural heritage management, revenues can be accrued by different activities that mostly relate to tourism but also some other industries as well (Geić, 2007).

Cultural characteristics of a destination play an important role in determining for

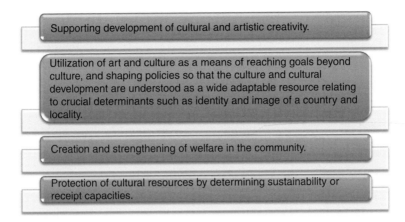

Supporting development of cultural and artistic creativity.

Utilization of art and culture as a means of reaching goals beyond culture, and shaping policies so that the culture and cultural development are understood as a wide adaptable resource relating to crucial determinants such as identity and image of a country and locality.

Creation and strengthening of welfare in the community.

Protection of cultural resources by determining sustainability or receipt capacities.

Fig. 14.3. Approaches to understanding and utilizing culture. (Pančić Kombol, 2006.)

management the capacity levels. The more unusual the culture, the more attractive the destination can be; consequently, the pressure from tourists may be stronger and have a negative impact on the destination. This is of particular importance for localities of cultural-historical heritage where once the damage is done it cannot be mended. In order to prevent such consequences or to reduce them, quality management of visitors (and attractions) is necessary. Specific tools and visitor management techniques include traffic management, control, limiting contact of visitors with artefacts, pricing as a form of regulating visitor numbers, encouraging visitors to 'leave no trace', ensuring quality experience, stimulating visits in the off season, different forms of interpretation, education of visitors on preservation of heritage, enabling easier circulation, creating a 'bond' with visitors, diversity of supply, etc. (Jelinčić, 2010).

Perhaps the most constantly present element of cultural resource management is the continuous raising of awareness for the need to preserve cultural-historical heritage. More precisely, all activities within the process of cultural resources management aim at preservation of samples of material and immaterial heritage for future generations.

14.6   Case Study of Dubrovnik

Besides a mild climate and attractive location on the Adriatic coast, the most important segment of Dubrovnik tourism supply is without doubt its priceless cultural-historical heritage. According to research results, when deciding to visit Dubrovnik as a tourist destination cultural heritage is, besides the beauty of the scenery and quality of catering facilities, one of the most influential elements (the percentage of respondents evaluating the influence of cultural heritage on their decision to visit the city was high or extremely high) (TOMAS, 2010). The city of Dubrovnik itself represents an exceptional example of a historical city (Vukonić, 2008) that has managed over the centuries to keep its appearance, with numerous historical buildings and monuments within centuries-old city walls. Apart from material movable and immovable monuments, Dubrovnik's heritage is rich with cultural manifestations, traditional customs, folklore performances and many other elements belonging to the immaterial cultural heritage of the region. The importance and role of cultural-historical heritage in Dubrovnik's tourism is statistically indicated in the number of visitors to well-known tourism sites and attractions in 2009 and 2010, shown in Table 14.1.

Breaking these data down further, Fig. 14.4, based on Dubrovnik's Local Plan (City of Dubrovnik, 2005), outlines the various groups of cultural-historical resources in the Dubrovnik area.

Dubrovnik is home to 285 cultural associations, 15 museums and galleries, 12 libraries, 13 culture houses and one theatre (City of Dubrovnik, Department for Culture and Heritage). At the

Table 14.1. Visitors to cultural monuments and attractions in Dubrovnik in 2009 and 2010 (in 000). (From Croatian Bureau of Statistics, Notices and Statistical Reports, Tourism, Visitors to Important Tourism Monuments and Attractions in 2009 and 2010, http://www.dzs.hr (accessed 25 August 2011).)

Monument/attraction	Total number of visitors		Domestic visitors		Foreign visitors	
	2009	2010	2009	2010	2009	2010
Dubrovnik City Walls	765.140	729.854	291.067	217.081	474.073	512.773
Special Reservation Lokrum	81.893	188.979	27.163	69.270	54.730	119.709
Biological Institute Aquarium	40.698	65.945	11.676	19.377	29.022	46.568
Dubrovnik Revelin Fortress	7.031	7.950	1.404	1.637	5.627	6.313

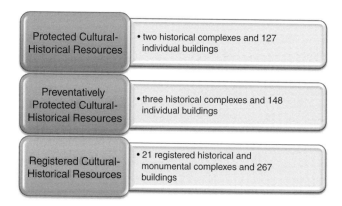

Fig. 14.4. Cultural-historical resources in the Dubrovnik area. (Dubrovnik Local Plan, 2005.)

national level, Dubrovnik-Neretva County was the number one county in 2008 with respect to the number of visitors to museums and galleries (1.1 million), this being yet another fact proving the importance of heritage in its tourism.

The main motivation for tourist arrivals in Dubrovnik, besides relaxation, is to learn about the historical heritage of the city and its surroundings. Such motives can be perceived not only in the form of cultural tourism but also as an additional motive in congress tourism, as well as spring–autumn relaxation tourism, which are very important for stretching the tourism season. However, valorization of cultural-historical heritage in tourism is not unified. The elements with the greatest representation in tourism valorization are the resources situated within the protected historical complex of Dubrovnik – the Old City, fortification system, civil buildings, sacral objects, movable material heritage displayed within museums, etc.

Elements of immovable material heritage to be found in the surrounding area, especially the system of old summer residences in the area of Rijeka Dubrovačka, are not at all or very rarely valorized. Conversely, perhaps the highest valorization applied to cultural-historical heritage relates to the immaterial heritage segment. Dubrovnik is a globally known destination because of manifestations such as Dubrovnik Summer Festival or St Blasius Festival, and numerous groups of tourists watch performances of the folklore ensemble Linđo. Also in this sphere, many famous people were born in Dubrovnik and marked historical periods by their activities, and their names are elements of a priceless heritage (e.g. Ruđer Bošković, Marin Držić).

Culture, i.e. cultural-historical heritage, must be a much more active and more recognized segment of quality tourism supply, and it must directly serve the functions of tourism. Taking cognisance of such an approach would result in a general increase in tourism supply in Dubrovnik, both in overall quality as well as development of specific forms of tourism, or more precisely cultural tourism. Thus, Dubrovnik as a tourism destination would keep up with trends of the international tourism market and retain the image of a desirable and modern global tourism destination.

14.7 Faults and Omissions in Management and Protection of Cultural-historical Heritage in Dubrovnik Area

Acknowledging its potential makes it even more difficult to identify faults and omissions in the management and protection of Dubrovnik's cultural-historical heritage. Dubrovnik and its institutions make large and costly efforts in the utilization of various segments of material and immaterial heritage for tourism purposes, aiming at enriching the existing tourism supply, stretching the tourism season, and finally affirming Dubrovnik as a cultural centre and cultural tourism destination. Such a title is fully deserved since Dubrovnik represents a key element not only of Croatian but also of European culture. Nevertheless, there are many faults that overshadow the numerous achievements of Dubrovnik as a cultural tourism destination.

Protection and preservation of cultural heritage organized by responsible institutions and organizations is mainly focused on the Old City, which does not represent a problem since a unique city monument like Dubrovnik requires and deserves this recognition. However, the problem arises when numerous summer residences, sacral buildings, historical cemeteries and similar monuments witnessing past periods, and situated in the surrounding area, are slowly suffering from time-related decay and neglect by the institutions in charge. Their subsistence and preservation presently depends on local associations and eager individuals usually lacking the funds for more extensive projects. Where initiatives are brought to life, they are often smothered in a whirl of bureaucracy that inhibits any further activity in that area.

The historical nucleus of Dubrovnik may be the priority in all protection and preservation projects as well as being a focus for sustainable exploitation by tourism, but this area is not spared from devastation and improper arrangements. Certain segments of Dubrovnik are slowly losing their authenticity. Negligent and improper attitudes towards cultural-historical heritage, and its tourism valorization in an unsustainable manner, do not necessarily have to result in significant negative consequences, but should such an attitude last there may be harmful consequences. The consequences here in Dubrovnik refer to physical damage to material movable and immovable heritage as well as distortion and loss of authenticity of elements of immaterial heritage belonging to a region. Moreover, where destinations mistreat their heritage such activity is usually condemned by the professions (both cultural and tourism related), impacts negatively on the inherent tourism valorization as well being received negatively by the public at large due to influence of the media, resulting finally in degradation of image and reputation.

The cultural supply of Dubrovnik is specific since for the most part it includes static cultural monuments that, although enjoying global fame, do not offer much more than sightseeing. Seeking a better way of satisfying tourism demands, Dubrovnik has offered new means of interpretation and presentation of cultural-historical heritage. Some of these have met with approval from tourism and cultural professions, as well as the local community, while others have caused a deviation from authenticity and quality. It is hard to understand and illogical that Dubrovnik as a destination with a specific form of cultural tourism is still missing the adequate infrastructure for interpretation of its cultural supply, which requires specific treatment and conditions. Furthermore, an inadequate choice of people participating in the presentation of cultural-historical heritage may cause damage to quality tourism heritage valorization. The reason for this lies in the main problem of Dubrovnik as a tourism destination – seasonality. Tourism demand is specifically oriented towards the summer season, which leads to a concentration of cultural events and increased number of visits to cultural monuments within only a few months.

In valorization of cultural-historical heritage in tourism and the related development of cultural tourism in a sustainable manner, a prompt and consistent cooperation of all institutions, bodies and organizations, whose activities include either presentation and interpretation of heritage or its preservation, is of key importance. Dubrovnik has a widespread network of cultural or tourism institutions that have not been cooperating at a level required for a city where living is extremely dependent upon the coexistence and intertwining of culture and tourism. However, the strength derived from a planned and purposeful tourism valorization of cultural-historical heritage has finally been recognized; consequently, cooperation between elements of the culture and tourism spheres has been gradually developing in order to bring an additional, high-quality tourism dimension to Dubrovnik. Such cooperation opens many possibilities for further development in valorization of heritage that has still not found its place in the central tourism presentation of heritage. An extraordinary advantage accompanying this valorization is the possibility of elaborating completely new concepts of presenting heritage elements in tourism, devoid of previous ways and customs. This leads to a completely new approach, which actually is needed in the development of modern cultural tourism. In addition, it is necessary in the same manner to exploit all other advantages offered by culture in tourism – independent of weather conditions or season of the year, and therefore, possibly stretching beyond the main season.

Unfortunately, there are threats that diminish the possible advantages and effects from tourism valorization of cultural-historical heritage, which will always be there. It is important to use all possible and available means to minimize their negative effects, but this will be possible only once the weakness of poor cooperation between subjects from culture and tourism are overcome, as well as subjects from other branches such as physical planning and entrepreneurship, for example. The accelerated development of cultural tourism as a specific form of activity is seen by many cities as their opportunity for development, and consequently they become direct or indirect rival destinations. Since these circumstances prevail in the tourism market and cannot be avoided, Dubrovnik as a cultural tourism destination

must find a way to stand out in the supply market. This is only possible with a quality programme of cultural tourism activities based on the specific characteristics of Dubrovnik cultural-historical heritage that can distinguish Dubrovnik within the group of cultural tourism destinations. It is exactly these characteristics that can make Dubrovnik, if correctly and thoughtfully valorized, a more attractive destination for quality cultural tourism.

Cultural tourism requires certain prerequisites for effective implementation of integrated management models: formation and foundation of managing and coordinating authority, organizational structure that is process-oriented, highly sophisticated computer support, management processes, actions and results, and knowledge about new management concepts such as tools to implement improvement projects. A suitable approach to improving the overall process of tourism development can be achieved by applying different management models. In this chapter a sequential model of integrated management processes is proposed (Fig. 14.5).

Each organization has the characteristics of an open dynamic system, which operates in a turbulent business environment. The fundamental purpose of environment analysis is an assessment environment that will be useful to management for immediate response, thereby increasing the chances of success of the company (SWOT analysis). Because of this information and communication are equally important for each step of the model (Buble, 2005).

The first step in introducing a model of integrated management processes for cultural tourism is linked to the strategic management process, and it is necessary to begin by defining strategic intention – vision, mission, goals, strategies and policies – in order to obtain a conception of development and positioning of the organization. Once you determine the long-term plans to develop, the next step is to establish a managing, advisory and coordinating authority that is responsible for implementing strategic plans through key processes and their components with potential problems and giving advice for improvement in order to successfully finish the integrated process management system.

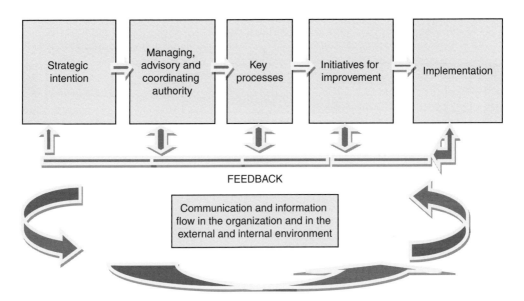

Fig. 14.5. Sequential model of integrated management processes. (From Authors.)

In Fig. 14.6 the process approach for determining workflows and their documentation as well as the satisfaction of setting the reference standards of integrated process control systems is presented. The key focus points of this integrated management system are extracted and outlined in Fig. 14.7.

Furthermore, management needs to complete a basic strategy for the integrated management process that adheres to the various criteria outlined in Fig. 14.8.

Establishment of an integrated management process is very important for the city of Dubrovnik and it will contribute to the improvement of relations, service, business results and the development of sustainable cultural tourism.

14.8 Summary

Cultural heritage as a main concept of culture is an integral part of cultural identity. Correlation between cultural heritage and tourism has benefits for both sides and for the local community. Cultural heritage enriches tourism products and improves the quality of the tourism destination. From the very beginning of

tourism development in Dubrovnik culture and cultural heritage were the most important segments of the overall tourist supply. Dubrovnik has recently turned to more intensive development of its specific tourism products and in particular its cultural tourism product. With the range of tangible and intangible assets, this is certainly one of the most important destination products.

In the valorization of cultural-historical heritage in tourism, and the development of cultural tourism in a sustainable manner, prompt and consistent cooperation of all institutions, bodies and organizations, whose activities include either presentation and interpretation of heritage or its preservation, is of key importance. Dubrovnik has a widespread network of cultural and tourism institutions that have not been cooperating at a level required for a city where living is extremely dependent upon the coexistence and intertwining of culture and tourism. However, the strength derived from a planned and purposeful tourism valorization of cultural-historical heritage has finally been recognized; consequently, the cooperation between subjects in culture and tourism has been gradually developing in order to bring an additional, high-quality tourism dimension to Dubrovnik. Such cooperation opens many possibilities for

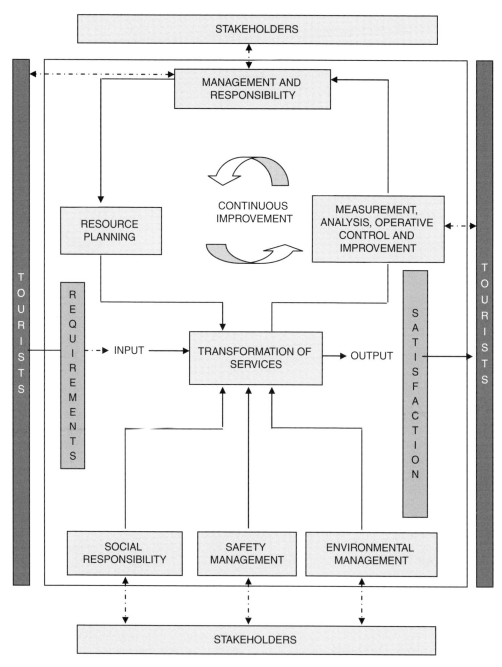

Fig. 14.6. Generic model of integrated management systems. (From Authors.)

further development in valorization that has still not found its place in the central tourism presentation of heritage. An extraordinary advantage accompanying this valorization is the possibility of elaborating completely new concepts of presenting heritage elements in tourism, devoid of previous ways and customs. This leads to a completely new approach, which is actually

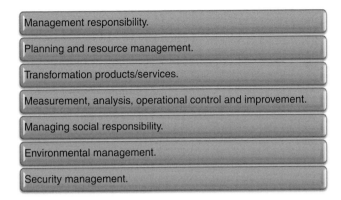

Fig. 14.7. The key focus points for an integrated management system. (From Authors.)

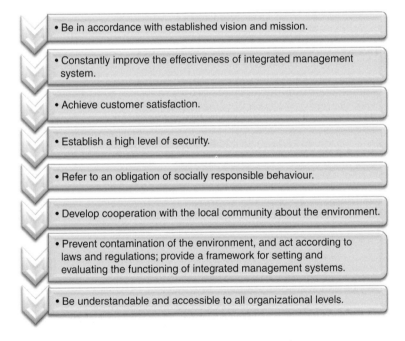

Fig. 14.8. Criteria for a basic integrated management strategy. (From Authors.)

needed in the development of modern cultural tourism. In addition, it is necessary in the same manner to exploit all other advantages offered by culture in tourism – reduced dependence on weather conditions or season of the year, and the possibility of stretching beyond the main season.

Therefore, cultural tourism requires certain prerequisites for effective implementation of its integrated management: the formation

and foundation of managing and coordinating authorities, the creation of organizational structure that is process-oriented, highly sophisticated computer support, management processes, actions and results, and knowledge about new management concepts such as tools to implement improvement projects. Establishment of integrated management processes is very important for the city of Dubrovnik and will contribute to the improvement of relations, service, business results and overall result in the development of sustainable cultural tourism.

14.9 Discussion Questions

- What are the four basic elements that are required for a high-quality development of cultural tourism?
- Describe the concept of consumption of heritage in tourism in the context of valorization of cultural-historical heritage.

- Explain why it is important to understand the development of cultural resource management and cultural tourism development policy.
- Identify the different categories of cultural-historical resources in the Dubrovnik area.
- Describe the main faults and omissions in management and protection of cultural-historical heritage in the Dubrovnik area.
- Describe the sequential model of integrated management processes.
- Explain the generic model of integrated management systems.

References

Alfier, D. (1994) *Turizam – izbor radova*. Masmedia, Zagreb, Croatia.
Antolović, J. (1998) *Ekonomsko vrednovanje graditeljske baštine*. Mikrorad, Zagreb, Croatia.
Bilen, M. and Bučar, K. (2001) *Osnove turističke geografije*. Mikrorad, Zagreb, Croatia.
Buble, M. (2005) *Strateški menadžment*. Sinergija, Zagreb, Croatia.
City of Dubrovnik (2005) Dubrovnik's Local Plan, Department for Urbanism, Planning and Environmental Protection. http://www.dubrovnik.hr/odjel_za_kulturu.php?id=40 (accessed 20 October 2011).
City of Dubrovnik, Department for Culture and Heritage, Cultural Institutions. http://www.dubrovnik.hr/odjel_za_kulturu.php?id=40 (accessed 20 October 2011).
Cooper, C. (2009) *Ekonomija turizma – načela i praksa*. Ekokon, Split, Croatia.
Croatian Bureau of Statistics (2011) Notices and Statistical Reports, Tourism, Visitors to important tourism monuments and attractions in 2009 and 2010. http://www.dzs.hr (accessed 20 October 2011).
Fairchild, D. and Silverman, H. (2009) *Intangible Heritage Embodied*. Springer, New York.
Geić, S. (2002) *Turizam i kulturno-civilizacijsko naslijeđe*. Veleučilište u Splitu, Split, Croatia.
Geić, S. (2007) *Organizacija i politika turizma: kulturološko – ekologijski i sociogospodarski aspekti*. Sveučilište u Splitu, Split, Croatia.
Gredičak, T. (2008) Kulturna baština u funkciji turizma. *Acta Turistica Nova* 2, 205–234.
Ivanovic, M. (2008) *Cultural Tourism*. Juta and Company, Cape Town, South Africa.
Jadrešić, V. (2001) *Turizam u interdisciplinarnoj teoriji i praksi – zbornik istraživanja*. Školska knjiga, Zagreb, Croatia.
Jelinčić, D.A. (2008) *Abeceda kulturnog turizma*. Meandarmedia, Zagreb, Croatia.
Jelinčić, D.A. (2010) *Kultura u izlogu – Kratki vodič za upravljanje kulturnim dobrima*. Meandarmedia, Zagreb, Croatia.
Marasović, T. (2001) *Kulturna baština 1*. Veleučilište u Splitu, Split, Croatia.
Marković, Z. (1989) *Osnove turizma*. Školska knjiga, Zagreb, Croatia.
McIntosh, R.V., Goeldner, C.R. and Ritchie, J.R. (2009) *Tourism: Principles, Practices and Philosophies*. Wiley, Oxford.
McKercher, B. and DuCros, H. (2002) *Cultural Tourism: the Partnership Between Tourism and Cultural Heritage*. The Haworth Hospitality Press, New York.
Mikačić, V. (1992) Turizam naslijeđa. *Acta Turistica* 2.
Mišić, A. (2000) *Rječnik filozofskih pojmova*. Verbum, Split, Croatia.
Moulin, C. (1995) On concepts of community cultural tourism. *The Tourist Review* 4, 35–40.
Pančić Kombol, T. (2000) *Selektivni turizam: Uvod u menadžment prirodnih i kulturnih resursa*. TMCP Sagena, Matulji, Croatia.
Pančić Kombol, T. (2006) *Kulturno naslijeđe i turizam, Radovi Zavoda za znanstveni rad – Varaždin* No. *16/17*. Hrvatska akademija znanosti i umjetnosti, Zagreb, Croatia. 211–226.

Pirjevec, B. (1998) *Ekonomska obilježja turizma*. Golden Marketing, Zagreb, Croatia.

Richards, G. (1996) Production and consumption of European cultural tourism. *Annals of Tourism Research* 2, 1048–1064.

Richards, G. (2005) *Cultural Tourism in Europe*. CAB International, Wallingford, UK.

Stavovi i potrošnja turista u Hrvatskoj (2010) *TOMAS – LJETO 2010*. Institut za turizam, Zagreb, Croatia.

TOMAS (2010) *TOMAS – Summer Survey*. Institute for Tourism, Zagreb.

UNESCO World Heritage Centre. *Convention Concerning the Protection of the World Cultural and Natural Heritage*. http://whc.unesco.org/en/conventiontext (accessed 14 March 2011).

Valls, J.F. (1997) Sustainable tourism and economy; territory heritage. *Revue de Tourisme* 1, 3–9.

Vrtiprah, V. (2006) Kulturni resursi kao činitelj turističke ponude u 21. Stoljeću. *Ekonomska misao i praksa No. 2*. Sveučilište u Dubrovniku, Dubrovnik, Croatia.

Vukonić, B. (2008) Povijesni gradovi i njihova turistička razvojna opcija. *Acta Turistica Nova, UTILUS – Visoka poslovna škola s pravom javnosti* 2, 111–122.

Vukonić, B. and Čavlek, N. (eds) (2001) *Rječnik turizma*. Masmedia, Zagreb, Croatia.

15 Case Study 7: Urban Regeneration and Cultural Development of Girona

Neus Crous-Costa and Dolors Vidal-Casellas
University of Girona, Girona, Spain

This chapter presents the case study of Girona's Old Quarter, the historical centre that includes, among other elements, the Cathedral, the ramparts and the Jewish quarter. This neighbourhood is not just a tourist open-air museum but an area of residence and work for a large part of the population. The Old Quarter was a very different place for most of the 20th century. It was a marginal area, with serious problems of crime and prostitution. Both people and business migrated to other quarters. From 1980 onwards a process of urban renewal started, aimed at benefiting the local population, which led to the termination of illegal activities and the recovery of historical legacy. A further result of this urban renewal is the increasing attraction of tourists from the coast and Barcelona, which has resulted in the city becoming a Spanish tourist destination in its own right.

15.1 Introduction

Old parts of cities have become some of the most relevant tourist areas, as they are felt to retain the identity of the community and the flavour of localness. These factors are increasingly drawing more and more visitors and cultural tourists to cities. The resulting situation is not without tensions (local–tourist, profit–cultural value, etc.), which are being discussed in the academic literature.

From the dual perspectives of tourism and the resident population, old towns serve the function of both identifying and differentiating urban areas; they form the space that was once the past and the collective memory of a given society. In this context, while tourism may serve to retrieve architectural heritage and contribute to functional regeneration (above all in the tertiary sector), it may also create notable imbalances in symbolic, cultural, social and environmental assets, despite these being precisely what attracted tourists in the first place (Brandis and Del Rio, 1998).

One of the distinctive features of old towns is their multifunctional nature, which facilitates the survival of living social realities. An old town that serves merely a single purpose is failing to adapt to the diversity required by the city that gave birth to it (Vicente, 1997). Thus, while the passing of time demands a reformulation and rethinking of the old town's uses in line with its inhabitants' new needs, one must bear in mind the various dimensions of the old town (social dimensions, those relating to personal and collective historical memory, etc.) and its potential uses (administrative centre, focus of tourist attraction, commercial and residential areas, etc.) so as to avoid its trivialization for either resident or tourist.

Spain as a whole contains over 900 historical and artistic heritage sites and almost 14,000 monuments that have been named Heritage Sites of Cultural Interest (Béns d'Interès Cultural) by the Spanish Government's Ministry of Education, Culture and Sports (2011). By 2012 44 sites had been declared UNESCO World Heritage Sites, 39 of them cultural and two mixed (both cultural and natural).

Regarding the protection and preservation of this vast cultural heritage, as early as in the 1980s a set of action guidelines were drafted in Spain, but these have proved insufficient as far as the protection of housing is concerned. Establishing a restoration culture is also proving complex in a country where private initiatives only take place selectively and following great public-sector effort (Troitiño, 2003). As we shall see, this is the case with Girona.

15.2   The Case of Girona

A provincial capital, the city of Girona has a population of almost 100,000. It is situated 100 kilometres north of Barcelona, the capital of Catalonia and one of the best-positioned cities from an international perspective. Girona is also some 60 kilometres from the southern French border, and the Costa Brava, one of Europe's main tourist destinations, is only 40–75 kilometres away.

The city centre has always housed numerous monasteries, convents and other church-owned properties, which have existed alongside palaces and other civil buildings. From 1835 to 1837 a set of decrees, promulgated by Juan Álvarez Mendizábal, resulted in the expropriation (and therefore privatization) of many ecclesiastic properties. This emptied many of them, and as a result in many places within the city walls Girona presented an image of grey and stony abandonment, often overgrown with plants.

The first noteworthy date in the process of the Old Town's regeneration is 1967, when the area was named a Historical and Artistic Heritage Site (Conjunt Històric-Artístic). Very little development took place at this time, but from 1982 to 1983 Girona City Council initiated the Special Plan for Old Town Conservation and Interior Reform (Pla Especial de Conservació i Reforma Interior del Barri Vell), the aim of which was to make this area comparable with the city's other neighbourhoods; in other words, to standardize the area without ignoring its own specific character.

Without doubt, the architectural grandeur of the Old Town forms a soul that both identifies and differentiates it. However, the Plan's constant rejection of mere picturesque conservation from the very beginning set it apart from policies the Franco regime had adopted towards historical buildings. The architects themselves recognized this, clearly stating that the basic value, and for which the Old Town was restored, was its architecture. Secondly, the neighbourhood's 'normality' was to be ensured, thus rejecting the idea of it becoming a mere living museum. Great efforts were made by the public authorities to promote commercial and residential activity (encouraging private agent participation), as well as to maintain institutional activity and site the university there. In addition to commerce, institutional activity was seen as a means of stimulating the area, not only as far as employment was concerned but also in revitalizing the restored buildings. The University of Girona was created in 1981 and two sites were chosen: the old Sant Domènec convent, situated at one of the highest points of the Old Town and abandoned by the army shortly beforehand, and the building known as Les Àligues. This achieved a dual aim: ensuring the conservation of the buildings and bringing life to the Old Town through the daily presence of students and teachers in the area. It must be pointed out, however, that initial results were not as expected.

Lastly, one must remember that the neighbourhood's residential function also underwent renovation. As opposed to the majority of old towns in southern Europe, housing in Girona's Old Town is of an acceptable standard and has important architectural qualities (Birulés, 2003). The restoration of the façades on the right bank of the River Onyar was vitally important for residents, who felt somehow reconciled with the Old Town, but also for tourism, which, over time, has come to view these façades as one of the city's iconic images, often compared with those on the Arno in Florence.

Municipal intervention also served to revive neighbourhood life in the Old Town. In 1986 Narcís-Jordi Aragó noted that recent months had witnessed the re-establishing of the popular festival in the Sant Feliu quarter, occupying an area stretching from the steps to the river, and including such activities as communal neighbourhood meals, dances, street shows and street decoration. In the same vein, All Saints' Day (1 November) saw the beginning of the Artisan and Antiquarian Fair (Trobada d'Artesans i Antiquaris) in Carrer de les Ballesteries and La Pujada de Sant Feliu, the very trades that originally gave their names to these streets. The fair continues fortnightly to this day.

From the mid-1990s the city began to appear widely in Spanish and international publications. The emphasis was placed not only on the care taken over the city's heritage but also on the considerations of citizen welfare and social balance. These publications contributed to traders recognizing that the singularity of the Old Town was something that would be beneficial to their businesses.

Private investment began in 1993. It is worth noting here that many developers and owners decided to restore buildings or neighbourhoods in exchange for negotiating or postponing obligations detailed in the Plan. Although these private agents were motivated by a complex set of economic factors, it is not true to say that the Old Town is a clear case of real-estate speculation or that a real social problem has been created.

Finally, we should also highlight the fact that the Plan meant the restoration of Girona's heritage and historical memory, also serving as an antidote to the feeling of 'grey and black Girona' that had previously been so widespread. In 2010, according to Girona City Council's Heritage and Architecture Round Table (Taula de Patrimoni i Arquitectura), the aim of the Plan, which remains in force, is and always has been for heritage restoration – to allow the residents themselves to live in and value the city.

15.3   Girona as a Tourist City

Tourism in the city of Girona may well date back to the Romantic vision of the 19th century, which fragmented the urban space and focused attention on some of the historical elements that remain the city's principal sights today: the Arabian Baths, Sant Feliu Church, the Cathedral and Sant Pere de Galligants Monastery. The first references to tourist agents present in Girona can be found in 1914, with the founding of the Girona Society for the Attraction of Foreigners and Tourists (Societat d'Atracció de Forasters i Turistes de Girona), similar to those already existing in various parts of Europe. The Society did not limit its activities to just information and publicity but also interacted with both the public administration and the private tourism sector, publishing the first travel guides and organizing several poster competitions (Galí and Donaire, 2006).

After the Civil War foreign tourism would not return to Spain until the 1950s, closely associated with the sun- and sand-related Fordist model of mass tourism. From 1950 to

1970 the city saw a decline in the number of visitors and tourist establishments. It should be clarified, however, that the city itself never really lost its interest in tourism, and 1964 saw the founding of the Centre for Initiatives and Tourism (Centre d'Iniciatives i Turisme), which took charge of promotion and visitor information. From 1976, with the initiative no longer in existence, the Costa Brava Tourist Board (Patronat de Turisme Costa Brava) focused its attentions on the coast.

As a result of restoration during the 1980s, while the Old Town lost its role as an urban economic centre (as happened in other cities) it still retained its central symbolic and cultural nature (Troitiño, 2003). At this time the restored façades of the houses on the right bank of the Onyar became (and are still) one of the most typical images for a kind of tourism that saw Girona as a half-day or day-trip from bases on the Costa Brava.

It would not be until the 1990s that tourism began to form part of the public urban planning strategy, helped by some well-known private initiatives and the 'Legends of Girona' guided visits. Originally designed as an enjoyable way for locals to rediscover their heritage, these guided tours were also offered in other languages and won the City Council FUTURES award, the prize money serving to build the Welcome Point information and booking office (Moreno and Vidal-Casellas, 1997).

15.4   Tourism Today

Girona's Municipal Tourist offices dealt with almost 140,000 requests for information in 2010. This figure has remained largely steady since 2005 (150,000 requests) and in 2007 was over 169,000 (Girona City Council, 2012). A 2009 study by the Municipal Observatory (Observatori de municipal) estimated the average amount spent by visiting tourists during their stay to be €765, while day-trippers spent an average of €108 per day. The following sections will deal with the activity and evolution of the main promoters and components of the local tourist industry that have provided these figures. The information is based on results obtained by various

researchers who have focused their attention on the case of Girona.

15.5   Public Tourism Management

The City Plan, passed in 1994, was one of the first strategic planning tools and was based on a profound change in the global conception of Girona and its own self-esteem (Donaire, 2002). During its drafting contributions were taken into account from all of Girona society as a whole. The objectives linked to tourism are contained in the second strategic guideline, under the heading 'Consolidating Girona as the tourist services capital of Catalonia'. This included the aim of making Girona a European centre of city tourism. It should be emphasized here that, from the very beginning, the idea was for tourism to be developed consensually between public administrations and the private sector, and to stimulate the setting up of tourism-focused companies, particularly in the Old Town. The city was, in addition, seen to be a resource that could contribute to the de-seasonalization of tourism throughout the province as a whole. The City Council's organizational chart stated that those functions corresponding to tourism would be the responsibility of the Promotion and Development Unit (Unitat de Promoció i Desenvolupament).

The year 1994 also saw the creation of the Girona Commerce and Tourism Commission (Comissió de Comerç i Turisme de Girona), a municipal initiative with joint public and private funding for the development of private initiatives and with joint financial responsibility for projects.

In 2004 the Local Development and City Promotion Department (Àrea de Desenvolupament Local i Promoció de la Ciutat) was set up. It took on the responsibilities pertaining to employment, indoor markets, flea markets, trade fairs, street markets, the Conference Centre and tourism. The tourism section arose from the evident need to promote existing local tourist products associated with culture, heritage, gastronomy and leisure. Its precise competences are technical services, information services and the management of tourist services.

Operating in parallel with agencies that are purely under municipal control, the Girona Tourist Board (Patronat de Turisme de Girona) was created in 1976. It was initially a joint public and private, non-profit public limited company. This is the official body for promoting tourism across the entire province (and includes the Costa Brava and Pyrenees as main brands) for both domestic and more importantly foreign tourists. It should be mentioned here that Girona is the only Catalan provincial capital that does not have its own specific tourist board (not including those that may cover the rest of the province).

Reflecting on the tourist products and services the city has to offer, Girona City Council states:

> Girona has all the charm of a large city but without the crowds; a very 'human-sized' city that will leave you walking around awestruck with your eyes wide open and your mouth agape at all it has to offer: its streets, festivals, cultural activities, restaurants, tourist services and events. Make the most of your visit at any time of year, and if you can, visit more than once, because the city is very much alive and there are always new things to surprise you.
> (Girona Turisme, 2012)

This is how Girona City Council introduces its website. As we can see, essentially the idea is to communicate a cultural product (the rest of the website promotes visits to the restored Old Town, where most events take place), with elements that cover gastronomy and shopping. The evident heritage component of what the city has to offer and its tourist image led the City Council to initially think of presenting Girona's candidacy as a World Heritage Site. However, the heterogeneity of the whole meant that it would prove to be a highly complicated task, and the initiative was finally abandoned.

It is the Jewish Quarter (Call) together with the Cathedral and Carolingian walls that have become the city's distinguishing features and iconic tourist images. The Jewish Quarter in particular has been one of the elements that has set what Girona has to offer in terms of heritage apart from those of competing destinations (Querol, 2009), and its primacy reflects the strategy recently adopted by many cities of aiming for singularity through the creation of thematic spaces (Tresserras, 2004).

One of the responsibilities of the Municipal Jewish Quarter Board (Patronat Municipal del Call) is promotion and stimulation of the Jewish legacy. For this reason, and in particular since the opening of the Jewish History Museum (Museu d'Història dels Jueus) in 2000, special emphasis has been placed on organizing guided tours to scenes of the community's daily life. The quarter has also joined the state Jewish Quarter Network (Caminos de Sefarad). The promotion of the Jewish Quarter has, it should be stated, regularly formed part of the election manifesto of parties that have governed the city since 1990.

The Jewish Quarter is not the only element of the city's heritage that has adapted itself to tourism. Santa Maria Cathedral is the most-visited site, receiving 230,000 visitors in 2011. Until 2005 visiting the Cathedral was free (except for admission to the museum) and the talks given by tourist guides were far from homogenized. The introduction of an admission charge formed part of a strategy for marketing the Cathedral and its museum designed by a multidisciplinary team from the University of Girona University Tourism School (Escola Universtiària de Turisme de la Universitat de Girona). The objective of the strategy was to provide guidelines that serve to professionalize the tourist management of a central feature of the city's Christian heritage, with a view to benefiting both administrators and tourists alike.

In the same vein, Sant Feliu de Girona church has been working for some time on making its tourism management services more professional, even though ownership-management issues make this more problematic than in the Cathedral's case. The Arabian baths, a national monument, are currently managed by Girona County Council, which has introduced admission fees and occasional guided tours.

The final element to mention in the cultural products and services Girona has to offer the tourist is the network that includes all the city's museums, with the exception of the Cathedral Treasury. These are the Tomàs Mallol Collection in the Cinema Museum (Museu del Cinema, Collecció Tomàs Mallol), the City History Museum (Museu d'Història de la Ciutat), the Jewish History Museum (all three municipally owned), the Catalonia Archaeology Museum, Girona (Museu d'Arqueologia de

Catalunya, Girona) and the Girona Art Museum (Museu d'Art de Girona) (owned by the Autonomous Government of Catalonia). In 2003 the museums set up a collaborative network, the aim of which was to work on dissemination and promotion. It includes a combined ticket, which, while not providing a combined admission price, gives users a 50% discount on museum admission fees after having paid the full fee at the first museum visited. The M5 ticket is given free of charge at the first site and is designed to stimulate the flow between museums as well as to act as an incentive for further museum visits. The M5 works, to some extent, as a city card. There are, however, some important differences in that it only includes public museums and a specific fee is charged at each site. It should be noted that, although providing a significant discount, admission fees to the city's cultural facilities are relatively low, the €5 fee charged at both the Cinema Museum and Cathedral being the most expensive. This may well make the offer less attractive.

15.6 The Tourist Image

The origins of the image offered by Girona can be found in the Romantic period, principally associated with the medieval city. Nevertheless, 'Girona is a city that is experienced more than evoked' (Galí, 2005b, p. 450), as, although the impression visitors take away with them is a very strong one, before visiting it was practically non-existent. Galí's 2002 study on the construction of Girona's tourist image, published in 'The tourist image of Girona's historical building heritage' ('La Imatge turística del patrimoni monumental de Girona': Galí, 2005a), analysed information available in travel guides and summarized the image of the city as being the Onyar riverbank houses and the two buildings that stand out behind them: the Cathedral and Sant Feliu Church. The river therefore acts as the boundary dividing the Old Town (the visited part) from the new city.

At the end of the 1980s the streets of the Jewish Quarter also started to be incorporated in the city's advertising. This was not spontaneous but rather answered municipal wishes

to explicitly promote this renovated area. It is very important to mention here the public spaces and everyday scenes that appear photographed in travel guides, since they project the image of a living city: 'to fill the eternal city with life and offer an authentic scene for tourist consumption' (Galí, 2005b, p. 198). In short, the tourist image projected by travel guides has been two-fold over the past 30 years: the Romantic image has been strengthened (not for nothing has the Cathedral become the city's classic icon), and new elements that were practically unknown beforehand have appeared (such as the 19th-century buildings, even if they play a marginal role in the tourist image).

The photographs that visitors take of Girona strengthen the positioning of these sights in the popular image, since these personal photographs form a different kind of advertising and complement word of mouth publicity. The most photographed image is the Cathedral (23.50% of the photographs studied), followed by the Onyar façades (20.44%), the streets in the Jewish Quarter (12.49%) and Sant Feliu Church (9.25%) (Galí, 2005b).

Complementing this study, Camprubí's doctoral thesis (2009) focused its attention on the images of tourist brochures published by different organizations. From this study we see that, as a whole, those brochures that serve to promote Girona present the city as a highly integrated site within its geographical area. This is shown by the fact that a mere 40% of those published by public bodies or tourist associations (Girona Museums, the Tourist Guide Association, the Shopkeepers Association [Gironamuseus, Associació de Guies, Associació de Botiguers], etc.) deal solely with the city. It is the city's heritage that is given greatest weight in these promotional photographs (56.78%), and their subjects only confirm the findings stated above with regard to tourist guides and the photographs taken by visitors. Thus, the Onyar façades appear in 26.32% of the commercially produced photographs, followed by panoramic views of the Old Town (10.53%), nature photographs (10.53%), the Cathedral (7.89%), Tapestry of the Creation (7.89%), Jewish History Museum (5.26%), Jewish Quarter (5.26%) and Sant Daniel valley (Vall de Sant Daniel) (5.26%).

15.7 Information Services

Girona's tourist office opened its doors in 1989, integrating the two previously existing offices: the one run by the City Council and the other run by the Autonomous Government of Catalonia (Galí and Donaire, 2006). It was situated at the top of the Rambla de la Llibertat, next to the Pont de Pedra, one of the city's main tourist access points and on the imaginary boundary of the tourist area (old city–new city). During high season (summer, Girona Flower Festival [Temps de Flors]), the tourist office also has an information stand at the train station.

The year 1995 saw the birth of the Welcome Point as a three-way initiative between Girona City Council, the Hotels and Restaurants Association of Girona (Associació d'Hosteleria de Girona) and the City Tourist Guide Association (Associació de Guies Turístics de la Ciutat). Its aim was two-fold: to act as support for the Rambla Tourist Office and also to become a booking centre for tourists on arriving in the city. Public administration participation proved key because it ensured the project's success and the continuity of its commercial activity (Querol, 2009).

A new tourist office was opened in March 2010, jointly financed by Girona City Council and the Autonomous Government of Catalonia. It was sited outside the Old Town, just a few metres from the Pont de Pedra. While the original intention was for this to replace the existing office on the Rambla, the latter's location within the city's tourist space proved so important that it was reopened in 2011 under municipal management (Fig. 15.1 illustrates the type of queries being dealt with by this tourist office).

15.8 Tourist Space in the Old Town: Itineraries

The empirical studies conducted by Galí in 2002 and 2003, measuring visitor behaviour inside the Old Town, are included in Galí and Donaire's 2005 book, *Tourist Itineraries in the City of Girona: Routes in the Old Town (Itineraris Turístics a la Ciutat de Girona: els Recorreguts del Barri Vell)*. Possibly the main change in visitors' attitudes since that publication has been seen at the Cathedral, where an admission fee was introduced in 2005. This has not, however, affected its position as the city's most visited site, which suggests that charging a fee is fully justified.

As is common in historical cities, tourists' use of space is fragmented, and within the overall tourist zone (the Old Town), in addition to the core elements discussed above, three marginal spaces are noted as being off the main tourist route: the neighbourhood of Sant Pere de Galligants, the old artisans' quarter and the space below the city walls. Galí's work identifies the route that tourists move within as

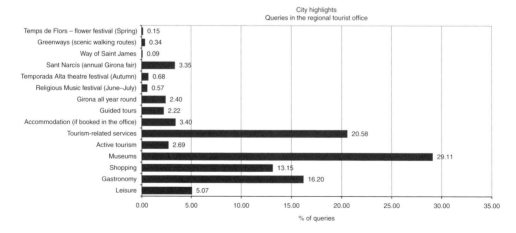

Fig. 15.1. Queries registered in the Catalonia's Tourist Office in Girona (2011). (From personal compilation based on Catalonia's Tourist Office in Girona data.)

forming a figure of eight that joins the main tourist sites through two main corridors: one is commerce-based, the other heritage-based (see Fig. 15.2). The commercial corridor has two branches, the first passes through Rambla de la Llibertat (where the tourist information offices are), while Plaça del Vi, Carrer Ciutadans and Plaça de l'Oli comprise the second. The heritage corridor starts at Plaça de Sant Feliu and ends at the Cathedral. The axes that connect the two parts of the tourists' figure of eight are Carrer Ballesteries and the more widely used Carrer de la Força.

The average stay in the city is, at 1 hour 33 minutes, notably low. This is, however, a common occurrence in historical cities and is perfectly in line with the number of sites that are truly seen (beyond taking the usual obligatory photograph). Continuing this analysis, the Old Town has 28 sites. Of these the following are identified as primary reasons for a visit: Cathedral (75.75% of visitors), the Onyar houses (39.85%), Sant Feliu Church (37.78%), the Archaeological Corridor (Passeig Arqueològic) (20.30%) and the Arabian Baths (20.11%).

The short time visitors spend in the city and the low number of sites seen is confirmed by research into museum use commissioned by the mayor in 2006 (see Alcalde, 2008). That research studied visitors' itineraries through their use of the M5 card, the order of their visits and time that passed between admissions. It also provided information regarding the role that museums play within the local tourist industry. According to the study, of the 12,983 tickets issued, a mere sixth were used at a second museum

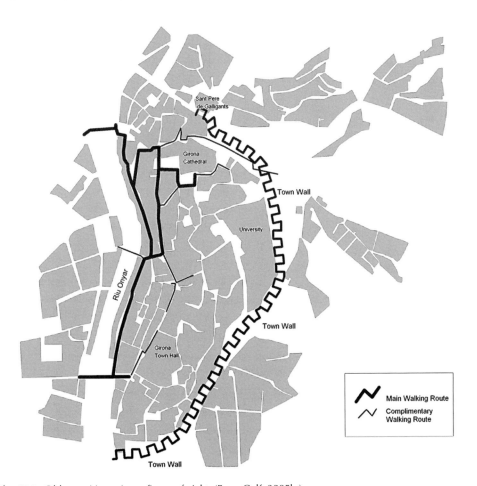

Fig. 15.2. Old town itineraries: a figure of eight. (From Galí, 2005b.)

(2164). Of those, just a fifth (433) ventured as far as a third site. A fourth museum was visited by only one in six of that group (72), while only a fifth of that group made a visit to another museum (15 people). It can therefore be seen that the majority of those who visit Girona individually and visit a museum rarely invest their time in a second, third, fourth or fifth museum visit. It should be mentioned that the city's museums, as pointed out in studies conducted by Galí and Camprubí, are secondary tourist sites, complementing the tourist's visit and secondary to other elements (Alcalde, 2008).

15.9   The MICE Segment

The 1991 manifesto of the Socialist Party of Catalonia (Partit Socialista de Catalunya) made express reference to congress and convention tourism, recognizing Girona's privileged position in this field. Promoting the MICE (Meetings, Incentives, Conferences and Events) segment would modernize the economy of both the city and the surrounding area. The Girona Convention Bureau was founded in 1992, forming part of the Girona Chamber of Commerce (Cambra de Comerç de Girona). The 1994 City Plan sought to stimulate the conference market as a strategic objective through promotion of the Girona Convention Bureau and the Girona Trade Fair (Fira de Girona). The Girona Trade Fair was created in 1984 in a new building outside the Old Town and the number of events and trade fairs that have been held there has increased over these 28 years.

First mentioned in 1991, the construction of a new Auditorium–Conference Centre was also planned but not inaugurated until 2006. Since its opening the facility has provided a great impulse for the development and boosting of business tourism in the city, contributing in a real way to stimulation of the local economy (Querol, 2009). Proof of this is that in the period immediately following inauguration, from May to December 2006, the economic impact of the Conference Centre was estimated at €941,640. Over its first 5 years the economic impact generated by the facility (€25.2 million) almost equalled the cost of its

construction and maintainance (€28 million) (Cultura 21, 2011).

15.10   Low-cost Flights

Fifteen kilometres from the city of Girona is an international airport, which was opened in 1967. In 2000 650,000 passengers passed through the airport, making it the 23rd most heavily used Spanish airport out of a total of 43 (Aena, 2012). This situation would change from 2002 with the arrival of low-cost flights, principally those of the Irish airline Ryanair (but also those of companies such as Transavia and Wizzair), and the establishment of regular daily connections with a number of European cities. This arrival of low-cost carriers caused a dramatic rise in passenger numbers between 2000 and 2011. From 557,000 passengers in 2002, the number rose to 3,000,000 in 2011, while 2008 and 2009 both saw over 5,000,000 passengers using the airport. Ryanair's 2011 move to Barcelona – El Prat Airport and the subsequent reduction in the number of routes to Girona caused this figure to fall. Passenger volume is, however, forecast to rise again in 2012.

Studies carried out by the Costa Brava–Girona Tourist Board and the University of Girona's Faculty of Tourism between 2003 and 2005 showed that the principal destinations of travellers arriving at Girona–Costa Brava Airport were Barcelona and the Costa Brava (Martínez et al., 2005, 2006). Two more recent studies were carried out in the summer of 2010 and winter of 2011. A third study, by the Higher Institute of Tourism Studies (Institut Superior d'Estudis Turístics [INSETUR]), led by Donaire and Ferrer-Rossell, revealed that the city of Girona was the chosen destination of only 4.3% of travellers, behind such tourist focal points as Barcelona (35.9%) and Lloret de Mar (11.7%), but ahead of other notable tourist locations like Figueres (0.5%) and Platja d'Aro (2.2%) (Donaire and Ferrer-Rossell, 2010). The most recent statistical data are from the winter of 2011, when the percentage of visitors naming Girona as their primary destination rose to 7.4% (21,000 people). The principal reason for the journeys was to visit relatives and friends (46.5%), followed by business tourism (23.3%) and then cultural interest (20.9%) (Donaire and Ferrer-Rossell, 2011). While these figures reflect the increasing position of Girona as a destination in itself (and taking into account the effects of climate and seasonality in these studies), the economic and social impact of these new fluxes is still to be determined, as is that of the loss of a sizable portion of Ryanair's routes in 2011.

15.11 Training Professionals: Tourism Studies

The Autonomous Government of Catalonia's Official School of Tourism (Escola Oficial de Turisme de la Generalitat de Catalunya) was created in 1989 and was the second to offer university-level tourism studies in Spain. After a short period outside Girona, the School officially became the University of Girona's Faculty of Tourism in 2007. On a municipal management level, among the aims of the 1994 City Plan introduced by the City Council was the offering of a higher Tourism Studies qualification by creating a Faculty of Tourism within the University of Girona. This would give these studies greater projection and create or stimulate a higher demand for graduates (Querol, 2009).

Throughout its existence, and particularly over the past few years, the Faculty of Tourism has participated in the professional sector in a number of ways. On one hand it has acted as a consultation and research body, carrying out specific studies that aid the understanding and redirection of the sector following the strategic guidelines of local and regional public bodies. Examples of this are the cited Girona Airport studies, where the role of INSETUR is particularly noteworthy. Secondly, the Faculty has Associate Lecturers from different professional areas who contribute a more applied focus to the knowledge passed on to the student, giving them a real vision of tourism within the area. An example of this is the participation, along with many others, of the Area Marketing Manager of the Girona–Costa Brava Tourist Board or the Area Product Manager of the Catalan Tourist Agency (Agència Catalana de Turisme) in the teaching programme.

The final, but no less important, participation comes from the fact that first-year Tourism Studies require at least two periods of practical work experience in tourist-sector companies. On one hand this gives the student a real-life tourist context in which to apply their knowledge; on the other it provides knowledge and is a source of innovation for the companies themselves.

Apart from the impact the faculty has on the city and its area of influence, mention should also be made of the dissemination of the 'Girona' brand that takes place indirectly within the international networks of which it forms part, examples of this being the Association for Tourism and Leisure Education (ATLAS) or the UNESCO/UNITWIN Network for Culture, Tourism and Development. In addition, student study exchanges with a range of European Universities via the ERASMUS scheme also disseminates the brand identity throughout a partner network of institutions.

Finally, aside from the Faculty of Tourism's influence, the siting of the University of Girona's Faculty of Arts (1992) in the Old Town has been identified as a decisive factor in the development of cultural tourism in the city. Although we lack quantifiable data on this influence, it should be borne in mind that the axes of tourism dissemination that spread in the form of literary creation, personal contacts and academic events are much more relevant than they may seem (Vidal-Casellas and Aulet, 2004).

15.12 Summary

The renovation of Girona city's Old Town was an initiative with public roots, and tourist consumption of it has been more highly conditioned by public than private management. The Special Plan for Renovating the Old Town (Pla Especial de Rehabilitació del Barri Vell) was the document that served to award value to the city's historical heritage and also that which stopped it becoming a mere living museum. The emphasis placed on restoring the neighbourhood for its inhabitants and the stimulation of housing and commerce are both to be thanked for this (Galí, 2005b).

Despite its status as a capital, Girona is a tourist city that has retained close links with its

geographical area of influence and is consequently seen as a day or half-day trip from
other parts of the province. Currently, as the
various components of the tourism sector have
positioned Girona as a tourist site in itself
because of cultural tourism and shopping and
as far as this image is concerned, the Romantic
image associated with its buildings has been
strengthened with many of the principal sites
maintaining their position (Arabian Baths,
Cathedral, Tapestry of the Creation, Sant Feliu
Church).

Girona offers a number of potential tourist
elements, both inside and outside the Old
Town; there are, however, many features that
have either yet to be considered as such or
have lacked sufficient promotion or positioning
in the tourist image. It is important to note how
the Jewish Quarter, one of the sites par excellence, forms an active part of the Spanish
Jewish Quarter Network, which serves as a
platform for dissemination and stimulation
under a brand umbrella at both national and
international level.

A key issue for the city and the future of its
cultural tourism is to lengthen tourists' stay and
increase their spending in the city, thus raising
the number of overnight stays and reducing
dependence on day-trips. The possibility should
be assessed of having a Municipal Tourist
Board responsible for product promotion and
development, coordinating the efforts of the
different public authorities and private bodies,
while maintaining the traditional link between
the city and its province.

Among the principal limitations of this
analysis, one should bear in mind that little reference is made to private sector intervention in
the local tourist industry. While it has been
shown that the main initiatives and determining factors in the development of this activity
have come from the public administration,
there have been times when private sector
action has provided a specific boost to the city.

A good example of this is increased accommodation available in the city (from 1410 beds
in 2008 to 2422 in 2010), or such events and
ideas as the recently held Girona10 (January
2012), organized by the Hotels and Restaurants
Association of Girona (Associació de Girona i
Radial), which offered accommodation or restaurants at greatly discounted prices.

The city's surrounding area benefits from
a wide offer of recreational and cultural events,
serving as an attraction for local, national and
international visitors. The generally positive
reception they have received has positioned
them in the collective image, and word of
mouth has helped increase the number of people attending them. Examples of annual events
are the Easter processions, Girona Flower
Festival (Girona, Temps de Flors) when parts of
the Old Town that are normally closed off are
opened to visitors, theatre festivals October–
January and the Gastronomic Forum (bi-annual,
held alternately in Girona and Santiago de
Compostela in February).

15.13   Discussion Questions

- Before the 1980s what was the situation
  of the Old Quarter of Girona in relation to
  the tourist sector?
- What was the core idea of the plan? Was
  tourism development one of its main
  elements?
- During the 1990s how did Girona City
  Council address tourism development
  within its strategic planning?
- How do tourists use this urban space?
  What are the main sites and what is the
  overall image of Girona as perceived by
  visitors?
- How have tourist stakeholders evolved in
  the city for the past 20 years, both in number
  and in terms of actions?

References

Aena (2012) *Estadísticas tráfico. Informes anuales.* http://estadisticas.aena.es (accessed 2 January
    2012).
Alcalde i Gurt, G. (2008) l Uso de los museos y la visita turística a la ciudad de Girona: un análisis a partir del
    tique m5 del Gironamuseus. *Revista de Estudios Turísticos* 177, 77–90.

Aragó Masó, N. (1986) La vida nova del barri vell. *Revista de Girona* 119, 7.

Birulés, J.M. (2003) *Girona: 20 anys del Pla Especial del Barri Vell: 1983–2003*. Ajuntament de Girona, Girona, Spain.

Brandis, D. and Del Río, I. (1998) La dialéctica turismo y medio ambiente en las ciudades históricas: una propuesta interpretativa. *Ería* 47, 229–240.

Camprubí Subirana, R. (2009) La formació de la imatge turística induïda: el paper de les xarxes relacionals. PhD thesis, University of Girona, Spain.

Cultura 21 (2011) *L'auditori de Girona genera 25, 2 milions en cinc anys*. http://cultura21.comunicacio 21.cat/2011/04/27/l%E2%80%99auditori-de-girona-genera-252-milions-en-cinc-anys (accessed 2 January 2012).

Donaire, J.A. (2002) Dossier. Els horitzons del turisme cultural. Girona, una ciutat amb turistes. *Revista de Girona* 212, 70–74.

Donaire, J.A. and Ferrer-Rossell, B. (2010) ícar. indicadors del comportament dels visitants a l'aeroport Girona Costa Brava. Estiu 2010 (unpublished report).

Donaire, J.A. and Ferrer-Rossell, B. (2011) ícar. indicadors del comportament dels visitants a l'aeroport Girona Costa Brava. Hivern 2010–2011 (unpublished report).

Galí Espelt, N. (2005a) *La imatge turística del patrimoni monumental de Girona*. Institut del Patrimoni Cultural de la Universitat de Girona, Girona, Spain.

Galí Espelt, N. (2005b) Mirades turístiques a la ciutat. Anàlisi del comportament dels visitants del Barri Vell de Girona. PhD thesis, University of Girona, Spain.

Galí, N. and Donaire, J.A. (2005) *Itineraris turístics a la ciutat de Girona: els recorreguts del barri vell*. Documenta Universitaria, Girona, Spain.

Galí, N. and Donaire, J.A. (2006) La història del turisme a la ciutat de Girona. *Revista de Girona* 239, 34–41.

Girona City Council (2012) Girona en xifres. http://www.girona.cat/observatori/fitxa_girona.php (accessed 16 January 2012).

Girona Turisme. Girona City Council (2012) Tourism. What to do. http://www.girona.cat/turisme/eng/activitats.php (accessed 10 February 2011).

Martínez, E., Prats, L. and Barceló, M.A. (2005) *El perfil de l'usuari dels vols de baix cost de l'Aeroport de Girona. Anàlisi comparativa anys 2003 i 2004*. Patronat de Turisme Girona – Costa Brava, Girona, Spain.

Martínez, E., Barceló, M.A., Caparrós, M. and Martínez, J. (2006) *El perfil de l'usuari dels vols de baix cos de l'Aeroport de Girona. Període: juliol i setembre de 2005. Anàlisi comparativa anys 2003, 2004, 2005*. Patronat de Turisme Costa Brava – Girona, Girona, Spain.

Ministry of Education, Culture and Sports. Spanish Government (2012) Bienes culturales protegidos. http://www.mcu.es/patrimonio/CE/BienesCulturales.html (accessed 1 December 2011).

Moreno, J. and Vidal-Casellas, D. (1997) La utilisation touristique du patrimoine culturel. Master's thesis. Université Toulouse, Le Mirail, France/Universitat de Girona, Spain.

Querol Puyo, E. (2009) Política turística de Girona. Bachelor degree thesis, University of Girona, Spain.

Tresserras Juan, J. (2004) El patrimonio judío como producto de turismo cultural: el caso del Ghetto de Venecia. In: Font Sentias, J. (ed.) *Casos de turismo cultural. De la planificación estratégica a la gestión del producto*. Ariel, Barcelona, Spain, pp. 79–107.

Troitiño, M.Á. (2003) La protección, recuperación y revitalización funcional de los centros históricos. In: Capel, H. (ed.) *Ciudades, Arquitectura y Espacio Urbano*. Cajamar, Almería, Spain, pp. 131–160.

Vicente, J. (1997) Viure a les ciutats històriques. Conclusions. In: Ajuntament de Girona, Universitat de Girona and Fundació 'la Caixa' (ed.) *La ciutat històrica dins la ciutat*. Universitat de Girona: Servei de Publicacions, Girona, Spain, p. 175.

Vidal-Casellas, D. and Aulet, S. (2004) Girona y el turismo cultural. In: Font Sentias, J. *Casos de turismo cultural. De la planificación estratégica a la gestión del producto*. Ariel, Barcelona, Spain, pp. 57–78.

16 Case Study 8: Reflection on the Constituent Elements of Cultural Tourism: Theatre Festivals. A Case Study of Temporada Alta (Girona, Spain)

Dolors Vidal-Casellas, Neus Crous-Costa and Milena Oliveras-Schwarz

University of Girona, Girona, Spain

This chapter describes the role played by theatre shows and, in particular, theatre festivals within the tourism industry, which have often been overlooked in festival analysis.

From a tourism studies perspective theatre festivals can be regarded as destinations in their own right. Domestic tourists and day-visitors seem to account for the largest part of the audience and, particularly in all-year-round destinations, it is hard to distinguish festival-goers from other visitors. As for the host region, usually a city or large heritage property, impacts have been extensively discussed from economics and marketing (branding and positioning within tourist imaginary) points of view, but other aspects such as new policies aimed at creating a win–win situation in which tourism and culture/arts can be mutually reinforcing must also be considered.

Both aspects (audiences and implications for the hosting area) are analysed in the case study of 'Temporada Alta' theatre festival, which is held in Girona (Spain) during autumn. Included in the exploration are its perception by visitors and locals, links with the tourist industry and the meaning of the festival for the host city.

16.1 Introduction

The relationship between theatres or theatre festivals and tourism has been studied by various authors from different perspectives and different disciplines, but more from an artistic and cultural point of view than a tourism one. Some authors who do include tourism in their research on theatre are Frew and Ali-Knight (2009), Bennett (2005) and Hughes (1998). It should be noted, however, that references to theatre and tourism can be found in articles addressing a wider subject area such as festivals in general. This study emphasizes the tourist dimension of these events, with the importance of a cultural perspective being implicit throughout.

As Prentice and Andersen (2003) establish, while citing Chacko and Schaffer (1993), Getz and Paliwoda (1991) and Rolfe (1992), performing arts and other festivals are nowadays a worldwide tourism phenomenon. It is widely recognized that these are one of the fastest growing types of tourist attraction (Crompton and McKay, 1997), as one can see in destinations such as New York, London or even Barcelona. While visiting a destination it is common that tourists – and more precisely cultural tourists – engage in this kind of activity, which is similar to that which they would do at home (Richards, 2001). Grappi and Montanari (2010) claim that festivals have become prominent events in many European cities and

elsewhere. The reasons they give for this proliferation are outlined in Fig. 16.1.

Festivals and events are therefore a very important motivator of tourism, and they figure prominently in the development and marketing plans and strategies of most cities and destinations (Getz, 2007).

The case study for this chapter is the Theatre Festival Temporada Alta, which takes place in Girona during the months of October, November and December.

16.2 Development of Cultural Festivals

In his *Dictionary of Concepts in Recreation and Leisure Studies*, Smith (1990) describes festivals as a celebration of a specific theme to which the public is invited for a limited period of time, annually or less frequently, and that includes single events. Art and cultural festivals, as the name clearly indicates, involve themes relating to creative activities in the arts and other cultural areas. Also, when one refers to a festival it implies that visitors are likely to be seeking cultural enrichment, education, novelty and socialization (Crompton and McKay, 1997). The search for novelty and cultural enrichment is something that is being adapted and used in many tourism and urban management policies,

New approaches to urban management.

The use of culture-led policies to positively restructure wealth creation.

Structural changes in economic production.

The progressive culturalization of traditional economic sectors.

Fig. 16.1. Reasons for the proliferation of festivals. (From Authors' compilation based on Prentice and Andersen (2003) and Getz (2007).)

mainly in cities but also in various other tourist destinations as a way of differentiating themselves from the fierce competition when it comes to tourism and culture. McDonnell *et al.* (1999) go further, describing special events and festivals as specific rituals, presentations, performances or celebrations that are consciously planned and created to mark special occasions or to achieve particular social, cultural or corporate goals and objectives.

Andersson and Getz (2009) and Grappi and Montanari (2010) have explored how festival tourism has been studied by many researchers from many different perspectives. Figure 16.2 identifies some of the key approaches in the literature.

In comparison, there is not so much academic literature on theatre or specifically European theatre festivals and tourism; although, as Hughes (1998) points out, the linkages between theatre and tourism are acknowledged in many studies, usually in the sense of identifying those audiences who are 'tourists' and determining the influence of theatre in the decision to visit the destination. Bennett (2005) on the other hand is much more critical of her

fellow scholars, emphasizing that academic literature must take into account the importance of this new segment of theatre public, the tourist. Theatre scholars, up until now, have concentrated on what one would call more 'profound matters' and clearly avoided any reference to commercial aspects or the increasing influence of the tourist on theatres.

16.3   Benefits of Festival/Theatre Festival for a Host City

A number of researchers in this field have dealt with the reasons why hosting a festival or special event is important and beneficial for the host city. The core of such studies is usually their economic impact and, in some cases, the capacity of these events to attract tourism or the ability of most festivals to improve the city's image. Frey (1996) also regards festivals as a way of keeping theatre and the performing arts alive and active.

Feifan Xie (2001) explains that, in terms of economic impacts, festivals and special events

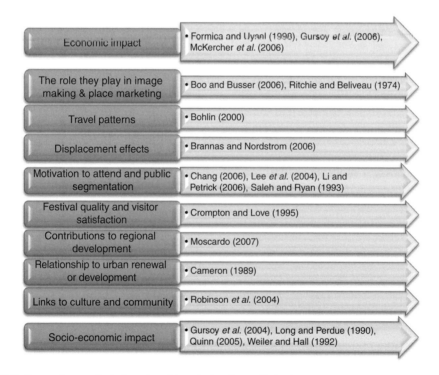

Fig 16.2. Perspectives on festival tourism. (From Authors' compilation.)

have long been regarded an impetus for economic development and job creation. In particular, event tourism can level-off seasonal variations. When referring to the economic benefit of the festivals, McDonnell *et al.* (1999) state that special events can also benefit under-utilized tourism infrastructures that visitors might not use if the existing festival were not there. Hughes (1998) explores economic effects, though in this case, focusing on culture in general, he sees culture as an instrument of urban economic regeneration that contributes to unadventurous cultural policy in cities:

> Tourism and culture are mutually reinforcing by virtue of the fact that tourism is also seen as an economic regenerator, part of the potential of which may be realized in 'tourism through culture'.
>
> (1998, p. 446)

While remarking upon the explosion in the number of festivals, Frey (1996) gives a general economic perspective on how festivals can be more profitable than theatres and how the cost is also less. In some cases though, with an old, well-known and well-established festival, the difference in cost between the festival and the permanent theatre is not so great.

Prentice and Andersen (2003), citing MacLellan and Smith (1998), see festivals as something necessary for repositioning a country as a place of interest for a variety of short holiday options for British and international visitors, thereby establishing festivals as a potential tourist attraction. Grappi and Montanari (2010) also consider festivals an enhancement of both the appeal and attractiveness of the city or destination to tourists, thus increasing the range of activities visitors can partake in and also increasing visitor satisfaction. Getz (2007) discusses the goal festivals have to attract tourists, especially in the off-peak seasons. The host city or destination offers a different kind of product, in this case a cultural event, to avoid considerable decreases in number of visitors during quieter seasons. On the other hand, Frey (1996) considers that the majority of festivals take place in high season, mainly summer, and most of them specifically to attract tourists, in some cases adapting their content to tourists' cultural needs and interests.

From a marketing perspective, festivals help to improve a city or destination's image. Stansfield

(1991) rightly observes that the positive potentials of local or regional festivals and special events are economic revenues and image-building, and Getz (1991, 2007) considers that festivals play a crucial role in improving the image of a host city or destination in a relatively short period of time and contribute to general place marketing (including contributions to fostering a better place in which to live, work and invest). This same author includes other benefits in hosting a special event, such as that it serves as a catalyst for urban renewal and for increasing the infrastructure and tourist capacity of the destination and animates specific attractions or areas, which would not be considered in another case.

Prentice and Andersen (2003) also refer to these aspects. They see the explosion in festival numbers as having multiple causes, ranging from supply factors such as cultural planning, tourist development and civic repositioning, to demand factors such as serious leisure, lifestyle sampling, socialization needs and the desire for creative and 'authentic' experiences by some market segments.

When just considering theatres Bennett (2005) believes theatre to be the logic of a transnational market economy. She establishes that although for tourism the importance of theatre is not as an artistic product per se, it does contribute literally and symbolically to the contextual commercial environment. She says that the presence of a flourishing theatre district contributes to increasing a city's significance in terms of urbanity, a rich cultural capital, a public life of art and pleasure, and an economy that spreads easily beyond the literal box office to encompass other activities.

In general, Grappi and Montanari (2010) establish that festivals are an effective strategy for cities to adopt in order to gain several potential economic, social and also cultural benefits.

16.4   Festivals as a Destination

Implicitly, a festival implies different motivations, experiences and groups of people consuming it. Prentice and Andersen (2003) establish that the recurrent importance of gregariousness may lead to the festival itself becoming a destination, rather than simply an attraction of a city or destination. They also consider, citing Getz and Cheyne (1997), that the experience of gregariousness may ultimately be independent of any specific place, and what has been found to make festivals special is their uniqueness, quality and atmosphere. These three factors are terms that could well be used when talking about a city or destination, clearly establishing then that a festival or a special event can be considered something alive, different and a part of the city or region. In fact, in the case of the Edinburgh Festival the authors Prentice and Andersen (2003) consider it has acquired the characteristics of a destination in its own right.

Other researchers observe the danger of festivals becoming a destination. When studying the case of London theatres, Hughes (1998) considers they have been criticized as being geared towards a tourist market with a consequent standardization, blandness and emphasis on spectacle. The West End (a generic term covering most of the central theatres) has been termed a 'theatrical theme park', part of the circuit that the tourist believes it is necessary to visit. Bennett (2005) in her research also writes about theatre districts and theatre standardization in London, New York and Las Vegas. She believes that commercial theatres are mostly clustered in large urban centres with the standard of comparison for the English-speaking world set by the theatre districts in New York City and London. The range and diversity of theatre products currently available on Broadway and in the West End certainly require a significant investment of production capital in terms of both dollars/pounds and people. This centralization of theatres in one district and the huge economic investment and costs for the theatres reminds one of the 'theme park effect'. It seems to suggest that theatre as a tourist resource becomes a 'theatrical theme park' (Hughes, 1998). Thus, a festival, theatre festival or a specific play (or musical) becomes a 'must see' spot in the tourist route around the city.

If festivals are to be considered destinations we need to understand how performing arts festivals (staged productions) are felt to be real by their audiences and divide festival-goers into different segments for the purposes of marketing (Prentice and Andersen, 2003). This idea of how the participants feel and perceive the festival, and how one, when marketing this type of event, has to consider different publics and segments, is similar to policies and management models for destinations and cities.

16.5 Competition Between Host Cities

One of the ideas that researchers agree upon is that festivals and special events, from mega-events such as the Olympic Games to local venues, are literally everywhere (Feifan Xie, 2001). Frey (1996) considers that in Europe nearly all cities and regions have their own festival. With this proliferation of festivals the level of competition between different cities wishing to organize festivals and attract potentially interested visitors has increased (Grappi and Montanari, 2010).

Cities, as central service loci, often have a particular concentration of theatres and associated leisure facilities and are thus likely to be of special significance in the relationship between arts and tourism (Hughes, 1998). With this concentration, cities would potentially seem to be a particular focus for this aspect of cultural tourism. In this case, cities that offer cultural activities and leisure, such as festivals, are therefore in competition with one another in attempting to attract a large number of tourists/cultural tourists.

In Prentice and Andersen's (2003) article on festivals as a creative destination they offer an extensive study of the Edinburgh Festival, explaining that in this particular case the city has sought to position itself as 'the world's Festival City' rather than solely as Scotland's capital, offering a unique selling point in terms of both creativity and heritage. In this example one can see the need for each city and region to offer a unique festival that differs from those offered by its competitors.

16.6 Festival Consumption

According to Getz (2007), the key issues that need to be answered when considering festivals and theatre from a consumer perspective are: who are the visitors that travel to a destination and why do they do so? Also one needs to ask: who attends an event and why? Considering the consumer perspective, Crompton and McKay (1997) define the decision to visit a festival as a direct action triggered by a desire to meet a need – which is explained through behavioural, cultural or social reasons.

In recent years the tendency in tourism is to emphasize performance and the ephemeral (Bennett, 2005); therefore, festival and special events fit in as this kind of attraction. As Hughes (1998) points out, the cultural tourist is much concerned in looking for a meaningful relationship with tourist sites and collecting different experiences. It is not so much acquiring goods but achieving cultural capital through a vivid experience, something more personal and subjective.

Prentice and Andersen (2003) identify three styles of consuming a festival or its host city, using the Edinburgh Festival to exemplify them: the first is consuming the city or region as a tourist destination or as a tourist-historic city; the second is consuming the place's performing arts in their context; and the third is consuming performing arts in general. The authors specify that the last type is, in its essence, independent of the location of the festival. Another aspect related to festival consumption, which Getz (2007) clarifies, is the appeal that no two festivals are ever the same – they are unique and one has to be there to enjoy and experience them. So again, the motivation for attending and consuming a festival is its uniqueness, the fact that it is unrepeatable and something one experiences and feels fully.

Performing arts festivals or cultural festivals in general offer, in the words of Prentice and Andersen (2003), a 'sensory experience' that entails feeling, thinking, participating, acting and relating. Until recently cultural tourism was seen as a passive means of consuming the unfamiliar and unknown. However, as the above authors explain, it can also be an active consumption of the already known and familiar, like art or performing arts. In this case Bennett (2005) also refers to the known and familiar when talking about her fellow theatre scholars or cultural scholars. Like Richards, she notes that

> theatre scholars in the academy are often avid cultural tourists, enjoying the benefits of conference and research travel to seek out opportunities to go to the theatre.
> (Bennett, 2005, p. 410)

Bennett uses this statement to remind scholars that in some cities or festivals tourists must be recognized as comprising a substantial part of the audience and that researchers must not generalize when talking about tourism, because when professionals of the liberal arts or academics travel they also become tourists.

16.7 Domestic Tourism and Festival Audiences

In Hughes' (1998) research the author comments on how the popularity of London theatre in domestic tourism is indicated by the number of specialist tour operators offering inclusive holidays with accommodation and theatre tickets, specifically targeting the domestic visitor market for short weekend breaks. Getz (2011) also refers to day-visitors and domestic tourism in cases where festivals take place outside big cities in a more rural area.

In cases where the festival and the city or region that hosts it are both potentially attractive to tourists, it is difficult to distinguish between those who are specifically visiting the destination or the festival. As Prentice and Andersen (2003) clarify, not everyone who is at a destination during a specific festival can be labelled as a 'festival-goer', and this is even more complicated when the destination attracts tourists all year round. This is exactly where the motivations and intentions of festival-goers start to be of vital importance in distinguishing the different target publics and segments.

Something festival organizers must bear in mind is that motives, which appear before the actual experience and are the starting point in the decision-making process (Crompton and McKay, 1997), can be physical, social or personal (Getz, 1991). Grappi and Montari (2010) suggest that festival organizers must take into account the festival environment; that is, external aspects that also involve the festival such as programme content, staff behaviour, location and atmosphere, information and facilities, the hotels and restaurants on offer and souvenir availability.

16.8   A Case Study of the 'Temporada Alta' Theatre Festival in Girona

Catalonia is one of the world's principal tourist destinations, and its main city Barcelona is one of the most important cities in Europe in terms of tourism. Approximately 100 kilometres north of Barcelona, and a similar distance south from the French border, lies Girona, capital of the province bearing the same name. Girona's main tourist area is its Old Quarter, including the Cathedral and the Jewish district (see Chapter 15, this volume). The city's tourist image is strongly tied to its historical and artistic heritage, and is often linked to its medieval past (Galí, 2005; Camprubí, 2009). In recent years some annual events have become major tourist attractions, particularly on a regional and national level.

Theatre had a fairly modest tradition in Catalonia up until 1980. Joan Oliver, one of the most relevant playwrights in Catalan literature, gave the following description in 1957:

> We have a modest but respectable tradition, which we have not known how to turn to our advantage in a positive sense. External circumstances have made the picture bleaker. And today we might say – exaggerating a little so that everyone realizes that Catalan theatre is a magnificent wasteland: debris, rubble, a few old shacks and a plasterboard kiosk here and there, in a vaguely Balkan style.
> (Joan Oliver, in Sala, 2003, p. 437)

According to Sala's (2003) analysis of recent history, the Catalan theatre scene from 1966 onwards experienced a boom in dramatic production that lasted throughout the 1970s and involved the emergence of numerous companies (directors, actors, scenographers, etc.) who conceived theatre completely differently to the way it had been understood in previous decades. The first independent theatre was created that differed from what was hitherto understood as commercial theatre.

Diverse non-textual theatre groups appeared (Els Joglars, La Fura dels Baus, among others) with clear connections to what was taking place in other countries like the United States. The other major new development was teatre-festa, or festival theatre, of which Els Comediants would be the best example. These two new trends, combined with other factors, would bring a profound change to the perception of the theatre space and scenography through the involvement of the audience.

The decade of the 1980s witnessed the normalization of Catalan theatre, coinciding with the arrival of democracy to the Spanish state (1978) and with it the refurbishing of Girona's Old Quarter and the gradual recovery of urban normality to the city as a whole. Resulting from this and other developments, the city of Girona currently has four facilities capable of staging theatre shows linked to the scenic arts. In addition, theatres in Salt, Sant Gregori, Celrà and Bescanó also host events during Temporada Alta. An integrated ticket sales service exists for the four facilities in Girona plus the theatre in Salt.

All four facilities in Girona have been inaugurated or substantially renovated in recent years. The Municipal Theatre, the original base for Temporada Alta, was closed for renovation from 2001 to 2006 (another building was temporarily equipped to host functions). The Mercè Cultural Centre opened under municipal patronage in 1984 in the old city, which at the time was undergoing a process of profound refurbishment. The independent theatre La Planeta opened its doors in 1987. And lastly, the Congress Auditorium, the only facility located outside the city's tourist area, was inaugurated in 2006. Therefore, we can say that over the last 30 years, and particularly over the last 20, cultural life in the city and its area of influence have experienced substantial improvements from both a quantitative and qualitative point of view.

Origins and aims of the festival

In 1992 the autumn festival 'Temporada Alta' was created with the objective of improving the local theatre scene. In its first year the event had a budget of a little over two million pesetas (about €12,000), which allowed the staging of four shows and attracted 4115 spectators.

The first year also saw the introduction of the Club del Mecenatge Teatral (Theatre Patronage Club), by which companies and organizations in the region could acquire a pack of tickets for each show in the festival, paying double the normal ticket price. This has a dual benefit: on the one hand it comprises an important source of funding and on the other Temporada Alta creates a solid link with business and society on a local or regional level.

Temporada Alta grew over the following 2 years in terms of the number of shows, budget and attendance (increased by almost 70%), but it remained a closed programme that served to initiate the local theatre season. However, premieres and foreign productions gradually began to be incorporated within the programme, and significant support was received from Girona City Council, with the budget reaching 18 million pesetas (€108,000) by 1995. The years 1996 and 1997 were of special significance. The number of foreign shows and companies grew and not surprisingly the festival was renamed as an International Theatre Festival. It now lasted throughout the whole of autumn. What is more, a new venue was added: Salt Theatre (Salt being a neighbouring town).

In 2005 the festival signed a 4-year agreement with the Autonomous Government of Catalonia and was recognized as a Scenic Arts Festival (in addition to theatre, it included other arts such as dance, music and circus). The following year the Spanish Ministry of Culture joined the organization, collaborating with Girona for the first time.

It was in 2008 that shows began to be co-produced with festivals and theatres from outside the country, in addition to the festival's own productions initiated in 2001. Nowadays, in addition to national and international scenic art shows, the Temporada Alta programme includes a wide range of parallel activities, among which the following stand out: cinema season, specialized courses, conferences, work in progress and multimedia arts. Thus, the festival has served to revitalize Girona's cultural life, offering a selection of shows for all audiences (from contemporary dance to children's circus, from experimental theatre to remakes of the classics). Some of the works included also form part of other theatre seasons like Escenaris Teatrals Transfronterers (which is held between theatres in Girona and the south of France).

In 2011 a new attendance record was set (reaching 93%) and the modus operandi of own productions, international co-productions and show premieres was maintained. To these we must now add new initiatives like the 1st International Developers Conference, the stage research laboratory LabCanal Argelès-sur-Mer (Havanera) and the Catalan Drama Tournaments.

Own communication channels

Temporada Alta has become a calling card for Salt Town Council and Girona City Council thanks to the broad range of audiences reached by the shows, international co-productions and parallel activities for public and professionals alike (see Figs 16.3 and 16.4). The festival is promoted partly through advertising, with the attention paid to the local audience being extremely important, particularly in Girona and Salt where banners are hung in the main streets. For the last 2 years a group of restaurants in Girona has also decorated its tables with tablecloths where diners can read the weekly Temporada Alta programme.

On a regional and Catalan level potential spectators are reached by means of adverts on local TV and radio stations. To complement this interviews and mini-reports are incorporated into different programmes such as the daily news. In addition to the audiovisual media, Temporada Alta also places ads in different written media, particularly newspapers. On occasion special promotions have even been offered to subscribers. Through these actions, along with journalists' attendance at shows, the written press has generated publicity for the festival in the form of articles on the shows as well as reviews that appear in both the general press and specialized magazines. An example of this is:

> If Girona is always worth a visit, Temporada Alta makes it unmissable for theatre lovers.
> (Juan Ignacio García Garzón, ABC, 20 November 2009, cited on Temporada Alta, 2012)

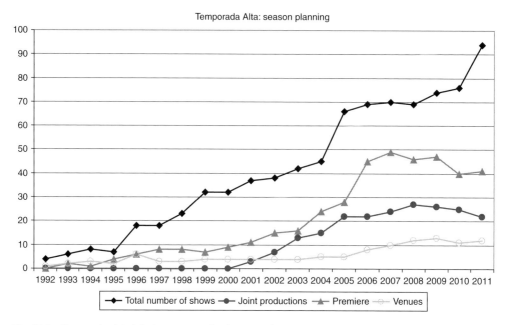

Fig. 16.3. Shows scheduled during Temporada Alta Festivals (1992–2011). (From Authors' compilation based on Bitò Produccions data.)

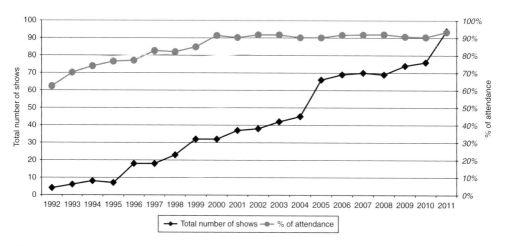

Fig. 16.4. Total number of shows (left) and percentage of attendance (right) (1992–2011). (From Authors' compilation based on Bitò Produccions data.)

With regard to online communication, Temporada Alta has its own website in four languages: Catalan, Spanish, English and French. As far as content is concerned, visitors to the website can consult the annual programme (calendar and description of each show); there is also an external link to purchase tickets, a section with information aimed specifically at the media (no registration required), a section acknowledging sponsor support, a section for volunteers and a section with practical information. This practical information section provides website links for transportation to Girona and Salt (including the train and

Girona–Costa Brava airport websites); there are also links to the websites of the two town councils and the Girona Tourism Board. Finally, with regard to the press, the website offers the possibility of subscribing to an RSS channel.

Online communication via Web 2.0 began in September 2009. The task of community manager was outsourced to the company Playbrand, and Temporada Alta is now present on four widely used social networks. Over this period of almost 3 years a total of 1639 tweets have appeared on Twitter (in Catalan), representing an average of almost two per day. Furthermore, a considerable amount of interaction is observed by followers (in total, 3157), who are proactive with the information they receive and/or they themselves generate. The Temporada Alta Facebook profile currently has 3769 'likes' and 115 people talking about it. Of the 'likes' it is worth highlighting that most are aged 25 to 34, although this must be noted with care because it is impossible to specify whether this is because most spectators and people interested in Temporada Alta are young people or among all the spectators and people interested in the festival only the younger ones use Facebook. Temporada Alta updates its status at least once a week (in Catalan), even outside the performance calendar, in order to maintain its presence in the social imaginary (the same is true of Twitter).

Since 2009 Temporada Alta has created a YouTube channel on an annual basis. This provides short videos of the shows to be performed each year, as well as TV ads and press conferences. The number of views received by each video, which are generally short, varies greatly: from a few dozen to over 2000. A Flickr profile was incorporated in 2011 and constitutes a photo bank of both the festival's shows and associated acts (award galas, press conferences, etc.).

Aside from the specific actions of promotion (see Fig. 16.5), the festival organizers reiterate year after year their gratitude to the festival-goers themselves (recent years have seen over 90% attendance), whom they consider their greatest ally in terms of promotion, thanks to the word-of-mouth they generate.

Promotion by tourism agents

Girona's tourism offices, of which there are two, plus one regional office in the city and one at the airport, receive the written Temporada Alta programme (in Catalan only) and act as promoters of the event. On the municipal tourism website the festival only appears in the Agenda section, which is on the page following the introduction. It is not included in any of the permanent links on this website or in the Culture and Leisure or Girona TV sections (which has videos of the city's various attractions under diverse headings). By contrast, however, on the Girona County Council's tourism website there is a permanent, although brief, page dedicated to Temporada Alta, with a link to the festival website. It is worth mentioning that this particular page is located deep inside the site, and this information will therefore only be found by potential visitors who are already interested in finding it. The website of the Costa Brava–Girona Tourist Board, the province's principal organization for promoting tourism, does not have space for Temporada Alta either, although on its inner pages it does include links to the websites of theatres and auditoriums, as well as listing music festivals.

Thanks to one of the promotion campaigns run by the aforementioned Tourism Board in 2012, Girona and the Costa Brava have been selected as one of the world's best destinations by the North American version of *National Geographic Traveller* magazine. However, Temporada Alta is not included among the diverse tangible and intangible attractions, which do include, for example, Girona's Temps de Flors flower festival. It is important to point out that during the months the festival is running, these three tourism agents (tourism offices, Girona County Council and the Tourist Board) do provide information regarding Temporada Alta via their agendas, bulletins and social networks. What is missing is a solid and permanent presence throughout the year.

When it comes to Catalonia the organization responsible for promoting Temporada Alta is the Catalan Tourism Agency (ACT), linked to the Autonomous Government of Catalonia's Directorate General of Tourism. However, Temporada Alta is not included on its list of

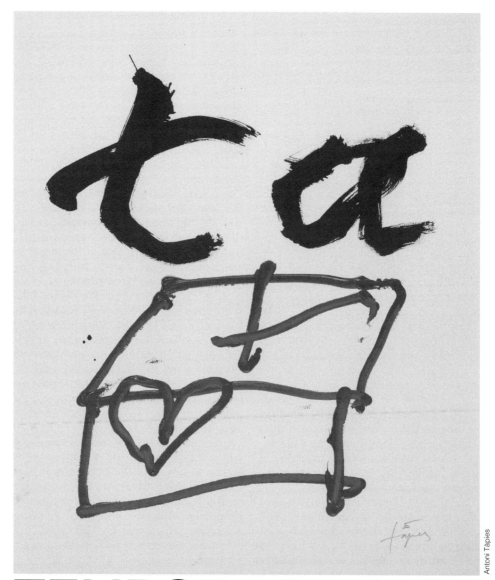

Fig. 16.5. Temporada Alta promotional poster by Antoni Tàpies (2008). (From Bitò Produccions.)

festivals, theatre and scenic arts. Within the ACT there are diverse product marketing clubs. Their aim is to unite the various stakeholders that comprise the tourism industry, to create a unified product and improve communication of it, particularly to international markets. Among these clubs, the Cultural Tourism Club unites, among other stakeholders, events such as the

Passion play La Passió d'Olesa de Montserrat and Peralada Castle Festival. Temporada Alta is not listed as a member here either.

Cultural events – advantages for local community

Cultural events with an international outlook are not only important from the point of view of cultural tourism, but rather very often they become a city or region's calling card and improve their image abroad. They also become integrated within strategic urban planning and bring not only economic but also social and cultural benefits. Temporada Alta has become the Autumn Festival that was lacking in Catalonia, from both a cultural and tourism viewpoint. For many years now, Temporada Alta has been emerging as a reference point on the European theatre scene, playing an important role in facilitating local creators to be seen, and placing special emphasis on co-productions with foreign theatres and companies. Not for nothing did the mayor of Girona say the following at the closing Temporada Alta press conference in 2011:

> The weight of Temporada Alta is perfectly recognizable in the value of the Girona brand ... and also in the value of the city and the region.
> (Carles Puigdemont during closing Temporada Alta press conference 2011)

The festival contributes significantly to promoting Girona as a region via, for example, the artists and specialists it brings year on year to the theatres of Girona, most of which are located within the Old Quarter, the city's main tourism centre. By way of example, the 1st International Developers Conference (2011) brought 65 professionals from eight different countries to the city. With regard to promotion, the festival has a very effective marketing policy for the local population, which has managed to involve both the public (who have become the principal opinion leaders) and organizations (which act as sponsors). Its link with tourism marketing stakeholders is, however, very weak and irregular, with no planned campaign in place throughout the year.

It is true that theatre presents a difficulty in the form of language that does not impact to the same extent on music festivals, which have become more strongly linked to the tourism industry in recent years. Despite this obstacle, however, it is worth remembering that the festival includes dance, music and circus acts, which do not suffer from this limitation. As for the theatre plays it is also important to note that many of them are performed in languages other than Catalan, particularly Spanish and English, which can be targeted at visiting audiences.

There is currently a lack of research into what proportion of Temporada Alta audiences are visitors, where they are from (Catalan, national or international) and the weight of the festival in the destination selection process. From the point of view of the local tourism industry, however, Temporada Alta is an interesting resource on which more work must be done, as it may help resolve two problems endemic to tourism: seasonality (which has dropped thanks to low-cost flights but is still very pronounced during holiday periods and weekends) and excursion tourism (whose linkage to overnight stays in the city could be improved if the total volume of visitors is taken into account).

For its part the tourism industry has shown a first expression of interest in the arts scene with the product Escapada Escènica (Scenic Gateway), created jointly with Girona Town Council and Girona–Radial Hotel Association. This is a package that includes: accommodation; two-for-one on tickets from the fixed theatre, music and dance programme; restaurants; entries to museums that are part of the Gironamuseus network; and two-for-one on tickets for Truffaut Cinema.

16.9   Summary

In summary, then, Temporada Alta needs to draft a strategic plan for its links with the tourism industry. Firstly, it would be interesting to conduct an audience study in order to determine the current level of tourists among Temporada Alta audiences and to achieve a permanent and easily accessible presence on the websites of the principal tourism stakeholders: Girona Town Council, County Council, the Costa Brava–Girona Tourist Board and the Catalan Tourism Agency. Joining the Culture Club is another option that the Temporada Alta management board should evaluate, taking into account its desire to convert Girona into the 'theatre city' missing from mainland Europe.

This study would allow analysis of whether the festival has become an actual tourist destination in itself (and whether this corresponds with municipal planning and that of the production company). Temporada Alta as a tourist destination can be focused on from the viewpoint of the local population (for whom shows can be considered a tourism space, creating a certain illusion of 'being on holiday', as it allows them to momentarily abandon their everyday lives despite being in the same geographical region) and that of visitors. In this respect, a significant difference has already been identified with regard to other European cities with a tourism positioning in the area of festivals and theatre shows (London or Edinburgh, for example). Generally speaking, the theatre districts in these cities become a place for tourist visits, whether accompanied by attendance at a show or not. In the case of Temporada Alta no theatre district exists but rather it makes use of existing facilities within the city of Girona and towns in its sphere of influence. This means that a certain type of inter-municipal cultural tourist route would need to be created: a special structure that would without doubt be of interest from the point of view of the academic literature.

Temporada Alta does not have any tourism products associated with it, not even, as found in the case of London theatres, a large number of specialized tour operators dedicated to selling tickets to visitors. Although collaboration with wholesalers may initially be complicated because of a lack of tradition and divergences existing in the tourism and cultural calendar, collaboration with the local or regional tourism industry would seem logical, taking advantage of workshops that are already organized, in particular by the Costa Brava–Girona Tourist Board and ACT.

Lastly, integrating Temporada Alta into the local tourism imaginary, proposing it as another attraction to visit or an attraction in itself, may lead locals to believe that Girona is committed to following the current trend of creating events in order to reduce seasonality and/or increase the number of visitors. In this case, it should be taken into account that we are taking as a basis a product that has been created with the clear intention of improving cultural life in the city, with a solid track record and that has given the city a character of its own (often linked to innovation in theatre, for which it has recently received awards), while at the same time aimed at a very broad spectrum of audiences.

16.10   Discussion Questions

- What aspects of festivals and theatre festivals relating to tourism have been less studied by academics?
- What are the main impacts (negative and positive) for a city or region that hosts a festival? Why do they compete?
- What are the expectations of visitors (day-visitors or tourists) regarding a festival?
- How can a festival be defined as a destination isolated from the rest of the city/region?
- Why has Temporada Alta become so important for the region and for Girona in particular?
- Are the links between Temporada Alta and the tourist industry strong enough to justify the presence of the festival in the tourist imaginary?

References

Agència Catalana de Turisme (2012) Tourist agenda. http://www10.gencat.net/pls/turistex/p03.recurs?dm=04&rcrs=AGC&tpsBarra=RD (accessed 1 February 2012).

Andersson, T.D. and Getz, D. (2009) Tourism as a mixed industry: differences between private, public and not-for-profit festivals. *Tourism Management* 20, 847–856.

Bennett, S. (2005) Theatre/tourism. *Theatre Journal* 57, 407–428.

Camprubí Subirana, R. (2009) La formació de la imatge turística induïda: el paper de les xarxes relacionals. PhD thesis, University of Girona, Spain.

Club de Turisme Cultural, Agència Catalana de Turisme (2012) Cultural Tourism Club. http://cultura. catalunya.com/ca/index.php (accessed 1 February 2012).

Crompton, J.L. and McKay, S.L. (1997) Motives of visitors attending festival events. *Annals of Tourism Research* 24, 425–439.

Feifan Xie, P. (2001) Festival and special event management. *Annals of Tourism Research* 28, 248–250.

Frew, E. and Ali-Knight, J. (2009) Independent theatres and the creation of a fringe atmosphere. *International Journal of Culture, Tourism and Hospitality Research* 3, 211–227.

Frey, B.S. (1996) Has Baumol's cost disease disappeared in the performing arts? *Ricerche Economiche* 50, 173–182.

Galí Espelt, N. (2005) *La Imatge turística del patrimoni monumental de Girona*. Institut del Patrimoni Cultural de la Universitat de Girona, Girona, Spain.

Getz, D. (1991) *Festivals, Special Events and Tourism*. Van Nostrand Reinhold, New York.

Getz, D. (2007) Event tourism: definition, evolution and research. *Tourism Management* 29, 403–428.

Getz, D. (2011) Festival places: revitalizing rural Australia. *Annals of Tourism Research* 38, 1671–1672.

Girona Turisme. Girona Town Council (2012) Tourism. http://www.girona.cat/turisme/eng/activitats.php (accessed 10 February 2012).

Gironès, Terra de Passeig. Consell Comarcal del Gironès (2012) What to see? Events and fairs. http://www. turismegirones.cat/uk/what-visit/m0/alls/1143a0ab54bed165878d7a0b7d2a7231/events-and-fairs. html (accessed 20 February 2012).

Grappi, S. and Montanari, F. (2010) The role of social identification and hedonism in affecting tourist re-patronizing behaviors: the case of an Italian festival. *Tourism Management* 32, 1128–1140.

Hughes, H.L. (1998) Theatre in London and the inter-relationship with tourism. *Tourism Management* 19, 445–452.

McDonnell, I., Allen, J. and O'Toole, W. (1999) *Festival and Special Event Management*. Wiley, Milton, Australia.

Patronat de Turisme Costa Brava–Girona (2012) Arts and culture. http://en.costabrava.org/categories/ default.aspx?t=arts-and-culture&com=QwBhAHQAZQBnAG8AcgB5AEkARABcADEAMgBcAA== (accessed 20 February 2012).

Prentice, R. and Andersen, V. (2003) Festival as creative destination. *Annals of Tourism Research* 30, 7–30.

Richards, G. (2001) El desarrollo del turismo cultural en Europa. *Estudios Turísticos* 150.

Sala, J. (2003) El teatre català dels anys 60–70: el llarg camí cap a la normalitat. In: *Museu d'Art de Girona: 60s versus 80s: literatura, música i arts visuals a Girona i a Catalunya (1960–1980)*. Museu d'Art de Girona, Girona, Spain, pp. 433–453.

Smith, S.L.J. (1990) *Dictionary of Concepts in Recreation and Leisure Studies*. Greenwood Press, New York.

Stansfield Jr, C.A. (1991) Festivals, specials events and tourism. *Annals of Tourism Research* 18, 350–353.

Temporada Alta (2011) RdP Tancament Festival Temporada Alta 2011. Temporada Alta edn, YouTube, Girona. http://youtu.be/eq21OkP0SPI (accessed 20 February 2012).

Temporada Alta (2012) Temporada Alta. Festival de Tardor de Catalunya, Girona–Salt. http://www.temporada-alta.net/ (accessed 28 February 2012).

17 Case Study 9: The London 2012 Olympic Games: The Cultural Tourist as a Pillar of Sustainability

Karl A. Russell[1] and Noëlle O'Connor[2]
[1]London Metropolitan University, London, UK;
[2]Limerick Institute of Technology, Limerick, Ireland

This chapter will examine the cultural background of the Olympic Games and the Contemporary Olympic Games movement. The chapter will also look at how, after 80 years of development, the Olympic Games have evolved substantially in terms of their significance, inclusion of participants, global media attention and the willingness of potential host cities to stage the games at quite a considerable cost. Finally, the chapter will discuss the impacts of the Olympic Games on Muslim faith. In recent decades the world has witnessed a global shift in geopolitical influence and socio-cultural acceptance of societies other than western, and the shifting of economic power bases towards emerging nations.

17.1 Introduction

Garcia (2008) suggests that the Olympic Games have long been regarded as the world's largest international sporting mega-event. The Games are also seen as a cultural phenomenon, supported by a global network of organizing and member organizations and National Organizing Committees (NOC) that seek to endorse an educational and intercultural remit promoting Olympism as a 'philosophy of life', headed up by the International Olympic Committee (IOC) (Garcia, 2008). The Games, which are considered to be the greatest peacetime event on earth, have a global scope, which cannot easily be understood but communicates cultural values in the form of signs, rituals and images (Garcia, 2008).

The 2012 Olympic Games were hosted and staged in London, United Kingdom (UK). This is the third time that London has hosted the Summer Games of the modern Olympiads (see Table 17.1). Only the USA has hosted the Summer Olympics on more occasions than the UK. The ancient Olympic Games were first staged in the holy city of Olympia, Greece, as a unique festival and 'cult of human essence', and as such was a non-secular way of paying homage by the ancient Greeks to their Gods in the form of sports worship (Liao and Pitts, 2006). Given the European origins of the Olympic Games and their historical significance, it is clear that they have a strong western and Eurocentric ideological and cultural basis, which for decades has gone alongside a western predominance towards the hosting of the Summer Olympic Games and an inclination towards a western cultural spectator and media audience.

The first 'modern' Olympic Games were staged in 1896 and held in Athens (see Table 17.1), the city that is traditionally called the home of the Olympic Games (Girginov and Hills, 2008). Liao and Pitts (2006) argue that the origin of the modern Olympic movement can be traced back to Coubertin's (1909) concept of creating a 'modern Olympia'. Coubertin had, as a visionary, perceived the long-term appeal of the ancient Olympic Games in the ancient Hellenic world as being deeply rooted in a unique festival form, as well as being located in a solid, physical setting, the holy city of Olympia. Coubertin also believed that if the modern Olympic Games were to extend beyond being a pure sporting event they should have an integral sense of culture and belief (Liao and Pitts, 2006).

During the first decade of their revival the modern Olympic Games did not attract the general public's attention as it does today. In addition, they were financially constrained, which meant the Olympic Games in Athens (1896), Paris (1900) and St Louis (1904) were little more than small spectacle affairs – but they were tied closely to the Olympic philosophy. The turning point in their popularity came about paradoxically in London in 1908, where the staging of the Games was linked to the great cultural Franco-British Exhibition of the same year (Liao and Pitts,

Table 17.1. Summer Olympic Game host cities since 1896. (Adapted from Rossenberg, 2012.)

1896 – Athens, Greece
1900 – Paris, France
1904 – St Louis, USA
1908 – London, UK
1912 – Stockholm, Sweden
1916 – Scheduled for Berlin, Germany*
1920 – Antwerp, Belgium
1924 – Paris, France
1928 – Amsterdam, Netherlands
1932 – Los Angeles, USA
1936 – Berlin, Germany
1940 – Scheduled for Tokyo, Japan*
1944 – Scheduled for London, UK*
1948 – London, UK
1952 – Helsinki, Finland
1956 – Melbourne, Australia
1960 – Rome, Italy
1964 – Tokyo, Japan
1968 – Mexico City, Mexico
1972 – Munich, West Germany (now Germany)
1976 – Montreal, Canada
1980 – Moscow, USSR (now Russia)
1984 – Los Angeles, USA
1988 – Seoul, South Korea
1992 – Barcelona, Spain
1996 – Atlanta, USA
2000 – Sydney, Australia
2004 – Athens, Greece
2008 – Beijing, China
2012 – London, UK
2016 – Rio de Janeiro, Brazil

*Summer Olympic Games were not held in 1916, 1940 and 1944 because of World Wars I and II.

2006). This co-hosting made the Olympic Games a centre-stage attraction. The Stockholm Games (1912) was a further landmark in proving a prototype of urban development as an element of hosting the Games and as a showcase of cultural diversity of the host society; this was achieved through the urbanization of the Game's site and the associated events. The cultural aspects of the Olympic Games became more prominent during the hosting of the Games in Antwerp (1920), Paris (1924) and Amsterdam (1928) (see Table 17.1), where cultural, aesthetic and symbolic expressions evolved into highly important themes within the modern Games movement.

Despite the costs, host cities expect significant benefits, not least being the opportunity to showcase the culture of the host city and country to a global audience (Low and Hall, 2010). Notwithstanding these laudable cultural goals, the origins of both the ancient and modern Olympics Games have remained deeply rooted in western ideology, culture and religion. This can be evidenced by the fact that since 1896 the Olympic Games have been hosted in 21 cities within 17 different countries (Liao and Pitts, 2006), of which the vast majority have been within Europe (14), followed by the Americas (6), Asia (3) and Australia (2) (see Table 17.1) (IOC, 2012).

17.2   The East and the Olympic Games

Since the 1990s the world has undergone a transformation with regards to its economic, socio-cultural and political power basis and influence. Fuelled by such concepts as globalization, capitalism and democracy, the influence of the western world has sought to impact upon traditionally closed and developing/'emerging' regions and markets of the world. This western influence was typified by the Moscow-hosted Olympic Games in the USSR in 1980, which preceded the spirit of Glasnost and Perestroika, the revolutionary movements that facilitated the eventual break-up of the Soviet Union. Such response was not immediate, since the Moscow Olympic Games were impacted by a boycott of several western nations, led by the USA and their allies, because of the Russian invasion of Afghanistan. A tit-for-tat boycott was then put into effect by Russia and its allies during the 1984 Los Angeles Olympic Games. The eventual political and cultural revolution, which has been attributed in some part to the Olympics 'effect', was to the forefront of 'the beginning of the end' of the cold war and the reduction in political, economic and social barriers that had remained between the less democratic countries known as the emerging East and the largely democratic, capitalist West. Olsen states that

> the fall of communism and the thrust to democracy and free market has without question reshaped the global landscape. This geopolitical shift has reworked the map of the world so that it looks nothing like what was in existence as recently as 20 years ago.

Nationalism, independence and individualism appear to be the forces that are fueled by this ideological shift ... (and) a global financial system that is evolving as the primary arbiter of wealth and power.

(Olsen, 1999, p. 323)

Within today's world decline in the economic and financial fortunes of the West, linked closely to the 2008 global financial crisis, has led to an economic and financial shift in global fortunes typified by the political, economic and socio-cultural growing importance of such countries as Brazil, Russia, India and China (BRIC), and the upcoming and developing nations of the Middle and Far East, all of whom have seen their importance and status grow on the global stage. This economic and financial movement in global influence and power has established an agenda and a shifting power base towards the emerging markets, who, sustained by economic growth and financial wealth, are making an impact in a globalized world in a way never before witnessed within contemporary times. The Middle East, geographical home to such economically powerful nations as Saudi Arabia (a member of the G20), UAE, Qatar and Bahrain, is a typical emerging region of the world, where wealth, economic growth and diversification, based on the sale of natural resources such as oil and liquefied gas that 'continue to drive the Gulf Economy' (O'Sullivan, 2008, p. 1), has seen their global profiles raised dramatically in terms of their political, economic and socio-cultural influence.

As the modern-day Olympic Games are required to demonstrate cultural inclusion for all (Douglas, 2012), the Olympic movement faces one of its toughest challenges in its western and Eurocentric ideology, culture and origins. Within this evolving world the movement must seek to embrace the changing order and seek growth within new 'uncharted emerging nations' and thus align itself towards seeking greater appeal to a wider global audience. Arguably the Tokyo Olympic Games (1964) marked the beginning of the Olympic Games movement into the east and this was further consolidated when Moscow played host to the 1980 Olympic Games. However, the anticipated changes were not as profound as expected, reinforced by the fact that only one of the Olympic Games between 1984 and

2004 (the Seoul, South Korea 1988 Summer Games) was staged outside of the western hemisphere. This meant that largely the Olympic Games returned to their western origins, supported by western economic growth at the time.

However, a radical change came about with Beijing, China, hosting the 2008 Games. This iteration was regarded as a second breakthrough event and a major turning point in Olympic history. This Asian-hosted event attracted over 10,000 athletes and millions of 'cultural sport tourists' in person as games spectators and tourists in their billions via the many media sources. As a global mega-event this provided China with the opportunity to broadcast a worldwide showcase of Asian heritage and culture. An estimated TV audience of 4.3 billion people (63% of the world's population) in 220 territories saw what has been called the 'biggest broadcast event in history' (Sponsorship Intelligence, 2009, p. 2). The audience was witness to a showcasing of 'culturally modern' China, portrayed within an electrifying opening and closing ceremony watched by an estimated global audience of 1.5 billion (Sponsorship Intelligence, 2009, p. 3). Furthermore, the hosts demonstrated their precision running of the Games, which contained both traditional and modern Chinese culture embodied within an event that showed China at its very best. Beijing 2008 marked a significant geographical shift of the Olympic Games and its movement. This has encouraged cities such as Doha, Qatar and Dubai, UAE, to announce to the IOC their credentials, willingness and readiness to 'bid' as host cities for future Olympic Games. However, one of the most often overlooked topics within this fundamental movement of the Games eastwards is the Olympic Games' appeal to a new market of spectators within new emerging markets. In these new destinations their cultural influence is markedly different to the Olympic Games' western and Eurocentric ideology, culture and origins. This brings about challenges to the Olympic movement and its future host cities as they must adapt in order to appeal to a new type of cultural traveller and tourist coming from the Far and Middle East as Olympic cultural tourists.

17.3 Cultural Movement and the Olympic Games

With the London Olympic Games (2012) the International Olympic Committee (IOC) faced one of its biggest challenges linked to its sustainability and legacy pledges, the need to broaden the Games' appeal within its ethos of inclusion for all, especially citizens outside of the western hemisphere. As many of the socio-cultural values and philosophies inherent within the Middle East and its predominantly Islamic society are different to those found within the west (Stephenson *et al.* 2010), cultural difference could present ideological contradiction with the intrinsic western ideology, cultural and philosophical basis of the Olympic movement and spirit. Predictions were that the London 2012 Olympic Games would witness a growing number of Muslim athletes, with some 3000 of the expected 11,000 athletes coming from Middle Eastern countries (Ferris-Lay, 2012). It was thought that this would also correlate to an increase in Middle Eastern Olympic visitors, many of whom would be Muslim Olympic cultural tourists, seeking to experience London 2012 as spectators. With advanced state-of-the-art media and communications, the Games were expected to also bring about an increased television audience within the Middle East.

17.4 Islamic Culture and the Olympic Games

Many Middle Eastern tourists are Muslims, who are followers of the third major monotheistic religion to have arisen in the Middle East, Christianity and Judaism being the other two. All three religions have Abrahamic faith at their foundation and as such all lay claim to a certain spiritual descent from a common ancestor – the Patriarch Abraham (Catherwood, 2011). Within Middle Eastern Muslim culture the beliefs and values that may impact upon the Olympic Games can be summarized as being related to (1) daily prayers, (2) gender segregation, (3) dress code and (4) dietary rules. Each of these cultural elements presents the Olympic movement with challenges in accommodating a Middle Eastern Olympic cultural tourist.

These elements will now be explained, and an examination will be undertaken to explore their potential significance in impacting the Olympic movement and the related cultural tourism.

Daily prayers: Salat

For Muslims communal prayer (Salat) is to be performed five times a day and is set at prescribed times: before sunrise (Fajr); after the sun has passed its zenith or highest point at noon (Zuhr); after mid-afternoon (Asr); after sunset (Maghrib); and after the onset of night (Isha). At these times the community is summoned to pray by the Muezzinm, who calls from a tower of the mosque (Ramadan, 2001; Bleher, 2009). Prior to praying worshippers must perform a series of ritual ablutions called 'Wudu', to prepare them to approach God in a state of external and internal purity (Hattstein, 2006, p. 22). Prayer can be performed wherever a Muslim is in the world, but he/she must face Makkah – the spiritual home of Islam. The subsequent prayers involve both body and mind, and involve a series of bows and prostrations that are performed together with recitations of the Qur'an and of praises to Allah (Ramadan, 2001). The Friday midday prayer, which in Islam is the Holy day of the week, is regarded as the most important prayer time.

Gender segregation

Islam holds that all men and women are completely equal in the sight of God (Badawi, 2011, p. 7). Allah says:

> For Muslim men and women, for believing men and women, for devout men and women, for true men and women, for men and women who are patient and constant, for men and women who humble themselves, for men and women who give in charity, for men and women who fast (and deny themselves), for men and women who guard their chastity, for men and women who engage in Allah's praise, for them has Allah prepared forgiveness and a great reward.
>
> (Al-Qur'an 33:35)

Concerning all religious obligations like daily prayers, fasting and pilgrimage, men and women have equal responsibility (Badawi, 2011). Therefore, the Islamic concept of gender relations can be described as complementary rather than competitive (Bleher, 2009, p. 14).

Within Islam there exist regulations that guide the behaviour and position of the genders within society and the home; these are regulated by Sharia Law. In Islam males have been given a greater degree of responsibility concerning economic factors, maintenance and protection and overall leadership of the family. However, this greater degree of responsibility does not imply superiority over women, which would go very much against the spirit of justice and equality in Islam (Badawi, 2011). In accordance with Sharia Law, the head of the family (the husband) decides on all major issues pertinent to the family. His duty as head of the household extends to maintaining his wife or wives, and in return his wife or wives are committed to obedience (Pfister, 2010).

In Islam one of the main points regulated by female deference to the male head of the household is the regulation of sexuality, which is controlled by gender segregation. The degree of segregation may differ between different Muslim societies and countries and their interpretations of the Qur'an. In some states like Saudi Arabia gender segregation is highly conservative, while in some states like Egypt the interpretation can be seen to be more liberal.

Dress code

Muslims follow the code of Islam that advocates that women and girls must adopt modest dress when in public, and to maintain this they have to cover their bodies, something that seems to guarantee gender differences and society hierarchies. Pickthall (2011) translates the Qur'an as stating:

> Oh Prophet! Tell your wives and daughters and the women of the believer to draw their cloaks close around them (when they go out). That will be better, so that they may be recognized and not annoyed.
>
> (Pickthall, 2011, p. 249)

While some women may be forced by the head of the household to wear a veil or the Hijab, by law within countries like Saudi Arabia and Iran, in other societies and countries women may wear it according to their own free will.

Dietary rules

Muslim cultural tourists all have beliefs and values relating to food and drink, with their faith dictating which food is lawfully consumed and which is not. In relation to the Qur'an, Pickthall translates:

> He has forbidden you only carrion and blood and swine flesh, and that which has been sanctified to (the name of) any other than Allah ... [that which] has been killed by (the goring of) horns. Eat not of that on which Allah's name has not been mentioned ... The beast of cattle is made lawful to you (for food).
>
> (Pickthall, 2011, pp. 20, 83)

Muslims will only eat meat where the blood of the animal has been allowed to drain fully from the animal's body (Bleher, 2009). This is known as the Zabiha (Halal) method. Islam also forbids the consumption of any substance that might interfere with the perception of an individual's senses or blur their judgement. This includes alcohol or mind-altering drugs (Bleher, 2009).

17.5 Evolving Ideas

The Olympic Games have become a mega-event costing billions of dollars to win the hosting rights, to build the infrastructure and to host the Games themselves. For many nations the billions needed are difficult to justify and raise, a fact even more acute in the face of the global economic downturn, which started in 2008. In recent decades the world has witnessed a global shift in political influence, socio-cultural acceptance of societies other than western and the shifting of economic power bases towards emerging nations. This has introduced new potential contenders as host cities and also new audience markets for the Olympic Games, both of these in emerging nations that are outside the western hemisphere. Many of these nations have both the financial resources and new audiences needed to stage mega-events and to a degree ensure sustainability of such activities within a new world order.

Emerging nations such as Bahrain, Brunei, Indonesia, Malaysia, Qatar, Saudi Arabia and the United Arab Emirates (UAE) are economically wealthy and are endowed with large sovereign wealth funds, controlled by their governments. The financial liquidity available to the emerging countries of the Middle East and East Asia have put these nations, with their mainly Muslim populations, at the forefront of those seeking to stage mega-events, becoming active participants within such events and the opening of new media audiences and markets that have often been untapped.

While many major sporting events (international tennis, golf and Formula 1 motor racing) have been staged in such countries as Qatar, the UAE and Bahrain, their financial strength is increasingly allowing them to exert a degree of socio-cultural influence on the controllers of mega-events (Ferris-Lay, 2012). Mindful of this fact, the Olympic Games movement needs to become acquainted with Middle Eastern cultural beliefs and values and to reflect on the challenges that these present to the Olympic Games movement. These issues not only affected the London 2012 Games but will have profound long-term implications for all future Games and their far greater global appeal to a wider audience outside of the western hemisphere.

Within the predominantly Muslim countries of the Middle East following Islam is a way of life for believers. Therefore, Middle Eastern cultural tourists should be respected and have their cultural beliefs and values accommodated to allow for their participants at mega-events, such as the Olympic Games, as Muslim cultural tourists. Regarding daily prayers, Olympic venues will have to provide mosques and clearly indicate the direction of Makkah for worshippers. This will allow Muslim cultural tourists to conduct their five daily prayers while at Olympic venues.

A number of female Muslim athletes were expected as participants in London 2012, with Qatar, Saudi Arabia and Brunei (Shane, 2012) expected for the first time in their IOC membership history to send female athletes. The number of female Middle Eastern cultural tourists was also expected to see an increase. The issue of female modesty at the Olympics has been raised in the past, with some sport federations not allowing athletes to wear a veil and cover their hair (Pfister, 2010). However, changes in many sporting federation rules now allow for athletes to compete while wearing a veil.

However, female modesty in terms of dress means that Muslim spectators may be offended by the attire of athletes in some sports, for example beach volleyball and swimming events. Equally it may mean that some of these sports are not broadcast on media channels where the clothing is contrary to the dress codes of the country.

Clearly, Islam prohibits Muslims from eating some foods such as pork and any food that contains port fat or pork gelatine, for example many ice creams. Also forbidden is meat from animals that have not been slaughtered in the way prescribed by the Qur'an. To accommodate Muslim audiences, food needs to be clearly labelled as 'Halal' to prevent individuals from unintentionally consuming foods that are contrary to their religious dietary beliefs.

The Olympic Games, while seeking to be a modern multicultural mega-event, like many major sporting events, is seen as a vehicle for the expression by both participants and spectators of patriotism and cultural belonging. This is borne out by the many acts of patriotism witnessed when an athlete is successful – by both the successful athlete and spectators alike. The IOC needs to be mindful of many factors and practices related to the culture of the Middle East (and of course other locations, which are not dealt with in this chapter), and this understanding is required to facilitate the popularity of the Olympic Games for the Middle Eastern, Muslim, cultural tourist, both in person at the venues and globally via the various media channels. These subtle changes in ethos may greatly influence a growth in participation at the Olympic Games by Muslim cultural tourists and thus may add to the Games' growing global appeal for Muslim audiences.

17.6   Summary

This chapter begins with a discussion that illustrates the Euro-centric nature of the Olympic Games and suggests that perhaps this western domination is now coming to an end, with global economic, socio-cultural and political changes. It then presents some basic background information on the Islamic faith, specifically highlighting those practices that need to be accommodated or at least considered if the Olympics are to become more attractive for Muslim visitors, viewers and athletes. These beliefs and values are important for many Middle-Eastern cultural tourists as 'Islam is not just a religion, but a way of life for Muslims' (Hattstein, 2006). Therefore, to progress the ideals of Olympic socio-cultural inclusion, the International Olympic movement and the IOC must embrace these challenges.

17.7   Discussion Questions

•   Should countries use mega-events to showcase their culture?
•   What are the implications for Middle Eastern female participants at the Olympic Games as either athletes or spectators?
•   What are the key cultural ideologies for and against staging major events such as the Olympic Games within the Middle East?
•   What benefit would cultural tourism gain from a country staging a mega-event?

References

Badawi, J. (2011) The Position of Women in Islam. Islamic Dawah Centre International, Birmingham, UK.
Bleher, S.M. (2009) Islam: A Brief Guide. Islamic Dawah Centre International, Birmingham, UK.
Catherwood, C. (2011) A Brief History of the Middle East. Robinson, London.
Coubertin, P. (1909) Le Cadre, Une Olympie Moderne ['The Setting, a Modern Olympia']. Revue Olympique October 153–156.

Douglas, E. (2012) Everest gets torched – how the Olympics ruined a peaceful, spring at the top of the world. http://adventure.nationalgeographic.com/2008/06/special-report/everest/ed-douglas-text (accessed 5 February 2012).

Ferris-Lay, C. (2012) Muslim athletes face Ramadan hurdles at London Olympics. http://www.arabianbusiness.com/muslim-athletes-face-ramadan-hurdles-at-london-olympics-439722.html (accessed 25 March 2012).

Garcia, B. (2008) One hundred years of cultural programming within the Olympic Games (1912–2012): origins, evolution and projections. *International Journal of Cultural Policy* 14, 361–376.

Girginov, V. and Hills, L. (2008) A sustainable sports legacy: creating a link between the London Olympics and sports participation. *The International Journal of the History of Sport* 25, 2091–2116.

Hattstein, M. (2006) *Islam: Religion and Culture.* Konemann, Koln, Germany.

IOC (2012) The Olympic Charter. http://www.olympic.org/Documents/olympic_charter_en.pdf (accessed 24 March 2012).

Liao, H. and Pitts, A. (2006) A brief historical review of Olympic urbanization. *The International Journal of the History of Sport* 23, 1232–1252.

Low, D. and Hall, P.V. (2010) The 2010 cultural Olympiad: playing for the global or the local stage? *International Journal of Cultural Policy* 18, 131–150.

Olsen, M. (1999) Macro forces driving change into the new millennium – major challenges for the hospitality professional. *International Journal of Hospitality Management* 18, 371–385.

O'Sullivan, E. (2008) *The New Gulf. How Modern Arabia is Changing the World for Good.* Motivate Publishing, Dubai, UAE.

Pfister, G. (2010) Outsiders: Muslim women and Olympic Games – barriers and opportunities. *The International Journal of the History of Sport* 27, 2925–2957.

Pickthall, M.M. (2011) *The Glorious Qur'an: An Explanatory Translation.* Islamic Dawah Centre International, Birmingham, UK.

Ramadan, T. (2009) *Islam, the West and the Challenges of Modernity.* The Islamic Foundation, Leicester, UK.

Rossenberg, M. (2012) Olympic Game cities – Olympic Game host cities since 1896 for Summer and Winter Games. http://geography.about.com/od/countryinformation/a/olympiccities.htm (accessed 25 March 2012).

Seymour, R. (2009) English football club attracts Arab buyer; one by one, England's most famous soccer clubs are being bought by foreign owners and now an Abu Dhabi investment group has entered the fray. http://findarticles.com/p/articles/mi_m2742/is_398/ai_n35552091 (accessed 26 June 2012).

Shane, D. (2012) IOC 'confident' Saudi will send female athletes to London. http://www.arabianbusiness.com/ioc-confident-saudi-will-send-female-athletes-london-450576.html (accessed 13 May 2012).

Sponsorship Intelligence (2009) Games of the XXIX Olympiad, Beijing 2008. http://www.olympic.org/Documents/IOC_Marketing/Broadcasting/Beijing_2008_Global_Broadcast_Overview.pdf (accessed 28 June 2012).

Stephenson, M.L., Russell, K.A. and Edgar, D. (2010) Islamic hospitality in the UAE: indigenization of products and human capita. *Journal of Islamic Marketing* 4, 9–24.

18 Case Study 10: Re-enactment as an Aspect of Cultural Tourism

Brendan Griffin[1] and Eimear Ging[2]

[1]Re-enactor;
[2]Re-enactor and living historian

This chapter is a case study of using re-enactment as an activity that can contribute to a larger cultural festival or historic site. The broader context of tourism in Ireland will be looked at, together with the impetus provided by the government-sponsored 'Gathering 2013' initiative, before moving on to a particular case that will be explored in some detail. The case looks at a festival in the twin towns of Killaloe and Ballina, located on the River Shannon in Ireland's midwestern region, where re-enactment has been reintroduced after an absence of several years. The purpose of this chapter is a focus on the unique brand provided by the historic figure Brian Ború. The approach will be focused on the practicalities of using re-enactment, in the particular festival, but will also attempt to cover some of the more abstract theoretical issues affecting this type of event design, and reflect on other events and activities involving re-enactment.

18.1 Introduction

In January 2012, despite its consideration for many years as an element of tourism (Johnson, 1999), the Irish Minister for Arts, Heritage and the Gaeltacht acknowledged heritage as a crucial area for developing the tourism sector in Ireland. He has committed his department, together with the Irish Tourism agencies (Fáilte Ireland and Tourism Ireland), the Heritage Council and other organizations, to developing heritage initiatives, and to contributing to the quality of the national heritage tourism product (Dáil Éireann, 2012). A second recent development has been a report by ITIC, the Irish Tourist Industry Confederation, which represents the tourism industry, refuting Fáilte Ireland's description of the capital city, Dublin, as the 'strategic cockpit for Irish tourism'. This report published in June 2012 claims that the €15 million spent on market-ing the city is not well focused and that Dublin has lost market share to other cities in recent years because of its lack of direction and iden-tity (TDI, 2012). The challenge it identifies is to spend money in a way that optimizes ben-efit to the community and boosts domestic and foreign investment extending beyond Dublin and Ireland.

Fáilte Ireland, the agency responsible for developing Ireland as a sustainable high-qual-ity and competitive tourism destination, both nationally and internationally, has identified cultural tourism as a key development area that responds to both the Minister's call above and the challenges of the ITIC-sponsored report. Their strategy (discussed in Chapter 9 of this book) focuses on developing customer needs-based tourism, targeting key markets and segments both nationally and interna-tionally. An important element of this strat-egy is promoting sustainable development through an emphasis on maintaining a strong local element to any cultural activity (Fáilte Ireland, 2010a). Furthermore, Fáilte Ireland have identified 'Shared Stories' as critical in interpretation of the past, drawing on the narrative of a place or its people as a means of generating a unique brand (Fáilte Ireland, 2010b).

The 'Gathering 2013' concept was launched across Ireland in May 2012 as a locally driven but nationally supported initia-tive to draw back people (tourists) from the Irish Diaspora overseas. This well-funded, culturally focused scheme has received strong support from Fáilte Ireland and other tourism agencies, which have provided guidelines on the sort of events they are targeting for the initiative (The Gathering Ireland, 2012). The primary focus is on 2013 but with an eye to sustainable development into 2014 and beyond. The deadline for submitting projects for inclusion/support as part of this national, year-long event was the end of June 2012 (rather than the usual year-end for such fund-ing) to ensure that initiatives will be fully up and running by September 2012, with the first Gathering events happening on 1 January 2013.

This chapter looks at the case of twin Irish towns Killaloe–Ballina, which have an established annual festival. They decided in 2012 to reintroduce a re-enactment element to the event as a differentiator and a method of focusing on a Unique Selling Point that has a direct connection to the towns' rich cultural heritage.

18.2   Killaloe and Ballina

Killaloe and Ballina are two small towns in the mid-west of Ireland, facing each other across the River Shannon and connected by a bridge, centrally located within a range of natural resources. Despite their physical proximity, the modern administrative land-scape means that these towns, which are located in different counties, are located in different governmental areas, so at times there has been a lack of integrated thinking, both in terms of general infrastructure and potential tourism development. In recent years, however, both communities have worked together to develop initiatives that will overcome physical and political barriers and thus benefit both areas.

While there are several interesting elements in Killaloe and Ballina, in terms of cultural tour-ism, the principle link to the past is as the birth-place of King Brian Ború. Brian Ború is a historical figure of the late 10th and early 11th century whose life and activities were first writ-ten down a century after his death. His palace (Kincora) was most likely located at the top of the hill in the centre of the present town of Killaloe, which during his reign was capital of Ireland. His name is known to every school-child in Ireland as the king who united all the people of Ireland for the first time, and under his banner they rose up and drove the Viking invaders out of Ireland at the Battle of Clontarf. This battle took place outside Dublin in 1014, and according to various accounts as many as 9000 people took part, with approximately half that number dying, including, in the best tradition of such stories, Brian himself and all of his immediate heirs (Downham, 2005). The reality of this preceding history/narrative of conflict is, of course, a lot more complex and a lot less black-and-white than any of the simple elements that make this such a popular tale in

Irish mythology. However, what is clear is that this individual is a significant figure in the history of Ireland in general and Killaloe and Ballina in particular. The story of Brian Ború is the premier story of this region and, in fact, probably one of the most significant stories in Irish history.

The towns of Killaloe and Ballina contain numerous other elements that are of cultural interest, including the early Christian churches/oratories of St Flannan and St Lua, the latter of which was moved to its current site in the 1920s, when the Shannon Hydroelectric scheme flooded its original island location. The original bridge between the towns is credited to one of Brian Ború's descendents, as is St Flannan's (12th century) Cathedral in Killaloe. Outside of the town, the fort of Béal Ború, located at a fording point across the Shannon, is associated with Brian Ború, being the place where he received his tribute. It was subsequently utilized as a site by the Anglo-Normans and in more recent times is linked with Patrick Sarsfield, who led a military unit across the Shannon as part of a relief effort for the Siege of Limerick in 1691. Killaloe also played a key role in the industrial use of the Shannon and related canal works for transporting goods, and in the 20th century the town had a role in the Irish war of independence that is commemorated by a monument on the Bridge (Kierse, 1983).

All of this cultural heritage and its present-day manifestation laid the foundation for Killaloe and Ballina to gain national recognition as a Heritage twin town. Throughout the early 1990s this Heritage Towns initiative (and other related financing mechanisms) gave the area access to funding that was used to improve local tourism infrastructure, including building an interpretive centre and library on the site of a former lock house at the bridge in Killaloe (Griffin, 2000). The Heritage Town designation also led to increased cooperation between the administrations and local people of the two towns and resulted in the development of a number of festivals and shared cultural events, as well as building up a sense of community in the area. The heritage/interpretive centre promotes all attractions of the area, but without doubt the element that would be most profitably promoted in a bid to attract tourists and casual visitors is the connection to Brian Ború.

18.3   Féile Brian Ború

The first Féile Brian Ború (Brian Ború Festival) took place in 1993 and was a local event to celebrate the culture and heritage of the area. Over the years the festival has grown in scale and scope to be a significant regional event that now runs over the course of two weekends and the week between them at the end of June and start of July each year. The festival covers a wide range of interests from sport to the arts and appeals to different demographics, with events targeted at young people, adults and families. A core organizing theme is focused on building a festival that retains its local focus and develops local identity, while also having a national and international appeal (Howard, 2003).

In 2011 the festival committee, working together with their patron and former international rugby star Keith Woods, put together a medium-range business plan focused on developing the festival as well as wider tourism potential in the area. The committee decided to look for increased funding to turn the festival into a truly national event, working initially to integrate it with the government-sponsored Gathering 2013 programme but with the intent of subsequently working towards a larger event in 2014. A key emphasis of the festival throughout the development process has been to celebrate the area's rich culture and heritage, with a view to establishing it on the international calendar as a significant event. The 2012 festival received more funding and a mentor provided by Fáilte Ireland, which facilitated an increase in scale of activities as well as more widespread marketing and more effective execution, with a focus on demonstrating real, measurable increases in tourism and tourist numbers as well as proof that the event has grown beyond its local and regional roots. There was a requirement in this expanded approach to actively reach out to groups and individuals in the area, as well as increasing the range and scope of activities available.

Re-enactment had been part of Féile Brian Ború in the past but was discontinued because of a lack of funding. The organizing committee were keen to reintroduce a re-enactment element to the 2012 festival, which they felt would make a strong contribution to the overall event and would generate a lot of public interest, especially in the lead up to 2014. The millennium anniversary of the Battle of Clontarf will take place in that year and, since it is the main event associated with the legend of Brian Ború, it is likely that there will be significant national events commemorating the occasion. Féile Brian Ború is conscious that it will need to present its own events but also link strongly into external activities and draw both publicity and future tourist numbers from the connection.

The historical person of Brian Ború was seen as a unique aspect of the festival that could not be matched elsewhere and an essential element of the overall brand, drawing on his fame and all that he achieved. The legacy of Brian Ború is a strong brand that has resonance locally, nationally and internationally with the Irish Diaspora. Working with the assistance of the Fáilte Ireland festival mentor, the committee identified a path to build on this unique brand towards provision of active learning opportunities specifically targeting overseas groups, in addition to the more general tourist population. The legend of Brian Ború would be the story promoted to sustain local interest and involvement in the festival and bring it to an international audience, following the 'Shared Stories' approach mentioned above.

For this reason re-enactors promoting and fostering the connection with the 1014 era were considered essential to build a direct link to that cultural heritage. The opportunity to reintroduce re-enactment came in 2012 following initial contact with Mogh Roith, a group based in the region. As a first step the group were invited to participate in the 'Discover Day' programme, where a small weapons display by a number of group members in costume provided the public an opportunity to interact with re-enactment as a trial for a larger event during the festival. The popularity of this feature within the Discovery festival demonstrated that a larger camp could be something that would

contribute to the overall aims and direction of the larger festival.

The festival committee decided that, while the time available to coordinate the reintroduction of re-enactment was short, it was important to do so in order to have this element optimized in time for the Gathering in 2013 and the bigger anniversary in 2014.

In order to manage the re-enactment element and ensure that it would meet the aims and objectives of the festival in an authentic way, the committee drew upon the expertise of its existing members and established a heritage subgroup, tasked to work on the 2012 festival and towards a larger event in 2014. The re-enactment group was invited to participate in this heritage subcommittee, which helped to ensure a creative flow of ideas and guarantee that this element was integrated into the overall festival.

18.4   Concept of Re-enactment

Before progressing it is important to reflect on the concept of re-enactment, which is a hobby in which the practitioners research particular historical periods extensively and assemble clothing, skills and knowledge, which enable them to portray an impression of that period in time as authentically as possible. It is a family hobby, in which babies and children often take part alongside their parents and add greatly to the representation (see Fig. 18.1). Clothing, weapons, craft equipment, etc., are often museum-quality replicas and represent a large investment of time and money.

Re-enactors are keen to share their knowledge and skills with the public at events such as Féile Brian Ború but must have a reasonable expectation that their personal kit will be safe. Also, as hobbyists rather than paid performers, they will only attend events that are of interest to them and an organizer is obliged to take this into account. Usually, they would expect to receive a small fee towards the cost of transportation and possibly food when attending festivals and similar events.

Within the broad category of re-enactment there are also individuals and groups who are paid professionals and who can be brought

Fig. 18.1. Training the next generation. This image includes Barry Gaynor and his son Lochlann of Fingal. Living History Society at Féile Brian Ború, 2012. (From Brendan Griffin.)

Fig. 18.2. Dave Swift of Claoimh dressed as an early 1600s musketeer. (From Niamh O'Rourke, 2011.)

into an event for a set fee, like any other performer. The standard of the display provided by these individuals is usually very high: it should be noted, however, that often the pure hobbyists are of an equivalent standard, but the level of authenticity varies between individuals and groups.

An example of professional re-enactment is exemplified in Claoimh (The Irish-language word for sword), which is a small but growing Irish business providing re-enactment-based services. Dave Swift, founder of Claoimh (see Fig. 18.2), made the transition from re-enactment as a hobby to re-enactment as a profession following the recession-driven collapse of the archaeology market in Ireland in 2008. Turning this economic challenge into an opportunity, he applied his knowledge and experience as an archaeologist to advance his belief that his product could make a real contribution to Ireland's heritage tourism sector. Discussing his vision and linkage to culture, Dave states: 'we serve as an interface between the cold stones of built heritage and the curiosity of the visitor' (D. Swift, 2012, personal communication). Thus, re-enactment can contribute to the cultural landscape by answering questions not only about the equipment the individual carries/wears/displays, and the place the event is

located in, but any of the many questions that the re-enactment stimulates in the minds of visitor. These questions often move beyond the narrow confines of history into broader questions about Ireland, its people and culture.

18.5   Re-enactment at Féile Brian Ború

In reinvigorating re-enactment as part of Féile Brian Ború, the festival committee decided to use the local re-enactment group, Mogh Roith: a small but experienced team of re-enactors with strong links to the local area, who also have demonstrable experience of organizing events in the region for festivals as well as major heritage organizations such as Shannon Heritage and the likes of the National Museum of Ireland. Part of Mogh Roith's aspirations for this event going forward includes the opportunity to build local capability and thus sustain and develop this event into the future (Ashworth and Larkham, 1994). In consultation with the festival organizing committee, Mogh Roith had a number of issues to take into consideration, ranging from the practical:

- providing a solution that meets stakeholder needs;
- choice of an era to represent;
- level of authenticity that would prove practical to provide;
- scale of the event within the funding parameters;
- availability of re-enactors at relatively short notice;

to more abstract problems:

- how best to represent the story of a historical figure who has become more legend than reality;
- finding the balance between satisfying public expectations and providing more challenging (and historically truthful) elements;
- addressing the desire for higher levels of authenticity held by many of the re-enactors while accepting that, for some, this is not the highest priority;
- how to create and maintain a sense of being in the past that is accessible to both children and adults; and
- engaging members of the public who may not be familiar with the Brian Ború legend and linking that legend with the local area.

As hobbyists rather than employed service providers, a central challenge for Mogh Roith was to provide an event that re-enactors would enjoy and find worthwhile, a different proposition than the norm for commercial ventures, wherein organizations use an event to promote themselves locally or attract new re-enactors. In order to provide an event of a calibre suitable to the aspirations of the festival it was necessary to draw most of the re-enactors from far afield – with most living more than two hours' driving time away from the event.

Festival organizers require 'bang for their buck' in order to maintain and increase funding and revenue, but also authenticity in terms of what is represented. These two elements are not always compatible and as a result the event design must balance both of these requirements. In addition, members of the public attending a festival bring different perspectives and needs. The organizing committee felt that families should experience activity that would heighten their experience of the weekend, with the focus perhaps more on entertainment and experience than education. It was felt that adults might enjoy the opportunity for a more detailed chat with the re-enactors, exploring the equipment, tools and crafts on display, taking advantage of various photo opportunities and updating their social media with the results. Young people would be engaged by a battle scenario with lots of noise and clashing swords, something that they can tell their friends about as well as turn into games once they go home.

Survey data have shown that main museum sites can be intimidating places for those who do not feel at home with the institutional code of such institutions (Merriman, 1991), and the opportunity to engage with a period of history in an outdoor festival environment can help to break down these barriers and encourage an interest in heritage. Experience from previous events shows that people of all ages and backgrounds enjoy experiencing equipment, weaponry and armour, with trying on helmets and chainmail being some of the most popular activities engaged in.

When choosing a time period to re-enact for Féile Brian Ború, it was necessary to decide between focusing on a specific era or going with representations from different eras significant in local history. In the case of the latter this could facilitate the opportunity to demonstrate elements of Anglo-Norman, later medieval, 1690s and War of Independence periods, since they all have explicit and well-known local connections and thus resonate with the people of the area. However, while all of these were possible, following discussions with the festival committee, Mogh Roith decided that focusing on the story of Brian Ború, the man and his time, would deliver a simpler, clearer message and experience for the public, as well as forming a basis for future events running towards 2014 and the millennium anniversary of Clontarf. This approach allows the festival to grow organically and link in with other historic anniversaries in the next 10 years, thereby maintaining a vibrant and living cultural experience.

Authenticity is a contentious issue in re-enactment, mainly among the re-enactors themselves. As hobbyists rather than paid professionals, presenting as authentic an impression as possible is one of the enjoyable elements for practitioners and can be used as a means of establishing 'superiority' of one group or individual over another. For paid professionals this aspect is of even greater importance because of the need to have a unique selling point or differentiator to their hobbyist counterparts. However, the basic reality is that it is not possible for modern people to present an entirely realistic representation of life lived 1000 years ago. Leaving aside the obvious physical differences brought on by modern nutrition, medical and dental practices, there are also physical environment obstacles to be overcome when presenting a historical time period: contemporary structures from the time will usually be lacking, as will animals, with many modern breeds introduced later in the medieval era, and also simple elements such as muddy roads rather than modern equivalents (hopefully).

Another more provocative example of the difficulty in attaining authenticity is that Viking slavery was an accepted norm, with Dublin as one of the principle slaving centres in Europe. The aesthetics of re-enacting this feature are not likely to appeal to the organizers of a family festival, and yet to leave out this element is to present a sanitized version of historical fact. Another example is the level of violence enacted on the population by people from all groups in the conflict of the time. People attending a festival that is primarily family focused are usually not looking to be provoked in this way.

In the case of Féile Brian Ború, Mogh Roith was asked to provoke interest and curiosity about the age but with a targeted approach to authenticity, creating a representation of the past that is consistent with aspects of the history and archaeological record while being in keeping with the theme of the overall event and the role of Brian Ború in the history and mythology of the region and country. Period-appropriate tents would provide a reasonably realistic substitute for built dwellings; clothing and equipment of participating re-enactors would be restricted to eliminate elements belonging to an earlier or later era, except where health and safety was an overriding concern.

The scale of the event was largely driven by the availability of re-enactors to take part, as well as available funding to pay for transport of people and their equipment. While those taking part in this event were hobbyists they would expect to receive a small stipend to cover expenses/travel when taking part in a funded event. Mogh Roith is a relatively small group and several of the members had prior commitments. As a result the group called upon other people from outside the region to deliver the required elements. As the event was organized at short notice, there was a high degree of likelihood that active re-enactors would already have committed to events elsewhere. Another key factor in deciding the scale of the event was the level of logistical support and associated costs required to ensure that the re-enactors were provided with the essentials necessary to run the event.

In 2012 there were relatively small numbers of re-enactors in Ireland with capability to participate in an 1014 era event, perhaps 100–200 individuals, with many of these limiting themselves to a small number of events each year. This compares with 800–1000 re-enactors annually attending the Battle of Hastings re-enactment and the 2000+ who took part in the 940th Anniversary of that battle in 2006. Later era events in the UK, such as the War of the Roses Battle of Tewkesbury, often have over 1000 fighters on the battlefield, while the tournament-style Battle of the Nations held in Warsaw, Poland, in 2012 attracted 300 competitive re-enactor combatants (see Fig. 18.3).

Battle of the Nations started off as a martial arts style competitive tournament for historical battle. The emphasis is on the later medieval time period, with re-enactors expected to have very high-quality armour and physical fitness to be able to take part. For several years the competition took place in the Ukraine, but in 2012 it was moved to Warsaw in Poland. The principle of the competition is that it takes bravery and courage to wear armour and face opponents at the level of intensity used in this competition.

How does it relate to culture and cultural tourism? The tourism element can be shown by the numbers of re-enactors and public involved. For the 2012 event more than 300

Fig. 18.3. Battle of the Nations 2012. Members of the Russian team close in on a team comprised of people from USA, Italy and the Ukraine. (From Vladlen Vasylenko.)

active participants from 12 countries competed, with at least as many more in support. In addition, 10,000 visitors viewed the fighting over the 4 days of the competition, with a significant number of people following live video feeds online and updates via social media from team members. Anton Trubnikov, the principal organizer of the event, highlights that for this event 'arms and armor are … made … in an authentic way' as a means of connecting the physical martial art aspect of the event with the culture and heritage of the medieval past. The modern relevance of this activity is seen by Anton as '[teaching] a person to socialize … support his friends, work shoulder to shoulder with his comrades, respect his rivals, love his friends and enemies both on the list and in life and generally to behave … [in a] chivalrous [manner]' (2012, personal communication).

This attitude and aspiration is found in most areas of re-enactment, where the underlying cultural significance of the period/event/individual being presented is central to the whole process. The significance of Battle of the Nations is shown by the rate at which interest is spreading: more than 20 nations have expressed an interest in sending teams for the 2013 event. Furthermore, the respect the event is receiving is impressive. For example, team USA, who sent more than 30 combatants in 2012, were presented by their country with a flag that had flown over the Capitol, and

this award was read into the Congressional Record in Washington DC on 24 June 2012.

Examining the scale of this international event provides an interesting contrast with the limited number of people engaged in re-enactment in Ireland. This is further compounded by the fact that individual re-enactors and groups specialize in very particular time periods and would have clothing, equipment and knowledge specific to that time. This is of importance to organizers, who must address the issue of limited resources when planning their events calendar.

18.6 The Event Proposal

Having considered the practicalities of providing an event populated by hobbyists that meets stakeholder needs, chooses the appropriate time period and has a high level of authenticity, Mogh Roith developed a proposal as to the scale of re-enactment event possible and the number of re-enactors who could be guaranteed.

The location for the re-enactment was felt to be crucial to the success of the venture. The chosen site was a small piece of land in the centre of the town that is owned by a government agency. The site is sheltered, secure and in the shadow of the ancient cathedral, creating a perfect sense of stepping into the past. For re-enactors this was a wonderful site, but it also had some limitations: due to its sheltered nature, the site is not immediately visible from the bridge or the main roads, and furthermore, access is via a laneway that is normally closed to the public, thus, getting people to realize that an event was taking place at this location was an issue.

Mogh Roith provided two re-enactment proposals to the festival committee – one for ten participants and the other for 20. The capacity to deliver these numbers was confirmed in advance. The cost associated with this proposal was based on this being a free, public event with the intention that it would lead to a strong role for re-enactment in the build up to 2014. Essentially, re-enactors would have their participation costs covered, with some additional costs to be met directly by the festival. A key element of funding was that the majority of people who took part in the re-enactment were either on site or in transit for 3 days. In many cases this involved individuals arranging to take time off using their annual leave from employers. It was found that the re-enactors who took part were willing to contribute to the event, partially because of their passion for their hobby but also because of the looming 2014 anniversary of the Battle of Clontarf, which has been a talking point within re-enactment circles for several years. There is great interest in generating support for a significant commemoration, and Féile Brian Ború is seen as a potential vehicle for such an activity.

While re-enactors will often embrace a wide range of the customs, practices, skills and occupations of the time period they are representing, the elements that are suitable for a public-facing event are often more restricted. A commonly used nomenclature within re-enactment is to divide activities between combat and living history, with the latter focused on craft and other 'normal' activities and often associated with a greater focus on authenticity. The public who attend festivals such as Féile Brian Ború appreciate being entertained and, while learning about skills and crafts from the past is always popular, undoubtedly the element that presents the biggest spectacle is the 'battle'. The living history element is provided by having displays that show the crafts and daily tasks as they are being performed or a static display that captures a snapshot of the activity shown but with a person to explain what is happening. Obviously re-enactors are limited as to what can be demonstrated in a safe manner and what is appropriate to a family show. For Féile Brian Ború it was decided to provide an event based on Brian Ború's Military Camp, therefore the displays would feature:

- The encampment layout itself as an example of what people on the move would live like.
- A simple domestic scene with a family going about their daily life.
- A blacksmith at work, as well as examples of other crafts including fibre craft and pottery, all of which were based on historical examples.
- An armoury display where people could interact with the weapons they see being used.

Re-enactment combat for festivals comes in several forms. Big events such as Moesgård in Denmark, Hastings in England or the Pennsic war in the USA involve large numbers of re-enactors and require suitable ground that can sustain battles that both meet the expectations of the public for large-scale spectacle and also serve to attract numbers of re-enactors. These battles can approach the scale of the originals on which they are based or inspired and range in intensity from fully choreographed fight routines or troop movements that are still quite realistic, at one end, to full contact competitive combat at the other (see Battle of the Nations above).

For the Féile Brian Ború event there were a limited number of combatants, so depicting or trying to depict a large-scale battle was not feasible. It was decided the focus should be on using the combatants in scenarios that would maximize their impact on the event and further the needs of the organizing committee. The approach adopted was to use the story of Brian Ború by having small-scale individual and group combats, wherein the warriors were looking to impress their lord and employer. In addition to this, a competitive tournament with the victor gaining glory and a small prize provided by the festival and commissioned from a local artist were arranged for the Saturday. The intention was that for the greater part of each day as a visitor arrived on site they would find combat in progress – whether a formal scheduled event or combat training in between. This allowed the combatants to show their skills in a safe and controlled way that included an element of the theatrical to engage with the public watching the event (see Fig. 18.4).

Living history displays were arranged around the perimeter of the combat in what was described as an 'encampment'. This prevented the public from expecting buildings and supported the illusion of an army on the move. The displays offered visitors the opportunity to interact with re-enactors, and some of the craft products, such as pottery and toy weapons, were available for purchase. An example of bringing the story to life was one of the festival committee seeing a young boy who had been to the encampment standing outside another event with the toy axe and shield he had bought demanding that those who wanted to enter

should tell him the password to get in. Another of the re-enactors from the area had his young nephew proclaim that he wanted to be a warrior like his uncle.

The final billed element involved a small team of re-enactors representing Brian Ború and his entourage (see Fig. 18.5). Their role was to bring the story of Brian Ború outside the site in a real and tangible way, by walking around Ballina and Killaloe 'in character'. While this reduced the number of people in the encampment it served to market the camp and provide members of the public with opportunities to interact with the re-enactors. As well as wandering around the town talking to people, they settled in locations playing a historically authentic form of chess and interacting as a king might with his subjects. This group acted as ambassadors for the main event while providing people with information in an engaging way. Sending the High King and his entourage out into the community also served the objective of integrating the event

Fig. 18.4. Warriors fighting to impress their lord – Brian Ború – Al and Stephen practise for battle. (From Brendan Griffin.)

Fig. 18.5. Telling the story of Brian Ború. (Note: Iain Barber as Brian Ború flanked by Andrew McCormick and Dave Caves as his entourage with Dave Mooney (left) from Mogh Roith.)

with the local community, something that can be lost in events that run to a standardized delivery model.

A number of extra, unannounced, events were added into the re-enactment to try them out. These included blowing 1014-era hunting horns from the top of the cathedral to announce the opening of the re-enactment event and children's combat training, where the children who were present at the end of a combat session were given the opportunity to form their own shield walls and practise the manoeuvres of the warriors. An additional unbilled and unplanned event was when a number of the re-enactors, including Brian Ború and his entourage, decided to walk to Béal Ború Fort on Sunday morning, moving from the place where Brian Ború would have lived to the place where he received his tribute. These sorts of activities and the simple movement of re-enactors around the towns in costume – going to the shop or bank, for example – provided a sense of what might be possible in the future.

18.7   Re-enactment as Part of the Broader Event

In order to deliver the planned re-enactment event, it needed to be fully integrated within the overall festival design with frequent communications between re-enactors and the overall coordinators. Both the festival and Mogh Roith appointed individuals to act as full-time liaison between these two stakeholders for the duration of the weekend. This ensured that any issues were dealt with in a prompt and efficient manner. In order to ensure that any potential issues regarding logistics and site preparation were dealt with, Mogh Roith were involved in the pre-event health and safety meetings and ensured that key personnel were aware of their activities and the type of potential risks. In addition, due to being based in the region, members of Mogh Roith were able to become more involved in the overall design of the heritage element of the festival, including a large festival pageant and similar activities.

18.8   Future Development of Féile Brian Ború

Organizing the re-enactment element of Féile Brian Ború 2012 has encouraged the authors to reflect deeply on ideas of authenticity and also the meaning and focus of such activity for the various stakeholders involved. This reflection resulted in a discussion with Scott Cross, a historian and archivist from Oshkosh, MI, USA, who has been involved in re-enactment for more than 40 years. Scott was initially drawn in by 'a desire to experience the past by simulating what people in the past experienced' (S. Cross, 2012, personal communication) and attended his first event at the age of 14 as part of an American Civil War group representing the 12th Illinois Volunteer Infantry. His interest in other eras brought him into re-enacting World War I, 1880s American West and World War II. Eventually his Irish heritage brought him to re-enact the Tudor time period of Irish history as a means of connecting with that past, and over the last number of years he has made strong contributions to discussions between Irish-based re-enactors on clothing and equipment of this time period.

Scott has always focused on authenticity, basing his American Civil War representations on original photographs before it was commonplace to do so. In the early 1970s this led him to find others with a similar interest and approach, to advance their shared interest together. Initially drawing on the research of others, he moved towards primary research, looking at surviving artefacts rather than relying on their description by others, and this resulted in various publications of his research findings. This process brought him more towards living history, the idea of living and doing as people did, and through such first-hand accounts he achieved 'a much better perspective of how life was in the past' (S. Cross, 2012, personal communication; see Fig. 18.6 for an example of such 'life in the past').

Scott has engaged in both first-person re-enactment, where the participant assumes the role of someone from the past, and third person, where they talk about the people of the past, and he finds that both are effective means of communicating with the public to show them what life was really like in the past.

Fig. 18.6. Mississippi River steamboat men. (This beautiful photograph of Scott Cross and Paul McKee portraying Mississippi River steamboat men not only depicts re-enactors in costume but was also taken on an authentic 'quarter plate tintype' by Claude Andre Levet, using the wet colodian process. The photograph was taken in Athens, Missouri, c.1996.)

According to him, re-enactors need to explain to the public what they are seeing. Engaging with the public is an art, and Scott emphasizes that it is 'important to "read" your audience and see who is interested and wants to learn more' (S. Cross, 2012, personal communication). This is a critical aspect of re-enactment at events because people are not there to be lectured to, and an interactive element to the interpretation of the past is critical.

On the subject of authenticity, Scott has a clear message that is of relevance to re-enactors and the public alike: 'The public really expects us to be the real thing, and if we are not, then they walk away with misinformation' (S. Cross, 2012, personal communication). It is the responsibility of re-enactors to ensure that this does not happen. In events like Féile Brian Ború the challenge is to maintain this authenticity, particularly in the context of Brian Ború, the person whose story has a strong element of legend.

18.9   Summary

This case study is limited to looking at the (re)introduction of a re-enactment element to a broader established festival. Early analysis of feedback from members of the public has been positive and showed that they enjoyed the re-enactment element of the overall event, with the interactive element foremost in what this contributed. As previously observed, better signage or people to direct visitors towards the re-enactment area would have been useful and will be taken on board for future events. Also, considering Irish weather, provision needs to be made for all-weather viewing facilities at the re-enactment, particularly the combat element.

Re-enactors enjoyed the festival, with early feedback to the organizing committee indicating that those who attended liked the site and the structure of the event and would want to take part again. One re-enactor said that the event 'met and exceeded [his] expectations'. Simple elements such as the festival committee providing food for the participants and the unexpected prize for the combat tournament were generally seen as strong expressions of respect for what the re-enactors were doing.

The Mogh Roith group were satisfied with what they achieved and have already identified ways in which they can build on the success of this event to deliver activities in the future. In Féile Brian Ború they have committed to working closely with the heritage subcommittee to make their future plans for the festival a reality.

The response from the organizing committee was positive and helped to crystallize the way in which they could use re-enactment and re-enactment-type activities in 2013, 2014 and beyond. This includes ideas as to how the 2012 single event model could be modified into a more ambitious schedule of delivering events throughout the year, targeting different people's needs. The presence of re-enactors dressed in period-appropriate clothing helped to reinforce the link between the local festival and the Battle of Clontarf/ Brian Ború story, which it is hoped will be useful into the future. The re-enactment also helped to draw-in and engage people who might not have been previously aware of the local cultural heritage.

Including re-enactment in an event can make a huge contribution, but it needs to be managed well. It works best when the event is linked to a tangible historical context and integrates both the re-enactors themselves and the community into a shared experience of the event. This is not always easy to achieve but serves to ensure that all of those involved will enjoy the event and want to return to it in future years.

18.10   Discussion Questions

- What is the benefit for Féile Brian Ború of having a re-enactment element as an integral feature of their festival?
- Look at a local historic site or event that does not currently have a re-enactment type of activity and work out the role that re-enactment might play.
- Discuss ways in which the use of re-enactors in an informal setting can encourage engagement by members of the public who might be put off or intimidated by a more structured presentation in conventional museums and interpretative centres.

Acknowledgements

Acknowledgements to: Aoife O'Connor for her invaluable assistance in determining the direction of this case study in the early stages of its development; The Féile Brian Ború committee for their willingness to allow this festival to be used as a case study (http://www. feilebrianboru.com/); Natalia Trubnikova for arranging an interview and translation with the Battle of the Nations team; Niamh O'Rourke, Scott Cross and Vladlen Vasylenko for providing images.

References

Ashworth, G.J. and Larkham, P.J. (1994) *Building a New Heritage: Tourism, Culture and Identity in the New Europe*. CAB International, Wallingford, UK.

Dáil Éireann (2012) Record of proceedings in Dáil Éireann 31 January 2012. http://www.kildarestreet.com/debates/?id=2012-01-31.63.0 (accessed 1 July 2012).

Downham, C. (2005) The Battle of Clontarf in Irish history and legend. *History Ireland* 13, 19–23.

Fáilte Ireland (2010a) *Cultural Tourism, Making it Work For You. A New Strategy for Cultural Tourism in Ireland*. Fáilte Ireland, Dublin

Fáilte Ireland (2010b) *Sharing our Stories: Heritage Interpretation Manual*. Fáilte Ireland, Dublin.

Griffin, K. (2000) Bord Fáilte's Heritage Towns, paper presented at Conference of Irish Geographers.

Howard, P. (2003) *Heritage: Management, Interpretation, Identity*. Continuum, London.

Johnson, N.C. (1999) Framing the past: time, space and the politics of heritage tourism in Ireland. *Political Geography* 18, 187–207.

Kierse, S. (1983) *Historic Killaloe: A Guide to its Antiquities*. Ború Books, Killaloe, Ireland.

Merriman, N. (1991) *Beyond the Glass Case: The Past, the Heritage and the Public*. Leicester University Press, Leicester, UK.

TDI (Tourism Development International) (2012) *Capitalising on Dublin's Potential*. Report prepared by Tourism Development International for the Irish Tourist Industry Confederation (ITIC), ITIC, Dublin.

The Gathering Ireland (2012) The Gathering Ireland 2013 main website. http://www.thegatheringireland.com (accessed 2 July 2012).

19 Case Study 11: Music, Money and Movement

Alan Clarke
University of Pannonia, Veszprém, Hungary

This chapter will consider the roles that music performs and is asked to perform in the construction of forms of cultural tourism around the world. Music is an integral element of culture and especially in the construction of communities' cultures and identities. There have been many volumes written about cultural tourism, but little attention has been given to the role of music or the ways in which music has been moved into different forms and formats to play a part in these cultural formations.

Therefore, this chapter will elaborate arguments concerned with the way that music has travelled and movement has been effected, which will mean looking at the issues of globalization and authenticity through a series of short micro cases – some of which may seem more significant to you than others. They have been selected because they highlight parts of the story about how music has been taken away from us and given back, and where we have actively endeavoured to change it.

19.1 Introduction

The dynamic of musical movement will be explored through the influence of commercialization – the impact of money – on the music itself.

One of the questions that every musician dreads is the simple and very common one: what kind of music do you play? In one of Terry Pratchett's Discworld novels this question is posed of a piper and his reaction stands as the starting point of the first section of this chapter:

> 'Kinds? There aren't any kinds. There's just music,' said Keith. 'There's always music if you listen.
>
> (Pratchett, 2002, p. 67)

In one sense this is the central tenet of this chapter, that this statement is both true and not true! Music has patterns, traditions and recognizable forms that have been passed from generation to generation from community to community, but this is not to say that there has been no change or transformation along the way.

This chapter arises from a particular conjunctural moment. I read the UNESCO report on cultural diversity (UNESCO, 2009), which made several references to the importance of music in cultural identity and the recognition of it. For example, it argues that

> The influence of African art and particularly music is widely acknowledged today. Jazz and other styles of Afro-American music, such as the blues, appeared in the 1890s, over a quarter century after the abolition of slavery in the United States. The syncopated rhythms of this music fused traits of African folk music with European popular music, but also Native American music, and reflected the mores and social situations of the first generation of African Americans born outside of slavery. African heritage is also a primary basis of Brazilian samba, Cuban rumba and Trinidadian calypso. Combining the skills of African storytelling, singing and instrument making, calypso usually involves some social commentary, typically in the form of satire, with an infectious beat. It has since been influenced by European, North American and other Caribbean cultures to produce reggae and the latest creation of black music today: rap.
> (UNESCO, 2009, p. 40)

This directly resonated with research into community festivals (Clarke and Jepson, 2011) that was at the forefront of my mind at the time because the research focused on why an officially designated 'community festival' had denied the cultures of the communities that actually constituted the host city. We were asking ourselves questions about the absence of Chinese and West Indian cultures and where the Campaign for Real Ale (CAMRA) festival fitted into the overview of the steering group. There was also a nagging question where all the music in the pubs and clubs on a very lively performance circuit had disappeared to. The answers are to be found in our papers documenting this experience (Clarke, 2010).

Then came the invitation to participate in a 'Town Gown' initiative and take a stage in the Utca Zene (Street Music) Festival in my adopted city of Veszprém in Hungary. Utca Zene is a free music festival that takes over the city centre for a week every July, with bands and performers producing music on ad hoc stages scattered throughout the city centre. The ultimate prize for the band elected by popular vote is a recording contract and more gigs. So, what connects an academic interest in cultural tourism and festivals with the street music audience more than a love of music and what it does with us. There was the catalyst for what you see now in written form, rather than its musical form from the day. I am indebted to the organizers for their invitation to think this through and perform it with an audience of friends and strangers in the midst of the festival. I am equally indebted to the editors of this collection for the opportunity to reflect on this in a more traditional academic written form that is presented here.

19.2 Music and Movement

Our journey begins with a map (Fig. 19.1), which will allow you to follow through the arguments.

This is a simplified representation of the dynamics of musical change, not least because it appears to be a one-way process, which it is not because music has travelled back and forth and continues to do so as both legitimate and illegitimate forms of culture. Moreover, the arrows can also be seen as where money has an impact on the dynamics of the music. They can also be seen as the points where tourism and music interact. It is the power inherent in tourism development that permits the changing of location, not only geographically but socially, as music takes on new forms that make it understandable to new audiences. Brown (2009) has explored the historical context of Celtic music's growth on Cape Breton Island, Nova Scotia, Canada, and traced the development of the offer from the initial investments of the federal government in tourism infrastructure on the island in the 1970s and the further investments in entertainment as a

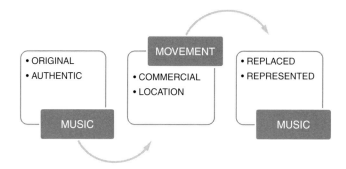

Fig. 19.1. The dynamics of musical change. (From Author.)

component of tourism in 1986. The success of the Celtic Colors International Festival has clearly identified a market for Cape Breton Celtic music and emphasizes that music festivals of this sort have the ability to enrich and to further extend the tourism season.

The first micro case illustrates this. Because I have been working in tourism, I have been fortunate to have the opportunity to travel widely over the last 30 years. My travels through Asia, China, the Middle East, the Caribbean and almost all of Europe have been supported by a musical score, consisting of music I have with me and the music that greets me. I have, in the best spirit of the cultural tourist, become a collector of local musics, but there is one song that has become a constant factor in my travels that seems to have nothing to do with where I have been. Once upon a time in 1977 there was a band called The Eagles, and they created a song called 'Hotel California' – a classic of its time, with its cryptic lyrics and long guitar solo. However, this has become a placeless, timeless piece that can be played on CD systems, acoustic guitars (rather than The Eagles' electric one), ukuleles, Bulgarian zithers, by mariachi bands, steel bands and, it seems, any other combination of instruments. It is included in every 'learn to play the guitar' syllabus and has come to outlive even the reformed Eagles. I loved it when it first came out, but now feel as though it haunts me as I travel. It has reached places where it does not belong and taken on forms that are not its natural ones. This is an example of what happens when music is re-placed and re-presented.

19.3   Cultural Contexts and Heritages

As UNESCO observed:

> Popular music is arguably the field in which the pressures of commercialization make themselves most strongly felt. Their impact is twofold: on the one hand, the pressures constitute an inducement to local artists to exploit their creative talents in an increasingly global market; on the other, they serve as a vector of acculturation processes related to the asymmetry of global cultural flows. In the case of popular music, four out of five of the major music industry conglomerates are located in the US, the other being in the UK; and the music sales market is dominated by the Western countries together with Japan and the Republic of Korea – Brazil being the only developing country to figure among the top 20 commercial outlets (Anheier and Isar, 2008).
>
> (UNESCO, 2009, p. 165)

When compared with other studies of culture and tourism, music moves beyond issues of authenticity constructed around the binary opposition of insider/outsider, front stage/back stage or destruction/salvation (LaBate, 2009). This moves the argument into the territory of commercialization and the influence that money has and will continue to have on the development of musical forms. There are many arguments about authenticity in cultural tourism, but it is not clear in music, and in particular in popular music, what this authenticity could refer to (perhaps authenticity refers to the type of music displayed in Fig. 19.2). As the first quotation from UNESCO demonstrates, the history of music has long been

Fig. 19.2. Medieval troubadours. (From http://www.pioneertroubadours.com/troubadoursonroadagainseries.htm)

about the movement of musical forms from one place to another, embodied often in the movement of the peoples of the music. More recently the capitalist system has found other ways of moving music from one continent to another in the form of the contract relationship, giving a new set of opportunities to artists performing in what is now recognized as the 'world music' scene or, as we could call it, the market for world music.

UNESCO goes further and asserts that

> In the field of popular music, diversity is everywhere. In the West, the range of often overlapping genres – including rock, pop, jazz, folk, Latin, blues, country, reggae and musical comedy – is virtually limitless. Musical traditions on all continents display a vast array of forms. Festivals offer great opportunities to sensitize the public to this diversity of expression. The 'world music' festival, where the audience is invited to move between performances representative of a variety of cultures and styles, is an especially good vehicle in this regard. In Australia, the WOMAD (World of Music and Dance) music festival franchise has greatly influenced the growth of interest in world music. Yet, while this expansion of musical tastes and encounters with often radically different musical traditions is to be welcomed, the potential drawbacks from the standpoint of cultural diversity should not be overlooked.
>
> (2009, p. 165)

Instead of tourism as the cause of permanent change, Stokes summarized the theoretical issues as

> how in modernity experiences of movement are valorised and aestheticised or demonized and pathologised, how difference is constructed and managed in situations of extreme commodification and cultural reflexivity, and how under what circumstances communication takes place across the gaps difference establishes.
>
> (1999, p. 141)

Another case can shed light on this and I have constructed it from the analysis of Flamenco music and dancing in Spain. Malefty (1998) studied how local people distinguish their private flamenco performances from public performances for tourists on gendered terms. The author asserted that in criticizing public performances of flamenco for tourists as inauthentic, flamenco aficionados actually used public performances to establish a relational opposition to their own private performances, thus authenticating their own performances.

Curiously, although peña aficionados appear to resist an encroaching tourism by scorning flamenco's commercial popularity, a deeper look at their private practice of tradition reveals a relational emphasis that actually embraces flamenco's popular exploitation. While aficionados deride flamenco 'for sale' in popular venues as 'inauthentic' compared with 'authentic' flamenco among locals, they exaggerate the differences between these social realms to establish a relation of mutual opposition. In the dynamic relationship between private and public flamenco, peña aficionados imply gender complementarity by means of performance contrasts. Flamenco 'tradition' practised locally among members in private peña clubs becomes a feminine construct of the 'inside', which opposes but complements flamenco performed for tourists in the public arena of masculine display and challenge 'outside' (Malefty, 1998, pp. 63–64).

Certainly it is no surprise to hear that the locals found the music and dance performances for tourists to be inauthentic. Malefty's research is interesting because it demonstrated that even when performances for tourists are considered inauthentic and commercialized, they do not necessarily degrade the same musical and dance genres for local people in their own spaces; in fact, by allowing people to construct contrasts about social and performance aspects of private versus public flamenco the presence of tourist shows appeared to invigorate local experiences and cultural expressions.

By directly appropriating aspects of the local culture one school of social regeneration, known as the 'culture for development' perspective, claims to be able to salvage development. This approach, according to Kleymeyer (1994), facilitates local development based on sustainable management of ethnic peoples' culture and thereby strengthens the cultural elements on which it is founded. However, this new sense of development incorporates local culture by objectifying the cultures into handicrafts that are easily sold to tourists. Examples from Healy and Zorn (1994) and others (Bryne Swain, 1989; Stephen, 1991; Meisch, 2002) illustrate that 'culture for development' projects conflate culture as the way of life of a community with the objects that index that way of life. Rather than a new model of economic development related to the way of life, 'culture for development' is simply following the old model of commodification. Local people become producers and retailers, and traditional objects become products. In this way 'culture for development' draws people and culture into capitalist markets. We can see this from a musician's point of view in the following case study from one of Botswana's leading guitarists.

Calistus Bosaletswe (2012) wrote a provocative piece in the *Sunday Standard* about Banjo Mosele, Botswana's famous guitarist, singer and composer, who became famous in early 2012 with his newly released album 'Across the Equator'. Mosele expressed his worry that the

structures and policies in place in Botswana were hindering development of ethnic music. According to him, the growth of the tourism industry has pushed indigenous music to the periphery of the cultural tourism experience. He believes that the music of the country and its people should be presented in live performances, introducing tourists to the authentic experience of Botswana music.

> We should use our music by playing live shows in hotels to show the tourists our culture. Currently, a tourist visiting Botswana has nothing to learn about our music and culture because hotels hire DJs who always carry laptops and play CDs. When tourists go back home they only talk about Okavango Delta, Chobe National Park and wildlife.
>
> (Bosaletswe, 2012)

He thinks that the tourist experience needs more than an animal safari and discos. Hotels and bars should provide venues for groups to showcase the actual music of Botswana. A further related issue is the loss of indigenous languages, which disempowers performers, and he feels it frustrates their attempts to express themselves, which they can do much better when singing in their 'mother tongue'.

He argues that failure to support a full infrastructure for artists is a hindrance towards empowering the youth who are seeking to turn their music into a profession. Mosele says that because there are no rehearsal places, musicians cannot practice before they go and perform on stage. He also commented that there are no good live venues:

> We learnt a lot before we could record and play music. There was a culture of live music and, at this juncture, they [are teaching] the youth the wrong things. It's very sad because you will see artists performing using CDs and it should be totally discouraged.
>
> (Bosaletswe, 2012)

His concern is about the short term focus of this approach and how it damages young peoples' career prospects. How can young people learn performance skills if they are trying to play instruments and sing while listening to a CD?

Treating culture for development as a commercialized set of commodities inherently ignores the complexities and specificities of history and economic relationships; therefore, the appreciation of culture in tourism has a less than politically liberating outcome.

> While seeming to celebrate cultural difference or the natural world, this paradigm dehistoricized certain people, practices, geographic regions, and their animal inhabitants, setting them up as avatars of unchanging innocence and authenticity, as origin and as ideal.
>
> (Desmond, 1999, p. 254)

Transformations have not only come from the geographical relocations of music but also from the technological changes that have impacted on the production of music in different forms and that have been channelled into forms of music that were previously technologically different. African musicians welcomed electricity for all manner of reasons because it brought a 'civilising' effect into townships, but one of them was that it also made possible the introduction of the electric guitar and synthesizers, which many in the West took for granted many years before they were available to musicians in Africa. This argument is apparently true, but there are also important questions to be debated about the use of amplification in any form for voices, never mind for instruments. We do not have to travel to Africa to find these questions debated, as we can see from the following example taken from the early career of one of America's most famous singer-songwriters.

19.4   Newport Folk Festival

Bob Dylan's performance at the 1965 Newport Folk Festival was always intended to be a straightforward, acoustic event: the then 24-year-old singer/songwriter had enjoyed a tremendously positive reception when he performed at the 1963 and 1964 festival, and was already firmly established as a top protest folk artist of traditional instrumentation (acoustic guitar, sparse backing). His decision to perform with an electric band came spontaneously the evening before his set. Dylan chose two tracks from his fifth album, Bringing It All Back Home,

including 'Like a Rolling Stone' and 'Maggie's Farm'. When Dylan took to the stage with that unprecedented amped-in performance, he intertwined folk with rock & roll. But almost immediately he was harassed by the audience, who booed him loudly and called him a traitor to the folk genre. Legendary singer/songwriter Pete Seeger watched from the sidelines and was dismayed by Dylan's electric ambitions; he complained to the audio technicians, 'If I had an axe, I'd chop the microphone cable right now' (that line spiralled quickly into the apocryphal story that Seeger actually had an axe and attempted to swing it at the sound system). After performing the three rehearsed songs Dylan stormed off the stage. He was eventually urged back by other festival performers and brusquely delivered two songs on acoustic guitar: 'Mr. Tambourine Man' and, not so subtly, 'It's All Over Now, Baby Blue'. The more traditional delivery satisfied the crowd, who cheered enthusiastically for the scowling Dylan. After that contentious performance he refused to return to the Newport Folk Festival for 37 years (to read more about this event see: http://www.rollingstone.com/music/news/this-week-in-rock-history-bob-dylan-goes-electric-20110726).

The electrification of music also caused furore in the UK and encouraged bands like Fairport Convention to adopt new ways to present traditional folk songs. Other bands attempting this adoption of technology had different understandings of what the 'tradition' would accept, with arguments about which different types of percussion would be acceptable. Ashley Hutchings, the founding (electric) bass player of both Steeleye Span and the Albion Country Band, would not accept using a rock and roll drum kit.

Figure 19.3 (derived from UIS UNESCO, 2009) attempts to depict the cultural cycle moving from Creation to Consumption (via Production, Dissemination and Exhibition), and again it is possible to locate this model within the cultural tourism markets.

Creation: The origination and authoring of ideas and content (e.g. sculptors, writers, design companies) and the making of one-off products (e.g. crafts, fine arts).

Production: Reproducible cultural forms (e.g. television programmes), as well as the specialist

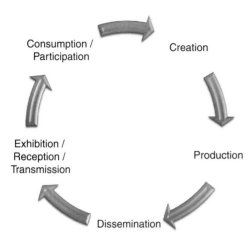

Fig. 19.3. The culture cycle. (Author's representation based on the analysis of the literature.)

tools, infrastructure and processes used in their realization (e.g. the production of musical instruments, the printing of newspapers).

Dissemination: Bringing generally mass (re)produced cultural products to consumers and exhibitors (e.g. the wholesale, retail and rental of recorded music and computer games, film distribution). With digital distribution, goods and services can go directly from the creator to the consumer.

Exhibition/Reception/Transmission: Sites of exchange of rights to provide audiences with live and/or unmediated cultural experiences by granting or selling restricted access to consume/participate in often time-based cultural activities (e.g. festival organization and production, opera houses, theatres, museums). Transmission relates to the transfer of knowledge that may not involve any commercial transaction and that often occurs in informal practices. It includes transmitting cultural identity from generation to generation, particularly in the form of intangible cultural heritage (ICH). It also includes festivals and events with open access.

Consumption/Participation: The activities of audiences and participants in consuming cultural products and taking part in cultural activities/experiences (e.g. book reading, dancing, participating in carnivals, listening to radio, visiting galleries).

One brief example demonstrates how this cycle can work. When the tourism industry began to take over in Jamaica the decision to promote all-inclusive resort hotels made a significant impact. The walled enclaves were successful at both keeping the tourists inside and the native Jamaicans outside. It has often been said that this was the industry's reaction to the threats of drugs and violence on the streets of Kingston, but what is not so well remembered is that this aversion to the authentic Jamaican also meant that Jamaican musicians were excluded. The music on offer in the enclaves was actually presented by musicians imported from North America – and these Americans were the touristic capture of the reggae moment (Bradley, 2001).

19.5   Globalization

The globalization of the economy promises greater choice of forms, new(ish) products for consumers and new opportunities for employment. However, this is weighed against the possible homogeneity of the cultural offers that are produced as a result of these forces. These arguments should not be read as saying that every place, everywhere will produce only the same cultural offer, because this is too simple a reading of the processes. It appears that there is a degree of what can be called 'glocalization', where the global themes are addressed and interpreted in local contexts and with local influences.

Dunbar-Hall (2001) analysed cultural tourism in Bali through two music and dance events designed for tourists, and a Balinese Hindu temple festival. All three cases allow tourists to hear and see performances constructed from the sounds and images of Balinese performing arts, which at the same time evoke cultural matrices that necessarily remain unfamiliar and unrecognized by tourists. Through these performance situations it is possible to see cultural tourism in Bali theorized through a map of boundaries and frontiers between culture bearers and tourists, created by entry to or restriction from knowledge these situations construct.

Globalization is often connected with cultural (very often western) hegemony. But as Johnson (2002, p. 26) usefully reminded us, the recent history of global consumerism has also produced non-American giants. Whether it is Japanese electronics or German luxury cars, industries such as these have the primary purpose to sell their product in markets that seem to be getting larger in terms of consumerism but smaller in terms of the spread of global consumerism. There are, of course, other products of global travel that have a recent history of being transmitted from one culture and then consumed in others. However, the difference between consuming a Starbucks' coffee (American?) and some sushi (Japanese?), for example, is that while both are very much the products of increasing global flows the former is analogous to many other consumer giants that dominate so many markets the world over while the latter is more likely to be the product of a local industry that is cashing in on the recent popularization of Japanese cuisine around the world.

The marketing of music across cultures is not necessarily always a product of globalization that provides profits to western companies. There are other global, national and regional flows that reflect global consumer practices but are not always connected directly to the western world. For example, the Japanization of some Eastern markets of 'Jpop' (Japanese popular music) is a phenomenon that on the one hand reflects global practices but on the other hand is, in effect, Japanization. Furthermore, some world musics have been transmitted from one culture to another many years before the concept of globalization was first coined and have continued to do so, not necessarily only for the purpose of making money. The adoption of western music by many non-western cultures is a fine example, where a performance and consumption of, for instance, Bach, Beethoven or Brahms is just as much part of local music culture as it is part of a European culture or western art music.

As a method of promoting tourism, heritage and identity, music as or in a performing art is increasingly used as a tool for representing a specific nation, region or culture through sound and symbol. There are both positive and negative consequences. For example, financial gain, bringing communities together and preserving traditional musics on the one hand but giving the visitor a false art, creating a financial dependence and driving communities apart through cultural competition on the other hand.

19.6 Selling the Irish

Finally the last arguments in this chapter focus on the repositioning of Irish music and dance. The winners of the Eurovision Song Contest have traditionally been invited to host the following year's event and produce an entertainment segment that provides an interval between the competition performances and the scoring. When Ireland won in 1980 they hosted the 1981 show and had the idea to commission a three-part suite of baroque-influenced traditional music called 'Timedance', composed by Bill Whelan, performed and recorded by members of Irish folk band Planxty with Dónal Lunny, and further augmented with a rock rhythm section of electric bass and drums and a four-piece horn section. The piece was performed, with accompanying ballet dancers, during the interval of the contest and later released as a Planxty single (http://www.youtube.com/watch?v=s_A4eODHvCM).

The Irish then made a habit of winning the song contest and considered revisiting the ideas and themes of Timedance in a different piece also composed by Bill Whelan. In a book about Planxty, Whelan is quoted as saying

> 'It was no mistake of mine to call it Riverdance
> because it connected absolutely to Timedance.
> It was a nod in the direction of where
> I believed it came from.'
>
> (O'Toole, 2007, p. 52)

Riverdance debuted during the Eurovision Song Contest in April 1994. It had been produced in almost total secrecy and only the immediate team had a sense of what they were going to reveal to the world. Although it was only just over 6 minutes long, the segment received a standing ovation from the studio audience, and it went on to become one of the most popular acts to ever enter the talent competition in 50 years (http://www.youtube.com/watch?v=3mC0rWgUqTc&feature=related). To his musical score Whelan added the world-renowned – though North American – Irish step dancers Jean Butler and Michael Flatley, and fame was found almost instantly. From this Eurovision segment the audio version of Riverdance hit number one on the Irish singles charts that May and reigned supreme throughout the summer. After breaking the record of remaining #1 on the charts longer than any other song, a video of the contest entry was turned into a fundraiser, which gave all proceeds to Rwanda relief work. Many of those who performed in the original Eurovision piece, including the previously mentioned principal dancers, later went on to appear in the original full-length Riverdance show that is still popular around the world. Jean Butler choreographed for the bulk of the dance troupe, as Michael Flatley focused on his solo work.

In February 1995 Riverdance – The Show opened at the Point Theatre in Dublin, making history as the first ever full-length Irish dance show. With a sold out 5-week performance run it broke every sales record. By September 1996 Riverdance had been performed 400 times and had been viewed by over 1.3 million people, both nationally and abroad. Now new generations are discovering Riverdance and many have been inspired to take Irish dance lessons themselves, as more studios have popped up all over the world to meet the trend's demand. (Read more here: http://www.ehow.com/about_5087265_ history-riverdance.html#ixzz1zH70HHk6).

The question to be asked about the Riverdance revolution is how far it moved the Irish music/dance tradition in order to create a successful cultural tourism product. Many doubt the authenticity of the dancing style – with arms outstretched, dancing with ballet shoes and touring without explaining the stories behind the tunes. It is undoubtedly successful, but what has it been successful as? In the small town next to me in Hungary we have an Irish dance centre that only does Riverdance-inspired sessions and routines.

19.7 Music and Movement – What is Wrong with *Titanic*?

The first part of this case is quite technical because it documents the introduction of a Greek instrument into Irish music, but the second part shows how this transference has now become an authentic part of the Irish music scene.

The Greek bouzouki, in the newer tetrachordo (four course/eight string, or τετράχορδο) version developed in the 20th century, was introduced into Irish traditional music in the late 1960s by Johnny Moynihan of the popular folk group Sweeney's Men, and popularized by Andy Irvine and Dónal Lunny in the group Planxty. In a separate but parallel development, Alec Finn, later with the Galway-based traditional group De Dannan, obtained a trichordo (three course/six string, or τρίχορδο) Greek bouzouki of his own. Almost immediately after the Greek bouzouki's initial introduction new designs built specifically for Irish traditional music were developed. The body was widened and a flat back with straight sides replaced the round, stave-built back of the Greek bouzouki. English builder Peter Abnett, who was the first instrument-maker to build a uniquely 'Irish' bouzouki – for Dónal Lunny in 1970 – developed a hybrid design with a three-piece dished back and straight sides. All of the initial Irish bouzoukis had flat tops, but within a few years luthiers such as Stefan Sobell began experimenting with carved, arched tops, taking their cue from American archtop guitars and mandolins. Even so, today the overwhelming majority of builders opt for flat (or slightly radiused) tops and backs.

With a few exceptions, bouzouki players playing Irish music tend to use the instrument less for virtuoso melodic work and more for chordal and contrapuntal accompaniment for melodies played on other instruments, such as the flute or fiddle. Because of this, it is common to use matched strings on the two bass courses, tuning to unison pairs in order to enhance the bass response of the instrument.

The Irish bouzouki has also become integrated into some other western European musical traditions over the past 40 years and is popularly used in the music of Asturias, Galicia, Brittany, Spain, and even the Scandinavian countries (in fact, there is even now a new Nordic branch of the instrument, having been modified further to suit the unique requirements of those musics).

The story of the *Titanic* has proved very popular since the majesty of its launch met with tragedy so quickly. The mixture beguiled James Cameron so much that he vowed to recreate the whole story in the epic film starring Kate Winslett and Leonardo DiCaprio. No expense was spared to tell the stories of the passengers and crew as honestly and accurately as possible, including the invitation of one of the first-class passengers to join in a party below stairs. A technically difficult sequence featured our two lovers spinning across the dance floor, with the music supplied by a traditional Irish band. Unfortunately the band and the producers accepted the line up as authentic because that was what dance bands had always been and would always be – except the rhythm section included a man playing an Irish bouzouki, which as we have just established did not arrive in Irish bands until the late 1960s. This means that the story of the iceberg has actually been augmented by a time-travelling musician as the ship sank in 1912!

In one sense it does not matter and the grand narrative of the film is not affected in the slightest by this oddity, but in another it becomes very significant because it serves to underline how this relatively recent import has become part of the fixtures and fittings of Irish music.

19.8 Summary

We began by looking at the UNESCO report on cultural diversity and the ways in which money can contribute to and underpin cultural identity. There was a discussion of the forms and genres of music in their original locations and then some comments about the relocation of these forms to other places. The argument presented proposes that it is the commercialization of culture, especially that from cultural tourism developments, which drives such movement.

This summary needs to remind us that actually 'IT'S ALL FOLK MUSIC' – this is taken from a comment delivered by Steve Knightley of Show of Hands, a band that had established a fine reputation for singing traditional songs from the south west of England. In one concert – and many more subsequently – they re-presented Bob Marley's 'No Woman No Cry' to some surprise, but Knightley comforted the audience by saying 'It's all folk music' and, of course, he is correct. The music belongs to the originators, but that includes the performers, wherever they are and wherever they are from.

Music is an integral part of our cultures and our cultural identities. It is also an important part of the cultural tourism offer because it offers a sense of entertainment and a sense of engagement. It is also possible to offer the commercialization of music to both the host music industry and its partners, but also conveniently to the tourists themselves. Music makes a souvenir that captures more of the senses than a postcard or a stuffed donkey and therefore carries additional value for the tourists.

19.9 Discussion Questions

- Why is music more than entertainment?
- Do touristic audiences care about authenticity?
- Would you walk out if one of your favourite musicians started playing different music? Why?
- How Irish is Irish dancing now?
- Do the benefits of globalization outweigh the dangers?

References

Anheier, H. and Isar, Y.R. (eds) (2008) *The Cultural Economy, Cultures and Globalization Series Vol. 2.* Sage, Thousand Oaks, California.

Bosaletswe, C. (2012) Banjo Mosele advocates for cultural tourism. *Sunday Standard* Online Edition. http://www.sundaystandard.info/print_article.php?NewsID=13012 (accessed 27 January 2012).

Bradley, L. (2001) *Bass Culture: When Reggae Was King.* Penguin, Harmondsworth, UK.

Brown, K.G. (2009) Island tourism marketing: music and culture. *International Journal of Culture, Tourism and Hospitality Research* 3, 25–32.

Bryne Swain, M. (1989) Gender roles in indigenous tourism: Kuna Mola, Kuna Yala, and cultural survival. In: Smith, V.L. (ed.) *Hosts and Guests: The Anthropology of Tourism*, 2nd edn. University of Pennsylvania Press, Philadelphia, Pennsylvania, pp. 83–104.

Clarke, A. (2010) Defining moments: cultures, power and communities. *Journal of Hospitality and Tourism* 8, 62–77.

Clarke, A. and Jepson, A. (2011) Power and hegemony in a community festival. *International Journal of Events and Festival Management* 2, 7–19.

Desmond, J.C. (1999) *Staging Tourism: Bodies on Display from Waikiki to Sea World*. University of Chicago Press, Chicago, Illinois.

Dunbar-Hall, P. (2001) Culture, tourism and cultural tourism: boundaries and frontiers in performances of Balinese music and dance. *Journal of Intercultural Studies* 22, 173–187.

Healy, K. and Zorn, E. (1994) Taquile's homespun tourism. In: Kleymeyer, C.D. (ed.) *Cultural Expression and Grassroots Development: Cases from Latin America and the Caribbean*. Lynne Rienner, Boulder, Colorado, pp. 135–148.

Johnson, H. (2002) Balinese music, tourism and globalisation: inventing traditions within and across cultures. *New Zealand Journal of Asian Studies* 4, 8–32.

Kleymeyer, C.D. (ed.) (1994) *Cultural Expression and Grassroots Development: Cases from Latin America and the Caribbean*. Lynne Rienner, Boulder, Colorado.

LaBate, E.A. (2009) Music and tourism in Cusco, Peru: culture as a resource. Presented to the Faculty of the Graduate School of the University of Texas at Austin in partial fulfilment of the requirements for the Degree of Doctor of Philosophy.

Malefty, T.D. (1998) 'Inside' and 'outside' Spanish Flamenco: gender constructions in Andalusian concepts of Flamenco tradition. *Anthropological Quarterly* 71, 63–73.

Meisch, L.A. (2002) *Andean Entrepreneurs: Otavalo Merchants and Musicians in the Global Arena*. University of Texas Press, Austin, Texas.

O'Toole, L. (2007) *The Humours of Planxty*. Hachette Books, Ireland.

Pratchett, T. (2002) *The Amazing Maurice and His Educated Rodents*. Corgi Books, London.

Stephen, L. (1991) Culture as a resource: four cases of self-managed indigenous craft production in Latin America. *Economic Development and Cultural Change* 40, 101–130.

Stokes, M. (1999) Music, travel and tourism: an afterword. *The World of Music* 41, 141–155.

UIS UNESCO (2009) UNESCO Framework for Cultural Statistics: Task Force Meeting Summary, May, Paris. http://www.uis.unesco.org/template/pdf/cscl/framework/TFM_Summary_EN.pdf (accessed 12 September 2012).

UNESCO (2009) *Investing in Cultural Diversity and Intercultural Dialogue*. UNESCO World Report. UNESCO, Paris.

Index

Note: page numbers in **bold** refer to figures and tables.